It is no exaggeration to say that the student of lesbian life cannot fully understand her own history without reading *Sex Variant Women in Literature* by Jeannette H. Foster.

The 2600 years of lesbian history through the pages of the contemporary literature of each era provides a panoramic sweep which establishes for all time the presence of lesbians in world literature from 600 B.C. through the middle of the 20th Century.

A fascinating journey, illuminated by the lives and loves of all manner of famous women. One comes away realizing that it is harder to find a heterosexual writer than a lesbian one . . . one realizes it with delight, of course.

Sex
Variant
Women
in
Literature

Jeannette H. Foster

Sex Variant Women in Literature

Jeannette H. Foster

The Naiad Press Inc.
1985

Printed in the United States of America

SEX VARIANT WOMEN IN LITERATURE was first published by its
author, Jeannette Howard Foster, through Vantage Press in 1956 in a
hardback edition. That edition was photo offset and issued by Frederick
Muller (London) in 1958. In 1975 Diana Press issued a photo offset
edition with the Afterword by Barbara Grier and Titles of Special Interest
through 1974. That was a paperback edition.

First Naiad Press Edition, 1985

Typeset by Sandi Stancil
Cover design by Tee A. Corinne

ISBN: 0-930044-65-7

Naiad Press

thanks the generosity and community dedication of

ANN R. STOKES

for making possible this edition of this essential book.

FOREWORD

The germ from which this book has grown was implanted nearly forty years ago when a student council voted one spring afternoon to dismiss two girls from a college dormitory unless they altered their habits. To one junior council member several features of the council session made it memorable. It was an unscheduled meeting and was convened quietly so as to render it secret. The absence of freshman and sophomore members indicated a "morals case," for in those days the younger students were thus sheltered from evil intelligence. Most striking of all was the utter incomprehensibility of the issue at stake.

The bewildered junior was herself younger than her peers, and outside the realm of books was ignorant to a degree incredible today. She had understood the earlier expulsion of a girl who stayed out all night, for after all one had simply accepted from childhood that such conduct was disreputable. But why should locking themselves into their room together lay two students open to rigorous discipline? To her private humiliation, everyone else appeared to know. The business was dispatched with embarrassed speed and by blind allusion rather than open statement. Her relief was great when opinion favored probation for the brief remainder of the year. For she could not have cast her vote for expulsion without understanding the cause.

She left the meeting with her mortifying ignorance undisclosed; but it rankled. She had never before been the most stupid in any group. And her curiosity was aroused. The two culprits were to her among the least attractive girls in college both physically and temperamentally. How could they be so obsessed with one another as to lock themselves in their room together at every opportunity? She was determined to learn. She went to the college library where day after day she had passed the row of worn tan volumes labeled *Studies in the Psychology of Sex* without once having the impulse to look inside. Now she explored tables of contents with the same slight nausea that had accompanied initial zoology laboratory dissection. Thus she met Havelock Ellis.[1]

Within her subsequent twenty-one years in women's dormitories as student or faculty member she had reason many times to be glad of all the study she was moved to undertake then and later, for it enabled her to help in averting more than one minor tragedy and to conduct her own life with some measure of wisdom. At first her study was confined to scientific and factual works; but as these sometimes cited pertinent belles lettres its scope gradually widened to include the latter. And, finally, because science and fact were so well listed in the bibliographic tools for specialists, and literature so sporadically or not at all, her investigation came to focus in the area of imaginative writing. The once-perplexed junior is the present writer, and what follows is a product of her extended search.

J. H. F.

PREFACE

For more than a century there has been a tendency to worship science as a key to knowledge and understanding. This preoccupation has served to determine the limits of potential knowledge. Science has created new problems almost as rapidly as it has solved old ones.

History records the phenomena of human life. It depends upon biographical data which are notoriously biased. Virtue or viciousness of character varies with the prejudice of the biographer. Most of what is told us in the realm of sexual behavior has been colored by, or has been a reaction to, social, moral, and religious convention.

Science proceeds by dissecting reality into its component parts. It has become so preoccupied with the study of these parts that it has failed to grasp the whole. Moreover, it is dependent upon knowledge which can be verified only through the use of the senses, with the result that its adherents have grown sceptical of philosophical and literary evaluations. Its study of elements and forces has led to abstractions, to a greater knowledge of unrealities.

In the realm of the sex variant, popular prejudice has reached and maintained its maximum height. The sex variant has always been with us and probably always will be. He has been thus classified, partly because of the arbitrary designations *male* and *female*. As I have shown in *All the Sexes,* there are any number of possible gradations of human behavior—from that of a theoretical masculine to that of a theoretical feminine being.

A particular person is always a complex of masculinity and femininity. Sex variants commonly are conspicuous through the exhibition of characteristics usually associated with the opposite sex. But science continues to recognize the fiction of male and female and has thrown little light on the problem.

The present work, Sex Variant Women in Literature, is a unique undertaking. The author was troubled in her student days by her lack of knowledge regarding female homosexuality. The need for understanding has resulted in a long search for evidence in literature, a field with which she was familiar. She has come to believe that imaginative as well as scientific writing is a mirror of human sexual behavior which should be given serious attention.

Some readers may question the propriety or the motives in associating the personal lives of authors with their writings. Poetry loses some of its charm through the suggestion that it might be an expression of the writer's sexual maladjustment. But as a matter of fact it is beginning to seem that all imaginative writings are attempts to find libidinous satisfaction in fantasy. Science may never be able to support this impression by its laborious methods of securing evidence, but the author's review of the literature of twenty centuries leaves little doubt of its validity.

In SEX VARIANT WOMEN IN LITERATURE the author has called attention to lesbian tendencies wherever she has found them. She has made no attempt to estimate what proportion of imaginative writing may be the work of lesbians. She has not confined herself to literary classics but has accepted the fact that human beings reveal themselves in whatever they read and write. Sexual variance shows itself in so many different ways that all types of imaginative writings have to be studied if we are to understand human motivations and behavior.

GEORGE W. HENRY, M.D.

ACKNOWLEDGMENTS

For help in pursuing this study the author owes many debts of gratitude, first to friends who added chance-read titles to the bibliography; especially to those who had no basic interest in the subject. An even heavier debt is due all the librarians who made available rare or restricted material, negotiated interlibrary loans, or merely rendered much ordinary service. Staffs of the following institutions deserve special thanks: the Union Catalogs of the Library of Congress and the Philadelphia Bibliographic Center; the libraries of Bryn Mawr College, the University of Chicago, Emory University, Indiana University, the University of Pennsylvania, Princeton University, Swarthmore College, and Yale University; the medical libraries of Emory University Hospital, the New York Academy of Medicine, and the Philadelphia College of Physicians; the public libraries of Chicago, New York City, and Philadelphia; and the Library of Congress.

Particular mention is due the special library of the Institute for Sex Research at Indiana University, of which the author was librarian for four years (1948-1952). It should be made clear that the present study is unrelated to that of the Institute, does not reflect its views, and has not been approved by members of its staff. The librarian's function was cataloguing, not sex research, and almost all of the material considered here was seen elsewhere. Nevertheless, acquaintance with what may be the largest extant library related to sex served to reassure the author that she had overlooked no important area of the field she wished to study. Gratitude is thus due also to the Institute and its Director, the late Dr. A. C. Kinsey.

CONTENTS

INTRODUCTION

This study is concerned with certain types of emotional reaction among women as these appear in literature. Its primary aim is neither psychiatric nor critical; that is, it does not pretend to solve the problems described nor to pass conventional judgment on the literature examined, though rudiments of aesthetic and psychological evaluation will inevitably be included. Its purpose is to trace historically the quantity and temper of imaginative writing on its chosen subject from earliest times to the present day, on the assumption that what has been written and read for pleasure is a fair index of popular interest and social attitude from one century to another.

Since new viewpoints and methods of study are constantly altering our sex vocabulary, some preliminary definitions seem advisable. First, what is meant by *sex variant?* The term was selected because it is not as yet rigidly defined nor charged with controversial overtones. Intrinsically, *variant* means no more than differing from a chosen standard, and in the field of sex experience the standard generally accepted is adequate heterosexual adjustment. But even this phrase lacks precision. Lawyer, clergyman, physician, psychoanalyst, biologist, sociologist, each will interpret it from his particular viewpoint. The meaning a layman meets oftenest in the literature of our western Christian culture is happy marriage and parenthood, but this is nearer to the churchman's and sociologist's ideal than to the working compromise by which average citizens worry along. Perhaps the highest practical common denominator is a heterosexual union agreeable to both its parties and not detrimental to them, to the society in which they live, or to the continuance of the race.

Possible deviations from this standard are many, but the present study will stay within the limits set by a work of 1941 entitled *Sex Variants,*[1] which was devoted to persons having emotional experience with others of their own sex. Under this head the author in-

cluded homosexuals, a term which he confined to those having only
such experience; bisexuals, capable of enjoying relations with both
sexes; and narcissists, attracted to both but able to achieve satisfaction with neither. The author of this work, Dr. G. W. Henry, was,
as his terminology indicates, a psychiatrist. His case histories provided very complete personal data, his volumes dealt with both
men and women, and he included only those who had engaged in
overt sexual activity. By contrast, the present study is not strictly
oriented to any professional school of thought. It is limited to relations
between women, and "relations" is substituted for "experience" by
intent. Because of the comparative sex reticence prevailing in our
culture, few details of sexual action are reported in nonscientific
writing, and in the peculiarly discredited field of sex variance authors
often avoid even implying action. For this reason scientists tend to
disparage studies based on literature, but where women are concerned
a lack of specific detail is not too serious. Current scientific work,
notably that of Dr. A. C. Kinsey,[2] has established the fact that women
as a whole engage in much less sex activity than men. But in spite of,
or perhaps because of, this relative infrequency of "outlet," passionate
emotion more often plays a dominant role in their lives.

Not all women recognize a sexual factor in their subjective emotional relations, particularly in the intrasexual field so heavily
shadowed by social disapproval. Still they often exhibit indirect
responses which have all the intensity of physical passion and which
quite as basically affect the pattern of their lives. Hence this study
includes not only women who are conscious of passion for their own
sex, with or without overt expression, but also those who are merely
obsessively attached to other women over a longer period or at a
more mature age than is commonly expected. If "commonly expected" is another nebulous phrase, a species of pooled judgment
is available to clarify it. During the past few decades—that is, since
Freudian concepts have become a part of the common background—
most works on sex guidance have taken some account of homosexuality. These agree in general that passionate attachments during
puberty and early adolescence may lie within the norm, but if occur-
ring later they constitute variance. Without here debating the absolute
validity of this opinion, one may borrow it as a working criterion.

As to women who habitually wear men's clothing or even for a
part of their lives pass for men, such transvestism is not in itself

variant. To be sure, many psychoanalysts consider it indicative of latent homosexuality, but to bring a woman properly within the scope of this study her transvestism must be accompanied by some evidence of fondness for her own sex. And, of course, mere sex disguise arising from pressure of circumstance, a favorite device for plot-complication from ballads to modern films, has no significance here.

With the meaning of *variance* clarified, the more familiar terms *homosexual* and *lesbian* need attention. In popular usage the latter implies overt sexual expression and so it will be used only where such implication is intended. *Homosexùal* is more ambiguous. Still in good scientific standing, it ordinarily has not Dr. Henry's restricted meaning, but is more nearly synonymous with his *variant*. For this reason and also because as a noun it is most often applied to men, it will be employed here only when needed to relieve verbal monotony.

To conclude the business of definition, the word *literature* has, of course, two common meanings: belles-lettres, and factual material relative to a given subject. Here it is used in the former, or, more accurately, not in the latter sense; that is, the impressive bulk of scientific writing on sex variance will receive only cursory attention, to provide background for the matter of primary interest. This latter comprises mainly fiction, drama and poetry, and might best be termed simply *imaginative writing*, since many works to be discussed can boast but little belletristic worth. Even such inferior items, however, are important in reflecting attitudes and providing quantitative evidence of interest.

Only a few excursions into the field of biography and memoirs will be undertaken. Though such works are frequently classed as belles-lettres, they suffer from too many limitations to provide a profitable hunting ground. Those claiming factual accuracy are seldom frank enough about sexual matters to be useful, a condition which applies to virtually all reputable efforts since the development of scholarly historical method in the early nineteenth century. As to items written largely for sensational appeal, months of research would be required in each separate case to winnow the sparse truth from chaff which might prove explosive if offered as seriously related to fact. Biographies will be examined, then, only if their subjects produced ambiguous or enigmatic literary works possible of clarification by reference to their lives; or if they were the subject of fictional works which represented them as variants; or even (very rarely) if persistent rumor or circumstantial evidence strongly suggests variance. Most of these will be treated in a separate section specifically labeled conjectural.

For each variant woman considered, as many as possible of the following points will be noted: physical appearance and temperament, with particular regard to "masculine" attributes; emotional history, including any suggestion of etiology for variance; social reactions to the variant expressed or implied within her milieu; and the author's personal attitude. Only occasionally are all these data found together in any single work, but from the aggregate written within a given period enough can be gleaned to reflect trends in sentiment from one generation to another.

The ideal scope of any study pretending to offer a quantitative picture would be complete coverage of its chosen field, but realistic considerations limit such an undertaking. Oriental literature, for example, though cited by a number of scientific writers on variance, is too unavailable in translation to receive more than passing mention. The same is true of certain areas in western European belles-lettres, for only such as have appeared in English, French and German, or have been adequately reviewed in these languages, are of avail to the present writer. Even within such limits, of course, completeness is a goal as elusive as the rainbow's end. First there is the difficulty of learning about pertinent items. Scientific material on sex variance has been recorded adequately in bibliographies, indexes and abstracts in the fields of psychology and medicine. Imaginative writing has not been similarly covered. Almost the only systematic listing was that attempted early in this century in a journal of varying title and frequency published in Berlin and edited by Magnus Hirschfield: *Jahrbuch für Sexual Zwischenstufen* (etc.), sponsored by the Humanitären Wissenschaftliche Komitee, 1899-1921. There, under the heading "Bibliographie der homosexuellen Belletristik," European titles were assembled for the years 1899-1917, with a scattering of retrospective items; however, even for current German material the list was not exhaustive.

As to the nonscientific bibliographies and indexes, the material listed under such sexual headings as appear in them is largely factual or controversial, not imaginative writing. Book reviews sometimes offer helpful leads, but variant works are all too often ignored altogether, or are treated with such squeamishness or caution as to obscure their sexual significance. And, though extensive discussions or notes of pertinent material occasionally appear in factual works, beginning roughly with Krafft-Ebing's *Psychopathia Sexualis* (1886) and coming down to Donald Corey's *The Homosexual in America* (1952), such windfalls are sporadic and disconnected. In short, however thoroughly a student may comb bibliographic sources, he will still happen by pure chance upon enough items not mentioned there to end with the certainty of others still undiscovered. He can only hope, then, that better informed readers will hasten to attack his short-comings and fill his lacunae.

Another difficulty is gaining access to titles of which record has been found. No class of printed matter except outright pornography has suffered more critical neglect, exclusion from libraries, or omission from collected works than variant belles-lettres. Even items by recognized masters, such as Henry James's *The Bostonians* and Maupassant's "Paul's Mistress," have been omitted from inclusive editions issued by reputable publishers. When owned by libraries such titles are often catalogued obscurely, or impounded in special collections almost inaccessible to the public, or they have been "lost"—most probably stolen—and not replaced. Of Catulle Mendès's *Méphisto-phéla*, for example, which ran to half a dozen printings in French and as many in English between 1890 and 1910, only four copies are recorded in the United States among the nearly fifteen million entries in the Library of Congress Union Catalog.

Despite such handicaps, however, persistent search eventually reaches a point where the majority of new references prove duplicates of older discoveries, and the jealous pursuit of new volumes produces diminishing returns in that the items when located prove of only trifling significance. Thus, while the degree of completeness attained is not that of the statistician, it is believed sufficient to provide a reliable historical overview.

Along with completeness another ideal in work of this sort is to include nothing which has not been seen at first hand, but because of the difficulties just outlined some inaccessible works have been admitted when reviews or other records clearly indicate their importance and offer an adequate account of their content. For works well known and easily available in English, such as the poetry of Sappho or Gautier's *Mademoiselle de Maupin,* a minimum of résumé will ordinarily be given, but in the case of scarce items, even when inferior, a fuller account will be necessary to render any discussion of them intelligible.

A final note on punctuation should be included here. Direct quotation from original texts in any language, or from published translations of foreign works, will be indicated by the customary signs. The present writer's own translations of foreign material will be enclosed in *single* quotation marks.

CHAPTER I.

THE ANCIENT RECORD

Sappho and Ruth

It is natural to begin a study of sex variant women with Sappho, Greek lyric poet of the early sixth century B.C., whose name and that of her native island, Lesbos, have supplied our popular vocabulary with its terms for female homosexuality. Plato, who lived only two centuries later and probably knew her work almost completely, pronounced her the Tenth Muse, and, happily, the high quality of her verse led classical writers to quote it freely. For what with the hazards of time and later prejudice, the twelve thousand lines she is believed to have written are now lost save for these quoted excerpts and some fragments on papyri salvaged during modern excavations in Egypt. The few hundred surviving lines consist largely of lyrics addressed to girls, among them the famous "Ode" which has been pronounced the most economical description of passion to be found in literature. These verses will be considered presently.

An amazing quantity has been written about Sappho, translating and re-translating her poetry, eulogizing her poetic genius, and arguing hotly about her emotional life. An exhaustive bibliography would fill yet another volume. The ultimate source upon which all the rest is based may be consulted in the Loeb Classical Library's *Lyra Graeca*,[1] where J. M. Edmonds gives (with translations) the text of all that is known of her poems, taking into account the latest archaeological findings, as well as every significant allusion to Sappho in classical literature from Plato to Suidas—some seventy references by more than forty authors. A more popular volume is that from the Peter Pauper Press [1948][2] in which an anonymous compiler has assembled for each of Sappho's poems and fragments the two or three soundest prose translations along with metrical versions by well-known English poets.

As is universally the case with persons so far removed in time, few details of the poet's life are established beyond question. The most comprehensive biographical effort to date is Arthur Weigall's *Sappho of Lesbos, Her Life and Times* (1932),[3] to which its author brings a wide knowledge of classical languages, history and geography. Although perhaps too conjectural in parts to satisfy the rigid scholar, this can be recommended for its careful documentation and its impartiality with regard to Sappho's emotional temperament.

The best-authenticated facts seem to be that the poet was a small dark woman sometimes referred to as "ill-favored," but endowed with sufficient grace and personal charm to inspire in several fellow countrymen and poets a passion which she did not reciprocate. She was of distinguished family and lived in a time of acute political strife. She suffered exile twice during her early years: once from Mitylene to the interior of the island of Lesbos, the second time to Sicily. Weigall believes she was already well-known as a poet before her Sicilian sojourn, and suggests that she may have spent her several years on the island in Sybaris, where she acquired something of that city's brilliant sophistication. He places in this period also her marriage, probably of short duration, and the birth of her daughter Kleis to whom she was devoted throughout her life. After her return to Mitylene in her middle twenties she seems to have had constantly about her an ever-changing circle of younger women to whom she taught the verse-writing, music, and dancing which constituted a well-born girl's preparation for marriage. Some of these pupils or protégées may have lived in her house; it is known they came from neighboring islands and mainland to be taught by her.

The incident most often connected with her name is her leap to death from the cliffs of Leucadia for unrequited love of a young ferryman, Phaon. Certain references in her work and that of others, however, indicate that she died peacefully at home at a relatively advanced age. In fact, modern scholars are inclined to pronounce the whole Phaon anecdote legendary; but since it persisted for a couple of millennia, Weigall attempts to demonstrate at least its possible truth. The tenacity with which the story has survived is undoubtedly due to Ovid's incorporating it in his *Heroides* or Epistles of Heroines (15: "Sappho to Phaon"),[4] since, thanks to his romantic qualities, he was the most popular of all classical authors for several centuries after the Revival of Learning. Ovid's epistle, though sympathetically written, represents Sappho as an aging and heartbroken woman deserted by her handsome young lover and still consumed by passion for him "as by a grass fire." Ridiculed by friends, reproached by her brother for such despondency while she still has a living daughter, desperate over her waning charms, she can think only of suicide; and all this plaint she pours out in a letter to the man who has left her without even a farewell. The lament shows less restraint than any of Sappho's known verse, for fervent though that often is, it never lacks dignity. There is always the chance, of course, that Ovid had access to poems now wholly lost and never mentioned elsewhere; it is certain that during the centuries immediately following her death Sappho was the subject of some dramatic works (possibly satiric) of which we now know only the author's names, but which Ovid may have known.

Wherever responsibility lies, there was certainly a legend subsequent to Ovid's day that two Sapphos had flourished in Lesbos, one the great poet and the other a courtesan of undisciplined habits. Weigall believes this tale was motivated by rumors of heterosexual irregularities, and was invented by her well-wishers to clear her name of their shadow. But one must consider also that during the period of this myth's crystallization homosexuality in either sex was no longer tolerated as it had been (within limits) in the earlier Greek period. In Rome its practice among women was associated only with courtesans; thus it may equally well have been rumors of lesbian irregularity which gave rise to the conviction that she must have been a courtesan.

When one turns from personal conjecture about Sappho to the text of her work, one is left with no possible doubt about her variant tastes. Consider, for instance, the "Ode" mentioned above:

> It is to be a god, methinks, to sit before you and listen close by to the sweet accents and winning laughter which have made the heart in my breast beat fast, I warrant you. When I look on you, Brocheo, my speech comes short or fails me quite, I am tongue-tied; in a moment a delicate fire has overrun my flesh, my eyes grow dim and my ears ring, the sweat runs down me and a trembling takes me altogether, till I am as green and pale as grass, and death itself seems not very far away ...[5]

Few of her other poems equal this in intensity, and the textual evidences that its object was a woman (the gender of the name Brocheo being for a time in doubt) are meager enough so that during the years when homosexuality was a heinous offense scholars could translate it as addressed to a man without too great a strain on intellectual integrity. Discovery of the Oxyrinchus papyri, however, (so called

from the Egyptian town where they were disinterred), added so much
variant material to that already preserved in quotations that it
rendered honest doubt of her variance impossible. In the many poems
and fragments addressed to girls her ardor is evoked oftenest by maidenhood, its moving aspect not virginity so much as physical grace and
delicacy and a certain light freedom of spirit. In one fragment, indeed,
she describes herself as "eternally maiden" at heart.

There is no comparable evidence with regard to her feeling for
men. Once, to be sure, in attempting to hearten a girl on the eve of
of her wedding, she says: "That night was sweet enough to me, neither
have you, dear maid, anything to fear . . ."⁶ Again she writes to a
man: "But if you love me, choose yourself a younger wife; for I
cannot submit to live with one that is younger than I."⁷ And finally:
"If my paps could still give suck and my womb were able to bear
children, then would I come to another marriage bed with un-
faltering feet; but nay, age now maketh a thousand wrinkles to go
upon my flesh, and Love is in no haste to fly to me with his gift of
pain . . ."⁸ (The complaint: "Sweet mother, I truly cannot weave
my web; for I am overwhelmed through Aphrodite with love of
a slender youth," cannot be counted as significant, for it was rendered by one translator even before the Oxyrinchus discoveries as
ending: "a slender maiden.")⁹ These are the total count of verses
referring to heterosexual love, and there is nothing in them to match
the "delicate fire" of the "Hymn to Aphrodite" imploring the goddess
to soften the heart of a girl; or of the "Ode" quoted above; of the
verses to Anactoria and Gongyla and the five poems to Atthis; or
of the numerous fragments that glow with vivid delight in the beauty
and love of girls. Significant too is the poem addressed to these girls
in her old age. She laments her fading charms more bitterly even
than in Ovid's fictitious epistle, and ends:

> But I, be it known, love soft living, and for me brightness and
> beauty belong to the desire of the sunlight [are as necessary to
> me as light] and therefore I shall not crawl away to my lair till
> needs must be, but shall continue loved and loving with you.
> And now it is enough that I have your love, nor would I
> pray for more.¹⁰

Thus on internal evidence it appears that despite marriage and
motherhood, opportunities for a second match, and much writing
of conventional hymeneal verses, her life-long preference was for
women. Nor does the meager quantity of surviving verse disqualify

such an assumption. A great part of it consists of quotations chosen by forty classical authorities on poetic style, who can scarcely be suspected of mass preference for variant subject matter. The remainder (barring one seventh century manuscript) comes from papyri which had been used to reinforce mummy-casings.[11] Altogether, no sounder random sampling could well be devised.

We have seen that during the later classical period Sappho was suspected of having been a courtesan, which in those times may also have implied lesbian activity. Just when lesbianism became the main charge against her has not been determined. To be sure, a heavy weight of disrepute fell upon her with the establishment of the Christian church, and led to the burning of her work more than once. This was ordered first about 380 A.D. by Gregory Nazianzen as the result of an earlier church father having pronounced her a *gynaion pornikon erotomanes*—lewd nymphomaniac—but the phrase does not necessarily imply lesbian excess. Subsequently Scaliger states that her books were burned in 1073 at both Rome and Constantinople, without specifying the reason.[12] As this date falls shortly after that on which the church had reimposed strict celibacy upon its clergy, it may be that society had been made sensitive to homosexual activity among celibates and turned its suspicion upon her also. But this last surmise defies proof.

The lesbian controversy became bitter only in the nineteenth century when homosexuality was a heated issue both in the English-speaking countries and on the continent, and Sappho's champions felt impelled to prove her innocence. The sole outcome of the voluminous quarrel is certainty that the issue can never be finally resolved without the unearthing of fresh evidence. There is no specific mention of active lesbianism in her verse. By way of implication there are two or three references to her girls as her own or each other's *hetaerae,* which, since it was the common term for *courtesan,* might be taken to connote physical intimacy. She also mentions more than once the "pure and beautiful things" they all did together, an emphasis which Weigall feels may imply that in her day rumor ran otherwise. But her defenders judge these and a few more tenuous allusions insufficient to support the charge against her. More definite is Maximus of Tyre's statement, made without animus, that three girls (whom he names) were to Sappho what Alcibiades and others were to Socrates;[13] then there is the epithet *mascula Sappho* used by Horace,[14] and last, a reference in Ovid's "Epistle" to "a hundred others [feminine] whom I have loved not without evil imputation." Certain translators of Ovid, however, omit the *not,* thus completely reversing the sense of the phrase; thus neither reading carries any real weight.[15]

It was not until 1909 that so considerable an author as Rainer Maria Rilke ventured to exalt Sappho's loves (without discussing their nature) as nearer the 'divine intention' than heterosexual passion, which he pronounced a 'temporal interruption' in the evolution of ideal human relations. Taking Ovid's "Epistle" as a virtual translation from some vanished poem of Sappho's, Rilke suggests that the original was a lament not for some actual lover, but for the nonexistent man who could satisfy her after her less sensual experience with girls.[16]

With this century's increasing tolerance of all sorts of sexual freedom, prejudice has softened to a relatively untroubled acceptance of Sappho's probable lesbianism, and to an effort to understand, rather than defend, such behavior. Weigall suggests that one description of her "tiny little body" implies underdevelopment and unfitness for easy childbearing, circumstances which psychiatrists consider likely to induce avoidance of heterosexual relations and motherhood. And Freudians might stress her devotion to her eldest brother, Charaxus. In two surviving poems she attacks him so harshly for marrying a beautiful Alexandrian courtesan, whose freedom he had purchased at great cost, that her vitriolic lines to him and the epithet "black she-dog" for his wife suggest acute jealousy as well as contempt.[17]

All this conjecture, like last century's battles, proves little save the impossibility of objective judgment until new evidence appears. In accordance with the temper of our own time, we may leave it that Sappho was certainly variant, and, quite probably, what modern authorities term bisexual. She experienced marriage and motherhood, and may even have enjoyed other heterosexual relationships, but passion for her own sex inspired most of her poems, to judge from the surviving fragments. Furthermore these poems have been called by some critics the greatest love lyrics ever penned.

Though the work of Sappho provides a natural introduction, chronological precedence must be granted to the biblical Book of Ruth, written perhaps a few centuries earlier and describing events that antedated King David by three generations. This great short story, long acclaimed as a masterpiece of narrative art, is the first of a thin line of delicate portrayals, by authors seemingly blind to their full significance, of an attachment which, however innocent, is nevertheless still basically variant.

Certainly as an "anonymous but exact description of love" there are few passages in literature to rival Ruth's appeal to Naomi be-

ginning "Entreat me not to leave thee . . ." To quote it is surely un-
necessary, but let anyone who learned it in childhood, who has
never subsequently considered it in the light of primitive tribal
custom, reread it for the force of Ruth's willingness to abandon not
only her native soil and her own family but even her God and her
hope of burial with her ancestors. The emotional significance of
this passage is reinforced by three others in the story. Ruth and
Orpah had been married "about ten years" at the time of their
widowhood and of Naomi's decision to return to Israel, so that Ruth
was then at least in her twenties, and her devotion cannot be counted
the clinging of a bereaved adolescent to her bridegroom's mother.
Orpah, moreover, remained in Moab without more than formal
protest, and with apparently every prospect of finding a second husband there.

Then when Boaz welcomed Ruth among his gleaners because "it
hath fully been shewed me, all that thou hast done unto thy mother-
in-law," the girl replied, "Let me find grace in thy sight, my lord, for
that thou . . . hast spoken to the heart of thy handmaiden."[18] And,
finally, when by carrying out implicitly Naomi's clever scheme Ruth
was taken as a wife and bore Boaz a son, "The women said to Naomi
. . . he shall be unto thee a restorer of life and a nourisher of thine old
age; for thy daughter-in-law, which loveth thee, which is better to
thee than seven sons, hath borne him."[19].

Viewed without prejudice, this is a masterly portrait of a somewhat passive young woman, twice playing the heterosexual role with
success, but dominated by another love at least as compelling as that
for the men she successively married. H. M. and Nora K. Chadwick in
their *Growth of Literature* point out that "it gives the impression
of being written primarily for feminine circles,"[20] and by comparison
with many treatments of the variant theme it might well also have
been written *by* a woman.

After Sappho's poetry and this one Hebrew prose masterpiece,
little that is pertinent to our subject remains from the half dozen
centuries preceding the Christian era. That male homosexuality was,
within limits, an approved pattern in Greek life, and that it occurred
in Rome whether approved or not, especially under the later em-
perors, are now accepted facts. About its prevalence among women
less is known. From Plato and Euripides to Ovid, women as individual
personalities did not often figure in well-known classical writing,
and of women writers, though Mary Beard enumerates references to
an impressive number,[21] most traces have vanished. A few fragments,

however, and a few allusions to works never recovered, indicate that
female variance existed.

Plutarch, for instance, tells us that Spartan girls under Lycurgan
law received the same athletic training as boys and were encouraged
in the same emotional expression.[22] Havelock Ellis (without citing
his source) mentions Miletus along with Lesbos as favorable to
female homosexuality.[23] The *Greek Anthology* includes some variant
epigrams of Nossis from the lower Italian town of Locris, an imitator
of Sappho, "one dear to the muses and equal to her." From the same
source we have Asclepiades' epigram on the beautiful Dorcion who
wore boy's garments and "with the chlamys clearly revealing her
naked thigh would flash the fire of love from her eyes,"[24] but this
may have been merely a device to attract male attention since the
costume described here was that of the *ephebi*—male homosexuals.
Elsewhere both Ovid and Appolodorus recount that Caenis of
Thessaly, having given herself to Poseidon, begged that in return she
be changed into a man.[25] These last two, indicating nothing more
specific than transvestism and dissatisfaction with a female role, are
not too significant. Equally outside our scope because in the category
of erotica, but written and illustrated by women, are lost manuals
on erotic techniques of all sorts written respectively by Elephantis and
Philaenis. The illustrations from the latter's work are said to have
been widely copied in the bedroom art of contemporary sophisticates.[26]

Weigall suggests that two of Sappho's protégées, like her, celebrated
love for women in their verses.[27] One is the Gyrinno to whom she
was particularly attached, who died at nineteen. Weigall identifies
her fairly plausibly with Erinna, a known poet from the island of
Telos near Rhodes, whose work was highly regarded in her day,
although only one poem of hers is known by name and all but a
few lines are lost. These lines, however, lament the death of a loved
girl, Baucis. The other poet, more certainly identified, is Damophyla
of Pamphilia, who is known to have stayed with Sappho and to have
written love poems and hymns to Artemis in imitation of her great
model's verse.

Mythology in Classical Authors

Secondary evidence that interest in female variance continued
through the period is found in the myths as recounted by Greek
and Latin writers at the beginning of the Christian era, though
details of these stories are probably more characteristic of the writers'
own times than of earlier centuries. One finds as much variety in

different authors' treatment as is found between Malory's and Tennyson's versions of the Arthurian legends. From any great compilation such as the *Mythology of All Nations* or Fraser's *Golden Bough* one learns that in all the interrelated Mediterranean mythologies there was at least one goddess among whose attributes were one or more of the following: virginity, aversion to male sexual approach, some masculinity in dress or interests (such as warfare or the hunt), intense fondness for maiden devotees, and a strict requirement of maidenhood in the latter. One finds also persistent legends of Amazons, exclusively female groups who suffered men only for procreative ends and made active war against the other sex[28] (cf. a random news note, April 1951, of a precisely similar legend from an island off the coast of Japan).[29] It is impossible to date the origin of these myths or to secure historical substantiation of the mores they reflect. But anthropologists assure us that female homosexuality is known in most primitive societies (e.g., there is a North American Indian legend of physical intimacy between two women which resulted in an amorphous birth),[30] and it seems likely that variant detail was current in early oral tradition but was omitted by writers to whom such phenomena was antipathetic, or eliminated by later censorship.

A comparison of the later classical writers supports this view. In Book XI of Vergil's *Aeneid* one of the vivid personalities is Camilla, leader of a cavalry troop which figures brilliantly in the military action and of whose members many, if not at all, were women. Of her favorite comrade-in-arms, Camilla says only that she was like a sister to her. The goddess Diana is described as loving Camilla long and intensely, and, when the latter is slain by a sly and unheroic man, Diana lends her own bow and arrows to another protégé, Opis, so that this demigoddess may avenge the favorite's death. But there is no mention of intimacy between the goddess and either Opis or Camilla.

Similarly the conscientious chronicler Apollodorus reports between Artemis and her nymph, Callisto, a great fondness terminated by the girl's lapse from virginity;[31] and Iphigenia, whom Artemis rescued from the altar upon which her father was about to sacrifice her, was equally cherished.[32] Of Athene and her boon companion, Pallas, he tells us that in their girlhood they were so equally matched in the practice of arms that Zeus felt obliged one day to interpose his aegis between them lest his daughter be slain. As a result, Athene's thrust killed Pallas, whereupon, overcome by grief, Athene herself fashioned a wooden statue of her friend, wrapped it in the aegis, set it up beside that of Zeus, and honored it as she did his image. Hence her later epithet, Pallas-Athene.⁵³ Apollodorus later illustrates Athene's antipathy to the male by the Hephaestus story.⁵⁴ But with all these suggestive incidents he never mentions active variance in the goddess.

Ovid, on the other hand, offers two reports of variance. That it was not a personal obsession with him is proved by his treatment of those devotees of Diana, Atalanta and Daphne. Though the latter was so averse to the male that she prayed to be free of the beauty which made gods and men pursue her and was transmuted into a laurel tree,⁵⁵ no woman enters her story. The same is true of Atalanta,⁵⁶ "maidenly for a boy, boyish for a maiden," her plainly dressed hair "caught up in one knot," and a bow and quiver part of her usual costume. The story is well-known of her evading marriage by challenging all suitors to a footrace in which defeat meant death, but in the end she finally succumbed to the youth who secured Venus's aid against her.

Concerning Callisto, however, of whom Apollodorus's account is so bare, Ovid is much more specific.⁵⁷ Jove, smitten with the charms of the young huntress, knows that the sure means of approaching her is to assume his daughter Diana's form. Thus disguised he says, "Dear maid, best loved of all my followers, where hast thou been hunting today?" and then "he kissed her lips, not modestly nor as a maiden kisses." With neither protest nor surprise Callisto begins to recount her doings, and not until "he broke in upon her story with an embrace and by this outrage betrayed himself" does she recognize that her lover is not the goddess. When the results of Jove's attentions become evident—amusingly enough Diana, the virgin, is the last to recognize the signs—the girl, though blameless, is expelled forever from the goddess's train.

Then there is Ovid's idyl of Iphis and Ianthe.⁵⁸ Iphis's mother, while carrying her child, is warned by the father that if she bears a girl it will be subjected to death by exposure. Consequently she manages to conceal the child's sex and raise it as a boy, giving it the name Iphis "which was of common gender." From infancy, Iphis is the inseparable companion of a neighbor's child, Ianthe, and by the time the two reach marriageable age, a little over thirteen, they are passionately in love. The two fathers have long since arranged a marriage. Iphis and her mother exhaust every pretext for delaying the ceremony, to the sorrow and anger of everyone else, for even Ianthe does not know her beloved's true sex. Iphis spends long days lamenting the cruelty of Nature, which "surely never before has cursed a living creature with a love so monstrous." Conscience bids her "do only what is lawful" and confine her love strictly "within a woman's

right." She and her mother pray frantically to Isis for aid, to the end
that when the wedding day can finally no longer be postponed Iphis
is transformed at the altar into a boy, her voice deepening, her color
darkening, and her body growing in muscular firmness. (As treated
later by Antonius Liberalis[39] the heroine of this same plot is the
mother, and the suspense centers wholly about her escaping her
husband's wrath, the daughter being of only incidental interest.)

In yet another of the *Metamorphoses* Ovid describes the birth
of Hermaphroditus,[40] thus indicating that he was much interested
in all variant phenomena, but from the quoted passage concerning
Iphis's pangs of conscience about expressing her love, it would seem
that his approval of overt lesbianism was not unqualified.

Later Classical Literature

All the remaining variant tales in Latin literature deal with courtesans. Probably the best known is Juvenal's scathing sixth *Satire*,[41]
generally thought to have been directed against the empress Messalina,
who figures in the text as Saufeia. It describes orgiastic rites in
honor of the Bona Dea during which women of the highest social
rank vie with prostitutes in erotic skill and endurance, with Saufeia
bearing off the palm. The performance ends with a frantic search for
men, since lesbianism alone cannot satisfy the participants.

With a much lighter touch Martial in the course of his *Epigrams*
describes unflatteringly two women who on his evidence would
modernly be classed as hermaphrodites. One, Bassa,[42] has gained an
irreproachable reputation by admitting no men to her house as either
lovers or servants, but the initiated know that with her feminine
domestic staff she practices every license. The other, Philaenis, the
erotic writer mentioned earlier, exceeds men in her prowess with
women, and also takes the active part in sodomy with boys.[43] Although Dioscorides has denied in his epitaph in the *Greek Anthology*[44] that she wrote the "obscene book" attributed to her,
Martial's repeated references throughout the *Epigrams* suggest that
enough smoke hung over her in his day to justify the suspicion of fire.
The specific sexual exercise implied by both Juvenal and Martial is
tribadism, and there is mention in Juvenal as elsewhere of the *olisbos*
employed by women less well equipped for a male role than Bassa and
Philaenis. Both authors purported to describe actual persons and
conditions immediately preceding the Christian era.

A couple of centuries later we find fictional contributions from
the minor Greek authors, Lucian and Alciphron, both of whom
claimed to be writing about a period nearer that of Plato. Though

doubtless they had at hand more literature from the century in question than has been available since, a glance at historical fiction from medieval romance to modern novel will remind us that the life pictured is probably much nearer to that of their own time.

Lucian, in his *Dialogues of Hetaerae*,[45] presents a tale told to her lover by a flute-girl hired as entertainer by two wealthy lesbians, one a Corinthian. After the banquet the hostesses persuade Leana to stay and share their bed, sleeping between them. The Corinthian removes a feminine wig to display close-cropped hair, and vaunts her ability to give amatory satisfaction. Physically she is entirely feminine, but she protests that "in my feelings and passions I am altogether a man." Leana admits have received proof of this, but when pressed for detail by her lover she says, "Now you want to know too much. It was rather nasty business. No, by the Goddess! I won't tell you any more." She has already gone far enough, however, to imply tribadism and to hint at cunnilingus.

In a later *Dialogue,* a lover accuses his mistress of having slept the previous night with another man. He says that stealing to her chamber to surprise her, he hoped the companion he found there was only her maid, but his exploring hand discovered a cropped head. She replies that it was her girl friend whose hair has been cut because of illness and who hides her disfigurement by day with a wig. The gentleman apparently takes no exception to this explanation, though whether the lover was maid or girl friend, the implication is obvious. Lucian's own attitude may or may not be that of the male lover of women in his *Amores.*[46] In the course of a long debate with a pederast on the relative merits of the two modes of sexual experience, the champion of heterosexual love says: "If it is becoming for men to have intercourse with men, then for the future let women have it with women . . . girding themselves with their infamous instruments of lust . . . in a word, let our wanton tribades reign unchecked."

As to Alciphron, in his *Letters from Town and Country* (2:12) [47] he describes a day-long picnic to which a courtesan has invited her friends at her lover's villa. After a meal of oysters and lettuce, "the sort Aphrodite is said to love," the guests pair off, a few with their male lovers, the rest with women partners "of random choice," and drift away into surrounding thickets. Whether the feminine coupling is from preference or *faute de mieux* is not made exactly clear. The author neither expresses nor implies any judgment on the activity portrayed.

That gleanings should be so comparatively meager from a full millennium is scarcely surprising in the light of later history. After the collapse of Roman power, repeated waves of barbarian invasion, famine, and plague reduced both social organization and literature to only what could be salvaged in the growing Christian monasteries. As the spoken language drifted into dialects of unlettered vernacular, churchmen clung to Latin as the medium of communication, but they withheld classical belles-lettres from laymen for many centuries and undoubtedly winnowed and expurgated it. Deeply ingrained in Christian morality were several factors making for obliteration of anything sympathetic to female variance. One was general asceticism, a natural reaction from Roman excesses during the later Empire. Another was the animus against all homosexuality which Christianity inherited from Hebrew mores. A third was the intolerance toward women in any sexual role, largely chargeable to the strong anti-feminine bias of St. Paul.

From the surviving classical records of variance the policy of later censors is easy to deduce. Ovid's tales stop short of objectionable detail and in any event include only mythical characters. Juvenal and Martial are vitriolic or contemptuous, Lucian and Alciphron are talking of courtesans. Sappho survives only in such fragments as were embedded in otherwise valued treatises. Any sympathetic treatments of lesbian love have been eradicated.

Even in the few scattering survivals, however, we find a great variety of persons: goddess, empress, great literary artist, wealthy sophisticate, courtesan, and bucolic adolescent. Their experience ranges from depraved exhibitionism through proud assumption of masculinity or unashamed feminine passion, to naïve and troubled innocence (or in the case of Ruth to devotion unconscious of its own deeper significance.) All of these types of personality and experience recur often in later literature, in such guises that it is sometimes difficult to be sure whether they are grounded in observation of universal human behavior, or in admiring imitation of ancient models.

CHAPTER II.

FROM THE DARK AGES TO THE AGE OF REASON

Introduction

That no variant material remains from the ten centuries following
Alciphron is hardly surprising, since so little record of any sort has
survived. An oral literature of heroic tales and folk humor must have
flourished throughout the Middle Ages; narratives in the earliest
vernacular manuscripts bear many marks of such ancestry. But if
anything was written down before the eleventh century it doubtless
shared the fate of Charlemagne's collection of Frankish tales, which
were destroyed by his son, Louis the Pious, because of their pagan
character.

By the twelfth century written literature was increasing rapidly,
and early in the thirteenth we find incorporated in a medieval romance the first known variant episode since Alciphron's light-hearted
and bawdy tale. Its appearance did not, however, herald any sustained use of variance as a literary theme, and to appreciate its significance and that of the few subsequent examples prior to the
eighteenth century, one needs for background some over-all view of
the status of woman in medieval society. To put it briefly, woman
was regarded in two antithetical lights: as angel and as devil. We
have already noted that from the outset Christian theology saw her as
responsible for the fall of man and, therefore, as the root of all sexual
evil. This derogatory opinion was reinforced after the third century by
infiltrations from the dualistic religion of Persia. Manicheism divided
the universe into God's divine and incorporeal kingdom of light and
the souls of men, and a realm of darkness comprising the material
world and men's bodies, the province of the Devil. Since woman's
reproductive function bound her closer to the flesh than man was
bound, her burden of original sin was so much the greater. In the
later Middle Ages serious philosophical debate arose as to whether

she was a complete human being possessed of a soul, or merely a breeder for the superior race of men.

If today such views seem incredible, they gain reality when one remembers the outbreaks of witchcraft from the fourteenth to seventeenth centuries and the dreadful measures taken to suppress witches as followers of Satan. Modern psychologists tend to diagnose those epidemics as hysteria on the part of the bewitched and of the culprits themselves, who frequently confessed to intimacy with the Devil. Certain historians of the occult, however, offer convincing evidence that organized witchcraft was a survival from ancient fertility cults widespread in Europe, of Druidic or even earlier origin; cults which had worshipped a god in the semblance of an animal—most often a goat—and whose rites, as in all known fertility cults, were sexual.[1]

Records of witches' trials show that leaders of covens and more especially of the great orgiastic sabbaths appeared as "black men," usually equipped with horns, tails and hooves, and that their followers credited them with supernatural powers and literally worshipped them as legates of a god or as the god himself. The animal disguise so exactly fitted the medieval concepts of Satan that Christian heretic-hunters quite naturally equated witchcraft with devil worship, recorded it as such, and reacted accordingly. No apologia for witchcraft is intended by this suggestion. If one grants "wise women" a knowledge of poisonous herbs and of rudimentary hypnosis, and also, as midwives, the opportunity to procure the bodies of stillborn infants for their horrid magic-working concoctions, the ugliest charges against them become plausible. Then, too, there is little doubt that sexual licence of all sorts was common at the quarterly sabbaths if not at all smaller gatherings. It is particularly noteworthy that the male leaders of these festivals had female partners, supposedly for the benefit of the few attending warlocks; but the record of at least one trial states that the celebrants "usually" consorted with leaders of the opposite sex,[2] an indication that at times they must have consorted with their own. And from secondary sources one learns that witches generally were credited with "masculine" sexual tastes and habits. Thus, homosexual practices, in themselves anathema, were associated also with witchcraft, the blackest of all possible heresies.

In sharp contrast to this negative view of woman there existed at the same time a cult of woman-worship first articulated by the Provençal troubadours and later immortalized by Dante. It celebrated the ennobling and exalting influence of love for a pure woman, who, since she had transcended both common human frailty and the special aptitude of her sex for evil, deserved a twofold reverence. In its religious aspect this worship centered about the Virgin Mary and found expression in the naïvely human legends which grew up about her.[3] As her invariable championship of the underdog, man or woman, innocent or guilty, appears to be merely an apotheosis of the maternal instinct, these legends do not concern us here.

On the secular side, adoration of woman flowered in the convention of courtly love, that concept of passionate devotion without overt reward which seems more often to have been celebrated in the breach than in the observance. From this idealistic code of sexual relations stemmed the copious literature of medieval romance, and indeed of subsequent romantic fiction, in all of which the parallel worship of purity and of overwhelming passion provides the basic conflict. And until the eighteenth century, romantic fiction was the almost exclusive vehicle—at least on the reputable level—for variant incident, which therefore remained technically beyond reproach.

Taken together, then, the two contradictory views of woman just outlined provide, as it were, a philosophical portrait of her as she appeared to the later Middle Ages. There is also a practical picture more difficult to delineate because less was written about it at the time. Its early background in particular is obscure, since so very little is known about women during the Dark Ages. Some anthropologists hold that among Germanic peoples women were highly regarded; monogamy was the universal practice even before the advent of Christianity; women fought beside men in emergency; and certainly the Teutonic Valkyrie are a match for the Amazons of ancient Greece. Other social historians point out that the earliest epics, sagas, and *chansons de 'geste* celebrate only the valor of men whose deeds insured the survival of their folk-groups, and in these tales women play negligible roles. It is known, too, that under feudalism in some parts of Europe women were treated as little more than adjuncts to the land holdings they inherited, and were promised in marriage by male relatives, sometimes when scarcely out of the cradle, with the sole end of cementing politically profitable jointures of territory.[4] Whatever the truth may be—and it is certain that no single truth can hold for so heterogeneous a geographic and temporal span as Europe in the Dark Ages—we come to relatively stable ground only with the crusades and the transition from feudalism to chivalry.

For perhaps a dozen generations from the eleventh through the thirteenth centuries many men of all classes were drawn off on ever-widening military campaigns, civil or religious. Thus, the management of affairs at home devolved to some extent upon women. Of the effect on lower-class women we know little that is specific, though the hysteria of witchcraft suggests one result of numerical imbalance between the sexes on that level. On the upper social levels history tells us that many women managed their lords' estates, dispensed justice, marshalled armed forces when necessary, and sometimes even led those forces against rival lords—a circumstance commoner in Italy and southern France than in regions farther north. Consequently, these women acquired considerable learning. Hitherto even literacy had not been too common among laymen aside from those destined for very high positions, but it is probable that during the twelfth and thirteenth centuries women were better educated than men of the same class, the latter being engaged in more strenuous pursuits. It is known that women were in charge of hospitals during this period, and a few rose to the status of lecturers in Italian universities.[5]

The long period of men's absences and women's widening responsibility resulted, as always under such circumstances, in a certain feminization of social outlook, evident in the burgeoning of courtly love. Today statistical reading studies show that sex is a prime factor in determining reading interests and that romantic fiction is predominantly a feminine taste.[6] Historic evidence of these facts can be seen in the rapid spread of chivalric romance between the twelfth and fourteenth centuries.

The earliest romances written down in the twelfth century were comparatively simple and direct, showing close relation to the epics and *chansons de geste* which preceded them. Subsequently, partly because crusaders brought home oriental tales of intricacy and sophistication exceeding any style current in Europe, plots incorporated magical and fantastic elements and developed greater elaboration. Still later, after the revival of classical learning in the early renaissance, pastorals developed in rough imitation of Latin models, but with plot structure nearer that of their medieval narrative sources.

Medieval and Renaissance Fiction

The first romance mentioned by students of this genre as containing anything relevant to sex variance is *Huon of Bordeaux,* which appeared in French about 1220. (It has been consulted by the present writer only in the English translation of Lord Berners, first printed in 1543.) The tale was basically a derivative from the Charlemagne cycle or "Matter of France," and the first part, though incorporating fantasy in the person of Oberon, King of the Fairies, runs fairly true to its source. But like many popular stories it acquired sequels, and when the action reaches the third generation we find Huon's granddaughter, Ide, serving among the Holy Roman Emperor's forces in the guise of a knight, a feministic touch alien to the original epic.

In recognition of her prowess Ide is given the Emperor's daughter in marriage, and cannot refuse the honor without dangerous offense to her overlord. The princess Olive is in love with her fiancé. Ide's own emotions are not described—one of the author's subtle devices for exploiting a piquant situation without involving his heroine in moral obliquity. Another is his weaving of an inescapable net of circumstance in preliminary chapters to prevent Ide's either fleeing as a lone knight errant or returning to her father's domains in her feminine role—the one course meant disgraceful death, the other involvement in incest. So the reader is free to follow with good conscience Ide's submission to the marriage ceremony, her pretence of illness as excuse for inadequacy on the bridal night, and the unelaborated account of her attempt to satisfy her bride with "clyppynge and kyssynge" throughout the eight days of the wedding feast. When this technique is pursued for another week, however, the bride's bitter grief forces Ide to confess her sex, and the confession, carried to the Emperor by an eavesdropping page, results in his decreeing that Ide be burned, "for he sayd he wold not suffre suche boggery to be used." The fire is actually kindled before Ide's frantic prayers to God and the Virgin save her (as Ovid's Iphis was saved at the altar) by miraculous transformation into a man. Beyond a doubt considerable physical intimacy is implied here, though none so specific as in Martial or Lucian. And it appears that death was not an excessive penalty for such intimacy if wilfully indulged in, though again the mores reflected must be taken as a hybrid between those of the tenth century, in which the story was laid, and the thirteenth, in which it was written down.

It is possible that this sequel to *Huon* owed something to a collection of oriental tales which doubtless entered Europe during the period of the crusades, though they were not published until the sixteenth century and are believed to have been rewritten at that time (as *La Fleur Lascive Orientale*).[7] One of these, "The Princess Amany," recounts the adventure of a daughter of the "emperor" of Tartary. Converted to Islam by a highly educated nurse, Amany avoids marriage to a "pagan" by flight in male clothing. During her wanderings, she has a liaison with a "farmer's" wife, and then rescues the Indian princess, Dorrat, from violation by slaying her abductor. For half a year she supports herself and the lady, who does not know her sex, by her prowess in hunting and marauding. Having arrived in India, the two marry at the emperor's decree. Up to this point, only Dorrat has been emotionally involved, Amany being still half in love with the Tartar prince from whom she fled on religious grounds. But when Dorrat, disillusioned on her bridal night, attempts suicide, Amany becomes physically excited in the course of the struggle to save her, and the two live in complete marital intimacy for a month. Then the Tartar prince, now converted, appears and marries them both (happy Islam!), whereupon both ladies discover that they prefer the embraces of a man to each other's. Even an elementary acquaintance with oriental literature will suggest that this tale is a hybrid well cross-fertilized with Christian chivalry, upon which it may have left its reciprocal traces.

An Italian renaissance example of female sex variance appears in Ariosto's *Orlando Furioso* (1531). Ariosto's predecessor, Boiardo, in treating the same Roland material, cast as heroine the completely feminine Angelica, but Ariosto gave the lead to Bradamante, a young Amazon in full armor whose exploits equalled and sometimes exceeded those of the male knights. Indeed, Ariosto's version has been cited as feministic because of her prominence in the plot.[8] We need consider only Canto 25, which tells how Bradamante while suffering from a head wound is shorn of her hair, and thereafter is universally mistaken for her twin brother. Sleeping one day in the forest she is discovered by "young Flordespine of Spain," whose instant infatuation is so violent that Bradamante is wakened by a passionate kiss. Since in the chivalric code "cravenhood it were, befitting man of straw" not to respond, she at once confesses her sex. The disclosure has no effect upon the young princess' ardor. Taking Bradamante home, Flordespine showers her with rich woman's apparel and gifts, and laments all day—in almost the very words of Ovid's Iphis—that she should be cursed with a love the like of which she has never met "mid mankind or herd." Bradamante feels no answering attraction, but nothing indicates that either girl considers this love to be sinful. It is merely "unnatural."

> The ladies had one common bed that night,
> Their bed the same but different their repose.
> One sleeps, one moans and weeps in piteous plight
> Because her wild desire more fiercely glows.
> And on her wearied lids should slumber light,
> All is deceitful that brief dreaming shows:
>   To her it seems as if relenting heaven
>   A better sex to Bradamante has given.[9]

In the morning Bradamante quickly departs, to relieve a misery she
cannot assuage.

And now follows an interesting inversion of the theme. When
Bradamante recounts her adventure at home, her twin brother, recognizing in Flordespine a beauty whom he has long admired but has had
no chance to approach, makes off in secret in his sister's knightly
trappings and seeks the Spanish castle in her place. The princess
welcomes him with rapture, again supplies woman's dress, and only
at night discovers his sex, which the boy, still posing as his sister,
attributes to a timely bit of magic. The two live together for several
weeks before the truth is learned by anyone else.

Comparison of this treatment with that in *Huon of Bordeaux*
points up the literary and social changes which have intervened.
Nothing could testify more clearly to the altered role of religion than
the absence of moral judgment and the sex change through benevolent
magic instead of divine intervention. This and the verbal echo of
Ovid throughout Flordespine's long lament (only partially quoted
above) show to what extent the Revival of Learning had bred
familiarity with classical word and temper. There is also here a
greater psychological subtlety, natural to growing humanism. Though
Flordespine's passion is roused by her mistaking Bradamante for a
man and satisfied only by sex-reversal, her initial emotion is unaltered
by her enlightenment, and the brother whom she accepts is so feminine in both appearance and action that an entire household is
deceived for weeks. Thus the Spanish princess exhibits definite psychological variance. It is interesting that the knightly Bradamante
remains unmoved throughout and that Flordespine, the petite, impulsive, eminently feminine member of the pair, takes the initiative
in the whole business.

Sir Philip Sidney's pastoral *Arcadia,* circulated among friends in
1580 though not published till a decade later, shows a similar relation
to both medieval and classical sources. Here, as in the second part
of Ariosto's episode, the hero masquerades as an Amazon, in order
to gain access to a princess whose family is living in pastoral seclusion
for political reasons. The heroine's father is completely taken in and
himself conceives a passion for the handsome stranger. His wife,
several decades his junior, is only briefly deceived but holds her peace
because she is similarly smitten. Thanks to the separate jealous machinations of these two, all the hero's efforts to reveal his secret to his
love are balked, but within a few weeks his passion has communi-
cated itself to the girl. And now we have the moral scruples which

regularly distinguish English from continental literature. They are given vividly in Sidney's own words:

> O me, unfortunate wretch (sayd she) what poysonous heates be these, which thus torment me? . . . O you Stars judge rightly of me, & if I have with wicked intent made myself a pray to fancie, or if by any idle lustes I framed my harte fit for such an impression, then let this plague dayly increase in me, till my name bee odious to womankind . . . No, no, you cannot help me: Sinne must be the mother, and shame the daughter of my affection. And yet these be but childish objections . . . it is the impossibilitie that dooth torment me: for, unlawfull desires are punished after the effect of enjoying, but impossible desires are punished by the desire itself... And yet . . . what do I, sillie wench, knowe what Love hath prepared for me? Doo I not see my mother, as well, at least as furiouslie as my selfe, love Zelmane? And should I be wiser than my mother? Either she sees a possibilitie in that which I think impossible, or else impossible loves neede not misbecome me. And doo I not see Zelmane (who dothe not thinke a thought which is not first wayed by wisdom and virtue) doth not she vouchsafe to love me with like ardor? I see it, her eyes depose it to be true; what then? And if she can love poore me, shall I thinke scorne to love such a woman as Zelmane? Away then all vaine examinations of why and how. Thou lovest me, excellent Zelmane, and I love thee: And with that, embrasing the very grounde whereon she lay, she said to her selfe (for even to her selfe she was ashamed to speake it out in words) O my Zelmane, governe and direct me: for I am wholy given over to thee.[10]

There could scarcely be a more economical record of how girls were taught to regard homosexual passion in sixteenth century England; of the heroine's ignorance that any satisfaction of the desire was possible; and of her blameless rectitude, for she has both her mother and her idol as examples, and the reader knows that she is under the spell of legitimate sex attraction. That Sidney's own moral attitude was not necessarily his heroine's is suggested only in his wording of an oracle's prophecy to her father earlier: "Thy youngest shall with nature's bliss embrace An *uncouth* love, which *nature* hateth most" [author's italics.] Still, he was careful that Zelmane's secret should become known to the princess before the pair had opportunity for so much as a kiss.

The *Arcadia* is cited in Iwan Bloch's *Sex Life in England* as the first instance of lesbian love in English literature, but Bloch bases his claim on a night the princess and her sister spent together. He does not mention that they were sisters; however, it is not the kinship which invalidates his statement. It is true that the text reads: ". . . there cherishing one another with deere, though chaste embracements, with sweet, though cold kisses; it might seem that Love was come to play him there without darte; or that weerie of his owne fires, he was there to refresh himselfe betweene their sweete-breathing lippes." But the reason for their embrace was that both were suffering from hopeless loves, and, too shy to share confidences even by candlelight, had agreed that "they might talke better as they lay together." Bloch, however, makes his point from the statement that "they impoverished their cloathes to iniriche their bed, which for that night might well scorne the shrine of Venus," interpreting this to mean that they made elaborate preparation for a night of love, however cold and chaste Sidney claimed it to be.[11] The proper sense of the elaborate Elizabethan conceit is, of course, simply that they released their own loveliness from their garments and laid themselves on the bed which was thus more "inriched" than a shrine bearing an image of Venus herself.

A French pastoral making use of the same theme is d'Urfé's *Astrée,* published serially between 1607 and 1620. This vast work, running to some 5500 pages, has not been examined, but Maurice Magendie's *L'Astrée d'Honoré D'Urfé* gives an adequate notion of its significant points. Laid in Merovingian times, it is bound anachronistically by the strictest rules of courtly love, which made a lady's lightest word law for her lover. Thus, once banished by his offended lady's decree, the hero Céladon may not re-enter her presence without specific summons. After a volume of misadventure he contrives to return by impersonating Alexis, daughter of a Druid priest whose casuistry reconciles him to this evasion of Astrée's orders. Since Astrée has long mourned him as dead she is unlikely to summon him, but until she does, "Alexis" cannot reveal his identity. Her new friend's phenomenal resemblance to her lost lover provokes in Astrée an infatuation which, however well accounted for, is our first example since classical times of a woman's passion without scruple for one believed from the outset to be of her own sex.

For a time the Druid manages to prevent too great an intimacy between his "daughter" and Astrée, but when the two are guests at the same castle and share a room, the hero cannot resist taking some advantage of his opportunity, his only concern being dread of his lady's reaction to these liberties when she is finally enlightened. This eventuality is postponed by enemy attack and a long embroilment during which "Alexis" fights as a heroic Amazon, saves Astrée's life, is wounded, and is finally spirited away by the Druid to recover without danger of disclosure. When the revelation finally occurs, Astrée is indeed outraged—but note the reason: people will believe she merely pretended to be duped in order to excuse her own complaisances, and 'in Forez a woman does not trifle thus with her honor.' She bids Celadon die in expiation for his crime. " 'De quelle mort vous plait-il que je perisse?' gémit Céladon écrasé. 'N'importe, pourvu que tu meures!' Et il s'enfuit pour la satisfaire."[12] The Druid intervenes by proposing a pilgrimage to a shrine of Diana whose lions and unicorns slay the guilty but spare the pure. These heraldic guardians are transmitted into statues as the pair approach, thus testifying to the young lovers' technical chastity. As everything short of the ultimate intimacy has pretty clearly occurred, it would appear that in France of the early seventeenth century, as in sixteenth century Italy, such relations between women were not regarded too harshly. Nevertheless, both this pastoral and Sidney's portray the "far away and long ago," not the authors' own period, and d'Urfé's tale is obviously more than a little satiric. Evidence will appear later that with regard to contemporary phenomena judgment is generally less lenient.

The Borderline of Reality

The five examples described above are all from the field of romance, in which no further variant flora have been detected until the early nineteenth century. Indeed, the whole field of fiction was largely fallow during the seventeenth and eighteenth centuries. From the renaissance on, thanks to a growing classical influence and the weakening of churchly prejudice, drama of actable length gradually supplanted long formless narrative. But the drama, too, yields a thin harvest during these centuries. In romantic plays sex disguise was fairly common, but it produced no variant situations comparable to those cited from romance and pastoral. Action on the public stage, of course, cannot go as far as in the printed volume; furthermore, theatre audiences included lower class spectators more apt to be shocked by homosexual implication than educated readers with classical literary background.

Let us look, for example, at the two most significant masquerading women in Shakespeare's plays. Viola in *Twelfth Night* is an unconvincing man, afraid of the sight of her own sword, and her scenes with Olivia never even skirt the anomalous, their interest centering on her verbal agility. In *As You Like It* Rosalind is much more boyish in appearance and temperament, and Celia's devotion to her is marked. Following her cousin headlong into banishment, Celia reminds her harsh parent that:

> . . . we still have slept together,
> Rose at an instant, learn'd, play'd, sat together,
> And wheresoe'er we went, like Juno's swans,
> Still we went coupled and inseparable.

Also LeBeau tells Orlando that Rosalind has been "detained by her usurping uncle To keep his daughter company; whose loves Are dearer than the natural bond of sisters." These passages suggest an intensity in Celia's attachment which the effeminate Frenchman is quick to notice, but no further word or action in the play reinforces them. Celia's infatuation at sight for Oliver, though it does not, like Rosalind's for Orlando, blossom before the spectator's eyes, is no less whole-hearted, and if passion is implied at all between the girls it is that early adolescent sort readily supplanted by the first heterosexual attraction. The other women of Shakespeare frequently cited as unfeminine, Beatrice and Katherine, express antipathy to men, marriage, and male domination but exhibit no interest whatever in women.

Two realistic plays of the early seventeenth century which have as their heroines real persons, one a known lesbian and the other suspected, are of special interest because no hint of variance appears in either drama. Middleton and Dekker's *Roaring Girl* (1611) was built around Mary Frith, a transvestist of the London underworld commonly called "Moll Cutpurse," who was about twenty-five when the play was written. She is portrayed as hearty, fearless and clever, a walking lexicon of thieves' cant and free tavern songs, but of blameless character—the sworn enemy of injustice, oppression and double-dealing in underworld and gentry alike. She befriends honest lovers of any class but makes short work of men who approach her; she would like to see all women "manned but never pandered," and she burns to right women's wrongs in general. Asked when she will marry, her impudent rhymed answer adds up to "Never!" In short, she is a kind of sexless and feministic Robin Hood.

In their epilogue the authors say that some will:

> Wonder that a creature of her being
> Should be the subject of a poet, seeing
> In the world's eye none weighs so light: others look
> For all those base tricks published in a book
> Foul as the brains they flowed from, of cutpurses,
> Of nips and foists, nasty obscene discourses
> As full of lies as empty of worth and wit,
> For any honest ear and eye unfit.

Their reference is undoubtedly to *A Booke called the Madde Prancks of Merry Moll of the Bankside, with her Walks in Man's Apparel and to what Purpose. Written by John Day*, which was entered in the Stationers' Register for August 1610. All copies of this document were so thoroughly eliminated by her friends that scholars have even questioned whether it was ever printed, and a *Life and Death of Mrs. Mary Frith* surviving from 1662, the year after her death, is somewhat less harsh. An editorial note to the 1885 edition of the play,[13] drawing on this biography and other sources, tells us that she was a shoemaker's daughter who from childhood would run only with boys, "taking many a bang and blow," and that she had·a lifelong aversion to women's occupations and to children. Against family opposition she educated herself far above her station, but in the end apparently found no outlet for her capacities except in the underworld, where even her bitterest detractors admit her masculine daring and success as "highwayman," forger, and fence. Havelock Ellis, in his introduction to another edition of the play and in his *Studies in the Psychology of Sex*,[14] quotes the 1662 biography as saying that "No man can say or affirm that she ever had a sweetheart or any such fond thing to dally with her," a mastiff being the only living thing she cared for. Ellis adds that though nothing is said of homosexual practices, "we see clearly here what may be termed the homosexual diathesis."

The second play is *La Monja Alférez* (1626) by Juan Pérez de Montalban, a literary disciple of Lope de Vega, and is included in a volume by Fitz-Maurice Kelly entitled *The Nun Ensign*. It gives a partial picture of the known life of Catalina de Erauso, a Basque woman who was alive at the time of its publication, and like *The Roaring Girl*, it was probably written to whitewash the heroine's reputation. Here also the heroine is a transvestist, but one who actually passes for a military man, the mainspring of the plot being her exposure by her brother, a fellow officer. One Doña Ana is represented as being infatuated to the point of presenting her beloved with her girdle, but the gesture is symbolic only. "Guzlan" evades the issue by pleading a vow of *castidad,* a term less exclusively feminine than its English equivalent, and the two are never alone together or involved in more than acceptable verbal exchange. The play can scarcely have been a dramatic success, consisting as it does largely of long retrospective speeches by other characters which review Catalina's past adventures and constitute her apologia. It is not known to have been produced more than once, at a critical period in her fortunes when it must have been badly needed.

Erauso's full history as given in Kelly's volume is compiled from an autobiography included *in toto,* certain "Relaciones" fairly well established as originating with Erauso herself, and references in the *De' Viaggi . . .* of Pietro della Valle. Relegated by her family to the life of a nun, which she found intolerable, though three of her sisters took their vows, the girl escaped from her convent in 1607 at the age of about fifteen by contriving men's garments from the stuff of her religious habit. Subsequently she shipped to South America, where for some time she lived by her wits and her sword. Later, to escape a prison sentence she joined the army, was promoted for bravery to the rank of ensign, and was entrusted with at least one special mission. For some ten to fifteen years she went unexposed and unrecognized even by her brother, under whom she served for a time in Peru. In 1622, however, he became suspicious, and assigned her to perilous duty, as a result of which wounds brought her so near death that she confessed her sex to a bishop, and her military career was naturally at an end. The alternative life as a nun was now more distasteful to her than ever, and within a year she sailed for Spain to obtain proof that she had never taken the final vows, and, if possible, to secure a pension from Philip III on the strength of her military service.

It was at this time that *La Monja Alférez* was written and presented, and perhaps partly through its sympathetic influence she had success in both her undertakings and was furthermore granted permission by Pope Urban VIII to continue wearing men's clothes, though not to practice further deception about her true sex. Her European visit was thus somewhat in the nature of a triumph, though her family still refused to recognize her. Accordingly she returned to South America, became a wealthy owner of horses and mules, and was still thriving in the business of carrier when she died in her late fifties.

Of her love life not too much is given, but it is all significant. At one point she tells of taking refuge, when wounded, with a half-breed Indian woman, a widow, who wished to keep her on as son-in-law. The daughter, however, "was very black and ugly as the devil, the very opposite of my taste, which has always been for pretty faces."[15] From this situation she quite simply ran away, as from a number of similar ones; but where the ladies were agreeable to her she postponed flight till the ultimate moment. While serving under her brother she even sometimes accompanied him to his mistress' house, but when she took to going there on her own he became so jealous—believing her a man, of course—that he had her transferred to a distant post.

Before joining the army she worked for a time as bookkeeper to a wealthy merchant in Lima, in whose house she also boarded, and she was dismissed in less than a year for "sporting and frolicking" with his wife's two unmarried sisters, "one especially whom I preferred." One day while she was "in the parlour, combing my hair, lolling my head in her lap and tickling her ankles," the employer observed the play "through a grating" and sent her packing.[16] The inferred activities are fairly unmistakable, but since she was believed to be a man, we can deduce nothing from the incident about local attitudes towards homosexuality.

A well-documented passage in the "Relaciones" tells us that after her return from Europe she was entrusted, by a couple in Vera Cruz who knew her to be a woman, with the responsibility of escorting their daughter to Mexico where the girl was to be married. Thus it is clear that her earlier emotional adventures had been well concealed. But during the journey "she became jealously attached to her charge, resented her young friend's subsequent marriage, and in a letter of incomparable arrogance challenged the girl's husband to a duel" because he forbade her the house. Friends managed to prevent the meeting, and it was after this that she "sheathed her rapier and set about earning an unromantic living as a carrier." She must have been in her late forties at the time of this episode.

Neo-Classical Aridity

Because so little variant material appears in reputable imaginative writing between 1650 and 1800 we must turn elsewhere for evidence that variance nevertheless flourished. For reasons mentioned earlier, biography and memoirs are not generally within our scope, but in the sixteenth to eighteenth centuries the chief aim of such writing was narrative interest, and certainly Brantome, Casanova and the rest are read and enjoyed now in somewhat the same way as is Proust's autobiographical fiction of the present century. As has been said, even historians grant that a very fair general impression of the writers' periods can be gained from these spontaneous records.

The wide and colorful canvas of Brantome testifies that court morals under the later Valois were free in every respect. At several points in the *Lives of Gallant Ladies* (1665) he implies that lesbian attachments were taken for granted in his time, and in Section 15 of his first Discourse he raises the question whether husbands are cuckolded when their wives engage in "the love that is called *donna con donna*."[17]. He also doubts whether the point has ever been raised before, living as he did three centuries before divorce was commonplace and lesbian activity actionable as one form of alienation of affection. The cases he cites are almost all bisexual, for though he has heard of women who would have nothing to do with men, these do not seem to have been celebrated for variance either. He says it was useless to seek one young girl in marriage because her "friend" would never let her go; but the friend, who was providing bed and board, was a married woman. Indeed, he maintains that husbands regarded such affairs lightly, since these could not lead to embarrassing questions about the paternity of offspring. With characteristic wit he manages to include among his anecdotes every possible means of satisfaction between women, impermissible of translation today outside a medical treatise. He maintains throughout that women come in the end to acknowledge the inadequacy of all such means, "for after all nothing is the equal of a man."

Anthony Hamilton in his *Memoirs of the Comte de Grammont* (1713) gives an amusing account of the rivalry between the Earl of Rochester and Miss Hobart, a maid of honor to the Duchess of York, for the affections of the rather stupid young court beauty, Miss Anne Temple. However, at the English court even under Charles II such affairs were not taken so lightly. When, after a long siege, the patient Hobart attempted to embrace her favorite, the girl screamed, other waiting women came running, and "this was sufficient to disgrace Miss Hobart at court and totally ruin her reputation in London."[18]

These affairs occurred in high society, but Montaigne—or perhaps his secretary, who is said to have written the *Voyage in Italy* (1581) —writing in the same period as Brantôme, describes the case of a young weaver, one of a group of six or seven transvestists engaged in that trade, who courted several women in towns near her own and was finally hanged for effecting a marriage with one of them. The union endured happily for half a year, however, before the offender was recognized and exposed by someone from her own village. This is interesting evidence of contrast in sexual mores at different social levels, for the country in this case was Italy, and Brantôme and others claim that homosexuality was rife there, particularly in the courts of Naples and Sicily.

What may be called a middle-class allusion appears in the memoirs of the Comte de Tilly (1800) when he tells of being drawn in as second in a duel by two young men in an inn at Chartres who wished to settle a quarrel at once. The matter involves a girl whom both had known intimately and one had promised by signed agreement to marry within the year, come what might. The prospective bridegroom learned that "the treacherous Julie was acquainted with a lady of this town who was suspected of having habits once much in vogue in Lesbos and which to the shame of our time have made alarming progress even in the provinces," and accused the other man of having known this when he foisted Julie off on him. Without denying the charge, the accused says to de Tilly: "I confess this sort of rivalry gives me no ill humor, on the contrary it amuses me, and I am so lacking in morals as to laugh at it."[19] Several other examples of lesbian activity, some of them involving nuns, are to be found *passim* in Casanova's memoirs.

From the viewpoint of mere numerical count the richest field for the gleaner of variant incident would be that literature—not quite reputable from the English reader's viewpoint—which is farthest removed from the romantic. In romance, sexual attraction is an experience so personal and subjective that true lovers can be satisfied only with one another, and separation or an extraneous attraction on the part of either constitutes tragedy. Woman's role often transcends that of man because any lapse on her part entrains personal and social consequences of extreme gravity. That is, the romantic viewpoint is relatively feminine.

In the other type of narrative, sometimes erroneously classed with realism, the sexual act is all-important, enjoyable with any adequate partner since sensual pleasure eclipses all subjective factors. Here a woman may be an enthusiastic and carefree playmate, a coy jade to be taken by trickery, or an aggressive, even sadistic, snarer of the hapless male. Her one requisite is a sexual appetite to equal her partner's, and she is apparently immune to physical, and indifferent to social, consequences. In short, the outlook here is masculine. If the percentage of women authors is low in all areas of literature, in this one it reaches the vanishing point. Not even Margaret of Navarre nor

Aphra Behn, famed as they are for a free approach, go all the way with their brother writers.

The ultimate limit of male-oriented literature is pornography, with which this study will not be concerned beyond defining it as writing of which the primary intent is sexual arousal. The category is difficult of sharp delineation for an English-reading audience, since relatively unseasoned readers may attribute pornographic intent to works which the more "sophisticated" continental takes in his stride and admits to the realm of legitimate belles-lettres. This is particularly true of that early French and Italian material which was written with wit, style, and care to avoid coarse terminology, and which is more properly termed erotic or *galant*. To account adequately for such racial or national inconsistencies in sexual tolerance is impossible here. Undoubtedly an earlier familiarity with classical literature in Italy and southern France, as well as a readier exposure there to oriental influences, had something to do with continental lenience.

Historians of erotic literature trace the genre ultimately to two hypothetical sources. One is a group of Greek tales called Milesian which originated about the sixth or seventh century b.c., satirizing religion as well as sex. They were particularly scurrilous in their portrayal of women. The other source is oriental literature, since in both Hindu and Islamic philosophy the inferior status of woman tends to depersonalize sexual relations. Whatever its origin, erotic literature has flourished steadily in modern Europe from the earliest renaisssance to the present day, and has been produced by authors of literary repute—Boccaccio, Poggio, Aretino in Italy; and, in France, LaSalle, Rabelais, Venette, not to mention a score of lesser names in both countries. In the seventeenth and eighteenth centuries it developed in France into the style called *galant,* somewhat less lusty and more verbally subtle than earlier works but nonetheless very free. In this class the names most familiar to English readers are probably Restif de la Bretonne and Casanova.

Naturally all erotic works concentrate mainly upon heterosexual activity, but intra-sexual episodes, particularly among women, are not uncommon. The women involved are never wholly, or even primarily, homosexual. An innocent girl may be initiated by one more experienced into the mysteries of giving pleasure to men. Ladies of quality may experiment with one another to alleviate boredom, or prostitutes amuse themselves in idle intervals. Nuns may console each other for lack of opportunity with priests, though the latter are usually also available. All these contacts are the fruit of propinquity rather than personal devotion, and the sexual play often involves more than two participants. In short, even these lesbian anecdotes are presented from the male viewpoint.

Erotic works involving religious celibates have been much more a continental than an English product. Such works always had as their secondary and sometimes as their primary aim, the discrediting of the Roman church, and may have begun in the Middle Ages after Gregory VII (1015-1085) first stringently imposed celibacy on the clergy. (It will be recalled that Sappho's works were burned by the Church in 1073.) With the growth of rationalism in the seventeenth and eighteenth centuries anti-clerical erotic writing increased in volume, and once the French Revolution had broken the hold of Catholicism in France, tales about the cloistered orders degenerated there into almost unalloyed pornography. In England, where Roman church and monasticism had been crushed by Henry VIII, the anti-clerical category of erotica did not flourish; in the Puritan-influenced American colonies it seems never to have taken root at all. Perhaps as a corollary of this religious conservatism, homosexual works were equally rare. Of the continental writers named above only Boccaccio and Rabelais are generally acceptable to English readers, possibly because of the absence of homosexuality from their works.

Even after the Restoration in England the natural anti-Puritan outburst of risqué drama and picaresque novel went no farther than heterosexual freedom. The only variant literary traces of the court's sojourn in France are Anthony Hamilton's lesbian anecdote cited above, and a vicious poetic satire written anonymously in 1732. It was actually penned by Sir William King, principal of St. Mary's Hall at Oxford, and was directed against a female relative who had done him out of a fortune. He describes the lady as one endowed with some of the attributes of a witch and addicted to indecencies with a titled woman friend who figured as her "familiar." The occult details Sir William seems to have incorporated not only to render his picture more repulsive, but to supply etiology for his subject's homosexual bent, which apparently he did not care to import gratuitously. England has little else to contribute to the early variant record save an incident or two included in stereotyped histories of prostitutes, and some rather juvenile whipping stories laid in boarding schools or in households dominated by sadistic step-mothers or governesses, and even in these lesbian activity is infrequent.

French literature, meanwhile, moved in quite the other direction, undoubtedly following tendencies at court. At the end of the sixteenth century Henry III was widely reputed to be homosexual. A generation later Louis XIII, ailing and neurotic, vacillated between a few feminine and several masculine favorites, and is said, by some French biographers, to have made little distinction among them. The house of Orléans was also generally credited with homosexual proclivities in both the male and the female lines. On the feminine side, too, we have Christina of Sweden's lengthy visit in France during the emotionally disturbed period of her life (1670-1680) following her abdication. It has been suggested that she brought about Monaldeschi's murder at Versailles because the "thick packet of letters" in his possesion contained damning evidence of her now almost unquestioned lesbian habits. A century later Marie Antoinette's relations with Lamballe, Polignac and others of her court ladies were the subject of numerous scurrilous pamphlets, and although the details must be largely discounted as political mudslinging, any wide reading of serious biographical studies shows the underlying charges to be quite plausible.

For whatever reason, as the Bourbon dynasty grew in power and extravagance and under Louis XV the great courtesans enjoyed high social standing, freedom among women even loosely connected with court circles became quite fashionable. By the middle of the eighteenth century several houses of pleasure were elite institutions. Private theatres were maintained by certain noblemen for the presentation of highly censorable drama, and the best-known actresses and courtesans—often synonymous—were credited with constant lesbian activity in memoirs of the gossip-column type. From better authenticated sources we know that numerous frivolous private societies sprang up, and at least one of them was composed of "Anandrynes" or lesbian women. The *galant* narratives, of which the eighteenth century produced a rich crop, included frequent lesbian episodes, and for the first time in many decades the variant interest sometimes predominated over the heterosexual.

As one example of such writing, let us glance at a comparatively inoffensive survival from the period just before the Revolution. It is taken from *L'Espion Anglais* (1777-1778), eleven rambling volumes probably from several pens. In imitation of the more reputable journalistic correspondence of the time, this work is cast in the form of letters from "Milord All'eye" in Paris to his friend "Milord All'ear" in London. Mayeur de Saint-Paul is credited with the authorship of three very long letters[20] recording the career of a young girl from the provinces who runs away to Paris, finds a place in the most elite *maison* of the day, and is there groomed for the service of a prominent lesbian actress. The latter's luxurious maisonette, which is secluded in a wooded park, is described in detail, as are the stages of the girl's initiation into the erotic services of her mistress and into a large lesbian cult whose temple is located within the grounds. Action and setting are portrayed with some art and the narrative seldom becomes indelicately specific. Unhappily for the lesbian, the girl's personal maid, who lives outside the grounds, gives her male lover an eloquent account of her young mistress's charms. By masquerading as a delivery girl from a modiste's shop the boy insinuates himself into the actress's paradise, converts the lavishly-kept prisoner to the superior delights of *jouissance* with him, and brings about her expulsion by her outraged lesbian lover. This rococo gem was said to be based upon actual persons and circumstances of the decade in which it was written.

As a kind of last gasp of the *galant* school's attempt to conform to later standards of acceptability one may cite the work of Felicité de Choiseul-Meuse, an author of uncertain identity who produced a number of racy novels just after 1800. Her *Julie, ou J'ai Sauvé ma Rose* (1807) is a lushly romantic tale in which, as its title suggests, a professional flirt contrives to be all but seduced by every type of lover from timorous stripling to middle-aged man-about-town, and in every sort of setting from her own boudoir to a Gothic cavern where she is held by a kidnaper. Throughout the story she is attracted by lovely women, but she becomes involved with one only in the final chapter. A woman of boyish type seems to have captivated the man Julie really loves, and, by way of revenge on both, Julie seduces her rival, who proves to be an already active lesbian. She finds this dalliance pleasanter than anything thus far experienced with men, and as it does not constitute defloration, she ends by marrying happily the original lover who advised her in adolescence that women's power over men consists in never sacrificing their technical virginity.

Erotic writing did not, of course, cease with the end of the eighteenth century. But what may be called the *galant* way of life suffered a sharp check with the French Revolution. Not only the divine right of kings but the allied privilege of court circles to be a law unto themselves was eclipsed for a number of decades. In all countries and at all times the possessors of enormous wealth have enjoyed considerable independence of public opinion, but literature celebrating such independence in the sexual sphere tended to bifurcate after 1800 into problem novels whose tone was condemnatory, and an underground stream of pornography unacceptable for open publication. However unavailable the latter material may have been to the growing number of middle-class readers, rumors of its existence

doubtless filtered into the general consciousness. Bisexual pornography continued to be written throughout the nineteenth century,
some of it fairly high in quality and attributed to authors of renown,
and the recurrence of lesbian activity in this subterranean stream may
well have contributed to the disrepute of variance of all sorts during
that century and the first years of the present one.

CHAPTER III.

FROM THE ROMANTICS TO THE MODERNS

Introduction

Imaginative works featuring variant women have thus far been few, widely separated in time, and for the most part written with literary intent only. Thus, it has sufficed to present them with slight orientation in literary history. During the nineteenth century such items averaged better than three per decade and the majority were novels, a form particularly apt to reflect drifts of contemporary thought and even to be written for ulterior ends. If even tenuous patterns are to be traced in this mass of material it will be necessary to sketch as background the general trends of interest from which the novels grew.

Probably the most significant feature of the decades just following the French Revolution was the rapid spread of democratic efforts toward political, economic and educational betterment of the common man. This was reflected slowly in variant literature, and then only indirectly as it multiplied readers, writers, and subjects of relatively modest social status. Outside the field of social reform the same revolutionary sentiment appeared under such different guises as the Romantic Movement in literature and a scientific rather than a philosophic attack upon the problems of human personality.

Most closely allied to practical politics was the Woman's Movement. The eighteenth-century French rationalists who championed the rights of man included women in their thesis; however, for various historical and psychological reasons their own country-women never as a whole embraced the feminist cause. In England and America, on the other hand, where the property rights of women or their inability to vote on such humanitarian issues as abolition of slavery were sore points, feminists embarked upon a battle for legal equality which ran on into the present century.

The Romantic Movement in literature represented a swing away from eighteenth century rationalism toward the glorifying of emotional experience. Whereas the sexual licence in pre-Revolutionary France had reflected a *galant* indifference to moral standards, the new and more general claim to emotional freedom was a matter of philosophic principle. However unsatisfactory from a pragmatic viewpoint the lives of such men as Rousseau and Shelley may have been, these "mad idealists" were acting upon conviction. The keynote of romanticism was, as always, the exaltation of Love and of every individual's right to follow its dictates, a theme which figured prominently in nineteenth century literature and which still persists in popular fiction and films. While this philosophic tolerance did not extend to homosexual love, it enabled the subject to be treated seriously in other than underground erotic literature.

Yet another aspect of the rebellion against hitherto revered authority was the extension of scientific method to the study of human consciousness. Ever since the renaissance, science had been advancing steadily in physical fields. Its practical applications had produced the Industrial Revolution, and its unfettered intellectual attitude had helped, via the French Encyclopedists, to sow the seeds of political revolution. During the late eighteenth century students of geology, biology, and human anatomy were accumulating the evolutionary data so dramatically systematized in 1859 by Darwin. At the same time scientific travelers, observing primitive societies, assembled the raw materials of what later became anthropology. Finally at the beginning of the nineteenth century a few pioneers, defying heavy odds of religious and popular prejudice, began to explore the relation of mind to body. In Germany laboratory experiment was concentrated on the neurological bases of sensory experience. In France medical aspects of the problem took precedence, focussing on mental aberration, and by the 1860s Charcot, best known for his therapeutic use of hypnotism, had founded the first great neurological clinic.

As to the objective study of homosexuality, nothing which could be called scientific by modern standards was attempted until the last third of the century, but the phenomenon was noted extensively in the pre-anthropological records mentioned above, and a considerable group of studies on human hermaphrodites antedated 1850.[1] A single descriptive article on homosexuality appeared as early as 1791, when a German periodical, *Magazin für Erfahrungs-seelenkunde,* published the biographies of two men who "manifested an enthusiastic love for persons of their own sex," and one of whom attributed his predilection to childhood experiences at home and at school. For the next fifty years the only pertinent contributions seem to have been some articles on "the Scythian madness" (male homosexuality) in the ancient Greeks. Then, in 1852, a Dr. Casper published in his *Vierteljahrschaft* a number of comments on contemporaneous pederasty,[2] and a few years later he brought out a volume of male case histories under the title *Klinische Novellen*. During the following two decades Karl Ulrichs (writing under the pseudonym Numa Numantius) produced upward of a dozen pamphlets, controversial rather than scientific, which defended male homosexuality as hereditary and therefore not justly subject to legal penalty. All these studies, it should be noted, dealt exclusively with men.

What is considered the first essentially scientific publication, however, was a clinical report in 1870 on a female homosexual patient by a German physician, Westphal, after which similar descriptive case studies multiplied rapidly. In 1886 Krafft-Ebing brought out his lengthy *Psychopathia Sexualis*, a large section of which was devoted to "contrary sexual feeling," and before the end of the century Albert Moll, Havelock Ellis, and Magnus Hirscheld produced even more extensive treatises.[3] Although all these later studies included female cases, women still did not receive much emphasis. A Spaniard, Casán, was apparently the only writer to treat women exclusively. (His volume, listed in the U.S. Surgeon General's Catalog as *El Amor Lesbio*, 1896, has not been available for examination.)

The mounting stress upon an objective approach to psychological phenomena had its effect on alert literary minds. (It was not restricted, of course, to sex or variance). Balzac was the first to embark deliberately upon a "naturalistic" study of human experience, and although literary critics observe that his plots are often based on more or less abstract concepts, none deny that his individual characters show the fruit of minute observation. By 1857 Flaubert also was maintaining that "it is time to give it (literary art) the precision of the sciences by means of a pitiless method,"[4] and later in the century Zola pointed out that his own practice, as well as his theories set forth in *Le Roman Experimental*, were "based upon the application of experimental science to physiology as developed in the writings of Dr. Claude Bernard."[5] Each of these three major novelists contributed to the understanding of female variance, and the same spirit can be detected in the fiction of several lesser writers who attacked the subject.

Even in the many·cases whcre direct connection cannot be demonstrated between scientific thought and the imaginative writing under consideration, there is a perceptible correlation from decade to decade between quantitative developments in both fields.

Precursors of Modern Fiction

The transition from *galant* writing of the eighteenth century to modern fiction with its psychological preoccupation and its elevation of women's roles to a position of romantic importance could hardly be better exemplified than by Diderot's *La Religieuse*. Superficially, this novel appears to be a typical pre-revolutionary anti-clerical effort. As it was undertaken in 1760, only a year after the second suppression of its author's major project, *L'Encyclopedie*, it is tempting to imagine that the Jesuits' share in that act of censorship may have been the immediate spur to its inception. Actually *La Religieuse* broke new ground, for Diderot's preoccupation was not so much the religious shortcomings of the convents depicted, as the morbid physical and psychological effects of celibacy upon women, especially when this way of life was not freely elected but enforced by church and family.

The tale was first conceived as a practical joke on an impressionable philanthropist, the Marquis de Croismare, who in 1757 had exercised his influence in behalf of a nun seeking release from her vows. Not even personally acquainted with the young woman, he engaged legal aid for her but had no success, and she was forced to remain in her convent. A few years later, when she was unobtrusively transferred to another religious house, Diderot, Grimm, and other friends of de Croismare's conceived the idea of pretending that she had escaped, and Diderot forged a series of letters in which she appealed to her former benefactor for some means of support in a place where her religious "persecutors" could not find her. The victim of the hoax was so moved by it that he offered her (by mail) a position as companion to his daughter, and the perpetrators were forced to fabricate an account of her sudden death. It was not till eight years later that the marquis learned the truth, and "was able to laugh at the incident over which he had earlier wept."[8]

In the meantime Diderot had invented a complete autobiography supposedly written by the girl during her last illness, and though this was not completed in time to become a part of the deception, it so engaged its author's interest that he continued to work on the whole story intermittently for a couple of decades. It was pretty certainly finished by 1780, but was not published until 1796, when it appeared in its present form, along with the account of its composition. Written as her own artless journal, it gives the story of an illegitimate girl forced into convent life by a guilt-ridden mother and her suspicious husband. The victim resists her fate with extraordinary intelligence and ingenuity, but her struggles are futile, and she is merely transferred from one religious house to another, each exemplifying some pathological aspect of conventual sex-repression. Under the best abbess she meets nothing worse than a rather hysterical exaggeration of piety with slight variant overtones; in the second institution she encounters outright sadism, and in the third rampant homosexuality.

The Superior in this last house is an overt lesbian, and her efforts to seduce the girl occupy nearly a third of Diderot's whole volume. The young nun, steadfast in her desire for freedom—and marriage, though she has not yet known love—remains almost wholly blind to the meaning of the other's blandishments and of her own partial response to them. The Superior is described as vain, frivolous, flighty, and wholly without religious feeling. The scenes in her quarters where her favorites gossip, fawn on her, and compete for her favors are more in the spirit of *galant* eighteenth century canvases than that of a religious house. Ellis says that for the Superior "Diderot found a model in the Abbess of Chelles, a daughter of the Regent (Philippe of Orleans, brother of Louis XIV) and thus a member of a family which for several generations showed a marked tendency to inversion."[7] Wherever Diderot gathered his material, his picture of fevered intrigue, jealousy, skilled seduction, and finally of the frustrated Superior's decline into acute neurosis, is unparalleled in fiction before the present century. Indeed, for clinical accuracy of detail it had no equal until Westphal's scientific case study of a homosexual woman was published in 1870. Thus it stands as a landmark in the literature of female sex variance.

Equally a landmark, though of a very different sort, is Mary Wollstonecraft's *Mary, a Fiction,* which since it appeared in 1788, actually antedated Diderot's from the viewpoint of open publication. It is the first novel on female variance to be written by a woman, and its significance is augmented by its being an English work, written before its author's lengthy soujourn in France at the beginning of the Revolution. The writer of this now forgotten volume (only a handful of copies are extant here or abroad) is more generally remembered for her *Vindication of the Rights of Women* (1798), for her liaison in Paris during the Revolution with Gilbert Imlay, an American soldier of fortune, and for her later and comparatively unromantic marriage to William Godwin. In their recent *Modern*

Woman, the Lost Sex.[8] Lundberg and Farnham devote much space
to establishing the *Vindication* as the germ of all subsequent rebellion of women against their normal social and biological roles.
But though Wollstonecraft strongly defended the right of women to
the individual liberty which was being generally claimed for all
men, an impartial review of feminism hardly appears to justify so
complete an assignment of responsibility to this single work.

The authors of *Modern Woman* have done an excellent job of
analyzing the unhappy home environment and early experiences that
made Wollstonecraft a champion of her sex and a mordant critic
of male dominance. They pass over, as not germane to their theme,
one major factor in her life, her consuming attachment to Fanny
Blood, a young woman slightly Mary's senior, which began when
the latter was about fifteen and continued until Fanny's death twelve
years later. Of this attachment William Godwin in his *Memoirs*
says that it was "so fervent as . . . to have constituted the ruling
passion in her mind."[9]

This friendship is the theme of *Mary,* though the fictional version
is less moving and significant than the known facts on which it
was based. As biographers and critics are agreed that Wollstonecraft
had little creative imagination and drew for all her fiction with almost
embarrassing literalness upon her own experience, a parallel analysis
of the tale and its source incidents will be enlightening. The fictional
"Mary" is the child of wealth, with a single brother and an ailing
mother sentimentally addicted to novel reading. In reality, Mary
was the second of six children of a violent drunken father and a
masochistically submissive mother. The family was so impoverished
that from childhood Mary was acquainted with the bitterest contriving, and in late adolescence faced earning her own living, a
problem not easily solved in her time for a woman above the
servant class.

The father in the novel, dangerous when in his cups and given
freely to wenching, is the only accurate family portrait aside from
the heroine herself. That "tenderness and compassion" for the
ill-treated mother became "the governing propensity in her heart
through life" was as true of the real as of the fictional Mary. As a
mere child Wollstonecraft had often slept on the landing outside
her mother's door so that her father should not misuse his wife
when drunk. Ann, the beloved friend in the novel, lives, as did
Fanny Blood, in wretched poverty and suffers from unrequited
love for a man who has trifled with her affections. Thus "Mary's"
passionate devotion to Ann is not returned in kind, and she is

"often hurt by involuntary indifference." Rushing to Ann with glowing delight and seeing no answering emotion in her friend's face, "Mary would check her warm greeting and seem of chilling insensibility." Then, perceiving her friend's hurt surprise, she forces a contrite and disciplined warmth.

Upon the death of both mother and brother, "Mary" submits to her mother's dying wish and to pressure from her father, and marries a boy who is joint heir to the family property. Her only thought is of providing a stable home for Ann. Without the marriage's being consummated—the mere approach of the husband sickens "Mary"—the weak and egocentric boy embarks on the conventional Grand Tour of the continent to complete his education, and Ann moves in as "Mary's" companion. "Before she enjoyed Ann's constant society she imagined it would have made her completely happy; she was disappointed, and yet knew not what to complain of."[10] At her father's death her husband proposes to return, but the thought of him still makes her ill. "There was no previous attachment to give rise to her revulsion. Her friendship with Ann had occupied her whole heart and resembled a passion."[11]

This husband, so pallid a figment, was extraneous to the real Mary's experience. Actually she and a sister had launched a school for young girls, for which she had had superficial preparation as a governess, in order to provide a home for Fanny. The latter had once expressed a wish to live with Mary, but after much procrastination and one brief trial of life with the two struggling sisters, she returned to her own wretched home. Presently she married her vacillating suitor, whom in fact Mary had brought to terms with a few privately delivered home truths—quite simply that Fanny's incipient tuberculosis was due to his long indecision. After achieving this selfless end Mary fell ill, for the second time in her life, the first having followed her mother's death five years earlier.

In the novel Ann, unmarried and ailing, is taken to Lisbon by "Mary," and dies there despite the beneficial change of climate. In reality it was her husband's business which took Fanny there, and pregnancy which aggravated her pulmonary weakness. Gravely ill, she sent a desperate appeal to Mary, who threw over her teaching, borrowed ruinously to finance the journey, and even so, arrived in Lisbon only a few hours before Fanny's confinement and a few days before her death.

The *Fiction* was written subsequent not only to that loss but to Mary's first efforts at journalism and her resulting encounter with the artist Henry Fuseli. Almost at once she loved Fuseli passionately. He, however, was married, and his wife quite naturally vetoed Mary's incredibly naïve proposal to become one of the household. The girl, now twenty-six, believed her own passion to be purely "platonic." One biographer of Fuseli reports her as saying to him, "If I thought my passion criminal I would conquer it or die in the attempt, for immodesty in my eyes is ugliness."[12] In the *Fiction* "Henry" figures as an ailing violinist met in Lisbon during Ann's last illness and loved later in maternal fashion, but made inaccessible by Mary's own married state.

> He told her that the tenderest father could not more anxiously interest himself in the fate of a darling child than he did in hers. . . . He had called her "My child!" . . . His child, what an association of ideas. If I had had such a father! She could not dwell on the thoughts, the wishes which obtruded themselves. Her mind was unhinged, and passion unperceived filled her whole soul.[13]

Another speech of "Henry's" is significant in the Ann-"Mary" relationship: "I would give the world for a picture with the expression I have seen in your face when you have been supporting your friend [in your arms]."[14] As to the final relation of "Mary" to her husband, after her return to England she faints at the sight of him, and finally, demanding her freedom, retires to the country where she devotes herself to good works and waits for death, in which she will be reunited with Ann, and "where there is neither marrying nor giving in marriage."[15]

This whole cathartic outpouring raises interesting questions as to the author's own understanding of its emotional significance. It was published anonymously, but her own name and that of Henry appear unchanged, their relations in the tale, as in life, being beyond question blameless. So were "Mary's" with Ann on the surface, though the author states openly that "Mary always slept with Ann, who was subject to terrifying dreams." Yet she substituted "Ann" for Fanny, even though the latter had passed beyond the possible reach of slander. Was she perhaps aware of criticism directed against their relationship? Mary had, at twenty, been governess to the children of Lady Kingsborough in Ireland, and was dismissed because the children grew too fond of her.[16] The fourteen-year-old daughter in particular was so attached as to become ill during a brief separation from Mary. In a letter preserved in Godwin's *Memoirs,* Mary refers to the pleasure she derived from the girl's "innocent caresses," an odd adjective had Mary not been aware of possible caresses between women that were otherwise.

The answer seems to lie in two passages, one from the *Rights of Women* in which she refers to physical love as "perhaps the most evanescent of all passions," and the other in a letter to Imlay written after it was all too plain that his infatuation had burned out:

> Ah, my friend! You do not know the ineffable delight, the exquisite pleasure, which arises from the unison of affection and desire, when the whole soul and senses are abandoned to a lively imagination that renders every emotion delicate and rapturous. Yes; these are emotions over which satiety has no power and the recollection of which even disappointment cannot disenchant, but they do not exist without self-denial. These emotions, more or less strong, appear to me to be the distinctive characteristics of genius, the foundation of taste, and of that exquisite relish for the beauties of nature, of which the common herd of eaters and drinkers and child-begetters certainly have no idea. You will smile at an observation that has just occurred to me: I consider those minds as the most strong and original whose imagination acts as the stimulus to their senses.[17]

Here is a summing up of the wisdom gained from three love affairs, two physically unfulfilled, the third disillusioning. The passage also foreshadows her relations with Godwin, whose own description of their courtship runs as follows:

> The partiality which we conceive for each other . . . grew with equal advances in the mind of each. . . . One sex did not take the priority which long established custom has awarded it, nor the other overstep that delicacy which is so severely imposed. I am not conscious that either party can assume to have been the agent or the patient, the toil spreader or the prey, in the affair. . . . It was friendship melting into love.[18]

In Mary's eyes, Fuseli, Fanny, and she herself evidently bore some of the stigmata of genius. Imlay, business man, extravert, casual adventurer, impetuous lover, was of "the common herd of child-begetters." Hers is definitely the feminine romantic ideal of the subjective aspects of Love outweighing the physical to a point where the sex of the partner is less important than his personality.

Thus, we have in the last dozen years of the eighteenth century two novels which sounded the keynotes of much that has followed. Diderot analyzed an overtly homosexual woman and pronounced her wholly pathological and destructive, even though he assigned much of the responsibility for her divagations to the environment in which her entire life was spent. Wollstonecraft's novel idealized an innocent variant relationship as the highest form of emotional experience. Numerous variations on both these themes appear in the succeeding century and a half.

The Novel Before 1870

For the first three-quarters of the nineteenth century variant fiction was so nearly an exclusive product of France that traces appearing elsewhere may be left for separate consideration. The first pertinent French item was a typical Romantic Period novel of indifferent literary quality, Philip Cuisin's *Clémentine, Orpheline et Androgyne* (1819). As its title indicates, intersexual anatomy is responsible for the heroine's variant personality, which is used merely as mainspring for a plot of the wildest extravagance. *Clémentine* is a beautiful child of unknown antecedents cast ashore near Carcassone as sole survivor of a shipwreck. With the approach of puberty her ambiguous sex makes her the object of so much superstitious hostility among the peasants of the neighborhood that she is sent by her wealthy protector to a physician in Cadiz who is glad of the chance to observe such an anomaly.

A child's unawareness of her own peculiarity had betrayed her to the peasants of Carcassone. Shocked into neurotic prudery she manages in Cadiz to avoid suspicion though not curiosity on the part of the physician's daughter, who becomes strongly attached to her and is hurt by her refusal of the easy intimacy common among growing girls. Clémentine canalizes her waxing male eroticism into strenuous physical exercise and becomes a proficient fencer. This unfeminine skill and her habit of going about occasionally in men's clothing produce violent infatuation in a bold young woman of the neighborhood who believes her to be a man, and who plays thereafter the role of villain in the piece. Because of this woman's advances, Clémentine is forced to leave her sceond home in Cadiz and is subsequently involved in a series of stormy adventures. She is too feminine to live out her life disguised as a man, too relentlessly pursued by her evil adorer to settle down as an independent woman and win a man she has come to love. An interim in a convent, where she takes refuge from the law after killing a man in a duel, naturally only produces fresh complications. Here she, herself, is passionately drawn to the urbane Superior who cherishes her, and a novice is similarly attracted to her; but she resists all temptations (and they are many) to give way to her feelings. At last obstacles are overcome according to the best romantic pattern—she marries her male beloved, who understands and accepts her anomaly, encourages her to fence and hunt with him, and enjoys her love, which has "la force reuni des deux sexes." The author must have read the contemporary literature on hermaphroditism, but was evidently shy of attributing his heroine's passionate intensity to her anomaly after once he had her settled as a married woman, and so lays it in part to prenatal influence. Her mother, we are told, had during pregnancy been very friendly with a Persian ambassador to the French court, and had been "saturated" with his oriental tales. Thus, the daughter was predestined to love "avec l'exaltation d'une Persane."

The second and slightly more artistic French narrative is a two-volume novel by Henri de Latouche entitled *Fragoletta* (1829), which is concerned primarily with the Napoleonic wars and anti-British propaganda. Emotional interest centers about the hero's love for the title figure, whom he first meets as a boyish girl of fourteen, daring, brilliant, and free of coquetry. Her Sicilian guardian, knowing himself pursued by political assassins, implores d'Hauteville to marry and care for Fragoletta, but d'Hauteville feels that his love for her has roused no response save lively friendship and so waits for her emotions to mature. On the guardian's death he becomes her protector until the misfortunes of war separate them. Later he hears she has returned to her native Austria from which she was removed as an infant.

She writes him of discovering there a twin brother, Adriani, who eventually visits d'Hauteville in his Paris home and falls in love with his sister, an untouched innocent a year Adriani's senior. Sent as a spy to Naples, d'Hauteville sees Fragoletta there at a court ball given by Queen Caroline, at which Lady Hamilton is a guest. He hears that Adriani is a spy on the English-Neapolitan side, but because of the need for concealing his own identity he can neither reveal himself to Fragoletta nor penetrate the mystery of her presence among the English and her brother's treasonous activity.

He then learns from a frantic letter from his sister that Adriani has seduced her and that she no longer wishes to live. Her mother also has fallen gravely ill of the shock. D'Hauteville pursues the boy to Paris only to find him gone again and his sister on her death-bed. Subsequently, he tracks the traitor-seducer back to Naples and challenges him to a duel. Fragoletta, still in Naples, begs him not to expose himself to certain capture by the enemy merely in order to avenge "un tort exagéré ou peut-être imaginaire," implying that only his sister's naïvete led her to believe herself ravished. D'Haute-ville persists in duelling, however, and overcomes his opponent without effort. Adriani retreats almost without resistance over the edge of a cliff and falls to death in the sea below with a feminine cry which reveals to d'Hauteville that Fragoletta and her twin are one. The reader is left in doubt whether Fragoletta was, like Clém-entine, a hermaphrodite, or (as seems more probable) was simply an exclusively lesbian woman. (Similarly the Chevalier d'Eon moved in international diplomatic circles alternately as man and woman, his true sex being known only upon his death in 1810.) In the course of the story the author incorporates a scene between Queen Caroline and Emma Hamilton which takes place in the former's sunken marble bath. The queen first plays the part of lady's maid in disrobing her beautiful friend, and later indulges in erotic play until the two drowse off in one another's arms in the warm pool. Latouche may have in-tended this lax court background to account for Fragoletta's transfor-mation from a rather engaging tomboy into an active lesbian.

Far superior from a literary viewpoint to either of these novels was Balzac's first venture in the intersexual field, *Seraphitus-Seraphita* (1834). The heroine of this tale has been mentioned by Natalie Clifford Barney, a twentieth century writer of lesbian verse, as one of those androgynes who lend rarity to the Human Comedy.[19] but Seraphita was not, like Clémentine, a physical anomaly. The novel of which she is the title figure is a lengthy excursion into Sweden-borgian philosophy, and the girl is raised in an undiluted atmosphere of that particular mysticism. The result is a sexless and wholly ascetic personality. To the man who loves her she seems the perfect woman. To a younger girl whom she leads in fearless ascents of rocky heights above the fjords and who loves her equally, she seems the perfect man, although there is never any mystery about her true sex. With neither man nor girl does she exchange even the most innocent of physical caresses. After her early death the girl and the man marry one another, their common half-mystical worship of her constituting a stronger bond than exists between ordinary lovers.

In the following year Balzac published his much better-known novel, *The Girl with the Golden Eyes,* a romantic tale involving an overt lesbian, though the latter enters the story only at the end, the main theme being her effect upon her passive victim. The story describes the conquest, by the very flower of Byronic heroes, of a mysterious beauty sequestered in a Paris mansion with all the vigilance surrounding a caliph's harem. Once reached by the hero, the golden-eyed girl proves a paradox of virginity and voluptuous sophistication until a *lapsus linguae* betrays that it is a lesbian of enormous wealth who has initiated her sexually and kept her hidden from the world of men. This woman, returning from an absence which made the adventure possible, at once detects the girl's infidelity and, in a jealous and sadistic frenzy, kills her. She then discovers that her rival is her own half-brother and almost physical twin (they were both illegitimate, their father but one step removed from royalty), and, consequently, it was his resemblance to her that made his fatal conquest of the girl so easy.

In the extravagance of the plot and the description of the hero, which occupies a good quarter of the tale, one might suspect satire upon the Byronism which was sweeping Europe, except for the romantic seriousness of the whole. Another long interpolated essay is an arraignment, mordant in brilliance, of the cruelty, stupidity, and license of Parisian life, in which one detects echoes from Rousseau: in such an "unnatural" milieu excesses of evil are only to be expected. Such romantic social philosophy concerned Balzac here more than the psychology of either woman. That the golden-eyed girl, sold by her mother at the age of twelve and a passive partner throughout, should first learn complete love from the hero, is barely credible. That after a decade in which she has suffered neither physical nor nervous ill-health she should be so instantly changed as to prefer death to her former life might be questioned by the modern psychologist. The lesbian Marquise is hardly better accounted for. Her cool purchase and long imprisonment of the girl, whose physical beauty is the only tie suggested between them, make poor preparation for her heartbreak and sudden desire for convent life because she has lost "that which seemed the infinite." Possibly her half-Spanish, half-royal blood are intended to account for both her lesbianism and her vagaries of temperament, for gossip credited the Spanish ruling dynasty as well as the house of Orléans with tendencies toward homosexuality.

In *Cousin Bette* (1846), Balzac, with a realism in sharp contrast to both his earlier tales and in keeping with literary trends of the

intervening dozen years, presents rather casually the half-realized
infatuation of the thwarted spinster, Bette, for Madame Marneffe, the
human instrument she employs to satisfy her much stronger passion
for revenge upon the family who have humiliated her. Valérie Marneffe, who "spent her days upon a sofa, turning the lantern of her
detective spirit on the obscurest depths of souls, sentiments and
intrigues . . . had discovered the true nature of this ardent creature
burning with wasted passion, and meant to attach her to herself."[20]
Both women have had lovers, Bette having striven in vain to hold a
Polish artist several years her junior. But "in this new affection she
had found food . . . far more satisfying than her insane passion for
Wenceslas, who had always been cold to her."[21] Little of physical
intimacy is implied between the two women beyond frequent kisses,
and since Balzac is not particularly reticent about such details, it is
not safe to assume any such relation as existed in *The Girl with the
Golden Eyes*. But later in the book he speaks of such attachments
as "the strongest emotion known, that of a woman for a woman."[22]

Thus, the faithful observer of the Human Comedy presented three
contrasting types of emotional variance and offered three distinct
explanations of it. In the first, intellectual conditioning was the
causal factor; in the second, a possible inheritance of temperament
plus the certain freedom for self-indulgence provided by limitless
wealth; and in the third, poverty of both circumstance and emotional
opportunity. The resulting experiences also show the writer's imaginative range. The first seraphic heroine is as innnocent and passionless
as the biblical Ruth. The Spanish Marquise is violent to the point
of melodrama. The warped spinster is confused and groping in
expression as well as feeling.

In the same year that *The Girl with the Golden Eyes* appeared,
Gautier published *Mlle de Maupin*. The former enjoyed a few
months' priority, but Gautier's volume had been promised to the
publisher a year before its appearance, and as the two men's long
friendship began only with Balzac's reading of the younger man's
story,[23] there is no question of influence in either direction.

From the standpoint of modern psychology Gautier's is the
more careful and complete study. Indeed, having humor, vitality,
and a tolerant bisexual attitude, it is probably the most generally
popular of all variant "classics." In it an orphaned heiress dons men's
clothes and sets out to discover how men live when uninhibited
by the presence of ladies. In the course of her adventures Maupin
is loved by a young man of poetic temperament who has had
mistresses but found them physically satisfying only, and by a

young woman of good social standing who has been one of those
mistresses. Maupin also has with her for a time a young girl
disguised as a page whom she has rescued from exploitation by an
old rake and on whom she lavishes a devotion both erotic and
maternal. The young man suffers from believing his passion abnormal
until he learns Maupin's true sex, but then recognizes that for the
first time he has found complete love because he has so many
more tastes in common with this girl than with his previous feminine
paramours.

As to the young woman, her passion survives the revelation of
Maupin's sex, her persistent caresses prove as exciting as the man's,
and Maupin finishes by spending half the final night depicted with
each of them and by riding off in the morning with markedly
unfeminine detachment. Physically, we have for the first time in
modern fiction the explicit description of a type which has since
become associated with homosexual tendencies in women—the tall,
wide shouldered, slim hipped figure endowed with perfect grace
and with great skill in riding and fencing. Temperamentally we
have Maupin's own description of herself as "of a third sex, one
that has as yet no name above or below." As a girl she was "six
months older but six years less romantic" than her bosom friend,
for whom her friendship had "all the characteristics of a passion,"
but for years she "burned in her little skin like a chestnut on the
stove" to satisfy what is described as an intellectual curiosity about
the lives of men away from women and their real attitude toward
women.[24] It is this unemotional detachment which Gautier emphasizes
as peculiarly masculine.

Scattered through the story is a quantity of very canny analysis
of intersexual characteristics, and though the tale is supposedly based
upon the life of a seventeenth-century actress, it departs so far
from the known facts about her that it must stand as a monument
to the author's pyschological acumen alone. Since he wrote it at
the age of twenty-four, one cannot escape the suspicion that it was
drawn from personal or at least close secondhand acquaintance
with George Sand, so newly come to Paris in her male costume and
so prominent in literary circles at that moment. It certainly marks
a long step forward in the serious study of a variant personality.
(The actual history of Madeleine Maupin d'Aubigny,[25] late seventeenth-century singer and actress, is perhaps worth attention because
of its contrast to Gautier's artistic modification. As a young woman
Maupin came to Paris from the provinces determined upon a stage
career, and married her vocal teacher, d'Aubigny, who was connected

with the Opera and who got her the position upon which she was set. The marriage was apparently a mere strategic move on her part and was short-lived. A tall woman, and a fencer of extraordinary ability, Mme d'Aubigny frequently played young men's parts, and soon took to wearing men's costume off as well as on the stage. One of her diversions was roaming the streets at night and provoking men to cross swords with her for the pleasure of worsting them. She inspired passion in many young women, one of whom, a girl of good family, ran away with her when her repeated embroilments forced her to leave Paris. The girl's parents overtook the eloping couple and put their daughter into a convent at Avignon.

Being apparently infatuated herself, Maupin resumed woman's dress and gained entry to the convent as a novice for the purpose of manoeuvering her friend's escape. The means which presented themselves were macabre enough. A nun died and was buried within the convent enclosure; Maupin exhumed the body, put it in her friend's bed, and set fire to the cell; during the resulting confusion the two young women escaped. But their subsequent precarious vagabondage apparently cured the girl of her taste for bohemian freedom and for Maupin; she returned to her parents. Maupin's later career was comparatively seamy and unromantic.)

In 1851 Lamartine included in *Nouvelles Confidences*[26] an innocent infatuation between two adolescent girls which is reminiscent of Wollstonecraft's Mary and Balzac's *Seraphita*. (Though a reference in Havelock Ellis seems to place Regina among Lamartine's poetic works, it is actually prose. His statement that here the theme is treated with "more or less boldness"[27] also appears unjustified.) Although the initial attachment between the heroine, Regina, and her school friend, Clothilde, might be considered "normal," since it occurs between the ages of fourteen and seventeen, its later effects compel attention. The two girls, thrown together in a declining Roman convent school where supervision is lax, contrive regularly to spend their nights together. Lamartine describes their hours of long talk and tenderness with such skill and delicacy that one can doubt neither the basic innocence of both girls nor the ultimate passion in their embraces.

During their years together Clothilde talks so much of a twin brother Saluse that Regina falls half in love with him vicariously, but at seventeen she is married unwillingly to a titled dotard. In the same year Clothilde's mother dies, and Clothilde does not long survive this double loss of her only parent and beloved friend. At Clothilde's grave Regina and Saluse meet and fall in love at sight. Their passion runs a stormy but blameless course, which leads eventually to Regina's seeking formal release from her marriage. While she is away from Rome her petition is granted by the church, but only on condition of Saluse's permanent exile from the city. Saluse decides in her absence on exile for her sake rather than on elopement and public scandal. On learning of his decision the girl cries out that he who would sacrifice love to conscience cannot be the brother of Clothilde. 'At Clothilde's tomb it was not she I found again, it was a phantom. . . . He had her features but not her heart.'[28]

Lamartine's effort to explain the girls' passionate friendship is interesting if seemingly somewhat confused. Primarily, like Diderot, he lays responsibility upon the convent environment, where not only are women segregated but every aspect of their life—music, incense, pageantry, solitude and idleness—inflames the 'imagination,' while the feeble pretense at education includes nothing to stimulate or discipline the intellect. Such life produces 'veritable orientals, fit only for the harem.' The specific occasion of their emotional involvement, however, he says, is Regina's identification of Clothilde with the unknown brother of whom the latter talks so eloquently. 'I should never have believed in this phenomenon, which reflects and thus redoubles the beloved object, I should have taken it for the imaginative creation of poets, had I not seen it with my own eyes in the spirit of Regina.'[29] This seems a rather feeble attempt to gloss over any homosexual implication, for Clothilde, though more intellectual and less passionate than Regina, is in no way masculine. And, in the end, it was precisely the masculine element in Saluse's sacrifice of their love which repelled Regina. It was a man's decision and not a woman's, 'of the head and not the heart.' Lamartine's treatment here of the variant theme gains added interest from the fact that earlier, in *Jocelyn*, he had sailed perilously close to the implication of male variance. In this story, popular enough to supply the libretto for Godard's opera, a hermit priest becomes so attached to the "boy" left in his charge that he suffers agonies of conscience before discovering that his ward is a disguised girl. Evidently the whole matter of possible intrasexual attraction held a kind of fascination for Lamartine, though he treated it with a reserve more Victorian than French.

Toward the end of this decade (1858) a novel appeared, *La Sapho*, cited by Lewandowski in *Das Sexual Probleme . . .*[30] as definitely lesbian, and of added interest in that it was written by a woman,

Céleste Venard comtesse de Chabrillan; but unhappily this has not been available for examination.

At the beginning of the following decade (1862) Flaubert published *Salammbo,* of which Krafft-Ebing says that the author made his heroine homosexual.[31] If this is true at all by modern standards the condition is latent and of short duration, but because of the expressed judgment of so prominent an early authority on sex variance the story will be examined in some detail. It will also be interesting to see with what "pitiless method" Flaubert dissects the emotional economy of an inhibited girl. To be sure Salammbo's adolescent devotion to the virgin moon-goddess Tanit (comparable to the Greek Astarte and the Roman Diana, and allied also to the Roman Bona Dea) verges upon passion, but it is so described as to suggest the sexual overtones in any ecstatic religious experience rather than to imply a variant element.

Daughter of Hamilcar of Carthage, Salammbo grows up in a time of such peril that she is raised in solitary seclusion; her only companions are an aged nurse and the eunuch who is chief priest in the temple of Tanit. She would like to become a "devotee," but Hamilcar designs a politically profitable marriage for her, and forbids her initiation into the inner mysteries of the cult (which would involve ritual defloration, though Flaubert does not mention this fact).

> She had grown up in abstinence, in fastings and purifications, always surrounded by exquisite and solemn things, her body saturated with perfumes and her soul with prayers. . . . Of obscene symbols she knew nothing . . . (she) worshipped the Goddess in her sidereal aspect.

She says to the priest:

> It is a spirit that drives me to this love of mine. . . . [The other gods] are all too far away, too high, too insensible; while She—I feel her as a part of my life, she fills my soul. . . . I am devoured with eagerness to see her body.

This may seem suggestive, but she denies physical interest when under the fires of spring and the full moon, she cries out to her nurse:

> Sometimes gusts of heat seem to rise from the depths of my being. . . . Voices call me . . . fire rises in my breast;

it stifles me, I feel that I am dying . . . it is a caress folding about me and I feel crushed. . . . Oh! that I might lose myself in the night mists . . . that I could *leave my body* [author's italics] and be but a breath, a ray, then float up to thee, O Mother [Tanit].[32]

Her nurse, wise in the signs of physical ripening, does not take this for religious ecstasy.

" 'You must choose a husband from the sons of the Elders, since it was [your father's] wish,' she says. 'Your sorrow will vanish in the arms of a man.' 'Why?' asked the young girl. All the men she had seen had horrified her with their wild bestial laughter and their coarse limbs."[33]

These men are her father's barbarian mercenaries, and Flaubert's picture of their drunken orgy after victory would revolt a stronger spirit than that of a sheltered girl. Her first direct encounter is with Matho the Libyan, "his great mouth agape, his necklet of silver moons tangled in the hairs on his chest." Crazed with passion for her, he steals the Zaimph [sacred veil of Tanit] from the temple as a love charm, breaks into Salammbo's chambers at midnight, and attempts to ravish and abduct her. Naturally terrified, she summons aid in time to save herself, but she does not understand what it is he wants of her. Later she tells him: "Your words I did not understand, but I knew you wished to drag me toward something horrible, to the bottom of some abyss. . . ."[34]

The story then centers around her personal conflict between her desire to retrieve the Zaimph and her horror of the barbarian who has fled the city without returning it. Finally, under religious compulsion to save Carthage by regaining its sacred talisman, she makes her way to the Libyan's tent. She has been instructed by the high priest to resist Matho in no way, and consequently she submits to his embrace.

Salammbo, who was accustomed to eunuchs, yielded to amazement at the strength of this man. . . . A feeling of lassitude overpowered her . . . all the time she felt that she was in the grip of some doom, that she had reached a supreme and irrevocable moment. . . . Some power from within and at the same time above her, a command from the gods, forced her to yield to it; she was borne up as on clouds, and fell back swooning.[35]

But on being questioned subsequently by her father as to what occurred, she is evasive.

> Salammbo told no more, perhaps through shame, or else because in her extreme ingenuousness she attached but little importance to the soldier's embraces. . . . Then she examined the Zaimph and when she had well considered it, she was surprised to find that she did not experience that ecstasy which she had once pictured to herself. Her dream was accomplished; yet she was melancholy.[36]

Although she does not see Matho again and feels only hatred for him ". . . the anguish from which she formerly suffered had left her, and a strange calm possessed her. Her eyes were not so restless, and shone with limpid fire. . . . She did not keep such long or such rigid fasts now. . . . In spite of her hatred of him, she would have liked to see Matho again."[37]

This is a master's account of the effect of physical release on an unawakened girl.

Considerably later Salammbo is married, according to her father's plan, to the effete prince, Narr' Havas.

> He wore a flower-painted robe fringed with gold at the hem; his braided hair was caught up at his ears by two arrows of silver. . . . As she watched him, she was wrapped about with a host of vague thoughts. This young man with his gentle voice and woman's figure charmed her by the grace of his person and seemed like an elder sister sent by the Baalim to protect her. She did not understand how this young man could ever become her master. The thought of Matho came to her and she could not resist the desire to learn what had become of him. . . . Although she prayed every day to Tanit for Matho's death, her horror of the Libyan was growing less. She was confusedly aware that there was something almost like religion in the hatred [sic] with which he had persecuted her, and she wished to see in Narr' Havas a reflection, as it were, of a violence which still bemused her.[38]

These two passages indicate quite the opposite of homosexual emotion.

When, after months of carnage, Matho is taken captive and literally torn to pieces by the people of Carthage, Salammbo is witness to his terrible death. Instead of sharing in the shrieking triumph of the populace, she "could once more see him in his tent, clasping his arms about her waist, stammering gentle words. She thirsted to feel and hear those things again and was at the point of screaming aloud." And when Matho "fell back and moved no more," Salammbo also collapsed into unconsciousness from which she never recovered. The concluding words of the book are: "So died Hamilcar's daughter, because she had touched the mantle of Tanit." Flaubert's novel carries symbolic overtones not apparent in brief summary, and since Tanit was allied to the Roman Bona Dea, goddess of sexual fulfillment and fertility, her Zaimph doubtless represents heterosexual passion. Salammbo, conditioned to asceticism throughout her early life, dies of the unresolved conflict between these two dominating drives.

A minor novel which Krafft-Ebing mentions as also "mainly lesbian in theme"[39] may shed some light on what he intended by the term. It is Ernest Feydeau's *La Comtesse de Chalis* (1867), in which a dashing Parisian beauty neglects her children and tubercular husband for a spectacular career in *le haut monde*. An idealistic and infatuated professor of the new *Ecole Normale*, who is keenly aware of belonging to a lower social class, ruins himself financially in his attempt to maintain a place in the countess's world. The story, told by him, is chiefly concerned with his efforts to save her from the frivolous and corrupt life of her circle. Her evil genius is a fabulously wealthy Prince Titiane, diseased and depraved at twenty-one, whom she repeatedly promises to dismiss from her life but to whose influence she continuously succumbs. She goes gradually from bad to worse, and ends by consorting *à trois* with him and one of the city's celebrated courtesans, his long-time mistress; however, this situation develops only in the last pages of a lengthy volume. The Prince is described throughout as so effeminate in appearance, dress, and appurtenances that it would be easy to imagine him a woman in disguise, but there is no textual support for such an inference. Late in the story it develops that it is solely his use of the whip which binds the countess to him, and that this flagellation is without sexual sequel, since Titiane is impotent.

Aside from being unusually tall and arrogant, the countess has no masculine attributes whatever, either physical or psychological, and it is never she who wields the lash. Her dominant motive is an egotistic compulsion to be the most dazzling figure in Paris. Since the fantastic young Croesus, Titiane, is the arbiter of social destinies in her particular world, she is slavishly submissive to him. Her interest in the courtesan, though it is charged with emotion throughout, appears to be the obsession of an ambitious woman with the techniques of a serious rival, and the emotion is predominantly jealousy. Her final indulgence in sexual promiscuity results from her determination to be outdone by that rival in no field whatsoever. Analyzed by a modern psychiatrist, the countess would be diagnosed as a complete narcissist, unable to care the slightest for anyone but herself.

Consideration of these two novels suggests that to Krafft-Ebing any failure of feminine heterosexual adjustment was included in that "contrary sexual feeling" which was equated throughout his later study with active homosexuality. As we have seen, modern psychoanalysts consider narcissim and homosexuality as closely related in etiology; yet it is confusing to have the more specific term applied to experiences which, like Salammbo's and the countess's, include relations with men and none with their own sex. "Mainly lesbian in theme" *La Comtesse de Chalis* certainly is not.

The fact that in a contemporary novel considered later, Feydeau's *La Comtesse* was bracketed with Gautier's *Mlle Maupin* and Balzac's *Girl with the Golden Eyes* may also have contributed to Krafft-Ebing's thinking it more "lesbian" than it is. Indeed, the modern investigator sometimes suspects that scientific writers had not read all of the belletristic titles they referred to but were satisfied to rely on the word of others with respect to them. Another detail which might have strengthened an impression of similarity to Balzac is Feydeau's denunciation of *le haut monde* in imitation of Balzac's earlier indictment of metropolitan life in general. The new element in Feydeau is acute class consciousness in his condemnation of the "idle rich." However second-rate from an artistic standpoint *La Comtesse de Chalis* may be, it is a remarkably exact contemporary record of "the mixture of splendor and misery . . . the sense of uneasy satiety, of restless torpor, of indefinable dread" described by the modern Albert Guérard as prevailing in the late Second Empire.[40]

Evidence from Poets

Although fiction made up so preponderant a part of variant writing in the nineteenth century, poetry also made a sizable contribution.

In 1816, Coleridge, who with Wordsworth is generally thought of as initiating the Romantic Period in England, published two parts of a narrative poem, *Christabel,* which was never finished. All college students of literature know that eerie fragment of medieval romance with its occult overtones.

Christabel, the innocent heroine whose betrothed is "far away" on a knightly quest, steals out from her father's castle at midnight to pray for her lover beneath a giant oak hung with mistletoe—a test of maidenly courage in the face of both natural and occult darkness, for oak and mistletoe still retain pre-Christian connotations. In the moonlit wood she finds a distressed lady, Geraldine, who tells a story of kidnaping and violence designed to win her sympathy. As she helps the fainting lady into the castle certain signs forebode evil to a reader acquainted with demonic lore: Geraldine's eyes gleam in the dark like an animal's, she is so faint that she requires Christabel's aid in crossing the sill, and once she is inside a mastiff moans in its sleep and embers on the hearth shoot out tongues of flame.

In Christabel's maiden chamber while the two are disrobing Geraldine (and she alone) sees the "spectre" of Christabel's dead mother come to guard her child, and bids the hovering spirit be off. Though she has shown fear at sight of a carven angel in the room and has made poor work of feigning prayer, Geraldine still has power to prevent Christabel's seeing the vision or being warned, and presently the two lie down together "in appropriate medieval nudity."[41] With fascinated loathing Christabel notes that Geraldine's "breast and side" are those of a withered hag; still she is powerless to resist the other's spell, and in Geraldine's arms she falls into a trance.

> With open eyes (ah woe is me!)
> Asleep and dreaming fearfully,
> Fearfully dreaming, yet, I wis,
> Dreaming that alone, which is—
> O sorrow and shame! Can this be she
> The lady [Christabel] who knelt at the old oak tree?

Afterward "Her limbs relax, her countenance Grows sad and soft," and in her sleep she both smiles and weeps, while Geraldine "Seems to slumber still and mild As a mother with her child."

In the morning Christabel wakes to find her guest already clothed, but "fairer yet and yet more fair!" for now her shriveled

bosom has the fullness of a young woman's, a subtle allusion to
the wide-spread folk superstition that sexual contact with innocent
youth heals sickness and restores old age. Christabel is troubled
by "such perplexity of mind As dreams too lively leave behind,"
and delivers her morning greeting in "low faltering tones." "Sure
I have sinned!" she feels, but is uncertain precisely how, and prays
merely that "He who on the cross did groan ᵀlight wash away her
sins unknown."[42]

Roy Basler, in his *Sex, Symbolism and Psychology in Literature,*
devotes a long chapter[41] to the poem which is recommended to the
reader for its minute analysis of Coleridge's skill in handling the
whole episode. As he points out, it is "too realistic psychologically
. . . for one to avoid an erotic implication." The remainder of the
poem contains nothing further of variant significance. The spell
of Geraldine's touch has made it impossible for Christabel to give
her father anything beyond the simplest objective account of how
the woman came there, and the action merely prepares for later
events never written.

Of the content of these three projected "books" we have only
a brief account by Dr. James Gilman, with whom Coleridge lived
later while undergoing treatment for his addiction to opium. The
relevant points follow: Complications force Geraldine to abandon
her feminine form and to assume that of Christabel's absent lover. In
this guise she woos the girl and gains the father's consent to a
marriage, even though Christabel is filled with inexplicable loathing
for her at the altar. Had Coleridge carried through this outlined
narrative, he could scarcely, as Basler says, "have avoided even
more harrowing suggestions of a sexual nature" in Geraldine's
disguised courtship. Significant of her sexual duality are repeated
references to her height and her arrogant bearing.

Basler points out that after 1801, Coleridge's moral reputation
was precarious because of his opium habit, and that "no man ever
feared calumny more keenly." Although the poet began *Christabel*
and had the entire plot worked out at that time, he published
none of it for fifteen years. When it finally appeared, the *Edinburgh
Review* attacked it with "charges of obscenity" and "implications
of personal turpitude," while "parodies and vulgar continuations of
the poem made the most of leering improbabilities." The dread of
further personal attack discouraged Coleridge from completing the
work, and no other English poet seems to have approached the
subject of variance for nearly a half century.

The next poem that appeared in England, however—Christina

Rossetti's *Goblin Market,* written in 1859—is so akin to *Christabel* in its overtones of folk magic and so alien to the temporally intervening French poetry on variant themes that it is best to examine it here. It is generally regarded as variant or even lesbian, but the vivid narrative is too symbolic for precise sexual interpretation. On the surface it recounts that two sisters, Laura and Lizzie, as they stroll at dusk are daily tempted by "goblin men" to buy the most luscious of ripe fruits. Though knowing the fruits to be forbidden, Laura succumbs, pays with a curl of her golden hair (having no money), and partakes alone, Lizzie having fled. "She sucked their fruit globes fair or red . . . sucked and sucked and sucked . . . until her tongue was sore. . . ." After this indulgence she can no longer see or hear the goblins, and wastes away with pining for their delicacies.

When she seems "knocking at Death's door," Lizzie, aware that another girl in like case has recently died, goes to purchase fruit for her sister with honest coin. The goblins refuse her money and use every means to force their wares between her own lips, but she resists and returns so dripping with crushed fruit that she is hopeful of bringing some satisfaction to her sister. Laura kisses her hungrily, but more in gratitude for the dreadful risk she has run than in greed for what lingers "in dimples of her chin." Indeed, the fruit now scorches Laura's lips and is wormwood on her tongue, so that from loathing she is seized with violent convulsion and falls unconscious. In the morning she awakes cured, and Lizzie suffers no ill effects at all.

As a translation of voluptuous experience into decorous terms the poem cannot be equaled, but any attempt at literal reconstruction of the experience bogs down in the symbolic details. Certain points however are implicit in the text: Laura's experience is a complete sexual release which it needs no acquaintance with Freud to recognize as oral-erotic. All the goblins are male, but they are grotesque, repulsive, more animal than human save for their ability to hawk their wares, and these irresistable wares take the shapes of ripe cherries, peaches, plums, melons, "figs that fill the mouth"—in short, the whole catalog of age-old symbols for female charms. Although the sisters are described as "Sleeping in their curtained bed Cheek to cheek and breast to breast," there is no more incestuous lesbian implication here than in Sidney's *Arcadia.* These embraces are plainly symbols of the innocence from which Laura lapses and to which she returns by virtue of Lizzie's steadfast purity. Perhaps the only safe inference is that Laura's "fall" is solitary, even subjectively in-

duced (psychiatric records prove fantasy to be an adequate agent).
Her subsequent neurotic inhibition is the product of guilt, and ends
in a releasing hysteric convulsion somehow brought about by Lizzie's
ministrations.

This mundane analysis of an exquisite work of art does reveal its
author's emotional pattern. It is known that Miss Rossetti had a
somewhat cloistered life, largely spent in the company of a mother
to whom she was intensely devoted and a sister who later became
an Anglican nun, all three women being almost fanatically devout.
She was twice passionately in love with men, but refused them
both on the grounds of religious incompatibility. The first of these
episodes occurred when she was barely seventeen. The man, a recent
convert to Catholicism, returned to the Church of England when
he discovered that Christina would not marry a papist, but later
reverted to Rome, and the whole affair seems to have constituted a
two-year span of acute emotional disturbance in the girl's life.
(She subsequently fainted upon meeting him unexpectedly in the
street.) It may well have been that any man's ability to switch
religious camps so readily under the stress of passion produced a
reaction to the whole business of sex such as we find in *Goblin
Market,* which was written when its author was nearing thirty.
Tragically enough, her life-long ascetic repression broke during her
last illness in a protracted delirium which revealed at what cost it
had been maintained.

France was as always more tolerant of sexual latitude in literature
than England, but even there the open-mindedness which made *Mlle
de Maupin* acceptable in 1835 was not constant. Since it is impossible
to give in short compass any account of the alternating waves of
liberalism and conservative reaction that swayed public opinion
there during the middle decades of the century, it must suffice to
note that Charles Baudelaire published his *Fleurs du Mal* during an
interim of clerical dominance, and in consequence the volume was
condemned by the *Tribunal Correctionnel* in August 1857. As early
as 1846 the publisher Levy had announced on advertising pages of
other works a forthcoming title by Baudelaire, *Les Lesbiennes,*[13]
which never appeared as such, probably because the title was too
daring. Only three poems in the *Fleurs* touch upon lesbianism, but
the longest of these was one of the six which were ordered removed
from the volume and which were not publicly printed again until
1911.

This poem, "Femmes Damnées, I," some twenty-six quatrains in length, describes rather explicitly the conquest of a feminine and passive young girl, half reluctant because still dreaming of hetero-sexual love, by a more aggressive feminine partner who decries the physical brutality and spiritual incompatibility of any male lover. In "Femmes Damnées, II" the poet watches a band of lesbians at a shore resort behaving much as any uninhibited heterosexual group might do, and accords them more than even his customary despairing compassion. Such love as theirs is doomed to go unsated, and they themselves, he says, will pass progressively to drink and drugs and "loveless loves that know no pity." And yet in "Lesbos" he holds Sappho guilty of a "crime of the spirit" when, faithless to her own earlier teaching and practice, she "flung the dark roses of her love sublime To a vain churl (Phaon.)" [44] (Note: "Lesbos" had appeared in 1850 in an anthology, *Les Poètes de l'Amour*, published by Lemerre. It was omitted from the 1858 edition of that volume, but reappeared in the edition of 1865.) [45] The Catholic Baudelaire was essentially a mystic, not a romantic with that faith in Love which had been the gospel of the preceding decades. Obsessed as he was by the failure of all passion to satisfy the human craving for per-fection, it is natural that homosexual passion, inevitably "unassuage-able, sterile and outcast," should seem to him the essence of pitiable futility. This negative judgment, however, is not given in terms of conventional morality.

Within a decade the wave of conservatism had so far receded that Paul Verlaine's *Les Amies, Scènes d'Amour Sapphique* (1867), though published in Brussels for safety, apparently encountered in France no harsher judgment than a comment in the *Bulletin Trimestriel* that they were by a poet of the school of M Leconte de Lisle, and were "fort singuliers." [46] The slim sheaf of sixteen pages contained six poems, subsequently included in his volume *Parallèle-ment*, which described lesbian love and its overt expression more explicitly than Baudelaire's condemned verses, or indeed than any other non-erotic work up to that time. The "Pensionnaires" are sisters in the middle teens, the younger of whom still 'smiles with innocence' despite the elder's far from innocent ministrations. The pair in "Sur le Balcon," dreaming only of the love between women, are 'a strange couple, pitied by other heterosexual couples.' "Prin-temps" and "Eté" reproduce the situation in Baudelaire's "Femmes Damnées, I" except that here the younger and more innocent girl is neither reluctant nor apprehensive. In "Per Amica Silentia" the poet applies for the first time the adjective "esseulées"—solitary, left alone—to those who 'in these unhappy times' are set apart by "le glorieux stigmate," thus foreshadowing the social isolation lamented sixty years later in the *Well of Loneliness,* but indicating by the adjective "glorieux" that his sentiment, unlike Baudelaire's, is one of championship. In the final "Sappho" he describes the poet, hollow-eyed, pacing a cold shore, restless as a she-wolf, weeping and tearing her hair over Phaon's indifference until finally she plunges into the sea in despair at the contrast between her present state and the 'young glory of her early loves.'[47] It is more than likely that it was from this poem that Rilke derived his interpretation of Sappho's "Lament" heretofore mentioned.

During the preceding year (1866) there had appeared in England Swinburne's *Poems and Ballads: First Series,* which raised an outcry on several counts—its general "paganism," its evidence of French influence (particularly that of Baudelaire), and its scattering of poems with a homosexual tinge. Swinburne had, in his youth, been intimate with the much older Sir Richard Burton, famous translator of the *Arabian Nights* and author of an appendix on that "sotadic zone" in the Mediterranean region which in his opinion favored the development of homosexual tendencies. Later Swinburne fell under the influence of Richard Monckton-Milnes, famous for a library of variant erotica. As both of these friendships were matters of common knowledge, when *Poems and Ballads* appeared, attention focussed naturally on such poems as "Erotion," "Hermaphroditus," "Fragoletta," "Hesperia," and the fairly numerous group with a lesbian coloring, though none of these were explicit or described a realistic contemporary situation in the manner of Verlaine.

"Anactoria" is a ten-page plaint from Sappho to a girl who no longer reciprocates her love, but it differs little from Swinburne's many laments celebrating all love as pain. The "Sapphics" describe life on Mitylene, "place whence all gods fled . . . full of fruitless women and music only." A half dozen stanzas scattered through other poems—notably "Dolores," "Faustine," and "Masque of Queen Bersabe"—echo the same note. Swinburne's attitude is unsympathetic, colder even than Baudelaire's and more scornful, with emphasis always upon the barrenness of lesbian love, as might be expected from a poet who occasionally made almost a fetish of baby-worship.

All of the longer biographies of Swinburne give some account of a projected narrative in mixed prose and verse upon which he worked intermittently between 1864 and 1867 but never finished. What remains of manuscript and galley proof is now in the British Museum, after a half-century in the possession of the notorious rare-book dealer and literary forger, Thomas Wise. It was finally edited and given private publication in 1952 by Langdon Hughes, an idolatrous admirer of Swinburne, for whom it held the promise of becoming, if completed, one of the greater English novels. Unhappily, neither the scant surviving text nor Mr. Hughes's overwhelming volume of annotation and championship convey to the reader much of that promise or of the author's projected intent. As Swinburne himself gave it no title it is generally known by the suggestive name of its central figure: *Lesbia Brandon*. Georges Lafourcade, in his scholarly two-volume study of Swinburne, suggests that this character was drawn from Jane Faulkner,[8] daughter of one of the poet's friends, who also inspired "The Triumph of Time" (fifteen pages of bitter reproach for failure to love him and save him from other fateful loves). For this dark, spirited young girl he seems to have nursed briefly his only "normal" passion; she responded to his half-hysterical romantic proposal with a helpless burst of laughter, and it needed but the one touch of ridicule to snuff out the hardly lighted spark.[9] Lafourcade believes that Jane herself "avait quelque chose d'anormal," and certainly the description of Lesbia is suggestive: dark, heavy-lidded, taciturn, Byronically proud, with a pathological hatred of men. When, on her deathbed, she is tenderly embraced by the man who adores her she shows only "mad repugnance, blind absolute horror." In her youth she had loved a governess and threatened suicide when the woman talked of marrying. Later she was an enthusiastic student of Sappho and wrote many love poems from the masculine viewpoint.

The emotional life of the hero, Hubert, up to the time of his meeting with Lesbia is said to be a quite frank parallel of Swinburne's own. The critical first encounter occurs while Hubert is dressed as a girl, and this disguise is responsible for Lesbia's immediate interest. Their subsequent relations are not developed in the portions of the story that Swinburne committed to paper, nor is much of Lesbia's experience save her eventual slow suicide by opium, in an atmosphere heavily fragrant with flowers and eau de cologne. Among the disconnected residual fragments are two: "Turris Iburnea" and "La Bohème Dédorée," in which the poet presents Leonora Harley, a beautiful but vulgar and stupid demi-mondaine. This character was said to be drawn directly from Adah Isaacs Menken, who was also the original of his "Dolores"—a fifteen page description of an insatiable nymphomaniac. There is reason, as will appear later, to believe that Menken's temperament included a variant strain. That Swinburne intended to make use of this in his plot is strongly suggested by the following:

Over their evening Leonora Harley guided with the due graces of her professional art [that of courtesan]. It was not her fault if she could not help asking her young friend [Hubert] when he had last met a dark beauty: she had seen him once with Lesbia.[50]

Further evidence that he planned to incorporate a lesbian element in the story is found in his correspondence of 1866, where he boasted that having won an undeservedly scandalous reputation because of that element in *Poems and Ballads,* he meant to live up to it in his current effort, which would give his countrymen real cause for Philistine horror.[51]

It is known that Swinburne was still at work on the manuscript in 1867 when his meeting with Mazzini deflected his interests into new channels. After the years of political discipleship which produced *Songs Before Sunrise,* he returned to the interrupted narrative. Following that, its history becomes confused. Certain passages in the hands of his publishers reached the stage of galley proof but became mixed with proofs of other incomplete work. Sections of manuscript entrusted to his good friend, Watts-Dunton, were "mislaid," and the poet's repeated pleas and complaints never stimulated him to find them. Though Langdon Hughes finds Watts-Dunton guilty of criminal rascality,[52] one cannot help wondering whether all this apparent carelessness may not have been well-meant discretion.

The text as it now stands is almost wholly in prose, and the few songs it contains have, like "The Triumph of Time" and "Dolores," been published among Swinburne's other poems. Nothing in it is at all daring; there is nothing to account for Lesbia's variance, nor any indication of how far the relations between her and Leonora would have gone. But it is clear that Swinburne, like his hero, worshipped the repressed, intense and melancholy Lesbia, and despised Leonora, the bisexual wanton. A reasonable conjecture is that Lesbia's early passions had been innocent; that even though despising Leonora she was unable to resist the other's seduction; and that self-contempt motivated her suicide—a plot allowing plenty of latitude for the author's intent to shock the British reading public.

CHAPTER IV.

THE LATER NINETEENTH CENTURY

Fertility in France

The sultry uneasiness in French society recorded by Feydeau in 1867 soon broke in the storm of the Franco-Prussian war, which ended monarchy in France. As is usual in time of war, all fiction concerned with emotional subtleties dwindled, and the years from 1870 to 1880 produced comparatively few variant items. One, however, was significant in being the first novel to attack lesbianism as a moral and medical problem. It was Adolphe Belot's *Mlle Giraud, Ma Femme,* and it began in 1870 as a serial in the newspaper *Le Figaro.* Westphal's clinical report on a lesbian woman had appeared in Germany early in the year, and it seems probable that Belot capitalized at once on the interest it aroused in medical circles, turning out instalments with journalistic facility, for he produced popular novels by the dozen. Westphal had concluded that his patient's compulsive homosexuality was not an isolated pathological streak in an otherwise sound nature, but a general state related to manic-depressive insanity (*"sogenannte folie circulaire"*), and Belot mentions early in his novel the sad difference between the French casualness with regard to lesbianism and the serious concern prevalent in Germany, although he does not enlarge upon the latter.

The serial was stopped "in the interests of morality," but it soon appeared in book form and ran to several editions (printings) before 1880.[1] All Belot's novels exploited sex, the boldest requiring anonymous private printing, so that he was experienced in skirting the limits of acceptability. When the serial version was censored he had only to delete or alter condemned passages, amplify the virtuous tone of the unpublished portion (there is a moral harangue inter-

polated baldly in the middle of the book) and profit by the publicity
which censorship always provides.

Mlle Giraud follows the course of a man's marriage to a girl who
stubbornly refuses to consummate the union. Adrien has been warned
against marrying Paule by a young matron of his acquaintance, but
since Mme Blangy will give him no reason for her warning, he
ignores it. After several months he suspects this woman, still his
wife's inseparable companion, of being a blind for some illicit affair
of Paule's. He tracks the two to an apartment which he examines
in their absence and finds to be a lush love-nest, with some details
reminiscent of the boudoir of the *Girl with the Golden Eyes.* Among
other things, he finds there that volume, along with Diderot's
La Religieuse, Gautier's *Maupin,* and "Feydeau's latest, *La Comtesse
de Chalis.*"

Adrien's life as a civil engineer has kept him out of Paris for
some years and left him so unaware of homosexuality among respectable women that none of these suggestive details arouses his
suspicion. It is only upon his meeting M Blangy, separated for
several years from his wife, that Adrien learns of the lesbian relationship between the two women. The two husbands institute a joint
campaign to separate their wives, but it is too late. For the few
months Adrien has spent in travel to escape insupportable domestic
tension, Paule has been free for the first time in her life to indulge
her tastes as freely as she likes, and her health has been gravely
affected. During the collapse which follows upon Adrien's taking
her to North Africa, Paule cries out one day against the wickedness
of segregation in boarding schools where loneliness drives girls to
emotional dependence upon their own sex. 'I believe it is not so
often men who ruin women,' she says. 'It is women who ruin each
other.'[2]

At this her husband begins to regard her as morally ill rather
than depraved, and his new sympathy brings her to the verge of
normal passion for him. But at this crucial moment, Paule's recapture
by Mme Blangy destroys all possibility of subsequent adjustment.
The conflict ends with Paule's complete subjection by her lesbian
friend and her death from meningitis, supposedly the direct result
of sexual excess. Adrien, learning later that Mme. Blangy has begun
the conquest of another girl, manages under the guise of accident
to drown the seductress. M Blangy, who guesses the truth, tells
him he has done the world a service in removing "cette reptile," and
the author leaves little doubt that he himself agrees.

Neither girl shows any sign of masculinity except that Paule's voice is unusually low and penetrating. Mme Blangy, the aggressor, is the essence of flighty femininity. But Paule shows a ripeness of figure unusual in an unmarried girl, which Adrien naively takes for promise of unawakened *volupté,* and both exhibit a cool and intelligent competence in dealing with practical details of their secret liaison which is overmature for their years. The cause of both girls' abnormality is the time-worn segregation in boarding school, Mme Blangy's having begun earlier in her life than Paule's.

Heterosexual frigidity as a direct result, however, makes its pioneer literary appearance in this novel. To the majority of variant women thus far encountered, heterosexual experience was also attributed, and of the handful to which it was not, only five—Mary Frith, Wollstonecraft's Mary, Lesbia Brandon, and one each in the poems of Baudelaire and Verlaine—have expressed antipathy to the male. Even in these cases revulsion was presented as a part of what Ellis calls the "homosexual diathesis," not as the result of previous lesbian activity. Although the present writer has not encountered earlier scientific authority for Belot's claim, his was not a mind likely to originate such an idea. His attributing meningitis to sexual excess was derived from contemporary medical theory, and it is probable that his holding homosexuality responsible for heterosexual failure was similarly grounded. Certainly the thesis was too popular with moralists and educators of the next half century to have stemmed from the passing comment of a minor novelist.

During the decade in which *Mlle Giraud* was the outstanding variant title, Barbey d'Aurevilly, nearing the end of a long career, published *Les Diaboliques,* and in one of these short stories, "The Crimson Curtain" there is a rather boyish girl, the pink of propriety when under the eye of her guardians, but unfemininely bold and aggressive with a male boarder in their house. Since none of her hidden sophistication is attributed to homosexual experience, and as the macabre end of the tale is her death from heart failure during a night of unrestrained heterosexual activity, the only implication seems to be that women with masculine traits are also "masculine" in the intensity of their sexual endowment, an idea previously hinted in Cuisin's *Clémentine.* The notion has reappeared more modernly in ordinary as well as variant fiction, but in the 1870's it would have run counter to growing scientific opinion that male secondary characteristics in women implied homosexuality.

In the course of the same years Zola's literary torrent was beginning to flow, and it is known that many of his novels, notably those treating of metropolitan life in Rome, London and Paris, include

incidental sketches of variant women. No pretense can be made
here to having read or even skimmed his entire output, but *La Curée*
(1874) may be cited as a sample appearing during the decade in
question. The significant figures are a pair of wealthy young married
women who appear intermittently among the numerous background
figures who are regularly referred to as "the inseparables" by their
friends, and by the author, and who are strongly reminiscent in
both appearance and behavior of Mlle Giraud and Mme Blangy.
As with the latter pair, their friendship is said to have begun in
boarding school and to have continued uninterrupted by their respective marriages, but it has no dramatic outcome nor any important
significance to the plot.

As was said in introducing the nineteenth century, the last two
decades saw a sharp increase in all sorts of writing on variance. In
the scientific field the great names were Krafft-Ebing, Moll, Ellis,
and Hirschfeld, the last three being crusaders for official leniency and
general tolerance on the grounds that homosexuality is inborn and
therefore should not be penalized. There was much talk of an
"intermediate sex," whose condition was referred to as "inversion"
(Ellis's term). The term *perversion* was confined to those who
were able to find heterosexual satisfaction and whose homosexual
activities were therefore judged to be willful and unjustified. This
hereditary view did not gain popular currency until late in the
century, but as it spread, the controversy it engendered began to
be reflected in fiction.

With 1880 the steady stream of variant fiction began to flow,
starting with Zola's *Nana*. In this well-known life history of a
courtesan the reader will recall the gradual progress of the robustly
heterosexual heroine from revulsion against an affair between her
friend, Satin, and Mme Robert and against the lesbian society of
the fat Laure's cafe, through indifferent tolerance of such activity,
to her own final active relations with Satin which end only at the
latter's death. (This premature death carries a faint implication
that Satin's long sustained lesbianism was less healthy than Nana's
predominantly heterosexual life). All the stages of Nana's habituation
to homosexuality are presented with the same naturalism which
marks Zola's portrayal of her other affairs, and there can be little
doubt that his material was drawn from direct observation of the
Paris underworld.

The physical types described at Laure's cafe are noteworthy. The
majority are women in their forties or over, obese and repulsive,

whose outcropping of masculine tendencies might thus seem to be a biological result of menopause. A few hoydenish younger women appear, but only one of them is a transvestist. None of their relationships is distinguished by love or constancy. Even Mme. Robert's superficially generous attempts to hold Satin by supporting her seem motivated largely by jealousy. While Zola's attitude is not one of approval, the lesbian episodes are presented with less harshness than several of the heterosexual affairs in Nana's career, and they entrain no tragic consequences to compare with the suicides and utter demoralization resulting from the latter. In the particular segment of Paris society portrayed, that of the high grade prostitute or courtesan, lesbianism is not only tolerated—Nana's titled lovers are well aware of her relations with Satin—but taken for granted. Evidently those cafés already flourished which were to be celebrated later on the canvases of Toulouse-Lautrec and in occasional cynical verses by Donnay.

In *Pot-bouille* (1883) Zola included two minor lesbian episodes at a respectable middle-class level. One involves the adolescent daughter of a mother so "particular" that the child is tutored at home for fear of evil influences at school. No account is taken, however, of the family servant, from whom the girl undertakes to learn 'what happens when you are married.'[3] The lessons are given in the daughter's room after the family has retired, and are apparently adequate. The second episode occurs between two young wives, each of whom has been drawn into a liaison with the same irresistible bachelor living in their apartment building. One of them, on the point of being caught by her husband before regaining her own apartment, takes refuge with the woman who has been her predecessor in the young rake's affections. Strangers till now, though curious about one another, the two women become much excited by their mutual exchange of unhappy confidences. It is three in the morning, and neither is fully clothed. They conclude by giving one another what comfort they can.[4]

In 1881 "Paul's Mistress" was published in de Maupassant's volume entitled *La Maison Tellier* and has appeared subsequently in only three editions in either French or English. (The English translations are very poor.) One of his lengthier short stories, it presents the tragedy of a boy of very good family, intelligent and sensitive, lost in infatuation for "a small thin brunette with a stride like a grasshopper's." At a riverside amusement park the couple encounters four women (two in men's clothes) who are hailed by the holiday crowd with enthusiastic shouts of "Lesbos! Lesbos!" That Paul

is revolted infuriates his companion, and in the course of the ensuing
quarrel the boy faces the hitherto unacknowledged fact that he and
Madeleine have nothing in common but their passion. Over his
protests they return in the evening to dance in the pavilion, and
his partner soon slips off with one of the transvestists. After an
hour of fevered search the boy comes upon the two in a thicket,
and in a frenzy of revulsion escapes unnoticed and throws himself
into the river. When some hours later his body is recovered Madeleine
weeps copiously, but then goes home with the lesbian, "her head on
Pauline's shoulder, as though it had found refuge there in a closer
and more intimate affection."

Here, as in *Nana*, homosexuality is pictured at the prostitute's
level, but an additional causal factor is suggested in Madeleine's
boyish build and gait. (One of the women in trousers, however, is
described with corrosive accuracy as fat-hipped.) De Maupassant's
judgment is quite clear. The exquisite beauty of the countryside,
evoked with all his genius for description, is presented as the symbol
of Paul's spirit, the strident vulgarity of the dance hall as that
of Madeleine's. Every phrase of this sustained contrast points up the
tragedy of fineness destroyed by depravity. Socially significant again
is the comparative tolerance of lesbianism and transvestism among
the respectable resort population. The two lesbian couples, living
in a riverside cottage and entertaining so noisily that their neighbors
protest to the police, are "investigated" with stupid solemnity.
However, there is no more serious result than "a voluminous report
of their innocence." This caricature of official action produces only
hearty laughter among the other cottagers. (Bernard Talmey, however, quotes a less complaisant report by Fiaux to the Municipal
Council of Paris in 1887 on lesbian prostitution.) [5]

Another short story in which lesbian action plays some part is
Dubut de Laforest's "Mlle Tantale" (1884), [6] one of a group of
psychological novelettes comparable to Casper's *Klinische Novellen*
of thirty years earlier in that the author gleaned his material from
his friend Charcot's clinic. Mary Folkestone, the "Mlle Tantale"
of the title, and the illegitimate daughter of a dancer, has, throughout childhood, been the witness of too many intimate scenes between
her mother and the latter's lovers to feel anything but loathing
for sex. As an adolescent she is revolted even when her friend Camilla
opens her blouse on a hot day; at the same time she is so aroused by
the sight of the other girl's breasts that she falls ill. The story
outlines her lifelong struggle to overcome her inhibitions. Following

a first experiment with her maid's lover, which disgusts her, she tries a second with an artist who is her social equal. Although this is less repellent, she finds no complete satisfaction. She then enters upon a liaison with Camilla who, after experience with men as disillusioning as her own, has become a lesbian. This effort, too, is a failure. Finally, neurotic from lack of emotional outlet she resorts to aphrodisiacs and dies of their excessive use; not, however, until the first scorned lover has found her in time to receive a contrite dying kiss. This ending indicates a belief in heterosexual passion, however unromantic, as the remedy for sex-engendered neurosis, and reminds one that Freud began as a pupil of Charcot.

Paul Bourget's *Crime d'Amour* (1886) will be touched on in passing only because Havelock Ellis mentions it as "dealing with the (lesbian) theme," but actually it offers only half a dozen lines on the subject. The night before becoming the lover of a good friend's wife, the hero reviews his very full amatory past. This reminiscence occurs early in the book and the cynicism about women which it reflects is an important factor in the story. The following quotation, however, gives the entire lesbian passage:

> On the mantlepiece between the likenesses of two dead friends he kept an enigmatic portrait representing two women, the head of one resting on the shoulder of the other. It was the constant living reminder of a terrible story—the bitterest faithlessness he had ever endured. He had been cynical or artificial enough to laugh over it earlier with the two heroines, but he had laughed with death in his heart.[7]

No further reference is made to the women, nor is there the slightest implication that this affair is more responsible for his disillusionment than his many others, some of which are recounted at length.

In contrast to the comparative realism of the last five authors stand such imaginative flights as those which follow. The first was the *Monsieur Vénus* of Rachilde (Marguérite Aymery Vallette), published in Brussels in 1884. According to André David,[8] the book was condemned, all available copies confiscated and the author heavily fined. Living in Paris, however, she was happily outside Belgian jurisdiction—the chief reason why so many daring French titles of the late century bore Brussels imprints. A year later the novel was brought out in Paris with some deletions and a preface by Maurice Barrès, and only this second version has been accessible for study.

It is the story of a wealthy orphaned girl, ward of an ascetic aunt who but for the necessity of raising her niece would have taken the veil. At the age of twenty-five Raoule encounters an effeminate man of the working class a year her junior to whom she is hopelessly attracted. Her pride is stung by her weakness, and to avoid accepting Jacques as an equal she virtually buys him and subsequently maintains him in luxury. By degrees she forces him to wear feminine clothing and play the woman's part, to which he proves readily adaptable after an initial rebellion. She herself assumes the masculine costume and role. Jacques' avaricious older sister is at first agreeable to his being kept, but when she discovers the real nature of the relationship she uses the threat of exposure to force a marriage which appears to her even more advantageous. This plebeian match estranges the aunt and most of Raoule's own world, leaving a handsome military man, a former suitor of the girl's, as the couple's only frequent visitor. But so completely has the husband become effeminized that presently he makes advances to the officer. A duel ensues which the jealous Raoule urges the latter to carry through to the death. After the loss of her faithless love she has a wax figure of him enshrined in the room that had been their "temple of delight," and she continues to visit it in secret.

In a significant early conversation with her military suitor, Raoule tells him that she is at last in love. "Sapho!" he cries. "Continue, Monsieur Vénérande, mon cher ami!" But she hotly denies the charge. Her intelligence and pride preclude that amusement of boarding-school girls and prostitutes. In Sappho such love may have had dignity because it was her invention, a new thing, but mere imitation is shameful weakness. She herself will also splendidly create a new vice. She then tells of meeting Jacques, with whom she fell in love as with Beauty. "She said 'Beauty' because she was unable to say 'Woman.' "⁹

Jacques is described elsewhere as a dazzling Titian blonde, well-fleshed in breast and hips, only his voice, hands, and coarse hair betraying his sex. Raoule herself is taller than he, a handsome brunette with level brows and a boyish figure. On the occasions when she ventures out in men's clothes her own sex is never suspected. That the method of satisfaction employed between the two is the kiss, and that only in its usual manifestation, is made unequivocally clear. Late in the story Jacques discovers that impotence has resulted.

Rachilde accounts with care for her heroine's behavior pattern. Throughout Raoule's childhood the aunt had harped upon the vileness of physical passion. At the same time the girl's emotional endowment was such that the mere reading of an erotic book threw her into a violent fever. Hence, both the compulsive experimenting with many lovers and the frigidity which prevented satisfaction. Raoule herself lays the blame for the latter squarely upon her lovers, whom she has taken as she has read books, in order to learn what passion is. But men, she says, offer a woman either brutality or weakness, never the one aphrodisiac—Love—which might teach her real passion. And to become the slave of mere sensation is unthinkable. If one is merely to indulge one's senses, then to preserve self-respect one must remain, like a man, indifferent to the experience and master of oneself.

Barrès, in his preface, says that Rachilde was only twenty when she wrote the tale, a well-bred and innocent girl with nothing but wishful dreaming from which to spin her fantastic plot. He singles out pride as the chief handicap of both heroine and author, pride which cannot endure domination of any sort by a man.

> To what mysterious cult are they pledged, these men and women whom love of self draws one to another [of their own sex]? . . . One sees with alarm men losing their taste for women, as Monsieur Vénus displays hatred of male traits. . . . It is *la maladie du siècle* . . . it smells of death.[10]

What he naturally dared not say more plainly is that the tale gives clear evidence of severely repressed homosexual inclinations on the author's part.

Additional, though less marked, evidence of her bias appears in Rachilde's second novel, *Madame Adonis,* which came out in Paris in 1886 without serious moralistic repercussions. From a literary viewpoint it shows some advance in maturity, being fairly free of florid description, vague philosophy, and erotic purple patches. There is even a touch of satire in the delineation of a miserly provincial woman lumber-dealer and her despotic persecution of her son and his Parisian wife, as well as in the Dickensian portrait of the girl's alcoholic father. But although comparative realism makes it more convincing, the plot is hardly less bizarre than that of *Monsieur Vénus.* It details the havoc wrought upon the young couple by a picturesque individual who first in the guise of a romantic artist woos the wife, and later as a *galante* and domineering woman captivates the man.

Continuing to pose alternately as twin brother or sister, this person convinces each of the young people that the other is unfaithful, and so manages to consummate affairs with both. Only when, goaded too far, the jealous husband surprises and kills his wife's lover, do they learn that only one person is involved—a woman. She has deceived the wife as to her sex by artificial means. No etiology is suggested for the woman's sexual dualism beyond her rebellion, like that of Raoule de Vénérande, against a feminine role. Light is shed upon the author by the tingling vitality of her descriptions of the central figure in the male role as compared with her parallel pictures of the same character as a woman, and also by the love scenes between the woman and the young wife. These are more convincing than the conquest of the man which is motivated largely by vindictive arrogance.

Seasoned readers of biography will not be surprised to learn that beyond her marriage in 1899 to Alfred Vallette, then editor of the *Mercure de France,* few facts about Rachilde's own emotional life are available. André David compares her personality to that of the Chevalier d'Eon, famous diplomat and transvestist of the eighteenth century, whose sex was an enigma to all Europe not finally solved until his death; Ernest Boyd refers to her assumption of men's clothing in her teens when she came to Paris and was befriended by Sarah Bernhardt;[11] but neither alludes to homosexuality. David does mention, however, her long and close friendship with Verlaine, whose homosexual connection with Arthur Rimbaud was a scandal in the late nineteenth century.

Rachilde continued for several decades to produce novels, in some of which lesbian women made brief appearances too slight to consider here. Her one later sustained treatment of homosexuality, (which ran serially in the *Mercure de France* as *Les Factices* and was published in book form as *Les Hors Natures* dealt with men.) In the reviews of fiction which she contributed to her husband's periodical from 1896 to the 1930s, she maintained the same attitude of superiority to female variance expressed by her own Raoule de Vénérande, but she regularly included lesbian novels in her review list and seldom failed to indicate their theme. Thus she provided an index of sorts to such fiction over a period of nearly forty years. When, during the 1890s, criticism was leveled at the *Mercure* for its consistent noting of fictional "decadence," Vallette replied in a sharp editorial that theirs was the only periodical whose reviews gave anything resembling an honest picture of contemporary writing.[12]

The Shadow of Feminism

In Rachilde's two novels just considered, women's deliberate adoption of male attire and outlook figures for the first time in half a century; that is, since the appearance of *Fragoletta* and *Mademoiselle de Maupin*. No significant rebellion against the feminine role is evident in Zola's or even Maupassant's references to transvestism among prostitutes nor in other variant French fiction before 1890. In other countries, however, what is now termed the masculine protest was receiving considerable attention. Oliver Wendell Holmes and Henry James in America, Olive Schreiner in South Africa, and August Strindberg in Sweden all contributed observations, even though the phenomenon appears in their work under widely differing guises and sometimes is only tenuously related to variance.

Dr. Holmes, versatile contributor to both medicine and letters, would today undoubtedly have been a psychiatrist. Throughout his life he was preoccupied with intersexual personality in women, and he explored it at least tentatively in each of his three novels: *Elsie Venner* (1859), *The Guardian Angel* (1867), and *A Mortal Antipathy* (1885). Of these a modern psychiatrist, Dr. Clarence Oberndorf, has observed:

> The theory of bisexuality and the importance of bisexual components in influencing the character of individuals is more than implied in each one of his abnormal personalities. The masculine traits in childhood of both Elsie Venner and Myrtle Hazard [in *The Guardian Angel*], something of a tomboy, are unmistakable. The bisexual theme becomes even clearer in *A Mortal Antipathy*, where Holmes repeatedly contrasts the femininity of Euthemia Tower with the masculinity of Lurida Vincent, and it is apparent that he has but little sympathy with the latter.[13]

Strictly speaking, Elsie Venner alone deserves the adjective "abnormal." Her eccentricity is due to her mother's having suffered a rattlesnake bite during late pregnancy of which she died shortly after giving birth to her child. The girl grows up unafraid of rattlers if not immune to their poison (there is no account of her being bitten), and possessing something of the reptile's power to hypnotize a sensitive individual with her steady ophidian gaze. As a result she is shunned by her mates, and develops a solitary and arrogant personality. She is a fearless mountain climber and not infrequently spends the night on dangerous and snake-infested rocky slopes above her home. During adolescence she exhibits for a teacher in the select female academy she attends "a special fancy" so intense it frightens the woman. On the girl's side the obsession seems more a desire to test her power than love. The reaction of the overworked and half-hysterical teacher is one of terrified revulsion until Elsie in her last illness calls upon her to act as nurse and companion. Elsie's only feeling of normal warmth is directed toward a young male instructor to whom she virtually offers herself, but he, too, is unable to respond as she desires, and she dies as an apparent result of subduing the innate drive to overpower those she loves.

Myrtle Hazard in *The Guardian Angel* was born in the tropics and lived her early years amid a luxury not only of natural beauty but of parental love and adulation from native servants. The strength and self-assurance thus bred enable her when orphaned to survive the efforts of a couple of puritanic aunts to break her spirit. At fifteen, precociously mature in both mind and body, she crops her hair, dons boy's clothes, and runs off to return to India where she spent the few remembered years of happy childhood. The accident which foils her plan wins her new friends, among them a young man whom she eventually marries. Although in appearance and behavior she is the most masculine of Holmes's heroines, variance plays the least part in her history. Her "best friend," the only person for whom she leaves any word upon running away, is merely the bosom companion natural to an adolescent, and there is no hint of passion in Myrtle's feeling for the girl.

As for Lurida Vincent in *A Mortal Antipathy*, despite Dr. Oberndorf's emphasis on her masculinity, she is physically fragile, under developed, and anything but boyish. We see her only in boarding school and learn nothing of her antecedents or early history. The factors conditioning her against a feminine role are that she is plain and unappealing to men and abnormally brilliant. Her only masculinity consists in a resolute ambition to best her male acquaintances in intellectual achievement. Envious of her schoolmates' charm and athletic prowess, she reacts by becoming the school prodigy and an ardent feminist. Jealously, and with unconscious passion, she adores Euthemia Tower, who returns her fondness with marked moderation and common sense. Euthemia is obviously more Holmes's ideal of womanhood than a convincing individual. She is beautiful with the wholesome beauty of youth, modest, warm-hearted, and admirably well-balanced. She is also the school's champion athlete, strong enough to carry an unconscious young man, whom she later marries, from a burning house without assistance.

From these novels one gathers that the good doctor was partial to women who were physically not much inferior to men, but he firmly believed that such equality did not breed masculine emotions. His scientific acumen had made him aware of passionate attachments between women[14] (a secondary character in *The Guardian Angel* is so devoted to her mother that the latter says, "I should think you were in love with me, my darling, if you were not my daughter,") but such attachments appear to concern him so little that one wonders if he was even aware of their ultimate potentialities.

The same question arises in reading Thomas Hardy's earliest novel, *Desperate Remedies* (1871), even though some early chapters give more details of a variant episode than anything in Holmes. Circumstances force the well-born Cytherea at eighteen into service as a lady's maid, and Miss Aldclyffe, a spinster of forty-six, employs her despite her frank admission of inexperience wholly from infatuation with her beauty and physical grace. Since both women are headstrong and mercurial, Cytherea's term as servant lasts a matter of mere hours, but its stormy ending promotes her to the status of companion and (ultimately) partial heiress of her mistress's fortune. This transition occurs during their single night together, in the course of which the older woman learns that the girl is already in love with a man and does her best to turn her adored against him and all of his sex. Miss Aldclyffe is a "tall . . . finely built woman of spare though not angular proportions,"[14a] but her aversion to men is the result of early seduction and desertion and not innate, and her passion for Cytherea, half-maternal, stems from years of emotional starvation. The girl, though also strong-willed and independent, is wholly feminine and quite unable to satisfy her mistress's pleas for some warmth of response to her caresses.

Although *Desperate Remedies* shows some immaturity in its Victorian elaboration of plot, its grasp of character foreshadows the mastery Hardy was later to attain, and an already developed ironic detachment saves the night incident from being either mawkish or offensive to British readers. Nothing in it betrays the least awareness of lesbian possibilities on the part of either Miss Aldclyffe or her author, nor is there any conscious feminism in her disparagement of men. Actually, she at once sets about contriving to marry Cytherea to a man of her own choice—her unacknowledged illegitimate son.

The variant episode is thus brief and incidental, but it is significant in having no known antecedent in British fiction save Wollstonecraft's *Mary* published nearly a century earlier.[15]

The feminist theme so uncongenial to Holmes's taste had been presented with passionate sympathy two years earlier in Olive Schreiner's *Story of an African Farm*. This novel is reminiscent of *Mary, a Fiction*, both in its championship of women and its naïvely autobiographical pattern. The similarity is due, however, only to the authors' comparable life circumstances and not to any possible influence, for by 1880 when Schreiner was writing, Wollstonecraft's volume was rare even in England, and Schreiner had not then left the Transvaal. She brought her manuscript to London in 1882 and it was published in 1883. *The Story of an African Farm* is a sensitive girl's outcry against the masculine violence and brutality of a frontier society, and its heroine is obviously a self-portrait of the author. Lyndall (Schreiner *mère's* maiden name) has been turned against men by the villainy or contemptible weakness of the only specimens of the sex in her lonely milieu, and equally turned against passion in women by her coarse and callous aunt's susceptibility to it. Snared later by her own emotions, she revolts against her lover's domination, refuses marriage, bears his child secretly and alone, and falls fatally ill in consequence. An effeminate boy, long in love with her, traces her to her hiding place, disguises himself as a woman, and without revealing his identity nurses her until her death.

All her life, at least on the conscious level, Lyndall has sought "something nobler, stronger than I, before which I can kneel down." Religion, the obvious answer to her need, has been spoiled for her by the pitiable weakness of the one man she has known who professed it. Her lover is stronger than she but signally lacking in the nobility she craves. Her only help, and subconsciously her only real love, is her own fearless strength. At one point she is reduced to crying: "Why am I so alone, so hard, so cold? Will nothing free me from myself?" But on two other occasions, notably the deathbed scene where she communes with her own image in a mirror,[16] her naïve and passionate narcissism reveals itself so clearly and is so lovingly transcribed as to betray it as the author's own. (One cannot help wondering whether Barrès had read the *African Farm* before writing his preface to *Monsieur Vénus* in 1885.) Schreiner's heroine is drawn to no individual woman save herself, but she is an impassioned champion of the whole female sex as well as a hater-of-men. The novel is filled with revolt against the subjugation of women and their limited opportunities for individual development.

Henry James's early novel, *The Bostonians*, published in 1885, stands in sharp contrast. This story ran as a serial in *Century Magazine*. Before it was finished Richard Watson Gilder, the editor, wrote James that "he had never published anything so unpopular." The novel came out as a book a year later but met with no warmer reception, and was not subsequently reissued until 1945, being omitted even from the twenty-nine volume Scribner edition of James' *Novels and Tales* in 1923. Philip Rahv in the preface of the 1945 edition of *The Bostonians* indicates several reasons for its unpopularity, but says that undoubtedly the "most disquieting" was its keen analysis of "the emotional economy of the Lesbian woman."[17]

Because of James's subtlety his work suffers more than most from condensation, but as the text of the novel is now readily available, its nearly four hundred pages can be reduced here to the barest skeleton. In essence, the plot is the eternal triangle. At its apex is Verena Tarrant, ultra-feminine, passive and suggestible, whose antecedents bear witness to James's interest in recently published theories of heredity. The rivals for possession of her are Olive Chancellor, Boston intellectual and feminist spinster a decade her senior, and the latter's cousin from Mississippi, a young man who has come out of the Civil War on the losing side with something of the present day's critical pessimism toward modern society. Olive sees in the girl, who has inherited a spell-binding oratorical gift, a powerful potential ally for the Woman's Movement to which she herself is devoted. Subconsciously, however, her motivation is a love-at-first-sight quite as passionate as that of her male cousin. Olive manages virtually to adopt Verena and by degrees to estrange her from her family and her previous suitors. Olive's cousin, Basil Ransom, is not so easily disposed of, so she must finally resort to exacting a promise from the girl that she will not marry. For several years the two women are wholly absorbed in their feminist efforts, traveling in Europe where they meet the prominent leaders of the movement, and studying intensively. Olive's emphasis is always upon the wrongs women have suffered at the hands of men.

Olive is increasingly obsessed by her love for Verena. Of Verena, James says: "Her share in the union, . . . was no longer passive, purely appreciative; it was passionate too, and it put forth a beautiful energy."[18] At last Verena is ready for public appearance, and invites Basil to her first lecutre, since he has been forbidden his cousin's house in Boston. He takes the opportunity to talk long and seriously to her about herself, Olive's influence, and his own love for her. He tells her that what the times need is not more feminization but less, that "it's a . . . hysterical, chattering . . . age of false delicacy and exaggerated solicitudes and coddled sensibilities. . . . The masculine character, the ability to dare and endure, to know and yet not fear reality . . . is what I want to preserve."[19] He tells her, too, that she has allowed Olive to imprison her in "a false thin shell" of devotion to feminism, when actually she has a genius for giving herself, not to a cause, but to normal life with a man. The girl is so moved that she dares not see him again and cannot hide her disturbance from Olive. The story then records a rapidly accelerating struggle between the man and the older woman for possession of the girl. The climax comes on the night of Verena's great Boston debut, when, just before speaking before an audience of thousands, she falls ill in the dressing room from inner emotional conflict. Basil attempts to reach her; Olive, beside herself, tries to keep him out; but Verena is aware of his presence and of her own accord chooses him in preference to public triumph and a potentially brilliant career.

As to the precise nature of the relationship between the two women, no more is specified than a good deal of quiet kissing and holding of hands, more symbolic than passionate except for a general "tremulousness." At one point the following appears: "It was a very peculiar thing, their friendship: it had elements which made it probably as complete as any (between women) that had ever existed."[20] This is included as part of a mental soliloquy of Verena's, and so Rahv, who comments on the "prescience with which [James] analyzed . . . the lesbian woman," may possibly be justified in adding that "one cannot be sure that James understood her precisely as such."[21] Had Verena's rumination above been presented as James's own, there could be no doubt of its significance, for he had spent a year in Paris during the 1870's, had known Flaubert, Maupassant and Zola, and could not have escaped awareness of all emotional potentialities between women. It is interesting that he was careful not to speak in the role of author, nor to venture recording any comparable fragment of the strongly variant Olive's stream of consciousness.

The last novel dealing with feminism, violent in its condemnation of the Movement and also of female variance, is Strindberg's *Confession of a Fool*. This story is now known to be a thinly veiled report of the author's relations with his first wife, Siri von Essen, Baroness Wrangel, whom he married in 1877. It was written in 1887-1888 as an *apologia pro vita sua* intended for publication after his projected suicide. When he decided instead to live and divorce his wife, he kept the manuscript sealed for five years, until public sentiment aroused by

the circumstances of the divorce led him to publish it "in self defense." In view of the fact that his second marriage in 1893 was
followed a year later by his second divorce and a third matrimonial
venture in 1901 came to a similar end in 1904, the *Confession* provides a valuable document on the psychology of the unhappy miso-
gynist, but scarcely an unbiased portrait of the wife.

The hero of the story, Axel, is a bookish introvert with what
today would be termed an obvious mother fixation. He falls in love
with the wife of an officer, his friend, partly from pity because her
husband is involved in a flirtation with her sophisticated young
cousin; the Baroness Marie, however, is rather less concerned about
the affair than Axel. "I'm in love with the little cat myself," she says
early in their acquaintance. Like Belot's Adrien, Axel is not warned.
In the idealism of first love he searches the art books in his library
for a likeness of his beloved. She is a goddess—not Venus, definitely
not Juno, not even Minerva, but Diana, "more boy than girl," who
never forgave Actaeon for seeing her nude. Axel is naïvely enraptured
by this seeming evidence of his love's purity.

Presently Marie leaves her husband for a stage career, living with
Axel rather incidentally and marrying him only upon discovery that
she is pregnant. It appears later, however, that the child is the
Baron's, conceived after their formal divorce. After a masquerade for
which she has dressed as a man, Marie is caught fondling a servant
girl. To Axel's reproaches she retorts that his suspicions are groundless and vile, as are police reports and medical treatises which term
"vicious" all caresses of any warmth. The birth of a second child—
Axel's, this time—briefly relaxes domestic tension; however, Marie
soon farms the child out to a nurse, installs an actress friend in a
neighboring apartment, and creates a scandal by caressing her new
love in public, though still protesting innocence.

The lengthy plot continues to oscillate between brief periods of
marital peace during Marie's pregnancies, and tempests over her
increasingly scandalous connections with women. Most of these are
with Marie's countrywomen, artists, and other bohemians who dress
and act as much like men as possible, make love openly to one
nother, and "wallow in the lowest depths." Many are militant
uffragists, and all are devoted to the cause. Once Axel reaches the
point of wanting to drown his wife, but he spares her for the sake of
their children. Most of the action thus far has occurred in Paris or
in Swiss resorts. There follows an interlude in Germany, "land of
militarism where the patriarchatc is still in full force." There no
one will listen to talk of women's rights, and, for the first time,

Marie is out of public life; consequently, Axel flourishes. Even his voice, "which had grown thin from everlastingly speaking in soothing tones to a woman, regained its former volume."[22] When his wife rages against his new dominance he reflects that he has always known it was the weakling in him, "the page, the lap-dog, her child" that she loved. He now makes an effort to leave her, but is helplessly bound by his masochistic passion. This sign of dependence softens her for a few months. Then Marie is caught caressing the adolescent daughters of guests, and the rupture is final.

Axel, intellectually concerned as to the cause of her aberration, tries to discover whether Marie had been a prostitute before her first marriage, but all evidence is negative. He does learn, however, that her lesbian habits and those of the Paris circle with whom she had most conspicuously misbehaved were common knowledge to everyone else. He finally decides to leave her and "to write the story of this woman, the true representative of this age of the unsexed." The novel was published in Berlin in 1893, two years after his divorce from Siri von Essen, but "in a corrupt and mutilated text, so crude in its language that it was suppressed."[23] The first authorized edition appeared in Sweden in 1912 after the author's death.

Before leaving Strindberg it will be interesting to return parenthetically for a moment to *Mlle Tantale,* since the modern analyst Dr. Clarence Offenbacher has suggested that it may have given Strindberg the plot of a much better known work, his drama *Miss Julie.*[24] To be sure the two have in common the unrewarding liaison of a girl with a man who is her social inferior, in Julie's case a groom. But in personality and in conditioning circumstances Julie differs sharply from Mary Folkestone. Julie is the daughter of a domineering feminist who, in her effort to equalize the sexes, assigns the labor on her estate to men or women with complete disregard of its customary division between them. Quite unlike Mary's parent, the sensual courtesan, Julie's mother scorns passion. She gives her senses rein as rarely as possible and then merely for the purpose of nervous catharsis. Julie also is wilfully self-contained, taking the groom in a callous spirit like her mother's.

Offenbacher points out that Strindberg was in Paris in the 1880s and probably knew of both Dubut de Laforest and Charcot. It is even more likely that he was aware of women like Rachilde and the more notorious Mme. Jeanne Dieulafoy, lifelong transvestist and author who was made a member of the Legion of Honor about 1890. At the beginning of the Franco-Prussian war, Dieulafoy was a girl of nineteen, convent bred, who had just married and who fought beside her husband during the siege of Paris wearing men's clothes, "to which she was long accustomed."[25] Subsequently, she accompanied him on archeological expeditions to Egypt, Morocco and Persia. To her grief she was unable to have children, but she devoted herself to those of her friends, and she and her husband for a time conducted a private school in which they educated the girls to be independent and fearless, the boys to show gentleness and consideration. This training they believed, doubtless from their own experience, would lead to better adjustment in marriage.

Since at the time of writing *Miss Julie* Strindberg was deep in the stormiest phase of his quarrel with Siri von Essen, he would have been more sensitive to masculine women than to clinical literature. No model for Julie's mother could have been readier to hand than this virile ex-soldier, archeologist, and "progressive" educator. *Miss Julie* may well be Strindberg's dark prediction as to the results of child-training by such a woman. The fact that there is no trace of variance in *Miss Julie* seems another reason for questioning whether it derived from *Mlle Tantale*. Strindberg was so exercised over that issue at the moment that he would not have missed a chance to attack it openly unless his models were actual persons and might conceivably be recognized.

The central figures of the more or less feministic novels considered above are not marked by unanimous sexual antipathy to the male. A number of them had husbands or lovers and bore children. Their common feature is rebellion against the domestic role imposed upon them in nineteenth-century society, and often their variance is merely one aspect of that rebellion. In contrast, the novels that follow have variance per se as their predominant theme, and the authors' attitudes toward variance are equally disapproving.

Fin de Siècle

Dubut de Laforest's second approach to the subject appeared in *La Femme d'Affaires* (1890), a vertical section of Paris life as sensational as was *Mlle Tantale* in the field of individual psychology. The title figure is a grasping Jewess, and her contrast to her Catholic daughter-in-law (almost the only irreproachable character in the book) would reward a student of religious and racial prejudice; however, neither of these women is directly concerned in the variant action. The latter involves a self-centered musical comedy star, bisexually promiscuous, and a lesbian amazon, Faustine, who supports her when necessary. Faustine, we learn, was expelled from a school at fifteen for corrupting its dormitory, and her subsequent excesses with a governess contributed to the latter's early death from tuberculosis (cf. *Mlle Giraud*). She then tried a couple of husbands, and at the time of this tale's action she still experiments with men—which is inexplicable since she never ceases to loathe heterosexual experience. She is violently jealous of her actress friend, especially of the latter's connection with a fantastic titled Englishman who has turned circus clown. During an ether 'drunk,' Faustine surprises the two together and cuts out the woman's tongue, thus destroying "the instrument of love." No etiology is suggested for her variance except her amazonian build. The unsavory trio are apparently incorporated in the novel to illustrate the types to whom the Business Woman will rent apartments at sufficient profit, but the author devotes more space to them than such reason requires. It was more probably his own literary profits due to sensationalism that he had an eye on. His is the most specific reference thus far to the techniques of lesbian activity, a detail doubtless reflecting his clinical connections, and one seldom repeated in openly published literature.

More concentrated upon variance is Catulle Mendès' *Méphisto-phéla* (1890), mentioned earlier for its long popularity and its present rarity. It is also notable for the immense detail of the lesbian life history presented in its more than five hundred pages. It must have escaped the censor in its day because of its heavily moralistic tone and its literary style. Mendès, like Flaubert and Maupassant—though artistically far from their equal—was more subtle than naturalistic, and veiled his lurid facts in generalities that might glitter or smoulder but were unlikely to put specific notions in a reader's head.

Its prologue gives a sinister sketch of a drug addict in the act of a self-injection of morphine—a reassuring indication that no matter how she may appear to flourish in the course of the tale, she will come to no good end. Wealthy and proud as the heroine of *Monsieur Vénus,* modish as the Comtesse de Chalis, she has the debauched remnants of beauty; however, her lack of natural brows and lashes implies syphilis. She takes morphine to blot out some abysmal horror which has left its scar upon her. The author then unfolds the heredity and the erotic career which have brought her to her present pass.

Sophie is the child of a bisexually promiscuous dancer by a Russian nobleman who laments his mistress's pregnancy because his 'rotten and accursed line' should never be perpetuated. He dies almost immediately and the dancer, now fabulously wealthy, takes a house in Fontainebleau and raises Sophie in strict respectability. But even in childhood Sophie becomes so attached to a neighbor's daughter,

Emmaline, that a temporary separation brings on hysterical convul-
sions, dangerous fever and somnambulism. The two children have
'played at marriage,' a game of innocent embraces which brought
vague shame to the other child, but seemed natural and acceptable to
Sophie. With the approach of puberty the game is discontinued.
During adolescence Sophie's powerful but still unconscious sex drive
leads her into emotional excesses, first in connection with confirma-
tion, and later in the study of music and poetry. Through all these
storms she sweeps the passive Emmaline along with hypnotic intensity, and the two girls are sometimes brought to the verge of fainting
through unrelieved excitement. Recognizing the danger signals,
Sophie's mother arranges her daughter's early marriage to Emmaline's brother. Sophie, still physically ignorant, is so delighted at not
losing her friend that she accepts the arrangement without question.

The disillusionment of her wedding night drives her to an attempt
to leap out the window, which her husband prevents. However, as
soon as he is asleep she flees to Emmaline. Awakened by marital
initiation to the significance of her feelings for her friend, she kisses
the sleeping girl's breast. The husband who has been searching for
her, surprises her in the act, reviles her, and beats her senseless.

Her brother's brutality moves Emmaline to run away with Sophie,
but in a cottage where they spend an idyllic week she is unwilling to
accept the caresses the other girl now consciously burns to bestow.
When circumstances finally overcome Emmaline's reluctance, she does
not share Sophie's transports. Somewhat repelled, and afraid for her
reputation, she slips away and returns home. Sophie is left broken-
hearted by her desertion. She realizes that she has failed Emmaline
exactly as her own husband has failed with her, and she determines
to find out how one woman can satisfy another.

Hiding in Paris from her husband, she allows herself to be
initiated by a lesbian show girl, Magalo, with whom she lives for
some time, physically captivated but hating herself for inconstancy to
Emmaline. The discovery that she is pregnant as a result of her
wedding night brings her to the verge of suicide. She loathes the very
thought of maternity; when her child is born, she consigns it to an
orphanage without a qualm. Her partner, Magalo, is shocked and
hurt, being genuinely in love with her and having envisioned a life
en famille for them and the child. Sophie turns against Magalo in
distaste because of the girl's interest in motherhood. Upon her
mother's death, Sophie, left enormously wealthy, makes plans to recapture Emmaline. She is confident that she can now both support
her and adequately fill the role of husband. In Fontainebleau, how-

ever, she learns that Emmaline has married, her family has dispersed, and her whereabouts are unknown. Once again, heartbroken, she returns to Paris.

Now she establishes a smart ménage and acquires an enormous lesbian following. Under her spell, actresses, artists and women of title neglect careers, male lovers, and husbands. She is known as 'a giver of incomparable joys, violent and sophisticated, deliciously and frightfully inventive.'[26] Into this spectacular brilliance breaks Magalo, destitute, broken, and ill. In a scene of deathbed repentance the girl, claiming guidance from Heaven, implores Sophie to give up her empty and miserable life and return to her husband and child. There can be no other happiness on earth. 'We both have had a demon in us," she says, "but for you it is not too late.'

Sophie's response is to go directly from Magalo's funeral to an orgiastic lesbian banquet where she glories in her role of presiding goddess (or demon). With this defiance, a third stage in her disintegration begins. Her liaisons, always loveless, now fail to give even sensual satisfaction, and she knows only boredom, relieved less and less frequently by flashes of desire. Haunted by memories of her only real love, she ferrets out Emmaline's whereabouts in the hope that even a brief encounter may rekindle her own jaded emotions.

In seeking to discover how she can reach Emmaline alone, she finds herself one evening spying through an open window upon a family scene centering about Emmaline's four children. The two men, father and uncle (the latter her own husband) are fatuously devoted to them. Emmaline has become wholly maternal, plump and placid. The climax occurs when Emmaline offers the youngest, an infant of six months, her breast. Revolted to nausea, Sophie plunges away through the darkness with demonic laughter.

> 'Now Emmaline was no longer worthy of her passion. Was her own life wrong? Must one be like such clods to be happy? Should she have had four children? . . . No! She repudiated such spineless notions. She was what she was. She thrust from her her old dream of Emmaline's breast, she jeered at Emmaline's bovine happiness.'[27]

This further repudiation of maternity heralds the final stage of her degeneration, a round of infamous adventures stimulated by drink and drugs. 'Unwilling to believe there could be so little pleasure in vice, she chose to think she simply had not learned enough,' and she frequents the most debauched Paris haunts, no

longer bothering to select her partners, but seizing indfferently on
servants and waitresses, to whom she becomes an object of terror. At
last, suffering from hallucinations, largely of sexual odors, she con-
sults a physician. His first advice is marriage; however, when he learns
that she has already tried that and even borne a child, he advocates
as a last therapeutic experiment the actual practice of motherhood.

Accordingly she fetches her sixteen-year-old daughter from the
convent orphanage. The girl is graceless and unappealing and on
sight awakens no sentiment but boredom. But while watching her
asleep and half-clothed, Sophie is stirred by violent desire. And now
in real horror of herself she leads the girl to the gate of Emmaline's
house where she can find her father and a true home, and entreats her
to enter it and stay there. The book closes with an epilogue almost the
literal duplicate of the prologue, for now the reader knows from
what nightmare the doomed woman was seeking to escape when she
plied her hypodermic needle.

Marred though it is by excess in length, incident and style, this
novel holds interest because of its effort to present a complete life
history and to account for its lesbian element. The chief trouble is
excess in this respect also. While the "morne demon" possessing
"Méphistophéla" seems at the outset an hereditary syphilitic taint,
the author says at one point:

> 'Why, if a scientist today diagnoses hysteria from the same
> symptoms that for Bodin [Attorney to Henri III and author of
> *Démonomanie des Sorciers*, 1580] proved demonic possession,
> should not current neuroses be, under other names, simply the
> old spells used by sorcerers? If divine grace is present in the
> bread and wine [of the sacrament], why not diabolic malice in
> opium, hashish, morphine? He who takes alcohol imbibes
> Satan. An emetic is an exorcist.'[28]

This could be sailing close to a biochemical explanation of psy-
chopathology, or, employed by Mendès who was at least a nominal
Catholic, it could indicate a half-serious suspicion of supernatural
influence.

At another point he distinguishes between relatively harmless and
"serious" homosexual activity.

> 'Rejected lovers, deceived wives, may console one another
> and forget to mention it to their confessors. Brilliant young
> belles dizzy with champagne and dancing may fall into each

others' arms as they undress at dawn. Prostitutes may seek the tender love they have never known, or consolation for men's brutality. Only the conscious, cool, deliberate players of man's role are courting damnation.'[29]

There is no indication of heredity bearing the burden here. Indeed, Mendès seems to absolve his heroine from responsibility for her actions up to the time of her desertion by Emmaline and her escape to Paris; that is, so long as she is physically innocent and motivated by love. But from that point on, each step in her downward course results from a deliberate refusal of motherhood, the final one involving repudiation of even her early love for Emmaline. Interesting to a modern analyst would be her obsession with Emmaline's breast, which had a parallel in Mlle Tantale's reaction to her friend Camilla.

Josephin Peladan, author of *La Gynandre* (1891) states differently the same thesis: there is no such thing as lesbian Love, it is simply one of the sexual vices. This novel is one in a long series designed to expose all these vices under the heading *La Décadence Latine,* which unless checked, he says, forebodes the end of French civilization. (He also proclaims the volume to be in part a satire on current lesbian fiction.) The hero of the tale, a young intellectual known merely as Tammuz, is, like his author, both Catholic and Rosicrucian, his mission the conversion of Lesbos to a constructive worship of Eros. The only other male protagonist is a novelist, Nergal. These names are derived from Assyrian-Babylonian mythology and represent sun gods and the generative principle, in opposition to all the female lunar divinities.

A prologue incorporates the two men's rapid survey of previous literature on female variance, from classical references through Catholic confessors' manuals to Balzac, Gautier, and Baudelaire. Sappho's influence, Tammuz decides, operated in so segregated a community of girls as to engender the cathartic intrasexual play common in such environments. In short, 'Lesbos is the story of a pagan convent.' The Catholic literature, of course, supports the thesis that lesbianism is merely 'female sodomy.' So also do belletristic works from Brantôme to Diderot. *The Girl with the Golden Eyes* is pronounced Balzac's weakest effort because it represents lesbian passion as a motivating force for murder. Gautier gives them momentary pause, because *Mlle de Maupin* records lesbian activity between two women of high social status; however, it is the Catholic Baudelaire who offers them the most convincing evidence that the lesbian experience may approach real passion. Tammuz claims that such error merely fore-

shadowed Baudelaire's mental collapse. After this formidable spear-
head of symbolism and avowed moral purpose, the novel presents,
with only faint satire, a cross-section of contemporary female variance.
Interestingly enough, it claims that the vice had become general in
Parisian society only within the previous decade, but it does not
attempt to account for that sudden burgeoning.

Tammuz, an impoverished nobleman enabled by a windfall to
spend a year studying life and love in Paris, is first introduced to the
Orchids. This group is no more than a salon, its hostess a woman
architect nearing forty. Her circle comprises a dozen idle young
women, some married, ranging from a wide-eyed orphan of seventeen who has been "taken" in her lonely innocence by the first man
who showed her any attention, to a beauty who worships her own
dazzling skin far too much to risk its damage by male caresses. The
presiding spirit, Aril, is sufficiently the diplomat to make each of her
protégées feel valued and to avoid tension by playing no favorites.
Tammuz is unable to discern much real passion among the group
for either Aril or one another, and no lesbian activity save as
outsiders stimulate it. A seductive actress-courtesan may strike a
momentary spark, or curious provincial women in Paris for a brief
fling may provoke some of the girls to exhibitionistic petting, but all
soon lapse again into emotional indolence. Their common need is
mainly companionship and freedom from the male aggression from
which all have suffered in one fashion or another. Aril's need is scope
for her powers of domination.

That the whole business is rather a pose is apparent in the
women's adoption of picturesque nicknames—not masculine—and is
further attested to by the confession of a senior member. While protesting her own and the group's willingness to die for Aril, she makes
clear to the young man that all of them are more thrilled by his
masculine interest than by anything happening among themselves.

Tammuz's next field for study is the Royal Maupins, a fencing
club housed and headed by a deserter from the Orchids too masculine
to submit to Aril's dominance. Whereas the Orchids were all passive-
feminine, even though one or two were tall, small-breasted and narrow-hipped, the Maupins consciously affect masculinity, in their
nicknames, and in wearing fencing hose and men's silk shirts
exclusively in the privacy of their quarters. Here the prime favorite
is not the hostess and nominal leader but "the Chevalier," a woman
who has avoided overt expression of all emotion, variant or normal,
and whose "purity" Orchids and Maupins alike hold in such reverence that they forbear trying to win her from it. She shows an

immediate predilection for the young man whose self-mastery in the
pursuit of an ideal equals her own, and this semi-defection from the
lesbian cause wakes violent jealousy among the pettier Maupins. A
trio of them provokes Tammuz to a match with their most skilled
fencer, fitting his opponent with a plastron beneath her tunic and
substituting untipped blades for regulation foils. Their apparent
plot is to kill him in the guise of accident. But the young man divines
the trick, makes the sign of the cross with his blade, and contrives
to break off the tip of it in his opponent's concealed guard, escaping
with a superficial wound. The exposure of the trick results in the
expulsion of the offending trio and in the Chevalier's betrayal of an
overmastering love for him. Although he feels an equal attraction, he
goes his way. He diagnoses the Maupins as poseurs whose prototype
is the swashbuckling male adolescent, still encumbered by feminine
weaknesses while lacking the male virtues of intelligence and impersonality.

His further "studies" in Paris lead him to a bathing club where
the sexual play of "socialites" is indistinguishable from that of
courtesans, and to the dressing rooms and studios of actresses and
artists where similar behavior is even more brazenly manifested. Along
the way he accumulates male gossip in the best clubs and sensational
stories from the yellow journals, all of which he holds heavily
responsible for nurturing the legend and cult of Lesbos.

There remains a famous lesbian group secluded in a chateau on
the coast of Normandy to which he makes an unannounced visit.
Here the leader is a Russian princess, whose name has become a by-
word for lesbian excess—possibly a satiric imitation of Méphistophéla.
Tammuz finds the Princess Simzerla a proud but pathetic stripling of
thirty whose excursions into vice have been, like Méphistophéla's, a
sterile quest for some satisfying love. Knowing all the gossip about
her before leaving Paris, he offers his sympathetic and seemingly
clairvoyant analysis of it to the princess while she is disguised as her
own brother and unaware that he knows her identity. This kindly
understanding, the first she has ever met, leads her—with time out for
a quick change into feminine costume—straight into his arms. Tammuz, as always, has sufficient control to treat her as a sister, for he has
decided that the way to 'save Lesbos' is not by converting any single
individual to heterosexual passion, not even the notorious archtype,
Simzerla, but by completely foregoing that physical victory against
which most of them have rebelled. If he gives himself to one, his
imaginative hold on all the rest is lost.

He finds Simzerla's group more mature and diversified than those previously encountered, most of them near thirty and fugitives from Parisian notoriety. He spends some weeks studying them individually and collectively, leading them into such literary and philosophical discussion as they are capable of, and spying for passionate attachments. He is unable to discover that more than one couple indulges in any physical expression, and that is rather anemic. Furthermore, in the course of their group effort to write a lesbian drama he obtains final evidence to support what he has felt throughout his study (and, one might add, before he began): women have no powers of impersonal or abstract thought nor any creative intellectual capacity. It is he who contributes as much of the drama as is written.

His final observation is made aboard the yacht of a Swedish-American transvestist known as the Phantom Princess, though she has acquired the actual name of Limerick from a British [sic!] peer, her deserted husband. Rumor has credited her with maintaining a floating 'Lesbos' to equal Simzerla's, but Tammuz finds it no more than a luxury craft of masculine simplicity manned by a hard-bitten male crew. "La Fantôme" has experimented with both men and women more lustily than Simzerla, and is completely disillusioned about the existence of Love. Weary of sensual indulgence, she now permits herself no more than occasional voyeurism, having her crew bring aboard waterfront women for orgies which she observes from the captain's bridge.

Because she is the most masculine of all the women he has encountered, Tammuz enjoys more intellectual companionship with her than with the others. He finds her capable of understanding his concept of woman's proper role in the scheme of things—that of Frea, goddess of fertility. She is quite in accord with his refusal to deify Love aside from its procreative aspect, and shares his unreadiness to sacrifice an impersonal quest or even personal liberty on the altar of Romance.

Informed early by one of the Maupins that many women's inability to respond to men is due to the ugliness of modern male garb, Tammuz has assumed on occasion a more graceful costume—modified Directoire—and with the Princesse Fantôme he dresses in gray silk fencer's hose and a jacket of violet velvet. She reciprocates by appearing at dinner in an evening gown of ivory moiré, above which her white shoulders, deeply tanned face and cropped hair create a ludicrous effect. Tammuz, however, is touched by this effort at refeminization, and before long the two are enjoying a passionate interlude against that grandest of all settings, the open sea.

The inevitable sequel is La Fantôme's holding him captive aboard the yacht in obedience to a newborn feminine hunger for permanence, and only a providential near-shipwreck frees him. Her desire is that they die in each other's arms; his, that he be spared to pursue his mission against Lesbos, and their escape from death can be attributed only to supernatural intervention in his behalf.

He now returns to Paris, and in completing his study of Lesbos he accumulates as it were the dregs of naturalistic data—lesbian sadism, gross exhibitionism, the gift to his mistress by an infatuated nobleman of his fifteen-year-old daughter, an excursion into lesbian prostitution on the part of a countess in order to earn a fortune for her beloved who is a "regular" prostitute. As his money and his time run out, Tammuz, as was foreseen, is convinced that his findings prove his initial thesis: lesbianism is not a distinct psychological entity but merely one of the sins of the flesh. Its causes are numerous—comparative frigidity, feministic rebellion, defiance of undeserved social opprobrium, cynicism about all love. And productive of, or augmenting, all these is the brutality or carelessness of men, their indifference to individual personality in their approach to women. Tammuz knows that by virtue of his sexless sympathy he could have had any one of the scores of lesbians he has studied. Believing, then, that he has achieved a fear-reaching psychological victory, he risks clinching it by a ruse which, as he himself observes, 'would make the angels of orthodoxy hide their eyes with their snowy wings.' In short, he stages a celebration of the rites of Eros, on the grounds that the proper cure for emotional aberration is not orthodox denial of the flesh but pragmatic trial of the normal.

With the aid of Nergal, who knows his Paris, Tammuz invites an attractive (and eligible!) male partner for each of his lesbian semiconverts, and amid a classical decor complete with Roman dining couches and phallic decorations, he treats the company to a banquet accompanied by aphrodisiac wines and incense. Then extinguishing the lights he leaves nature to take its course. Peladan fails to record the percentage of error in this quantitative experiment. (But at least one sadistic lesbian survives to figure in *La Vertu Suprême*.)

Easy as it is to ridicule Peladan's second-rate symbolism and although his *reportage* may not be dependable, there is much psychological soundness in his analysis of lesbian types, however melodramatic the personal histories he fabricates to account for them (and perhaps also to forestall attempts to identify their originals). The composite personality of Tammuz and Nergal is sound—the idealistic, somewhat effeminate man such as variant women are often drawn to. And in *L'Androgyne*,[20] the complementary study, in his "épopée," of homosexual tendencies during male adolescence, he shows sympathy with the very type he scorned the Maupins for imitating, so long as it is a passing stage in male development. Just as evolutionary ideas were in the air long before Darwin systematized them, so the theory of emotional maturing now attributed to Freud was antedated in literature.

Even after discounting Peladan's and Mendès' Catholic bias and their romantic extravagance, their canvases give evidence to widespread lesbianism in *fin de siècle* Paris, and echoes of it and of the crop of fiction it bred must have been far reaching. Amusing proof of this fact is at hand in a light-hearted farce written in 1892 by two Americans, Archibald Gunter and Fergus Redmond, entitled *A Florida Enchantment*. A transvestist tale, it involves no real intrasexual experience (in this respect harking back to medieval and renaissance romances), but its intent must have been unmistakable burlesque of such novels as Rachilde's and Peladan's. In Part I, "The Metamorphosis of Miss Lillian Travers," the heroine discovers that her fiancé is dallying with a ripe widow, and at about the same time she acquires four seeds from an African "tree of sexual change." Since the casket containing these is a relic from a slave-trading grandfather long dead, there is no chance of replenishing the supply. Embittered by her lover's faithlessness, Lillian decides to move from the category of deceived woman into the obviously happier one of philandering man. To gain an ally in the venture she persuades her negro maid to join her in swallowing a seed, and both become sexually male, though to all ordinary appearances they are still women.

Part II, "The Boyhood of Lilly Travers," recounts the hilarious and salacious adventures of the two 'trans-sexists,' to coin the only appropriate term. Lilly's young cousin Bessie falls in love with her, as does also the widow hitherto involved with her fiancé. Lilly wholeheartedly reciprocates Bessie's love, but the cousins' bedroom scenes are kept at the level of farce and never go the implied lengths of Ariosto's or d'Urfé's in similar circumstances. At one point Lilly attends a ball where she dances exclusively with women, apparently without incurring social criticism—a detail which, if as realistically accurate as the rest of the winter resort setting, gives evidence of American naïveté in the 1890s. The negro maid's adventures are naturally somewhat more rabelaisian than those of her mistress but stop short of being censorable.

Part III, "The Wonderful Adventures of Mr. Lawrence Talbot," presents Lilly's life after she has managed to assume male garb and name. The former fiancé suspects Lawrence of having murdered his cousin Lilly for her fortune, and challenges him to duel intended to be fatal. To protect himself Lawrence forces the man to swallow the third magic seed, whereupon he becomes a grotesquely masculine woman, just as Lawrence is a beautiful and beardless youth. Now Lawrence and Bessie marry and set out for Europe, but the unhappy ex-fiancé pursues them, threatens Lawrence with exposure, and points out that Bessie, on learning the truth, will certainly swallow the fourth seed in order to learn the delights of being a man, and will thus be lost forever as a wife. The only solution is to present the villain with the means of regaining his manhood, so that he can get the widow, who is still infatuated with Lawrence, out of his way by marrying her. There is no evidence that this jolly bit of satire (discovered quite accidentally by the present writer) was reviewed or otherwise noted either at home or abroad, nor did it deserve to be from a literary viewpoint. It is worthy of mention here, however, as showing that America was aware of variant fiction other than that of Henry James.

To return once more to France, during 1896 the *Mercure de France* carried serially Remy de Gourmont's *Le Songe d'une Femme,* a work of higher quality than any since James's *The Bostonians.* In the form of correspondence among some dozen persons it presents an exhaustive analysis of what constitutes a satisfactory sexual relationship. The central figures are a sensitive intellectual, Paul; a simple, sensuous, and radiantly happy Annette; and a fascinating but physically inhibited Claude whose emotional pattern closely resembles that of Mlle Tantale without being similarly accounted for. Claude is married and has also experimented sexually with an artist for whom she posed in the nude, but she has never achieved satisfaction. She exerts an irresistible charm over women but has found relations with them equally unrewarding. For a time she falls under the spell of Annette's open-hearted warmth, but Annette scorns lesbianism as childish. Claude dreams of a perfect love which will be more than fleshly, and for a time she is hopeful of realizing her ideal with Paul. During what might be called a probationary period she holds him captive by giving him "all her thoughts," and permitting generous caresses without complete surrender. Paul has cherished a similar dream and has found Annette too exclusively sensual. In the end, however, he abandons Claude for the simple and more "natural" woman. Claude, he finds, can bring happiness to no one, not even herself. The implication is that for anyone who seeks romantic perfection all love must end in failure—a direct echo from Baudelaire. De

Gourmont's title pronounces such an ideal typically feminine: a woman's dream.

The last important negative item before 1900 was Henry James's "The Turn of the Screw" (1898). If his delineation in 1885 of the Bostonian Olive Chancellor was moderate enough to leave critics dubious whether he intended her as a lesbian, there is nothing ambiguous in his later story. In one of his letters, James himself says that his intention was to give "the impression of . . . the most infernal imaginable evil and danger."[31] In this novelette, an innocent young governess goes to a remote English country estate to take charge of two orphans, a boy of ten and a girl of eight. The children's precocious beauty and charm strike her at once as more than normal, and apprehension dawns with her learning that the boy has been expelled from his school for reasons carefully evaded in the letter of dismissal.

Soon she has glimpses about the grounds of a repellently attractive man and an equally sinister woman, who prove to be apparitions visible only to herself. From a reluctant housekeeper she extracts that the man, a former groom now dead, had "had his way" with any woman in the household or neighborhood that he chose, and that the female spectre, in life her predecessor as governess, had departed pregnant by him and died in London of an abortion. These indelicate facts James characteristically conveys by indirection, never by the bald word. Both these personalities had been evilly intimate with the children.

Discovering that her awareness and antagonism can hold the spectres at bay, the governess devotes herself to protecting the children from them. She soon learns to her horror, however, that the little girl not only sees the dark woman but exerts self-control and histrionic talents beyond the capacity of most adults in order to conceal the fact. The boy becomes genuinely devoted to the governess and tries to cooperate in resisting the male ghost, but, always fragile, he succumbs to the emotional conflict and dies of a heart attack. The little girl, more completely dominated—might an affectionate man have weakened the spell for her as a woman did for the boy?—realizes now that only she and the governess can see the apparitions. With precocious acumen she accuses the governess of insanity, sensing that a child's word will stand against that of a potentially hysterical spinster, and achieves her enemy's removal.

This is the first literary appearance of lesbian corruption of a child by an adult, and is probably attributable to the increasing publication of clinical case studies, for the theme has recurred at least twice in the subsequent half-century. James's aversion can be explained on a number of counts. Where in *The Bostonians* he studied well-bred women, his antagonists here are debauched members of a lower class. Then, too, it is known that he had abandoned an original plan of taking up permanent residence in Paris because he found the atmosphere there morally uncongenial, and he had settled in England, which had been rocked only three years earlier by the scandalous trial of Oscar Wilde for homosexuality. It is conceivable that a desire to deny unequivocally any sympathy with that phenomenon helped to motivate *The Turn of the Screw*.

The final French writer of importance to treat of lesbianism before the turn of the century was Pierre Louÿs, who wrote more in the spirit (though not the style) of Gautier, Verlaine or Zola than in that of his contemporary anti-lesbian crusaders. His *Chansons de Bilitis* (1894) and *Aphrodite* (1896) purported to be the fruit, respectively, of translation and intensive classical research, and to give accurate pictures of life in early Greece and Alexandria. Classicists promptly exploded his claim and accused him of sensational exaggeration; nevertheless the two works enjoyed enormous popularity at the time and have since been reissued every few years in English as well as French. The *Songs of Bilitis*, in free verse reminiscent of the Greek Anthology, pictures the life of a girl from her bucolic childhood in Pamphilia, through young womanhood on the isle of Lesbos, to her end as a prosperous courtesan in Cyprus. In her teens she bears a child but leaves it behind without a qualm when adventure leads her on. The emotional highlight of her roving existence is the period in Mitylene, during which she loves and marries another girl with whom she lives happily and faithfully for a decade. However spurious their Helelnism, the poetic quality of the *Chansons* is high, and they have been repeatedly imitated and translated in English, German, Swedish, and Czech. One German translation of twenty-four of the songs was made by Richard Dehmel, a poet in his own right.

In *Aphrodite* lesbianism is only incidental, but still it recurs throughout, including the daily ministrations of a slave girl to a courtesan mistress who accepts them as she does her bath or food; the courtesan's intermittent play with a pair of younger flute-girls; and the flute-girls' marriage, like that of Bilitis, in which they find solace for the depravities they must see and endure as paid entertainers. That Louÿs was aware of every possible sort of lesbian activity is evident, but confining his attention as he does to courtesans, he adds little to an understanding of variant relationships among

other classes of women. It is the taller and stronger of his pairs who
always plays the male role, and the only other suggestion of etiology
is the excessive worship of female beauty, dominant in the cults of
Isis or Aphrodite. It was in this respect particularly that he was
accused of distorting historic fact. As Louÿs pictures this worship, it
is closely related to feminine narcissism.

Louÿs's *Adventures of King Pausole* published at the turn of the
century is a rollicking tale, supposedly contemporary, but wholly
fanciful in setting. One of its characters preaches the saving grace
of healthy promiscuity as opposed to the prudish constraints of
romantic love. Wholesome citizens, he says, come from the slums
where children run loose. Strictness in raising the young, breeds
maladjustment and neurasthenia. Voluntary exclusive devotion to
one individual leads to the madness of an Orestes, the tragic end of
a Marguerite, or the suicides of Romeo and Juliet.

The lesbian pattern in his fantastic design is woven about Mirabelle, a danseuse reminiscent in physique and temperament of
Maupin. She easily captivates the kings' daughter, Aline, for, although the royal Pausole himself has a harem of 365 women, he has
kept his child as secluded as Salammbo. Brought to his senses by
Aline's "elopement" with Mirabelle, and by several adventures he
has while searching for the pair, the king embraces the doctrine of
freedom for the young to the extent of smiling on Aline's marriage
(at fifteen) to a page who speedily converts her to the joys of
heterosexual love. The dancer happily encounters a young noblewoman who, like herself, has known men but has dreamed of a
woman partner, and their union apparently becomes permanent.
Thus, Louÿs compromises between the promiscuity advocated by his
spokesman in the book and the current romantic ideal.

In the factual literature on homosexuality one finds ambiguous
allusions to more variance in French fiction between 1880 and 1895
than it has been feasible to pursue, but considering the returns on
those verified it is unlikely that any important lesbian works even of
low quality have gone undetected. In 1896 Rachilde's signed reviews
began in the *Mercure de France* and a little later the first bibliography
of belles-lettres in Hirschfeld's *Jahrbuch* listed a few retrospective
titles along with current notes. These two systematic sources show that
perhaps a dozen minor French novels appearing during the last half
dozen years of the century (none were available for examination),
dealt with variance to some extent. Such titles as *Mlle Wladimir,
Mon Mari* and *Satana* indicate close imitation of such earlier suc-
cesses as *Mlle Giraud* and *Méphistophéla*. The majority seem to have

made at least a pretense of condemning lesbianism, but Rachilde
remarked acidly in reviewing one of them (Jane de La Vaudère's
Les Demi-Sexes, the theme of which was ovariotomy undergone by
women sufficiently eager for masculinity) that she wished novelists
would stop peddling sensationalism under the guise of medical in-
struction or moral preachment.[32] The cheery insouciance of *King
Pausole* was clearly an innovation and marked the beginning of a
new period. As for the few novels published in Germany before
1900, since they were the first of their kind they will be left for
consideration with twentieth-century material from which they are
indistinguishable.

Summary

Before leaving the nineteenth century a brief summary of its
variant writing will be illuminating. That a preponderance of the
material was in French will not surprise English readers, who have
long recognized the comparative frankness of France in matters of
sex, at least until our own last decade or so. In view of the quantity
and variety of attention devoted to the subject, however, the proportion of sympathetic treatment is low. Of the more than a dozen
authors who took overt lesbianism as a major theme, seven—Coleridge,
Baudelaire, Belot, Mendès, Peladan, Strindberg, and Gourmont—
condemned it explicitly, though with differing degrees of severity.
Seven others—Latouche, Balzac in *The Girl with the Golden Eyes*,
Rossetti, Swinburne in *Lesbia Brandon*, Maupassant, Rachilde in
Mme Adonis, and James in *The Turn of the Screw*—made lesbian
affairs responsible for murder, suicide and ruin, and so implied
equally strong condemnation. Only three were tolerant, and of these
Louÿs, for all his championing of sexual freedom generally, hurried
Aline in *King Pausole* into a heterosexual match at fifteen, and depicted Bilitis as promiscuous from puberty to death save for her lesbian interlude. Gautier was sympathetic to a single lesbian experience
but predicted an unhappy future for Maupin. Verlaine alone, himself
homosexual, let his portraits stand without comment. The several
authors who included minor lesbian episodes pictured them as
involving gravely maladjusted women or as the pastime of prostitutes
and other questionable characters.

Of the four novelists who used variance as a major theme but
avoided or denied lesbian implications, James in *The Bostonians*
considered it a menace to society, Lamartine showed it as contributing
to failure in heterosexual adjustment, Balzac in *Seraphitus-Seraphita*

made it a mystic apprenticeship for marriage, and only Wollstonecraft exalted it above experience with men.

Quite as notable as this limited sympathy for variance is the
frequency of heterosexual action. Some eighty primary and as many
or more secondary characters are involved in the total of variant
scenes, and of these only half a dozen indubitably never knew men.
(For a number of the minor figures definite evidence is lacking, but
indications are that they belonged in the bisexual group.) To be
sure, several women had involuntary and/or, distateful experience
with men, but the majority eventually found such experience preferable to variant relations.

When it is noted in conclusion that the proportion of male to
female authors is even larger than that of French to English, one
cannot avoid inferring some causal relation between the fact and the
statistics above. This impression is confirmed by noting that the four
feminine writers, Wollstonecraft, Schreiner, Rossetti and Rachilde,
pictured no successful heterosexual relations. "Mary" refuses to consummate her marriage; Lyndall commits slow suicide to escape hers;
Raoule achieves a fantastic evasion, and Mme Adonis takes the man
of the couple she captivates in a spirit of vindictive sadism. The
hypothesis of a very natural sex bias with regard to feminine variance
will be amply supported in studying twentieth-century authors.

CHAPTER V.

CONJECTURAL RETROSPECT

Four women among thirty-odd nineteenth-century authors dealing with variance may seem a meager fraction until one recalls that Mary Wollstonecraft was the first of her sex to appear in this record since Sappho. What accounts for this dearth of feminine authorship? Since the renaissance, many women have been published; factual literature attests that female variance has always existed to a greater or less extent; and surely it is a subject in which, if any, one would expect women to show more interest than men. But thus far, only one literary attitude toward variance has enjoyed freedom from censure: disapproval, whether it was conveyed by satire, exhortation, or tragic example.

To such derogatory expression it is natural enough that few women should contribute. Equally obvious are the factors inhibiting feminine expressions of sympathy. For one thing, women have suffered too many critical handicaps on the score of their sex alone to embark lightly upon a venture which lays men of established repute open to attack. More important, a man writing tolerantly of female variance can be accused of nothing worse than tolerance, but a woman is at once suspected of being variant herself, which to the man-in-the-street is tantamount to being lesbian in the most damning sense of the term. This is not mere armchair theorizing. Havelock Ellis in his volume on sexual inversion observes that women poets of his day who had contributed variant histories to his record regularly changed the gender of pronouns in love lyrics destined for publication, in order to conceal the homosexual inspiration of their verses. And the present writer has amusingly enough been viewed askance by certain librarians after demanding from their "restricted" cases novels no more questionable than those of Radclyffe Hall. If this was the state of affairs well into the twentieth century, a time presently to be shown more tolerant of variance perhaps than any since the classical period, how much more stringent must have been the need for caution when to be suspect incurred moral opprobrium and complete social ostracism?

It seems certain, then, that there have been women of variant inclination through the centuries who also possessed literary gifts, and it is probable that exhaustive research would reveal traces of variance in a surprising number of feminine authors from the renaissance on. The purpose of the following chapter is to consider those few whose lives most readily yield suggestive hints, and to correlate such hints with corresponding traces, however carefully masked, in their writing.

Louise Labé. The first promising subject is Louise Labé, lyric poet of the early sixteenth century and one of a group of brilliant young women who brought considerable distinction upon their native city of Lyons. Until the middle of the last century the best biographical encyclopedias stated as fact that in 1542 she took active part in the Dauphin's siege of Perpignan and acquitted herself so well that she was thereafter nicknamed "le capitaine Loys."[1] With advances in historical method, the authenticity of this episode has been questioned (though never flatly disproved), the alternate probability being that she took the part of a knight in a tournament celebrating the same victory. In either event, her horsemanship and conduct of arms are described as masterly.

Scholars have expended much effort in attempting to identify the persons to whom her passionate lyrics were addressed. Internal evidence favors the assumption that she had a number of lovers; yet, even the critics who find this idea acceptable have not managed to identify more than one, her fellow poet Olivier de Magny. Several other leading questions also remain unanswered. Why, in view of Labé's marked poetic gift, does so slim a volume of her verse remain, in comparison to her surviving prose, which is excellent but of lower vitality? And what was the cause of her quarrel with Clémence de Bourges, a younger woman poet to whom she dedicated a volume published in 1555, and, in that dedication, proclaimed as being more gifted and showing brighter promise than herself?

Her biography, like those of many nonpolitical figures so far removed in time, is not rich in documented detail. It is known that she was born about 1520, the daughter of a wealthy cordage merchant. Despite her middle-class status, as a girl she studied music, Greek, Latin and Spanish, and seems also to have known Italian well, especially the work of Ariosto. In 1542—that is, in her twenties, late for those days—she married Ennemond Perrin, another cordage

merchant and a friend of her father's. Her husband was twenty years
her senior and the marriage was childless; however, it endured for
more than a quarter of a century, and on his death Perrin left her
all his property. Both father and husband being men of wealth,
Labé had a large house with pleasant gardens which became a rendez-
vous for poets and artists. Her liaison with de Magny apparently
stirred no scandal, but 'so brilliant a position naturally excited
envy,' and she was rather spitefully nicknamed "La Belle Cordelière."
After her husband's death in 1565, the noblewoman of Lyons set
upon "la petite bourgeoise" for having eclipsed them intellectually
and socially, and during the brief year before her own death Labé
was accused of being "livrée à toutes sortes de désordres."[2]

Until the time of her marriage Labé was certainly skilled and
active in all the arts of an *homme de guerre*. Even later (about
1547) when Diane de Poitiers accompanied Henry II on a visit to
Lyons, Louise seems to have been one of the moving spirits, if not
the organizer, of a fête honoring the favorite, in which young women
of the town assumed the costume of Diana the Huntress and exhibited
their skill with bow and dart. (It is interesting to find Brantôme
alluding to this event in passing, though he mentions no names and
no precise date.)[3]

In her thirties Labé rebelled against the limitations of feminine
education, proclaiming that women should study all the "sciences"
pursued by men, and in the letter of dedication to her friend which
prefaced her volume in 1555 she begs them to 'lift their spirits a
little above their bobbins and distaffs.'[4] Shortly after the publication
of this work she was estranged from Clémence de Bourges by the
aforementioned "éclatante" quarrel of uncertain origin, though until
then 'their union was cited as one rare between two women.'[5]

Apparently no one has suggested that she may have been homosexual. But in her "Elégie I," we find the following:

> Encore Phébus, ami des Lauriers vers . . .
> Chanter me fait . . .
> Il m'a donné la lyre, qui les vers
> Souloit chanter de l'amour Lesbienne . . .

If in sixteenth century France the final adjective carried its present
meaning, and there seems no evidence to the contrary, this passage
is certainly suggestive. In "Elégie III," a kind of apologia for a life
of emotional *Sturm und Drang,* she says she was only sixteen when
she first suffered a devastatingly tragic love, but that she had already
loved deeply twice before. She implores her townswomen as they
read of her 'amorous pains, regrets and tears' not to condemn that

"erreur de ma folle jeunesse—Si c'est erreur. . . ."[7] This confession has disturbed some critics profoundly because it seems to imply that she must have been a courtesan.

Only a few of her lyrics reveal the sex of the person to whom they were addressed, an evasion more difficult in an inflected language than in English, and among those which do not betray it is the group that is acclaimed by critics as most distinguished by sincerity, frankness, and 'an amazing freshness compared to her contemporaries.'[8] The descriptive touches in some of these sonnets, moreover, picture a loved one of more delicate beauty and a passion of less harsh and painful violence than the others. The assumption that she was a lesbian would explain her precocious passions and the number, variety, and anonymity of these later flames better than the hotly disputed courtesan theory, although she was undoubtedly bisexual and very ardent—"tous ses gouts furent des passions," says one biographer. It would also explain the many, although comparatively unimpassioned, tributes written to her by male poets, for artists incline to be more tolerant of sex variance than the public at large, and they may possibly have gone on record in her favor because she suffered from social persecution.

And finally, lesbianism would account for her estrangement from her younger friend, "of noble family and spotless reputation," as well as any of the other theories advanced to that end. Until late in the nineteenth century a legend persisted that in the same year that Labé's volume was published Clémence submitted verses of her own to her friend for criticism, but the latter instead of giving it "enleva a Clémence son amant,"[9] and it was suggested that Clémence's death within the year was chargeable to this blow. This tale was fairly well discredited in 1877 by the Dutch scholar Boy;[10] however, nothing plausible has replaced it.

Let us consider the case if that rare union *was* a passionate one. With the older woman married and famous, the younger formally engaged (as Clémence was), their friendship would excite little comment. If the married woman had also had as lover the most distinguished poet of the period, and if, as there is reason to believe, Clémence had married at twenty, and lost a husband, they would be even safer from suspicion. Then Labé publishes the volume of poems described above. She dedicates it to Clémence in a letter lauding the girl's poetic promise to the skies and deploring a married woman's humdrum life. If, as commonly happens, identities were inferred at the time for the subjects of Labé's verses, Clémence's "noble family," and her fiancé as well, may have frowned on further intimacy between the girl and the devoted friend who seemed so little in favor of her marrying.

Clémence might still, however, submit her own work for a more practiced writer's criticism. What happened? Despite the fact that scholars have unhappily been unable to trace de Bourges' volume, several conjectures are legitimate. Did it contain impassioned verses to the fiancé which stirred Labé to reckless jealousy? Were there cryptic love poems to Labé herself which convinced her that marriage would be unhappy for her beloved protégée? In either case she might have enlightened the young man as to the nature of her relation to Clémence. Unhandsome behavior, but no more so than the legendary stealing of the lover for herself (which Boy believes did not occur). There is a kindlier alternative: she merely warned Clémence that certain poems would be indentified as written to her; the less experienced girl, suspecting her of literary jealousy, published them anyway; Labé's apprehensions proved correct, and the result separated the lovers. But such involved psychology belongs more to the twentieth century than to the sixteenth. All this is conjecture, to be sure, but no more implausible than the several conflicting theories already advanced by Labé scholars. Furthermore, it has the advantage, conclusive with experimental scientists, of providing answers to more questions than any other single hypothesis.

Charlotte Charke. A sadly different life story is recorded in the autobiography written nearly two centuries later by Charlotte Charke, daughter of the erratic actor and playwright, Colley Cibber. (An account of that irresponsible egomaniac's family life would shed light on his youngest child's temperament and fate, but cannot be included here.) Though Havelock Ellis expresses uncertainty that Charlotte was actually homosexual,[1] there are elements in her adventures which more than compare with significant passages in the lives of Mary Frith and Catalina Erauso. Like these two women, Charke was a transvestist, and at several points in her story she mentions connections with women which promise definite significance had they been expanded. But at the time of writing she was forty-five, unable to get work, and more than half-starving in a bare single room near a refuse dump in London. Survival depended on her standing well with her readers—her tale appeared in weekly installments—and on her hope of reconciliation with her father, who had long refused aid. Hence her narrative is so full of discreet elision as to be sometimes incoherent or even contradictory. This is particularly evident in regard to her "wearing breeches," one of the sorest points between her

and her family, and also to all her personal relations except her early
and unhappy marriage.

Her history is a veritable psychiatric case study. Born when her
mother (the actress Jane Shore) was forty-five, she was the youngest
of a dozen children and the object of violent jealousy among her
elder siblings because of the mother's favoritism. Charlotte, on her
part, was intensely devoted to her mother as long as the latter lived.
Precociously brilliant, she was sent to boarding school at eight and
within two or three years was crammed with three languages, music,
dancing, and geography, all of which she later pronounced useless in
aiding a woman to earn her keep. From the age of five she was given
to donning boy's clothes and engaging in the most daring and
original exploits, sometimes to the point of grave danger. These
make enthralling reading but are not pertinent here. At sixteen she
married a worthless bandleader in her father's theatre—the Drury
Lane—and had a daughter within the year; but even before the
child's birth her husband was "running with a plurality of common
wretches [women] that were to be had for half a crown,"[2] and at the
end of the year the two separated. Her trenchant comment on her
marital relations is that both she and her husband "ought rather have
been sent to school than to church, in regard to any qualification on
either side towards rendering the marriage state comfortable to one
another."[3]

She made her debut as an actress shortly before her marriage and
continued on the London stage for perhaps two years after her
separation, taking men's parts at least half the time. Then apparently
she went on the boards in her father's favorite role and one he had
made famous, Lord Foppington in *The Careless Husband*. Perhaps
this fact led Cibber to cut off financial support and to spoil her
chances with all London producers. More likely it was her travesty
of his acting that enraged him, for his vanity was morbid and she
inherited his wicked and heartless wit. As long as her mother lived
she was sure of some funds, but death soon closed that channel and
she was driven to a variety of shifts that would have been tragic had
she been capable of taking anything very tragically. These experiences,
too, are diverting, but only the most significant can be touched on
here. For a time she ran a grocer shop in London, living meanwhile
with a young widow who lent her money for her business. Later,
when arrested for debt, she was saved by contributions from women,
once from a Mrs. Elizabeth Careless whose name suggests her profession, and again from "all the ladies who kept coffee houses in and
about Covent Garden . . . for the relief of poor Sir Charles, as they

were pleased to stile me.''⁴ Twice women lost their hearts to her and
she was forced to reveal her sex, but her mere word was not sufficient.
In the first case we are not told how she managed to be convincing.
In the second, she was working as a waiter, and her inamorata came
to Charlotte's room to give her the lie, saying she "could never have
made advances to one of her own sect [sic]." When Charlotte asked
if she was sure she "understood what she meant," it led to a physical
brawl so violent as to cost Charlotte her position.

Intermittently she acted in the provinces with strolling companies
of low calibre and continually bankrupt, and for a long time she and
another actress stayed together through thick and thin, the friend
caring for her during three years of "nervous fever and lowness of
spirits." At one point she lets slip that this woman passed in a tight
place as "Mrs. Brown," and since "Mr. Brown" was the name Charlotte took whenever she needed an alias, it may be that they lived
outside the theatre as man and wife. Finally, they abandoned acting
for a time at Chepstow in Wales because Charlotte "met with many
friends," particularly another widow who lent her considerable sums
of money, and a younger woman who gave her the use of "a very
handsome house with a large garden, near three quarters acre of
ground" which had just been inherited. The latter also wrote her
"very friendly letters" when she went on short trips. At that time, she
attempted to run a bake-shop, still with her faithful friend the
actress, who she says now stayed on "only out of sincere friendship
and an uncommon easiness of temper," a suggestion that might well
imply a more cogent previous reason. As was said, none of these
passages mentions variance, but taken all together and in conjunction
with the dark mystery she makes of her first experience in men's
clothes,⁵ as well as her family's relentless disowning of her, they
make a picture which seems to justify her inclusion in a conjectural
record.

"The Ladies of Llangollen." Charke's history brings us to the
late eighteenth century, a period when the Age of Reason had passed
its peak and the deifying of emotion which characterized the Romantic Period was beginning to appear. Blanche Hardy, in a biography of
the Princess de Lamballe, says:

It was the age of great friendships: girls and even grown
women carried the miniature of another woman about with
them in a locket, bracelet or other ornament, would draw it
out occasionally when in company, gaze fondly upon it, and

press it to their lips; wrote long and loverlike letters to the beloved object, awaited her coming ardently, and wept storms of tears at her departure.[1]

One such passionate friendship was born in Ireland, though the parties to it are universally known as "the Ladies of Llangollen," the picturesque valley in Wales where they spent the greater part of their lives. The journal kept for forty years by the elder of the two is now all that survives of their writing, though references to them in the work of friends suggest that both wrote some nature essays and verses. The younger was something of an artist as well. Both Lady Eleanor Butler and Sarah Ponsonby came of titled families. They met first at a school in Kilkenny, probably when Eleanor was nearing twenty and Sarah entering her teens, for there seems to have been about seven or eight years' difference in their ages. Their friendship apparently flourished for nearly a decade before Eleanor's harsh and prudish mother tried to force the boyish young woman into either a distasteful marriage or a convent. Sarah's mother, a second wife, had died in the girl's infancy. After a third wife increased the already large family, Sarah lived with a cousin whose husband made advances which were disgusting and gravely disturbing to the adolescent girl. Her older and more independent friend, given to wearing men's clothes, proposed an "elopement," but the two were without resources, and after spending several nights in a barn they were apprehended and brought back in disgrace. Sarah at once fell gravely ill. Eleanor was forbidden to see her, and Sarah's cousin accused Eleanor of having

a debauched mind, with no ingredients for friendship which ought to be founded on virtue, whereas hers every day more and more . . . was acting in direct opposition to it, as well as to the interest, happiness and reputation of one she professed to love.[2]

This cousin also attempted to keep Sarah from receiving Eleanor's long letters, which she said only aggravated the girl's illness.

The romantic pair had an ally, however, in a servant, Mary Caryll, known as "Molly the Bruiser" because of her marked masculinity. With this girl's help, Eleanor was hidden in Sarah's bedroom closet for several days, whereupon the latter promptly recovered, and as soon as she was well enough the pair staged a rebellion—they simply refused to live any longer at home or apart from one another. Both families being by now worn down, the girls were given a small allowance and invited to remove themselves permanently from the neighborhood. They managed to get as far as Wales, and, once established, they sent back for Molly, who remained their servant until her death many years later.

Though "poor as church mice," the two women were radiantly happy, and "of a personality so powerful" that they were known as the Platonists. "Their retreat became a kind of court at which all the great ones of their time presented themselves. Wordsworth, DeQuincey, Scott, the Duke of Wellington and Mme de Genlis were among their guests,"[3] and they had a half century of idyllic happiness before they died, Eleanor in 1829 and Sarah in 1831. The journal which Eleanor Butler kept from 1788 until her death records the placid course of their mutual existence, detailing financial stress lightly borne, small village tensions faced with equanimity, and again and again "a day of sweetly enjoyed retirement."

On the precise nature of the relation between them the journal is naturally reticent. The modern French analyst of all feminine emotions, Colette, devotes better than twenty pages to it in *Ces Plaisirs,* and epitomizes neatly the distinguishing feature of all such attachments.

> 'It is not sensuality that ensures the fidelity of two women but a kind of blood kinship. . . . I have written kinship where I should have said identity. Their close resemblance guarantees similarity in *volupté*. The lover takes courage in her certainty of caressing a body whose secrets she knows, whose preferences her own body has taught her.'[4]

If English readers of Eleanor's journal want to see in a single mention of "our bed" an impure significance, says Colette, then let them.

> 'What is purity? Why is it "pure" to stroke a cheek but not a breast? Yes, yes, the breast responds. But what of it, if above it the lover merely dreams? "It is the victim who is almost always responsible in emotional crimes," says an old magistrate. How one would like to have the journal of Sarah Ponsonby, the younger girl! Eleanor Butler was the practical one, the possessor, the male. Sarah Ponsonby was the *woman*.'[5]

Karoline von Günderode. During the same years that saw these willing exiles living out their rapturous idyll, a very different life was swept along on the tide of romantic *Sturm und Drang* in Germany. Karoline von Günderode was still unborn when the Ladies of Llangollen settled in their Welsh elysium, and suicide ended her quarter-century of life two decades before their death. Outside her native land this distinguished young romantic poet is most likely to be remembered through her brief connection with Bettina Brentano von Arnim, sister of the poet Clemens Brentano and the "child" of *Goethe's Briefwechsel mit einem Kind.* The mercurial and precocious Bettina was undoubtedly a very remarkable young person, but scholarly research has proved her published correspondence with Goethe to be largely spurious, and even the superficial reader can detect signs of *post facto* interpolation in her letter to Goethe's mother describing Günderode's death and the two girls' previous relationship.[1]

Equally copious expansion is evident in the correspondence with Günderode,[2] a really remarkable volume of philosophy, poetry, and romantic "sensibility" made human, however, by the small ordinary preoccupations of the two very busy young women. Nine-tenths of the volume is occupied by Bettina's own letters, supposedly written during a number of brief absences when she was a guest at various country estates. Had these voluminous outpourings actually been penned under such circumstances the girl would have had no time for meals or sleep, let alone the normal social exigencies of house-party life.

Karoline von Günderode was one of several daughters of a moderately affluent widow, who spent the latter part of her short life in a "Kloster" (not a religious house but a dignified retreat for well-born spinsters such as has been charmingly pictured by "Isak Dinesen" in *Seven Gothic Tales*). She was, by all acounts, an interesting mixture of emotional mysticism and sceptical "masculine" intellect, and both are reflected in her poems.[3] At least one of these, "Wandel und Treue," suggests that there is no certainty save that all is uncertain, no ultimate Truth because life and universe alike are in constant flux and inexpressible in terms of any constant pattern. It might almost have been written today rather than a century and a half ago.

The context in which the poem is quoted shows that it grew out of long-sustained discussions between her and Bettina on the nature of love. It is cast in the form of a dialogue between Violetta, who embodies Bettina's championship of romantic constancy, and Narziss, who represents Günderode's own viewpoint. The latter holds that love, like all else, is subject to change; therefore, one should not attempt to fix it upon a single person or thing, but should love only Love and follow its dictates wherever it leads. The amount of stress laid upon this composition by Bettina, who compiled and inflated the correspondence for publication, suggests an effort to throw upon the other woman all responsibility for any inconstancy which ensued.

The sixty-page biography of Günderode in Ersch and Gruber's *Allgemeine Encyclopädie der Wissenschaften und Kunste*[4] records several variant attachments in her life. Previous to her acquaintance with Bettina she enjoyed a very close friendship with Frau Karoline von Barkhaus, to whom she wrote oftener than weekly in the warmest terms, and in one of the quoted letters she mentions that 'a room is ready where we will sleep together when you come.' Another woman, Frau Susanna Maria von Heyden, mentioned as her most intimate friend, fell heir to Günderode's portrait and two paintings of the scene of the unhappy girl's death. She 'never recovered from her grief over her unlucky friend, and lived secluded from the world in joyless solitude.'

As to the relationship with Bettina, their correspondence shows it to have been warmly emotional as well as intellectual. Bettina wrote at length to Madame Goethe of Günderode's extreme sensitiveness and intensity, describing the latter's pallor the first time that Bettina kissed her on the mouth, and generally betraying awareness of unpleasant gossip and eagerness to deflect it from herself.[5] The facts of the case seem to be that, like Labé and Clémence de Bourges, the two girls had a serious quarrel, and Günderode's suicide followed closely enough upon it to create some unpleasantness for the survivor. Here, too, the cause of the quarrel was a man, and editors of Günderode's poems and letters claim that it was the tragic end of this romance with him which led the poet to take her own life. The man involved had, while fairly young, married a widow thirteen years his senior, who had several children. When he and Günderode found themselves deeply in love, the wife, with "sterbende Gute," agreed to release him, but under emotional stress the already tubercular young man suffered a serious hemorrhage, and since he was not yet free it was the wife who nursed him back to health. In penitent gratitude he swore that if he lived he would never leave her, and he kept his vow. This version of Günderode's tragedy is offered by the conventional biographies.[6]

In Bettina's letters and elsewhere, however, the story survives of the man's being a fellow guest of hers at one of the house parties which spacious living and difficult travel fostered in the eighteenth century. Full of his love for Günderode, he paid much attention to a child in the house who reminded him of his beloved, and in Bettina's presence he called the little girl "his Karoline" (her name was

Sophie) and caressed and kissed her. The fiery Bettina, furious that he 'used expressions in speaking of Günderode as if he had a right to her love,' told him off roundly, and this contretemps apparently led to some difficulty between him and Günderode—the only reasonable explanation being that Bettina must also have talked as if *she* "had a right to her love."

The quarrel between the two young women followed, and one summer evening a few weeks later Günderode strolled unobtrusively to the bank of her favorite stream and there shot herself. It is not suggested that any overt scandal occurred, or that the quarrel with Bettina was the immediate cause of this act. Günderode's poetry is minor-keyed and full of a romantic preoccupation with early death. But certainly something in the relation between the two girls was a contributing factor. And that variant inferences are not far-fetched is evidenced by a German lesbian novel of 1919,[7] in which the memory of Günderode is worshipped with passion by a brilliantly educated lesbian, while Bettina is the object of jealous hatred. The author of this tale (of which more later) is known to have had access to much German material not available to the present writer, which apparently supported the lesbian inference.

Only a few years after Günderode's death a tragedy in Edinburgh was directly attributed to homosexual scandal. Two mistresses of a private school, Marianne Woods and Jane Pirie, were accused of tribadism by Dame Helen Cumming Gordon on the evidence of a young relative (or ward) who was a pupil in the school. The young women brought suit for slander and after a long and bitter battle apparently won their case, but their reputations were damaged to the extent of ruining their educational enterprise. It is upon the court record of their trial that Lillian Hellman based her Broadway success of 1934, *The Children's Hour,* and their story will receive further attention when that drama is considered under twentieth-century literature.

George Sand. In France the spectacular figure of George Sand invites attention, both because of her adoption of male costume in the 1830s, and because critics are agreed as to the pronounced masculinity of her always semi-autogiographical heroines. She wrote nothing to be classed as variant, but special note is due her *Gabriel-Gabrielle,*[1] the title an obvious echo of Balzac's *Seraphitus-Seraphita,* which antedated it by only five years. Sand's title-character is definitely an inter-sexual, but the author avoids variant emotion and concentrates upon psychological ambiguity. Gabriel, an orphan, is not only raised as a boy, but by a somewhat strained device is made to believe that she actually is one until she attains her majority. Learning at this point that the deception has been contrived by her grandfather, to secure for his branch of the family a fortune which can be inherited only through the male line, she sets out to find her defrauded male cousin and make restitution. The two fall in love, marry secretly, and live abroad in the hope of avoiding family interference. Their effort is futile, and after much tragic misunderstanding and dangerous intrigue, Gabrielle is finally set upon and killed by her grandfather's hirelings during one of the periods when she is again, as during her youth, posing as a man.

The most pertinent passage describes a masked ball which Gabrielle attends dressed for the first time as a woman. The cousin, who still believes her a man, speaks recklessly of how easily he could love "her." Her reply is:

> "This sort of entertainment should be morally frowned
> upon. It all goes to excite impure ideas, the whole purpose
> is to shake our composure. The joke has gone too far. I am
> going to take off this costume and never put it on again."[2]

Later she implores him not to duel with a fellow-reveller who has insulted her, as when it is known that she is "really a man it would be ridiculous. And who knows? Wicked minds could even find in it matter for odious interpretation." Her cousin replies: "That's true. May my honor and reputation for courage perish, rather than that flower of innocence which graces your name. I will turn it all off as a jest."

As it is common knowledge that, though never a compulsive transvestist, George Sand wore men's clothes as frequently as women's from her girlhood in Nohant until she approached middle age, her treatment of this incident is rather surprising. But this, and her careful avoidance of so much as the mention of female homosexuality, carry a suggestion of the caution observed by all potentially suspected variants. The circumstances of Aurore Dudevant's childhood and puberty were enough, in all conscience, to produce any or all of the aberrations in a psychoanalyst's manual. Her heterosexual affairs were so numerous, open, and dramatic that few students have looked for other emotional incidents in her life. By her own statement, however, she never achieved complete satisfaction with any of the men she loved,[3] and there are a number of suggestive incidents which crop up in one after another of her biographies.

During her last year in a convent school in Paris—at about seventeen, that is—she suffered what in modern parlance would be called a violent "crush" on an Irish schoolmate. In the 1830s she was "for a long time . . . fascinated by the great romantic actress of the day, Dorval. . . . Dumas and Vigny loved her (Dorval), and she had been Musset's last mistress. George had seen much of her in those years, so much that Vigny had become jealous of their intimacy."[4] (André Maurois quotes a letter in which Vigny refers to Sand viciously as "that Lesbian.")[5] Many years later, after Dorval's death, Sand took over the responsibility for her children. During Sand's sojourn in Switzerland in the middle 1830s she met Mme d'Agoult—known to literature as Daniel Stern—and was so strongly attracted that she entertained her new friend at Nohant for several months after their return to France. Subsequently the two lived but a few doors apart in Paris and for some time held a joint salon. Still later she experienced a friendship of similar intensity with Pauline Garcia, Malibran's sister and a noted singer. Even after Garcia had married Viardot, Sand continued to see so much of her that Mme Viardot was generally referred to as "Mme Sand's friend" first, "the great singer" second.

Given Sand's passionate temperament and her lack of restraint, it seems reasonable to assume that she had several variant experiences, which were overshadowed in the public eye by her more dramatic heterosexual ones, and about which she preserved discreet silence in her writing. It may be argued that such silence is out of character with her fictional volubility about her other affairs. But the noted men of her day with whom she became involved had little to fear from her advertising their relations with her. For her own reputation she was apparently not much concerned, being a true and courageous child of the period; however, she may well have felt consideration for women whom she loved and who had more to lose. Possibly her variant attachments were *not* physical liaisons; nevertheless, if she had presented them fictionally in their true intensity, because of her other notorious experiences it is unlikely that they would be credited with innocence.

Emily Brontë. In England an even more complete discretion was guarded by the enigmatic Emily Brontë. All four of the Brontës wrote with talent which in Charlotte and Emily approached genius; yet their lives as children of a poor clergyman in a remote country

village were almost empty of outward event. Emily's was barren
even of a love affair, a paradox to critics in view of the emotional
power in her writing. In the century since their deaths, some hundred
critical and biographical studies have attempted to solve the Brontës'
riddle. In Charlotte's case the task is relatively simple, since her
letters reveal without much reticence two passionate attachments,
one to Ellen Nussey, an early school friend, and the second to
Constantin Héger, master of the school in Brussels where she twice
stayed briefly, as student and as teacher. The first love was of such
intensity that E. F. Benson, in his biography of Charlotte, frankly
pronounces it homosexual, though he is quick to add that considering
the frequency of such experience among adolescents of both sexes,
it should be regarded as more normal than otherwise.

It is true that this friendship began in the years between fourteen
and sixteen when Charlotte and Ellen were together in boarding
school, but it seemed to grow rather than diminish over the subsequent decade, until Charlotte was writing to Ellen in her twenties
of "trembling all over with excitement after reading your note."
In 1836, when she was twenty-one, Charlotte wrote:

> Ellen, I wish I could live with you always, I begin to cling
> to you more fondly than I ever did. If we had a cottage
> and a competency of our own I do think we might love until
> Death without being dependent on any third person for
> happiness.

And again in the next year:

> Why are we so divided? Ellen, it must be because we are
> in danger of loving each other too well—because of losing
> sight of the Creator in idolatry of the creature.[1]

From the very openness of these transports it must be obvious
that the relationship was an innocent one, and indeed that she
herself was ignorant of any other possibility. Moreover, all the
fire went out of it as soon as she had met and fallen in love with
M. Heger.

Emily's case is more complex; consequently, all manner of solutions
have been advanced for the puzzle she presents, from a most secretly
hidden liaison of the ordinary sort to an incestuous relation with
her brother Branwell. The most illuminating suggestions from
the viewpoint of the present study are found in Romer Wilson's

All Alone and in Virginia Moore's *The Life and Eager Death of Emily Brontë*. Miss Wilson analyzes in Emily what she terms the "Dark Hero ideal," a male alter ego which she very plausibly claims to be the most significant feature of Emily's personality, and of which she shows Heathcliff in *Wuthering Heights* to be a projection. Employing a different approach, Miss Moore assembles objective testimony that from earliest childhood Emily was boyish in appearance, temperament and behavior, and suggests that many of her lyrics were inspired by a person of her own sex.[2] In Emily's own day, of course, *Wuthering Heights* was the one novel published by the pseudonymous "Bells" whose feminine authorship critics longest refused to credit, and Moore's chapter advancing the theory of Emily's variance is very convincing. Adverse critics have attacked Moore's soundness on the score of her misreading the title of a poem in the British Museum Brontë manuscript; however, all the Brontë handwriting is virtually illegible, and Moore was the first to study the document. In her zeal to consider all conceivable evidence for a man in Emily's life, she read as "Louis Parensell" a title shown later to be inserted in Charlotte's hand and deciphered as "Love's Farewell," but at least her exhaustive search for records of Mr. Parensell has reduced the likelihood of any subsequent scholar's unearthing evidence of a lover.

Surprisingly enough, Moore failed to capitalize on one important episode in Emily's life—the girl's reaction at fifteen to her first meeting with Charlotte's bosom friend, Ellen Nussey. At the time of Ellen's first house-visit to the Brönte's she was, on the evidence of a surviving portrait, a bewitchingly pretty and very feminine young woman. Thus the adolescent Emily, who had had opportunity of meeting virtually no one outside her family, was thrown into contact with an older girl of great physical appeal and one patently capable of variant emotion. The house was small, and sleeping arrangements involved Emily's sharing a bedroom with Charlotte and her guest.

> But Emily had sensibilities too delicate to intrude on bosom friends. While Charlotte and Ellen whispered far into the night, she bundled up and went and slept in the little cubby over the peat room with Tabby the servant.[3]

One day Charlotte was ill and unable to entertain her guest.

> But to their surprise, Emily, whose dislike of strangers

had always been violent, volunteered for that office. On their return from the moors Charlotte was nervous. "How did Emily behave?" she asked eagerly as soon as she could get Ellen aside. "Why, Emily had been very, very nice," said Ellen in surprise.[3]

Later in her life Ellen described Emily as maddeningly unsociable, but as having "a brilliant and very appealing sudden gaze when she allowed her eyes to be seen."

Immediately upon Ellen's departure, Emily suffered an attack of erysipelas so severe that her arm had to be lanced, "accompanied— unromantically—by liver complaint." The indication that her general health was not good Moore considers puzzling.

> Though living next to the pollution of an ancient graveyard and exposed to the unhealthy environment of Cowan's Bridge [the original of the dreadful boarding school in Charlotte's *Jane Eyre*] she had remained hale and strong from the age of five to the age of fifteen.[4]

In view of modern psychosomatic theory, this illness is highly revealing, for skin and gall bladder complaints are recognized symptoms of emotional tension or disturbance. It seems fairly evident that Emily was strongly (even if perhaps unconsciously) drawn to Ellen Nussey. Under the circumstances the latter's visit would have been a period of intense stimulation and strain. At the withdrawal of the exciting presence the nervous reaction was equally intense, and her body registered a deprivation which her proud and in- independent spirit would not willingly have admitted to con- sciousness.

There is also internal evidence of variance to be gleaned from Emily's poetry, despite the angry insistence of one critic that "Emily Bronte's own voice turns to nonsense the hundreds of pages of biography based on [such] subjective interpretation."[5] The critic is Fannie Ratchford, whose separate volume, *The Brontes' Web of Childhood,* skillfully reconstructs the two sequences of remarkable legend composed during adolescence by Charlotte and Branwell, and Emily and Anne respectively. But in her impatience with sub- jectivity Mrs. Ratchford goes to the other extreme of regarding these creations as spontaneously generated and quite unrelated to the lives of their creators. Thus, her discovery that cryptic initials heading Emily's most "masculine" poems stand for male characters in the Gondal epic leads her to the outburst quoted above. Yet she herself points out that the poems in question were composed over a period of twelve years, and that "lack of agreement between chronology of composition and story sequence shows that they were not written as progressive plot incidents but were merely the poetic expression of scenes . . . and emotions familiar to her inner vision. . . ." Ratchford also admits that "only a small percent of the poems carry headings, and [these] . . . raise as many problems as they solve. Varying sets of initials appear for the same character . . . G. S. in one poem is a boy, in another a woman."[6]

Thus it seems probable that Emily's lyrics sprang from her own experience, and that the confused initials represent an effort to incorporate them into some whole which would not betray their intimacy. (In the end she achieved her catharsis in prose through *Wuthering Heights.*) For lyric poetry is the most personal of all modes of expression, and Emily was morbidly reticent. All Brontë scholars know the story of Charlotte's "accidental" reading in 1845 of her sister's jealously guarded manuscript, and of the violent quarrel which followed. In Charlotte's own moderate words:

> My sister Emily was not a person . . . on the recesses of whose mind and feelings even those nearest and dearest to her could with impunity intrude. It took hours to reconcile her to the discovery I had made, and days to persuade her that such poems merited publication.[7]

It is certain that many poems, along with many letters, were sacrificed to Emily's passion for privacy.

The most enigmatic chapter in Emily's history covers the years from 1835 through 1838. All critics agree on the evidence of her poetry that during this time she underwent the major emotional experience of her life, one which gave rise to poems of nightmare, guilt, tragic separation and desire for death, and one which also contained the seeds of the mutually destructive love of Catherine and Heathcliff in *Wuthering Heights,* written nearly a decade later. Emily's correspondence from this period has been lost or destroyed, Charlotte's few surviving letters have undergone cutting on her part which leaves them barren, and one must infer pointed expurgation. The precise dating of Emily's poems written before 1839 might help solve the mystery, but for such precision scholars have striven in vain. The latest and best established chronology, that of Hatfield, will be accepted here.

It is known that for three months in late 1835 Emily was a pupil at Roe Head, a boarding school where Charlotte was engaged as teacher. Her speedy withdrawal was laid to Charlotte's concern for her health; and as her poems before that date indicate that she could not be happy away from the moors and could not endure any sort of constraint, she may well have been literally sick for the freedom of home. Upon her return there, Anne went to Roe Head in her place, and Emily was left in Haworth with Branwell, who must have been sad enough company. He had just failed neurotically in his intention to study at the Royal Academy and was spending his time as a drunken idler at the village tavern. It is because so few poems and so few letters to or from her absent sisters remain from this interim that the hypothesis of a questionable relationship between brother and sister has grown up, and of course, Emily's rapid decline and death within a year of Branwell's in 1847 lends some support to the theory. But her poetry bearing the date of 1836 is emotionally thin and immature, and critics are agreed that the major change in it dates from the following year.

The single external event in her life at that time was a teaching engagement at Law Hill, of which all that is known certainly is that it continued for at least six months during 1837. Some scholars hold that it began in the fall of 1836, others that it continued well into 1838. There are traces of evidence to support both contentions, but whether it lasted six months or sixteen, it was, beyond question, Emily's longest absence from Haworth till then. Following Hatfield's dating of her poems, one can trace first the impact of new scenes (February 1837), nostalgia for the moors, and a wish to "be healthful still and turn away from passion's call." Then in sequence (how rapid one cannot say) come abysmal self-distrust; nightmare; melancholy; the agony of separation (November, 1837); more desperate melancholy (through 1838); and finally in late October and early November, 1838, two poems of passionate and bitter reproach to a faithless feminine love: "I knew not 'twas so dire a crime To say the word adieu," and "Light up thy halls—and think not of me!" Whatever experience produced these intense, immediate and certainly autobiographical outcries must have occurred during a period when, as a letter to Charlotte testifies, her boarding-school responsibilities absorbed her from six in the morning until sometimes eleven at night, and where supervision would have made association with a man impossible. In view of her earlier quick withdrawal from Roe Head, the fact that she endured such conditions for even six months is remarkable.

It is reasonable to imagine that at Law Hill she met and fell ardently in love with another woman—whether teaching colleague or senior student—and that the emotion was sufficiently mutual for Emily to envision some such lasting companionship as Charlotte dreamed of with Ellen Nussey. (Indeed, Moore's emphasis upon the beauty, intellectual and social capacities, and personal charm of Miss Elizabeth Patchett, the school's forty-four-year-old headmistress, suggests the possibility of Emily's superior having lit the flame reflected in her verse.) The pattern of such dormitory dramas, whoever the actors, is fairly constant. One young woman is aglow with excitement and an often illusory sense of complete rapport; the other is flattered and genuinely responsive until the emotional voltage runs too high. Then withdrawal follows on the one side, hurt and misunderstanding on the other. Whether Emily encountered Victorian admonition from a colleague, or the news from some charming young creature (as she toyed with her new ring) that *she* was about to enter love's *real* province, it is certain that Emily felt herself "betrayed." Actually, this proud woman of twenty or twenty-one, in the grip of authentic passion, must have been brought to see her feeling through other eyes as something between a juvenile *Schwarm* and that horror the very name of which Saint Paul forbade to be uttered. It is probable that she became at once either physically or nervously ill and perhaps left the school, (inexplicable in the middle of a term), hiding jealously the reason for her going, and blotting it from all records. (Interestingly enough Moore tells us that Miss Patchett married a local vicar "shortly after Emily's departure from Law Hill." Was it her halls that were lit, and for her wedding, in November 1838?) [8]

A blow like this—the realization that the only love of which she seemed capable was regarded by the world as either frivolous or sinful—would explain her subsequent melancholy and her stubborn refusal to enter again into any personal relationship. It also colored her memories of Law Hill so that a decade later she used details of the buildings and environs to describe Wuthering Heights farm, the setting in which, as the dark-spirited Heathcliff, she finally wrought vicarious revenge upon a vain and inconstant Cathy.

George Eliot. The eye in search of variance inevitably turns next to the George in England who had not yet assumed her masculine cognomen—Mary Ann Evans. This novelist was undoubtedly masculine in many ways, both physically and psychologically; which of these traits were inborn and which bred of the childhood adoration of father and brother so vividly reflected in *Mill on the Floss,* it is impossible to say. But George Eliot's masculinity does not seem to have affected her emotional life. There are, to be sure, a handful of very close women friends cited in the Hansons' recent biography:[1] Sara Hennell, near her own age and, like her, rather masculine; Mary Sibree, the first young girl she tutored; and later Bessie Parkes and Barbara Leigh Taylor, young feminists a half dozen years or more her junior. All of these are mentioned as parties to friendships which were briefly more or less emotional on one side or both. But even so, two considerations exclude their subject from a list of variant women until more evidence is at hand. The concern felt by two of the girls' families about Mary Ann Evans's influence was caused not at all by her emotional temperament but by her religious unorthodoxy. Furthermore, nothing in George Eliot's work reflects any interest in emotional connections between women or even an awareness of them. Her life, as soon as she was freed from enslavement to her invalid father, was a succession of excitements involving men, men who captivated her emotions regardless of whether they were married or (like Herbert Spencer) incapable of passion. She was that case so disheartening to the hereditary theorist—an extremely mannish woman not obsessed with women but with men.

Margaret Fuller. The life of an American contemporary of George Sand and Emily Brönte offers similar suggestions of variance, while her surviving work is almost equally empty of it. Margaret Fuller, New England transcendentalist, feminist, and journalist, is remembered for her *Woman in the Nineteenth Century,* which played a part in this country comparable to Wollstonecraft's *Vindication* in England; for her editing of the short-lived *Dial,* and for her work at home and abroad on the staff of Horace Greeley's *New York Tribune.* She is also remembered for her friendships with Emerson and Carlyle and her efforts to familiarize her countrymen with Italian and German literature, especially the work of Goethe. She is thought to have been the model for Holmes' Lurida Vincent and for the Zenobia of Hawthorne's *Blythedale Romance.* Catherine Anthony, in one of the first "psychoanalytic" biographies of this century,[1] reveals the rigorous asceticism and intellectual forcing imposed upon her during childhood by that puritan idealist, Timothy Fuller, and argues for a father fixation as the key to her later emotional life.

It was not until the age of thirty-four that she experienced her first romantic love for a man, the German Jew James Nathan, whom she met during her first year in New York. When he expressed passion for her, she was deeply disturbed, even shocked, and he soon returned to Europe, partly, it is thought, to escape from her stubbornly "platonic" hold upon him. Four years later in Italy she lived for a season with the Marchese d'Ossoli, whom she married secretly after discovering that she was pregnant, as Wollstonecraft had done in the case of Godwin. Versions of both these heterosexual experiences were permitted to survive by Emerson, William Ellery Channing, and James Freeman Clarke, who edited her *Memoirs*, but, says Mason Wade in a later biography, "These friends of Margaret, in their regard for her memory, inked out, scissored or pasted over a third of the never-to-be-duplicated mass of material they had before them."[2]

The first thirty-four of her fifty years were not, however, emotionally empty. At the age of thirteen she fell deeply in love with an Englishwoman visiting in Cambridge, the first member of a more cosmopolitan society than she had before encountered. When after a few months her adored departed she fell into melancholy, was unable to eat, and declined so much in health that her father packed her off to a boarding school to find companionship of her own age. She was far too precocious and self-absorbed to be popular with the girls, and her chief interest was in a sympathetic teacher with whom, as with her English idol, she afterwards corresponded for years. Family cares and financial stress after her father's death apparently filled her late teens and early twenties to the exclusion of personal contacts, and no emotional record survives from the year when she taught in Bronson Alcott's school. At the end of a succeeding period as headmistress of a school in Providence, however, she parted from the boys without emotion, but the girls, whose adoration had been precious to her, all wept at losing her and she wept with them. (Most of these incidents were not expurgated from her *Memoirs*.)

Her next five years, between the ages of twenty-nine and thirty-four, were devoted to her famous "Conversations," hybrids between a French salon and a modern seminar. For a course of these two-hour sessions held in the homes of the participants her fee was twenty dollars, in a day when tickets to as many lyceum lectures cost only two; still her group never numbered less than thirty. Her intellectual brilliance and the magnetism she exerted upon her exclusively feminine audiences have become legendary, and it is quite evident from the various accounts of them that a strong emotional rapport

with women contributed to her success. It is notable that the evening
course given one winter to a mixed group which included many
distinguished intellectual men was a comparative failure.

Considering her emotional inhibitions as shown in her affair
with Nathan, and, more particularly, in view of the rigorous prudery
of Boston at the time, it is unlikely that any of her numerous
feminine attachments reached the point of overt expression. But the
student of variance must forever regret the loss of those confessional
passages obliterated by the three moral vigilantes who edited them.

The only other episode of possible variant significance in her
life (aside from her translating a part of the work of Günderode)
was the effort she made to meet George Sand when she reached
Europe in 1846. The famous woman was for a month or so away
from Paris, and after her return she failed to answer Margaret's note
begging an interview. After a week of silence Margaret "took her
courage into her hands" and risked a call. A servant's error in reporting her name might even then have sent her away disappointed, but
she persisted, and finally reached Sand in person. Writing to a friend
about the encounter, she says:

> Our eyes met. I shall never forget her look at that moment.
> . . . Her face is very little like the portraits, but much finer;
> the upper part of the forehead and eyes are beautiful, the
> lower strong and masculine, expressive of a hardy temperament
> and strong passions, but not in the least coarse. . . . What
> fixed my attention was the expression of *goodness*, nobleness,
> and power that pervaded the whole. . . . As our eyes met
> she said, "C'est vous," and held out her hand. I took it and
> went into her little study. . . . I loved, shall always love her.[3]

Though pressed for time, Sand kept her for the greater part of the day
and talked freely to her. Afterwards Margaret decided that despite her
hostess's constant smoking, and the fact that she had undoubtedly
had "something of the bacchante in her life," she had never liked any
woman better than she liked George Sand.

Adah Isaacs Menken. The difference in emotional climate
between puritan Boston and exotic New Orleans could not be
better illustrated than by setting against Margaret Fuller's life that
of the actress, dancer, poet and adventuress who attained fame as
Adah Isaacs Menken. Encyclopedias are monotonously insistent that
she was born Dolores Adios Fuertes, daughter of a Spanish Jew.

Various other sources, among them the preface to an 1890 edition
of her poems,[1] claim that she was Adelaide McCord, daughter of a
storekeeper in a small Louisiana town. The truth is perhaps obscured
forever by what another authority describes as "her own habit of
romancing about herself and her origin."[2] Thus some of the following picturesque details offered by Clement Wood should doubtless be
liberally salted, but many are demonstrably true.

Although, like Margaret Fuller, Menken was precocious enough
to be translating the *Iliad* at twelve, she was also dancing in the
New Orleans Opera House, and by the age of fourteen "she was
a woman, whose sensitive beauty was the pride of the town." By
the time she was twenty she had the following adventures to her
credit: marriage at sixteen to "a nobody whose very name has
vanished," who abused and abandoned her; a season of dancing
which made her the darling of the Tacón Theatre in Havana; a
tour with an amateur theatrical company in Texas, followed by her
founding a newspaper in the town of Liberty; being captured by
Indians, and rescued by white rangers. A year after the first publication of Walt Whitman's *Leaves of Grass* she brought out a volume,
Memoirs (or *Memories* [?] now lost) which is said to have "received
the placid fervor it deserved."[3]

A few months before she was twenty-one she married a musician
in Galveston, Alexander Isaacs Menken, adopted his faith and his
name, and retained both to the end of her short but crowded career,
though this included several later marriages. She subsequently returned to the stage and toured the south, part of the time in Edwin
Booth's company. In Cincinnati she paused long enough to study
sculpture, and became the leading contributor to the *Cincinnati
Israelite*. Her article on Baron Rothschild's admission to parliament
won her his epithet of "inspired Deborah of her adopted race."
Moving north to Dayton, she took up military drill and was elected
captain in the Life Guards. Here she met a pugilist, John Heenan,
known as the Benicia Boy, whom she married a year later in New
York, but, like her first unlucky choice, he was brutal, and she
subsequently tried matrimony with the humorist known as Orpheus
C. Kerr, and again with "one John Barclay." Menken died, Kerr she
divorced, but in what manner she freed herself of her other mates
is uncertain.

Her success as an actress seems to have been moderate until in
New York in 1861 she accepted the part of Mazeppa in a dramatiza-
tion of Byron's melodramatic poem. This male part involved being
bound to the back of a fiery Arab steed, feet in his name, head

hanging from his crupper, and "she glittered in this role from
Albany to London, Paris and Vienna." In Europe she enjoyed social
and literary, as well as dramatic, success. "Nobility and royalty paid
court to her; the aristocracy of art thronged to her salon." She was
the intimate friend of Gautier, Dumas, Charles Reade, Swinburne,
and Dickens, and in 1868 dedicated to the last of these her second
volume of poems, *Infelicia*.[4] Within a few months of its publication
she fell ill and died at the age of thirty-three.

　　Menken's place in the present study is due to James Gibbons
Huneker's comment in *Steeplejack:*

> The grave of Ida [sic] Isaacs Menken, poet, actress . . .
> greatest of Mazeppas, is there [Père La Chaise cemetery in
> Paris]. . . . Her letters to Hattie Tyng Griswold, published after
> the death of the notorious and unhappy woman, revealed
> another side of her temperament. Extracts were printed in
> the newspapers. She was a Mazeppa doubled by a Sappho. Her
> slender volume of verse entitled "Infelice" was credited to
> Swinburne, but that is nonsense. The poet of Anactoria, while
> he sympathized with Lesbian ladies, never wrote bad poetry.
> . . . A strikingly handsome woman according to the report
> of her day, her figure being the "envy of sculptors." . . . A
> tormented, morbid soul, a virile soul in a feminine body. . . .[5]

　　Upon examination, the volume *Infelicia* reveals no more obvious
lesbianism than do the poems of Brontë or Labé. Its impersonal
poems, pleas for the Jews or for industrially exploited women, explain
the interest of Dickens and Reade, champions of social reform.
The tragic desperation in most of the love lyrics suggests, along with
her twice marrying sadistic men and her success as the victimized
Mazeppa, a strain of masochism which may account for her appeal
for Swinburne (who was not, craving Huneker's pardon, too sympathetic to lesbian ladies, but who was obsessed by pain). Three
poems, however, are obviously addressed to women. "Dying" and
"Answer Me" allude to soft and tender hands, warm bosoms. "A
Memory; To a Dead Woman" says:

> Too late we met. The burning brain,
> The aching heart alone can tell
> How filled our souls with death and pain
> When came the last sad word, Farewell![6]

In "The Release," a subjective autobiographical fragment, she says:

> Wherefore was that poor soul of all the host so wounded?
> It struggled bravely . . .
> Can it be this captive soul was a changeling, and battled . . .
>   in a body not its own?[7]

These poems to, or about, women come nearest to serenity and peace of any in the volume. The rest reproach men for their cruelty to the women who bear their children, or, like "Resurgam," they represent the author as dead though still beautiful, crowned with flowers, and fêted—her spirit murdered by the man she loved.[8]

As to the Hattie Tyng Griswold mentioned by Huneker, she is listed in Frances Willard's *Woman of the Century*[9] as a successful Wisconsin journalist and a friend of Violet Paget, the British art critic and philosopher, who wrote under the name Vernon Lee. No record seems to exist of her connection with Menken outside the newspaper articles mentioned by Huneker, which have not been consulted here. As in the case of Sand and Wollstonecraft, interest in Menken's spectacular career has diverted attention from possible variant experience, but it appears to be precisely such stormy and passionate spirits who turn to women for the happiness they are unable to find with any number of men. It is interesting that Clement Wood should say, in contradiction to Huneker, that she deserved as much poetic acclaim as Whitman, but "was a woman, with a softer voice."[10] The volume alluded to, *Memoirs,* has not been seen by the present writer, but honest critical judgment compels some qualification of Wood's praise in view of the known *Infelicia,* though there are many pages in the latter which are not "bad" poetry.

"Michael Field." Another "poet" in the present group is Michael Field, pseudonym of two late-Victorian Englishwomen, Katherine Bradley and Edith Cooper. They were aunt and niece, but actually they were much closer than this relationship indicates, for when Edith's mother was left an invalid after the birth of a second child, Katherine and her mother moved in to care for the family, and Katherine assumed complete responsibility for the three-year-old Edith. Katherine was then seventeen and had studied at Newnham and in Paris, where she had been in love with the older brother of a French friend. This man died, and the loss is reflected faintly in her first published poetry a decade later. There is no indication of any other heterosexual interest on either woman's part throughout their lives.

By the time Edith had reached late adolescence and Katherine was approaching thirty, their relation had become one of adult equality, and they were active together in university life in Bristol, though apparently more in debating, woman's suffrage, and anti-vivesection societies than in formal university courses. In 1881, when one was thirty-three and the other nineteen, they published jointly a first book of verse, "by Arrand and Isla Leigh," which received little critical comment. It was two years later that they hit upon the pseudonym of Michael Field, and when *Callirhoë and Fair Rosamund* appeared in 1883 it was hailed as the work of a new and promising talent. They published, in all, eleven volumes of verse and nineteen or twenty poetic dramas, mostly on classical or historical themes; but, as Sturge Moore says in the introduction to their joint memoirs, *Works and Days:*

> After the first flush of acclamation their work was treated with ever-increasing coldness by the literary world, and there is no doubt that the discovery that Michael Field was no avatar . . . but two women, was partly responsible."[1]

The handful of volumes which have been available for inspection seem far from works of genius; nevertheless, the poems have as much freshness and lyric charm as those of many other minor writers who are repeatedly included in anthologies. The plays, though they exhibit careful historical scholarship, are weighted with moral or feministic message and seem artificial and heavy. The one that reached the stage in their own day was an immediate failure.

There is evidence in the luxurious format of their privately printed volumes, and in the description of the house in Richmond where they lived after Mr. Cooper's death, that they were blessed with ample means, and beyond doubt their thirty-five years of adult life together were happier than the lives of most Victorian spinsters. They cultivated the acquaintance of all the surviving nineteenth-century poets, and derived much excitement from moderate friendships with the aging Browning and Meredith. But the Victorian era as a whole was disinclined to honor two "Platonists" as the previous century had done, and their closest friends were a pair of Royal Academy artists, Charles Ricketts and Charles Shannon, who lived together near them in a relationship evidently comparable to their own. That they did not escape disapprobation is indicated indirectly in several of the entries in *Works and Days*. When they first recognized Ricketts and Shannon at an art exhibition they hesitated long before speaking, uncertain how such a gesture might be received, even though Ricketts had designed the cover for one of their recent volumes. After attending another "private view" one Sunday afternoon in 1889, Katherine made much in their journal of being greeted by Fairfax Murray. "We recognized that he was proud to manifest to the world that we were his friends."[2] And in connection with one of their volumes of verse, *Long Ago* (1889), based on fragments from Sappho, Katherine told Browning that "we meant to do no more harm than George Herbert, when he took a text from Holy Writ and wrote a hymn thereon." The harm they were accused of having done is not mentioned.

The relation between the two women is more difficult to analyze than any so far encountered. Some time before the publication of their first volume of poems they were moved to a step best described in a later poem of Katherine's:

> It was deep April, and the morn
>   Shakespeare was born.
> My love and I took hands and swore
>   Against the world, to be
> Poets and lovers evermore.
> To laugh and dream on Lethe's shore,
> To sing to Charon in his boat,
> Heartening the timid souls afloat;
> Of judgment never to take heed,
> But to those fast-locked souls to speed
> Who never from Apollo fled,
> Who spent no hours with the dead;
>   Continually
> With them to dwell,
> Indifferent to heaven and hell.[3]

This, along with certain other poems (notably the "Third Book of Songs" in *Underneath the Bough*), leaves no possible doubt about the intensity or the variance of their mutual emotion. Not even Colette, however, could assign a masculine or a feminine role to one or the other. Sir William Rothenstein, in his preface to *Works and Days*, describes "Michael" (Katherine) as "stout, emphatic, splendid and adventurous in talk;" "Field" (Edith) as "wan and wistful, gentler in manner, but equally eminent in the quick give and take of ideas."⁴ A good photograph of the two women shows Edith's features to be of a decidedly boyish cast and her hair short. In the memoirs the two use a wealth of nicknames, masculine, feminine or neuter, and either may refer to the other by the male pronoun. It seems as though they tried to think of themselves as a single bisexual personality, and in one place Katherine says of the Brownings: "These two poets, man and wife, wrote alone; each wrote, but did not bless and quicken one another at their work; *we are closer married* [italics hers]."⁵

They exhibit consciousness of the physical possibilities between women more frankly than any other writers except for the portrayal of fictional characters. This is particularly striking in Edith's account of an attack of scarlet fever she suffered while they were travelling in Germany. Katherine fought an entire hospital staff in order to occupy a room with her, and Edith writes later: "I have my love close to me. . . . Looking across at Sim's little bed I realize she is a goddess, hidden in her hair—Venus. Yet I cannot reach her. . . . I grow wilder for pleasure and madder against the ugly Mädchen"⁶ (the nurse who kept her in bed). Yet when another nurse, middle-aged, becomes infatuated and annoys her with constant caresses, she says:

> My experiences with Nurse are painful—she is under the possession of terrible fleshly love she does not conceive as such, and as such I will not receive it. Oh, why will Anteros make one cynical by always peering over the beauty of every love—why must his fatality haunt us?⁷

Much later in their lives, Edith, whose health was never robust, failed steadily, learned she had cancer, and turned to the Church of Rome. Katherine followed her into that church more slowly and, one infers, partly to reassure the younger convert that they would never be separated here or hereafter, just as she concealed the fact that she also was suffering from the same dread ailment as long as Edith lived, in order to spare her added vicarious pain. This religious move resulted from the influence of a brilliant Jesuit, who had made their acquaintance through enthusiasm for the mystic exaltation of their verse. There is no hint of struggle, change of habit or attitude, or anything resembling "repentance" in either woman, and this fact, along with the "Anteros" allusion above, suggests that the two had achieved some sort of limitation upon expressing their love which satisfied their stringent Victorian consciences.

Probably the complete manuscript of *Works and Days* included other psychological and philosophical discussion of such relationships, and perhaps also more details of the poets themselves, for Sturge Moore mentions having reduced the text considerably in the interests of good taste, and of omitting matter likely to be of little interest to later students of literature. Unfortunately, biographers and literary historians often prune material of foremost interest to students of emotional psychology.

Emily Dickinson. If Emily Brontë was for a century a British enigma, Emily Dickinson has for almost as long been New England's "little sphinx." Many who do not know her poems will have heard of her self-cloistration at thirty in the family house in Amherst, her wearing only white thereafter, and her habit of communicating even with old friends through the open door of a room in which she remained stubbornly invisible. Favoring the growth of such legends are a life as empty of outward event as the earlier Emily's, poems with a higher emotional charge and no fictional disguises, and a history of publication mysteriously complicated by family feud. Some critics have observed that in nineteenth century New England recluses and eccentrics were not uncommon, particularly among old maids and old bachelors who sometimes worked at becoming "characters." Some have elucidated in detail the family quarrel between surviving sister and sister-in-law which blocked publication. But none have dared to pretend that Emily's life was absolutely normal.

A tragic love affair has been the natural hypothesis, and search for clues has produced an embarrassment of possible candidates. All Emily's letters resemble her poems enough in economy and intensity so that despite her own elision and the subsequent editing many still approach love letters in effect. On their internal and some external evidence, she seems to have felt real warmth for a number of men with whom she enjoyed intellectual communion, from her near-contemporary George Gould in the late 1840s to Judge Otis Lord, her father's friend, eighteen years her senior, in her later life. To each of a half-dozen potential candidates, one biographer or another has assigned responsibility for the heartbreak in her poetry and her willful seclusion. But in every case, objective support is meager, and the necessary assumptions have reflected the theorist's predilections quite as much as his subject's.

As the quantity of poetry and correspondence in print has increased, however, the different editors' versions of some duplicate material have invited comparison, and from this and much peripheral research Rebecca Patterson has suggested in *The Riddle of Emily Dickinson* (1951) a pattern of departure from the norm which brings its subject within the range of the present study. Mrs. Patterson presents the integrated results of three separate investigations. First, she has studied Emily's life story exhaustively: the puritan background in Amherst; emotional tensions in the family circle (Emily's father, whom she both loved and inwardly defied, forbade at least one marriage and tried to prevent her writing); Emily's feelings, convincingly diagnosed as ambivalent, toward the men who captured her interest; and her sometimes more absorbing attachments to certain women. Second, Mrs. Patterson has compiled the objective and emotional biography of Kate Scott Anthon of Cooperstown, New York. This tall, striking, and passionate woman she shows to have been the product of a relatively cosmopolitan milieu, to have been emotionally attracted to women from adolescence in boarding school to ripe old age on the continent (despite a couple of satisfying if short-lived marriages), and to have met and violently loved Emily Dickinson when both young women were about twenty-nine. Third, she has collated all available versions of Emily's poems and letters (in some of which the sex and number of pronouns were altered or lines omitted by the poet herself or censoring editors), and has re-established chronology which was either deliberately falsified or wishfully confused by the editors to support the legend of a male lover. However unpopular Mrs. Patterson's hypothesis of a variant passion for Kate Anthon may be, it partly explains the erratic behavior of both the poet herself and her surviving relatives as motivated by fear of scandal. (Sue Gilbert Dickinson in particular, whom Emily's sister Lavinia branded a procrastinator and obstructionist in the matter of publication, had her reasons.)

From minutely assembled external evidence as well as careful interpretation of poems and letters, Mrs. Patterson reconstructs the following emotional history. During late adolescence Emily was passionately attached to Sue Gilbert, afterward her sister-in-law, a girl who had similarly attracted Kate Scott during their boarding school days. But Sue herself was cold in both relationships, and left Emily wholly unaware of the true nature of her emotion. A decade later, Kate Scott Anthon appeared, the widow of a loved first husband who had died after only two years of married life. Kate was beautiful, socially and emotionally mature, hungry for love, and much taken with Emily at sight. The two women's association was not protracted, probably amounting in all to less than two months; however, it was highly concentrated during Kate's semi-annual visits over a period of two years to Sue Gilbert Dickinson who lived next door to Emily.

The contact begun in March 1859 flowered then and during August of that year into an intense mutual absorption. Emily even showed Kate the poetry of which her own family still knew nothing. This flowering included some demonstrativeness, apparently Emily's first congenial experience of caresses, and therefore an electrifying revelation. In March 1860, during Kate's third visit to Sue, Emily's sister Lavinia was absent from home, and the two young women spent a night together. This experience enlightened Emily as to at least the nature of passion (a lesson of which many Victorian spinsters died ignorant), but to Kate's desire for complete intimacy, Emily reacted with shock and withdrawal. Kate knew herself well enough to be aware that she could not continue a close association on Emily's puritanic terms, and she avoided visiting Sue again for more than a year, though for a time she continued to correspond with Emily. The latter was too inexperienced to understand quite what had happened, and for six months she continued to be—as she had been since first meeting Kate—happier and more out-going in her personal relationships and correspondence than ever before or after.

Then, at the beginning of 1861, Kate ceased to reply to Emily's letters, of which only three have been published and probably few more survived. Kate was not silent from indifference; Mrs. Patterson assembles sound evidence that she too suffered bitterly. But she was apparently convinced that their relation had reached an impasse, and by April 1861 Emily's pain and veiled reproach so troubled her that she wrote terminating their connection. This month marked the beginning of Emily's withdrawal from social contacts. She refused particularly to see anyone who might mention Kate's name, for fear of her own reaction if she heard it spoken. Meanwhile, Kate had turned for comfort to her friend, Gertrude Vanderbilt, wife of a New York judge and some six years her senior, on whom she evidently could depend for complete understanding. Mrs. Vanderbilt seems to have offered sane advice—which may even have preceded Kate's final letter to Emily—and some religious consolation. When in the fall of 1861 Kate felt constrained to visit Sue Dickinson, knowing that to sever the connection without reason would arouse awkward conjecture, she played safe by bringing Mrs. Vanderbilt with her. To the still uncomprehending Emily, this effective preclusion of private interviews was a bitter final blow.

All this, it must be admitted, is a fairly detailed reconstruction

of events for which proof positive can never be produced. But it
did not deserve the wholesale damnation which critics accorded Mrs.
Patterson's volume when it appeared. Other biographers had noted
the meticulous omission of any descriptive detail in Emily's love
poems which could give a clue to the beloved's identity or personality. The present writer, still little acquainted with Dickinson (to
her shame be it said) when *Bolts of Melody* appeared in 1945, was
assured by several lovers of Emily's poetry, on the internal evidence
in that volume, that the poet belonged in this study. Let us grant,
then, that Emily may in her early life have felt "idealistically amorous"
(as one critic phrases it) toward certain young men, notably Gould
and Newton, with whom her associations came to nothing. (Both died
quite young, which might partially account for Emily's concern
with death.) She also probably fell in love with the Reverend
Charles Wadsworth whom she met in Philadelphia in 1854. (This
has the vote of Mark VanDoren, specialist in historical research.) But
she saw Wadsworth no more than three times again, probably only
twice, and then only for a few hours. In her late twenties—a dangerous age for emotional spinsters—she met the first woman whose mind
matched her own. She was off guard precisely because her new friend
was a woman; but Kate Anthon had virtually a man's emotional
approach. An explosive result was almost inevitable. Mrs. Patterson's
demonstration of how closely a new out-going happiness in poems and
letters paralleled Emily's meeting with Kate Anthon, how exactly
the beginning of her period of "agony" coincided with Kate's withdrawal, is too apt to be dismissed as absurdly biased special pleading.

CHAPTER VI.

TWENTIETH CENTURY

Introduction

The early twentieth century has already been cited as relatively tolerant of homosexuality. To the extent that it prevailed, this tolerance was due to popular acceptance of hereditary theory. We have noted Karl Ulrichs' defense of male homosexuals in the 1860's on the ground that their proclivities were innate. Within the next three or four decades, scores of case studies, current and historical, were accumulated to support or to oppose this claim. On the one hand there were exclusively homosexual histories of persons whose physical traits approached those of the other sex. On the other were records of homosexuals cured by hypnosis in the clinics of Charcot and Magnan. The majority of cases fell between these two extremes. Many were bisexual. Many persons reporting obsessive homosexuality were somatically normal. Following the lead of the biological sciences, students of the problem attempted to classify homosexuals. The subjects were variously divided into "true" or born and "pseudo-" or elective; "masculine" and "feminine" in general appearance; active and passive in the sexual role; homosexual and bisexual. But the determining data were less objective than is desirable for close classification. And although each dichotomy was independently more or less sound, there was little correlation among the logically related groups from the several divisions.

The resulting confusion seems now to argue against, rather than for, the claim of somatic causation of variance. But at the time the recent or current publications of Darwin, Mendel and Galton provided rich soil for the cultivation of any hereditary theory; so the men best remembered today for their work on homosexuality are Krafft-Ebing, Moll and Hirschfeld in Germany, and in England Symonds, Ellis and Carpenter, all of them strongly inclined toward a hereditary explanation of the phenomenon. By 1900 most of these men's contributions to the subject were in print and widely disseminated, so that in scientific and intellectual circles there was much talk of an intermediate sex whose condition was referred to as *inversion*—Ellis's term, as noted earlier.

The effect on homosexuals was naturally pronounced. From being generally regarded as moral lepers they felt themselves restored to human dignity, as biological sports, perhaps, and in a distinct minority, but no more reprehensible than albinos or color-blind people. Many were encouraged to write, many other authors took a more liberal view of them, and the public began to accept the new outlook in literature. Tolerance was by no means general, however, even in the great metropolitan centers where for years a certain degree of it had obtained. In the medical profession negative opinion was strong, and, of course, conservatives in all fields battled against the new "demoralizing" influence as long and bitterly as their predecessors had against Darwinian evolution.

Geographic infiltration of tolerance was markedly uneven. France, where interest if not sympathy was already widespread, was comparatively hospitable to the new attitude. Germany, despite its being the birthplace of the hereditary viewpoint, was somewhat less so. Sentiment there might have developed more favorably if, in 1906, military interests had not used the charge of homosexuality as a weapon against Philip von Eulenberg, whose pacific influence on the Kaiser they wished to eliminate.[1] Even so, the effects of the Eulenberg affair were not so sweeping as those of the Oscar Wilde case in England a decade earlier.

A retrospective glance at England shows that during the 1880's the publisher, Vizetelly, had managed to get into circulation a million copies of current French fiction before legal battles with the censor impoverished him, and, also, that a number of major critics had supported his efforts.[2] All were fighting for greater general liberality in matters of sex, but after the Wilde scandal in 1895, the public reacted strongly against homosexual activity. Havelock Ellis had to publish his volume on sexual inversion (1896) in Germany, and even there its appearance was not welcomed; consequently, his other *Studies in the Psychology of Sex* came out in America a decade before England would permit their publication.

America was the scene of no dramatic inhibiting episodes; however, our intellectual isolation retarded awareness of relaxing European attitudes towards inversion until Freud's influence had also been felt. While the wave of tolerance was spreading slowly from its continental origins, a counterforce was growing there. Sigmund Freud had begun his work with Breuer and Charcot before 1890 and was a practicing psychoanalyst by the turn of the century. The year 1905 saw the publication of his first important treatise; and in 1909 G. Stanley Hall, psychiatrist, and president of Clark University, invited Freud to lecture at a conference in celebration of that institution's twentieth anniversary.

Almost immediately the foundations of the hereditary theory were threatened. For Freud's thesis, as no one needs reminding in this generation, was that the human personality passes through several phases of sexual development, beginning in earliest infancy, and reaching maturity only with complete heterosexual experience. All individuals, he said, are potentially bisexual. In some, the homosexual component becomes conscious and active, and unless this phase gives way with the passing of adolescence to the heterosexual, the personality remains arrested and immature. Such an arrest constitutes neurosis, whether or not it becomes troublesome enough to demand psychiatric attention.

As is obvious, this view contradicts the hereditary theory at several important points. It holds that the homosexual is not born, but made by conditioning factors in his early life, chiefly family relations before he is five years of age. He can usually overcome his neurosis if he earnestly wishes, at least with the aid of psychiatry; therefore, he may be considered more or less responsible for his state if he persists in it. Furthermore, the bisexual is nearer to maturity than the homosexual. This conclusion is particularly opposed to the tenets of the Ellis-Hirschfeld school, which classed frigidity to the opposite sex as a mark of "true," that is, innate and blameless, homosexuals. The battle between the hereditary and the Freudian theories can be detected in a good deal of twentieth-century variant fiction.

The pendulum swung again toward physical causation with the development of endocrinology, which at first held the individual's glandular endowment responsible for his sexual inclinations. This science began as a branch of general physiology, and acquired major sexual importance only with Steinach's and Voronoff's famous experiments in rejuvenation through graft of sex glands or other reinforcement of sex hormones. In the variant field, endocrinologists were first concerned with glandular influence on secondary sex characteristics—breast development, hair distribution, vocal register, et cetera. Thus, during the 1920s and 1930s a number of physicians were attempting to cure homosexuals by dosing them with hormones which reinforced their biological sex and tended to decrease variant traits. These experiments enjoyed some publicity in medical literature but had only limited success. In the meantime, disciples of Freud were bringing in evidence that psychological disturbances alter endocrine balance. The final compromise is the current school of psychosomatic medicine.

To bring scientific opinion on homosexuality up to date, attention must be given to four further attacks upon the problem. Most closely in line with early search for physical causation are accumulations of exact somatic measurements by such different agents as the so-called Harvard group in their *Explorations in Personality—a clinical . . . study of fifty men of college age* (only a partial publication of their findings), and G. W. Henry in his *Sex Variants*. Neither of these studies has, so far as published material indicates, established significant correlations between homosexuality and any somatic factor or group of factors measured.

A statistical study limited to genetics was made in Germany during World War II by Theodor Lang.[3] On the ground that the offspring of a large group of parents should by the law of probability be equally divided between the two sexes, he made a statistical count of the siblings of several thousand homosexual men. He found a greater proportion of males among these than among siblings of a control group of heterosexuals. From this he argued that the homosexuals, though somatically male, possessed more than the average number of female genes, their brothers having in the aggregate more of the male determinants. Like all such studies this has been attacked on the grounds of its statistical soundness, but it has not been discredited. More conclusive in the same field is J. F. Kallman's study of twins, *Heredity in Health and Mental Disorder* (1953). Dr. Kallman compared, among other things, the incidence of homosexuality in identical and non-identical twins. Identical twins showed an enormously larger percent of similar sexual behavior than the latter, and his evidence is conclusive that "a genetically oriented 'imbalance' theory . . . can no longer be regarded as an implausible explanation for certain groups of . . . homosexuals."[4]

In the psychoanalytic field such dissenters from the so-called pan-sexualism of Freud as Jung, Adler, Horney and others have assembled evidence that sex is not always the prime cause of neurosis. Freud found it to be so, they say, because in his day social taboo made it the most common cause of insupportable tension. Now that sexual standards are less rigid (thanks in part to Freud's work), other factors such as the thwarting of the ego or long-continued insecurity appear of almost equal importance. To account for the homosexual, these later psychoanalysts suggest such causal factors as early social humiliation resulting in withdrawal from heterosexual competition, acute anxiety with regard to childbearing, or reluctance to assume responsibility for a family. Still regarding homosexuality as a neurosis, that is, an abnormal way of escaping an untenable situation, they leave unanswered the question as to what predisposes an individual to the choice of this particular solution of his difficulties.[5]

Most publicized of this century's contributions are undoubtedly the monumental statistical studies of sex behavior by the biologist A. C. Kinsey, which have shown homosexual experience to be more prevalent than hitherto claimed even by Ellis or Hirschfeld. Insofar as Kinsey attacks causes, he is with the Freudians in holding that all individuals are potentially bisexual, but there the agreement ceases. Kinsey's contention is that the human sex drive will find outlet according to its strength in a given individual, and that its satisfaction via the same sex is due to the sensitivity of erogenous zones to any adequate stimuli. This explains satisfactorily the behavior of bisexuals and of homosexuals whose opportunities are largely confined to their own sex, but to account for those who are frigid to the other sex Kinsey is obliged to admit the importance of subjective factors.

This brief survey indicates how much the social attitude toward variance has relaxed since the days of Belot and Peladan. Today the sternest counsellors of youth—outside perhaps a few religious groups—no longer talk of homosexuality in terms of depravity and corruption. And the psychiatrist's charge of arrested development weighs comparatively lightly upon such variants as are fairly well adjusted to their condition.

Factors other than the scientific have also affected this century's output of literature dealing with variant women. Until the beginning of World War I, the Woman's Movement figured sporadically in fiction, but not in variant novels after 1900. As a force in practical politics, however,—sometimes, as in England, a very noisy one—it had by the end of the war won the suffrage battle throughout much of the western world. Even where this end was not achieved, the movement widened women's educational and occupational opportunities, and thus tended to multiply the total number of feminine authors. Next, the war opened a number of men's jobs to women, increased their financial and personal independence, and encouraged tendencies toward masculine simplicity in dress. It also brought about that relaxation of sexual standards in general for which the 1920s have

become notorious. Taken together, these alterations in women's status
are held by some social historians to have increased female variance.
Certainly what may be called a first peak in variant literature was
reached between 1925 and 1935.

Thus, it is not surprising to discover that during the first third
of the present century, literary titles dealing with variant women
averaged more than one per year, that at least half were written by
women, and that a majority were more favorable to variance than
otherwise.

Poetry—French

Since the discussion of conjecturally variant women closed with
a consideration of lyric poetry, the same literary thread will be
traced first in the twentieth-century pattern. More than a dozen
poets have celebrated love between women, three-quarters of them
feminine and all but two sympathetic. The earliest were two expatriates who adopted Paris as their residence and wrote almost
exclusively in French.

The lesser, from a literary viewpoint, was Natalie Clifford
Barney, an American with New York and Bar Harbor background
who was able to live independently in Paris and to maintain her
own yacht. Born in 1877, she had by the late nineties made contact
with Pierre Louÿs, and she introduced to him her British-American
friend, Pauline Tarn. Both young women were enthusiastic about
Louÿs's *Songs of Bilitis,* and seeing in him 'the champion of the
young girls of the future,' they submitted manuscripts for his judgment. They found him more inclined to admire *"jeux latins et
voluptés grecques"* than the 'exaggerated preoccupations" of *femmes
damnées* whose sense of sin he suspected of giving an edge to their
passions. He pronounced Barney's novel, *Lettres à Une Connue,*
unsuited for publication because of its outmoded poetic diction, but
concerning Tarn's verses, which he praised, he afterward wrote
to Barney: 'You must write your story and hers. It is the indispensable
first chapter to your complete romance.'[6] The implication of some
previous emotional connection between the two is supported by
evidence in the poetry of both.

Barney was a Maupin type, with 'a fencer's grace noticeable in
an all-too-feminine Paris; moonlight-blonde hair, blue eyes with a
glint of steel, made to observe and not (like most women's) to be
gazed into; white gowns and a cape of ermine'—a composite descrip-

tion from later articles by her fellow authors "Aurel" and Lucie Delarue-Mardrus, quoted by Barney herself in her *Aventures de l'Esprit*.[7] In the garden of her luxurious Paris residence she built a Temple of Friendship and welcomed there many of the literary personalities of the day, evidently in conscious imitation of certain esoteric groups of the eighteenth century. Though many men were admitted, it was recognized that this was an Amazonian cult dedicated primarily to women. In her Chart of the Realm of Friendship she placed Remy de Gourmont first and Renée Vivien (Pauline Tarn) second.

Barney's literary output was comparatively meager, perhaps because she did not care to publish too tangible evidence of her emotional bent. The complete record of publication is as follows: *Quelques Sonnets et Portraits de Femmes* (1900), described by critics as sensuous poems of restrained passion; *The Woman who Lives with Me*—possibly a version in English of the novel Louÿs criticized—listed without date as a "roman abrégé, hors commerce"; *Cinq Petits Dialogues Grecs*, printed in the periodical *La Plume*, 1901; *The City of the Flowers*, "poème avec enlumières, à un seul exemplaire"; *Actes et Entr'actes*, 1910; *Poèmes—Autres Alliances*, 1920; *Pensées d'une Amazone*, and *Adventures de l'Esprit*, 1929, both in prose.

She is probably best remembered in French letters for having inspired two volumes by Remy de Gourmont, *Lettres à l'Amazone*, essays which first ran serially in the *Mercure de France* and were translated into English by Richard Aldington (1931), and *Lettres Intimes à l'Amazone*, 1927.[8] The first volume, comparatively impersonal, includes considerable analysis of Barney's temperament, which has 'the superiority of a profoundly pagan spirit, determined to obey Nature only in so far as it gives its consent.' This, Gourmont says, is 'so different from . . . Christian morality that . . . some courage is needed to express it so openly and so strongly.' He defines as "chaste" any action prompted by Love rather than by what Verlaine calls 'the obscene mechanism,' and observes that women, who feel passion only when they love, are spared men's bondage to 'that tyrant, sexual need.' He says that l'Amazone sets out to conquer without coquetry or any other passive or impulsive feminine motivation, and he judges her self-willed and egotistic.[9] Both he and the feminine commentators mentioned above, picture Barney as merciless in her intellectual judgments, wanting in tenderness, impatient of men, and scornful of all who abandon themselves to their emotions. Despite Gourmont's analytic clarity, in the *Lettres Intimes* we find the spontaneous record of what he terms "une amitié violente," springing from Barney's being not only "une amie mais un ami." His volume includes a good bit of his own verse, "des poésies sapphiques" about two women of ancient Greece written earlier but not previously published, and several poems to Barney herself, whom he describes as "un page et une femme . . . Natalie qui aimes tes soeurs et tes pareilles, Plus que toi même, et plus que tout, l'Amour . . . Natalie préférant bure et cuire à la soie, Natalie souriante au bord de la géhenne."[10]

His friendship with Barney began in 1910 and drifted along less and less satisfactorily for three years. By 1913 Gourmont betrays continual distress because she is so often absent, traveling with "une amie" and leaving no address, since most of the time, she and the friend are on the yacht he had helped her to procure. He owns to a resentment which surprises him, and implies that had he been able to divine her temperament at the outset he would not have permitted himself to become so involved. Yet we have here a close copy of the situation he himself had analyzed so clearly a dozen years before in *Un Songe de Femme.* There could be no stronger testimonial to the truth of Proust's later contention that each individual follows repeatedly a compulsive emotional pattern, and does not profit by experience. Nor could there be a better picture of the difficulty the two sexes experience in mutual comprehension, even when both parties are psychologically so close to the intersexual borderline and have so many interests in common.

Barney's *Aventures de l'Esprit* record primarily her association with the more or less notable literary figures of her day, and the judgments expressed are clear-headed and relatively merciless. *Actes et Entr'actes,* the only other volume available for examination, consists of four poetic dramas ranging from twenty-five to seventy pages each, and a dozen or so lyrics. One of the dramas, "Equivoque," was presented in her garden in 1906 with the film star, Marguérite Moréno, in the leading role of Sappho. It represents Sappho's death as resulting not from love of Phaon but from the loss of a beloved girl, Timas, who marries Phaon but subsequently, disgusted by her wedding night and overwhelmed by nostalgia for her great earlier love, follows Sappho to death in the sea.

Two of the lyrics, "Virelai Nouveau" and "Filles," represent the poet as following young *filles de joie* on their twilight strolls and taking a man's sensual pleasure in their consciously seductive beauty, but the enjoyment is detached, that of the *voyeur* only. "Couple," however, explicitly champions variance in its description of a loving pair:

> Se tenant par la taille—ainsi que deux bouleaux
> Reliés par leurs branches—
> Elles vont, ondulant leurs têtes et leurs hanches . . .
> Elles tachent de fuir l'été, son corps doré
> Versant, comme une essence . . .
> Sa mâle adolescence.

(Compare Peladan's Tammuz the sun god.)

> Il leur fait peur . . .
> Et la brune qui parle á sa blonde compagne . . .
> Est-elle la dryade au long corps maigrelet
> Qu'emprisonnant l'écorce
> Et qui garde d'instinct la crainte de la force,
> De la brutale force?
> Elles sont dans la nuit ainsi qu'au seuil d'un temple,
> D'un mystérieux temple . . .   .
> Si quelque homme, épiant ce couple insidieux,
> De son mépris le couvre . . .
> Qu'il sache que tout don de beauté plaît aux dieux;
> Que les lois ordinaires
> Ne peuvent s'appliquer á ces noces lunaires . . .
> Elles ont, d'un élan plus divin qu'animal
> Dans les vastes silences
> Joint avec des baisers leurs ressemblances,
> Toutes leur ressemblances.
> Et par delà la terre, et le bien, et le mal,
> Elles vont, diaphanes
> Et troublantes, et ceux qui les jugent profanes
> Sont eux-mêmes profanes.[11]

In three short "Paroles de Maîtresses" she depicts well the misery of a woman awaiting passively the pleasure of a male lover. In a dozen "Paroles d'Amants," she pictures and rejoices in a man's more active pursuit, even though painful, of the dream and illusion of love, "sublime, immense et limité."

> Je ne regrette rien, ni son bien ni son mal.

> Sa douleur m'est utile et son mal nécessaire . . .
> . . . Je n'ai peur
> Que de ne plus souffrir . . .[12]

"Te Deum" expresses the same satisfaction:

> Tes yeus cernés de noir
> Et ta face plus pâle
> Que n'est pâle le soir,
> Et ma bouche—pétale
> Entr'ouvert, frais piment
> Trop rouge—un peu brutale,
> Disent étrangement
> A la bonne Déesse
> Des féminins amants
> Et des males maîtresses
> Une long remerciement.[13]

A "Quatrain" sums up the debit side of her resolute assumption of masculinity:

> Je ressemble à ces rois qui vivent séparés
> De la vie, et malgré leurs plaisirs, misérables
> Et seuls, tendant en vain leurs bras lourds et parés
> Vers quelque pauvre joie humaine et désirable.[14]

There remain a group of poems addressed to Renée Vivien, published after the latter's death, which will be mentioned later.

Of greater literary importance is Renée Vivien, whose poetry has been pronounced most perfect in form of any French verse written in the first quarter of the century, and this quality is the more remarkable in that her native language was not French but English. As she died at thirty-two, its quantity also deserves mention, for her collected poems run to five hundred pages; besides she produced two volumes of "prose-poems" which a decade later would have been called free verse, a prose satire, and an autobiographical novel. In addition she and a friend collaborated on a number of similar volumes of verse and personal narrative under the pseudonym of Paule Riversdale. As originally published her work appeared in this order: *Etudes et Préludes*, 1901; *Cendres et Poussières*, 1902; *Evocations, Sappho,* and *La Vénus des Aveugles*, 1903; *Kitharèdes*,

1904; *A l'Heure des Mains Joints,* 1906; *Sillages* and *Flambeaux Eteintes,* 1908; and posthumously in 1910, *Dans un Coin de Violettes, Le Vent des Vaisseaux,* and *Haillons.* Prose-poems: *Brumes de Fjords,* 1902, and *Du Vert au Violet,* 1903; *La Dame à la Louve* (a collection of short stories), *Le Christ, Aphrodite et M. Pépin* (satire), and *Une Femme M'Apparut,* (novel), 1904.

Vivien was more openly lesbian than any woman so far encountered, but the few selections and biographical notes found in anthologies are careful to conceal this fact, and since further text and comment are not readily available in this country, she will be discussed here at some length. Almost the only sustained account of her personal life is included in a critical volume by her good friend André Germain; however, as it was published in 1917 when most of the persons concerned were still living, it omitted all personal names and many details of the poet's troubled history. Her publisher and friend, Edward Sansot, has attested that all her work was autobiographical in its inspiration, and so from internal evidence and scattered fact it is possible to supplement Germain's picture.

She was born (1877) Pauline Tarn, daughter of a Michigan heiress and an English gentleman of a Kentish family distinguished in law and the church. The girl was born in Hawaii and spent her first dozen years in travel, in French and German schools, and in Paris. From the fragmentary accounts one infers a background to equal any of Henry James's pictures of international marriage and difficult childhood. Between twelve and sixteen she was happy for a time with another English girl housed in the same Paris *hôtel,* whom she met through the intimacy of their respective governesses. Violet Shilleto was already a precocious mystic whose conern with "the meaning of life" made a lasting impression on her young companion. No shadow seems to have fallen on their passionate friendship before Pauline was removed to England at sixteen.

There for several years Pauline underwent conventional preparations for debut and marriage, including presentation in the Queen's drawing room. On this occasion she is described as a tall slim girl with delicate features, a luminous halo of fair hair, and eyes of "brun doré," which court gown lent her the air of a "princesse de légende."[51] But the demure exterior concealed rebellion. She was still nostalgic for Paris and Violet. The stuffy formality of social life in Chislehurst smothered her. Above all she was revolted by "coquetry" and the prospect of marriage. All this she poured out in letters to Violet, and the interception of certain of these produced an uproar of which Germain says that her later poem, "Sous la Rafale," is not an exaggerated picture:

> De la nuit chaotique un cri d'horreur s'exhale.
> Venez, nous errerons tous trois sous la rafale . . .
>
> L'éclair nous épouvante et la nuit nous désole . . .
> O vieux Lear, comme toi je suis errant et folle,
>
> Et ceux de ma famille et ceux de mes amis
> M'ont repoussée avec les outrages vomis.
>
> Comme toi, Dante, épris d'une douleur hautaine,
> Je suis une exilée au coeur gonflé de haine . . .[16]

According to Germain's implications and evidence in her poetry, her relations with Violet, like those of Lamartine's Regina with Clothilde, were essentially innocent. But if her letters matched her subsequent verses to Violet in loving eloquence, they would scarcely have sounded innocent to conventional Britons in whose ears the Wilde scandal still reverberated. It is certainly from this same experience that "Le Pilori" grew, for the two poems are unique among her collected verse:

> Pendant longtemps, je fus clouée au pilori,
> Et les femmes, voyant que je souffrais, ont ri.
>
> Puis, des hommes ont pris dans leurs mains une boue
> Qui vint éclabousser mes tempes et ma joue . . .
>
> J'ai senti la colère et l'horreur m'envahir.
> Silencieusement, j'appris à les haïr.
>
> Les insultes cinglaient comme fouets d'ortie,
> Lorsqu'ils m'ont détachée enfin, je suis partie.
>
> Je suis partie au gré des vents. Et depuis lors
> Mon visage est pareil à la face des morts.[17]

Whatever actually happened, peace seems to have ensued only with her attaining her majority and returning to Paris, where she lived alone save for a formal companion. She was obviously wealthy in her own right, for within a few years she acquired residences in Paris, Nice, and Mitylene, the first of which became legendary for its treasures of antique and oriental art, and to the end of her days she was an inveterate traveler.

At the outset of Pauline's Parisian life, drunk with her new freedom and the means to enjoy it, she found her old friend Violet too serious for her mood, and some sort of "puerile" misunderstanding occurred. Through Violet, however, she had met a 'fellow-exile and nascent poet' who was undoubtedly Natalie Clifford Barney. Her new friend introduced her to Sappho, as yet unknown to her. Until now, says Germain, she had been a *jeune fille,* 'doubly unawakened either as poet or as woman.' The new contact proved a double revelation, as well it might. Here was a beautiful sophisticate whose poetic gifts and interests, wordly resources, and emotional tastes matched her own; here, too, at last, was the great classical poet who glorified those tastes. In order to know Sappho better she set herself to learn Greek, and in her 'passionate fervor' mastered it "avec une facilité qui stupéfiait ses professeurs." She and Barney lived together, and it must have been during these years between 1898 and 1900 that she acquired the villa above Mitylene where intermittently "for months at a time she attempted to recapture the golden age of Sappho."[18] We know from Gourmont's account that both young women were writing poetry, and as soon as she considered publication (possibly even earlier) Pauline adopted the new name under which thereafter she lived as well as wrote—Renée Vivien, suggesting a radiant rebirth.

Two poems published in the same volume with those already quoted convey her exaltation at this time better than any account of them can do. One was "Ainsi Je Parlerai:"

> Si le Seigneur penchait son front sur mon trépas
> Je lui dirais: O Christ, je ne te connais pas.
>
> Seigneur, ta stricte loi ne fut jamais la mienne,
> Et je vécus ainsi qu'un simple païenne . . .
>
> Le monde était autour de moi, tel un jardin.
> Je buvais l'aube claire et le soir cristallin.
>
> Le soleil me ceignait de ses plus vives flammes,
> Et l'amour m'incline vers la beauté des femmes . . .

Pardonne-moi, qui fus une simple païenne!
Laisse-moi retourner vers la splendeur ancienne

Et, puisque enfin l'instant éternel est venu,
Rejoindre celles-là qui t'ont point connu.[19]

Far from being the mere defiant sacrilege this seemed to some
readers, it was the confession of a new faith to replace the one in
whose name England had damned her. In its entirety, much too long
to quote, the poem is also an apologia for her first love so slandered
by her "persecutors." She elaborated her creed in "Psappha Revit,"
among whose fourteen quatrains appear such lines as these:

Celles que nous aimons ont méprisé les hommes . . .
Et nous pouvons . . .
Etre tout à la fois des amants et des soeurs.
Le désir est en nous moins fort que la tendresse . . .
Et nos maîtresses ne sauraient nous décevoir,
Puisque c'est l'infini que nous aimons en elles . . .
Nos jours sans impudeur, sans crainte ni remords
Se déroulent, ainsi que de larges accords,
Et nous aimons, comme on aimait à Mitylène.[20]

Of this faith from then on she was the dedicated priestess.
    Inevitably her attainment of the Golden Age was imperfect.
Her poems are full of evidence that from the start her second love
was not too happy, as exemplified by the following:

Nocturne

J'adore la langueur de ta lèvre charnelle
Où persiste le pli des baisers d'autrefois.
    Ta démarche ensorcelle,
Et la perversité calme de ta prunelle
A pris au ciel du nord ses bleus traîtres et froids . . .
Sous ta robe, qui glisse en un frôlement d'aile
Je devine tons corps—les lys ardents des seins,
    L'or blême de l'aisselle,
Les flancs doux et fléuris, le jambes d'Immortelle,
Le velouté du ventre et la rondeur des reins . . .[21]

Sonnet

... Tes lèvres ont pleuré leurs rhythmiques douleurs
Dans un refrain mêlé de sanglots et de pauses.
Et la langueur des lits, la paix des portes closes,
Entourent nos désirs et nos âpres pâleurs ...
Tes yeux bleus aigus d'acier et de cristal
S'entr'ouvrent froidement, ternis comme un métal ..."

La Fleur du Sorbier

... Le couchant qui blêmit et rougit tour à tour,
La campagne morbide et l'heure de tristesse
Semblant nous reprocher d'avoir, o ma Maîtresse,
Accompli sans désir les gestes de l'amour ...
Ton regard sans lueurs paraît agonizer ...
Une phalène, errant dans le jardin, se pose
Sur la fleur du sorbier, d'un or pâlement rose
Comme la fleur secrète où j'ai mis mon baiser ..."

These carry no record of "désir moins fort que la tendresse," nor indeed of tenderness at all in the poet's cold blonde partner. But it is not difficult to understand the two girls' basic incompatibility. Barney's refusal of self-surrender, her contempt for abandon in others, were aspects of a resolute masculinity. Vivien, by nature feminine and romantic, needed to give herself wholly and to be cherished in return. An apparently love-starved childhood and an antipathy to everything male sharpened her hunger for a feminine response. Nothing less than the initial experience of passion, induced by beauty and blessed by Sappho, could have bound her to Barney at all.

In 1900 the spell that held her was broken by tragedy. Early in that year Violet Shilleto fell into acute depression, "finding her intellectual mysticism empty" and doubtless also wounded by the loss of the intimate friendship, and in the autumn she secretly joined the Catholic church. Whether spiritual conflict undermined her health or whether incipient tuberculosis precipitated the religious crisis, she fell ill and was ordered to winter in Cannes. Vivien promised to visit her there, but was too deeply entangled in her own affairs to sense the gravity of the other girl's condition. She seems instead to have made a trip to America. When at last she responded to an urgent summons, it was too late—her friend was dead before Vivien reached her.

Vivien's grief and remorse were shattering. The fact that Violet was given a "cold" Anglican funeral and interred beneath a church in the Avenue de l'Alma instead of under clean earth and sky increased the poet's agony, and "for a long time she spent hours each day at dusk" in the subterranean gloom beside Violet's grave. This state of affairs quite naturally moved Barney, who was nothing if not proud, to accuse her of being more in love with Love than with reality, and to depart for a protracted stay in the States. Thus Vivien was left doubly deserted, and from this period stem many poems in her early volumes. In *Cendres et Poussières* (1902) we find "Devant la Mort d'une Amie Véritablement Aimée":

> Ils me disent, tandis que je sanglote encore:
> "Dans l'ombre du sépulchre où sa grace pâlit
> Elle goute la paix passagère du lit,
> Les ténèbres au front, et dans les yeux l'aurore . . .
> Dans une aube d'avril qui vient avec lenteur
> Elle refleurira, violette mystique."
> Moi, j'écoute parmi les temples de la mort . . .
> J'écoute, mais le vent des espaces emporte
> L'audacieux espoir des infinis sereins.
> Je sais qu'elle n'est plus dans l'heure que j'étreins,
> L'heure unique et certaine, et moi, je la crois morte.

And in *Etudes et Préludes* (1901):

> J'attends, o Bien-Aimée! o vierge dont le front
> Illumine le soir de pompe et d'allegresse . . .
> Notre lit sera plein de fleurs qui frémiront . . .
> Et la paix des autels se remplira de flammes;
> Les larmes, les parfums et les épithalames,
> Les prières et l'encens monteront jusqu'à nous.
> Malgré le jour levé, nous dormirons encore
> Du sommeil léthargique où gisent les époux,
> Et notre longue nuit ne craindra plus l'aurore.

In *Evocations* (1903) she is proclaiming a "Victoire Funèbre:"

> Dans le mystique soir d'avril j'ai triomphé.
> J'ai crié d'une voix de victoire: Elle est morte . . .

> —Quel sourire de paix sur tes lèvres muettes,
>   O soeur des violettes!
> J'ai brulé de baisers des pieds blancs de la Mort
> Car elle t'épargna la souillure et l'empreinte,
> L'angoisse de désir, les affres de l'étreinte,
> Les ardeurs de vouloir, l'âpreté de l'effort.
> —L'amour s'est éloigné de tes lèvres muettes,
>   O soeur des violettes![24]

The contrast between these devoted elegies and the poems to her second love is striking, and one is aware of a revolt against passion *per se*. For the first time the poet voices a longing for death which recurred with increasing frequency in her later work.

Completely sobered by her double loss, Vivien seems to have spent some part of 1901 in Scotland with her family. On her return to Paris she leased the large residence which had housed her and Violet during their early association, and made it her permanent home. Here she must have worked on the three volumes which appeared in 1902 and on the translation of Sappho which was among those of 1903. This last and *Kitharèdes* (renderings into French of all fragments from the Greek Anthology written by or about women) were lauded by critics both as translations and as poetry, the only adverse comment being that they were so much wordier than the originals. What she apparently attempted, however, was to expand fragments into plausible wholes, as many other translators have done before and since (cf. especially Marion Mills Miller).

The year 1902, says Germain, was probably the calmest of her life. She was suffering from disillusion as to her own powers of emotional constancy, and believed that the serious loves of her life lay behind her. If in mid-twentieth century this sounds adolescent in a young woman of twenty-five, one must remember that in the English-speaking countries the emotional ideal popularly given lip service at the turn of the century was still "One Great Love in a Life." For a year she strove for emotional quiescence, but there are signs even in *Evocations* (1902) of encounter with a new personality:

Sonnet

> Ta royale jeunesse a la mélancolie
> Du Nord où le brouillard efface les couleurs.
> Tu mêles la discorde et le désir aux pleurs,
> Grave comme Hamlet, pâle comme Ophélie . . .
> Mon coeur déconcerté se trouble quand je vois

Ton front pensif de prince et tes yeux bleus de vierge,
Tantôt l'Un tantôt l'Autre, et les Deux à la fois.[25]

Twilight

Les clartés de la nuit, les ténèbres du jour
Ont la complexité de mon étrange amour . . .
L'ambigu de ton corps s'alambique et s'affine
Dans son ardeur stérile et sa grace androgyne . . .

In *La Vénus des Aveugles* (1903) "La Perverse Ophélie" and "Sonnet à une Enfant" are addressed to the same person, and they show Vivien struggling to spare both the other girl and herself the fevers of such an alliance as her second had been. This volume also reflects a more bitter struggle which would have remained an enigma except for Germain's discreet sketch of what occurred during 1903. He describes the new beloved as endowed with a cameo profile, a keen if 'exclusively practical' intelligence, and a temperament in every respect different from Vivien's. It is clear that he did not like the girl, and he attributes to her much of the suffering and catastrophe in Vivien's later life, although he grants that the poet produced the greater part of her published work under the stimulus of the new association. She was, in fact, the Hélène de Zuylen de Nievelt who collaborated in the "Paule Riversdale" volumes, and to her (in part) Vivien dedicated several original volumes and her collected poems of 1909. No biographical data are discoverable, but the Hamlet and Ophelia references above, and the fact that *Brumes de Fjords* (1902), the first volume dedicated to her, was announced as translated from the Norwegian, suggest that she was from Northern Europe. (Her name, of course, sounds Dutch.) A difference in the dedicatory initials between 1902 and 1909 suggests that the girl may have married in the interval.

In 1903, Vivien was apparently just entering with delicacy and caution upon this new emotional adventure when Barney reappeared on the scene. Like all women who know themselves weak, says Germain, 'Renée armed herself with a strong resolution' not to see her old love. But Barney was not one to be "congédiée" at another's pleasure. When Vivien, at the end of her endurance, left Paris and took refuge in her villa at Mitylene, wanting only peace, she was run to earth even there. (This may, of course, be a euphemistic version of the episode. It is not impossible that Vivien went to Greece by secret pre-arrangement with Barney.) In any case some weeks of renewed intimacy ensued of which *La Vénus des Aveugles* reflects the bitter and poisoned entrancement. To her tormentor Vivien writes, among much in the same key:

Sonnet

Tes cheveux irréels, aux reflets clairs et froids
Ont de pâles lueurs des matités blondes;
Tes regards ont l'azur des éthers et des ondes.
Pourtant je ne sais plus, au sein des nuits profondes
Te contempler avec l'extase d'autrefois . . .
Je vis—comme l'en voit une fleur qui se fâne—
Sur ta bouche, pareille aux aurores d'été,
Un sourire flétri de vieille courtisane.[24]

Cri

. . . Vers l'heure où follement dansent les lucioles,
L'heure où brilla à nos yeux le désir du moment,
Tu me redis en vain les flatteuses paroles—
Je te hais et je t'aime, abominablement.[25]

Full reaction came with return to Paris and to Violet's grave:

La Nuit Latente

La luxure unique et multiple
   Se mire à mon miroir . . .
Ma visage de clown me navre.
Je cherche ton lit de cadavre
Ainsi que le calme d'un hâvre,
   O mon beau Désespoir! . . .
Mon âme, que l'angoisse exalte,
Vient, en pleurant, faire une halte
Devant des parois de basalte
   Aux bleus de viaduc . . .
Et, lasse de la beauté fourbe,
De la joie où l'esprit s'embourbe,
Je me détourne et je me courbe
   Sur ton vitreux néant.[26]

Other poems in the same volume make it evident that at this time she longed for the courage to kill herself, and in reverie dwelt upon the death of both her current loves.

By 1904 she had apparently freed herself of the old entanglement
and yielded to the inevitable ripening of the new. *A L'Heure des
Mains Jointes,* published in 1906 but reflecting this emotional period,
opens with the idealistic title poem:

> J'ai puérilisé mon coeur dans l'innocence
> De notre amour, éveil de calice enchantée . . .
> Ma doucel je t'adore avec simplicité . . .
> Tes cheveux et ta voix et tes bras m'ont guérie.
> J'ai dépouillé la crainte et le furtif soupçon
> Et l'artificiel et la bizarrerie.
> J'ai abrité ainsi mon coeur de malade guérie
> Sous le toit amical de la bonne maison. . . .

This poem and many others in the volume have, indeed, a new
simplicity, occasionally sacrificing to it something of her earlier verbal
magic. They evoke the image of a soft-spoken, light-footed pale girl
with tawny hair who turns to her for comfort and peace as well as
reciprocating them. One sees, too, a garden above Nice, surrounded
by pines and full of pale iris, for Vivien carried symbolism into daily
life—violets for the first love, lotus and tiger lilies for the second, iris
for the third. The love celebrated here seems complete and happy,
combining passion with companionship, and it was during 1904 that
Vivien tried to link her friend's life to hers even in authorship with
the "Paule Riversdale" experiment. From this year come three volumes under Vivien's name and three or four of joint authorship,
justifying Germain's statement that this alliance was fruitful.

But the collaborative prose-poems, narratives, and verses were not
well received. Of "Riversdale's" *Echos et Reflets* the reviewer of
poetry for the *Mercure de France* said merely, 'Renée Vivien is no
longer alone in evoking the glorious and tragic shade of Sappho.' On
L'Etre Double, one pseudonymous narrative, Rachilde's total comment was:

> Que de vers! Et que d'histoires japonaises. Le roman, peu
> chose du reste, un amour de femmes, est complétement noyé
> par ce déluge de citations. Trop de vers! trop de fleurs! trop
> de lucioles, trop de poissons bleus![27]

Vivien's own autobiographical tale, *Une Femme M'Apparut,* fared
thus:

> . . . Le texte est du même ordre avec . . . le vieux style dit

décadent, mort hier, déjà horriblement pourri, et la pluie des androgynes, y compris la Saint-Jean-de Vinci. Tout cela sent l'héroïne de *La Passade* de Willy, qui se tenterait de se faire prendre au sérieux.[28]

The last comment is particularly interesting inasmuch as Willy (the novelist Henri Gauthier-Villars, of whom more later) had called the heroine of *La Passade* "Mona Dupont de Nyewelt," a name too like Hélène's to be a matter of chance, considering his notorious penchant for including real persons in his fiction. He described her as a *gamine* given to roaming the streets of Montmartre at night and tossing pebbles through fanlights for sheer deviltry—altogether, far from innocent.

It may have been the critical cold douche of 1904 that kept Vivien silent during 1905 and restricted her output during 1906 and 1907 to a single volume per year, but it was more probably unhappiness. The drift of her personal life is not difficult to discover from poems in *Sillages* and *Flambeaux Eteintes* of 1908. "Malédiction sur un Jardin" bids the flowers fade, since her love no longer cares to walk among them. "Vêtue" begs the beloved not to discard a gown, but

> Garde-moi, parfumée ainsi qu'une momie
> Ta robe des beaux jours passées, o mon amie!

"Amata" voices that ultimate plea of the desperate woman which tougher spirits always take for hypocrisy:

> Dis, que veux-tu de moi qui t'aime, o mon souci!
> Et comment retenir ton caprice de femme?
> . . . Ton vouloir est mon voeu, ton désir est ma loi,
> Et si quelque étrangère apparaît plus aimable
> A tes regards changeants, prends-la, réjouis-toi!
> Moi même dresserai le lit doux et la table . . .
> Je mets entre tes doigts insouciants mon sort,
> O toi, douceur finale, o toi, douleur suprème.

That this time the defection was not hers, that she had at last attained to her own ideal of self-effacing constancy, seems to have saved Vivien from bitterness. Only one later poem is tinged with it, "Terreur du Mensonge," in which her resentment is not for the defection itself but for the lie which sought to conceal it.

Was this lie perhaps responsible for the gender of "prends-*la*" above? For as was suggested earlier, the "ambiguë" Hélène may have married before the end of 1908. It is certain that, in that year, Vivien prepared the edition of her collected poems which she dedicated to her friend under the new initials. It is also known that she made an unprecedented visit to her family in England, and soon afterward attempted suicide with laudanum. One biographical note[29] mentions that during her last year she was suffering from "Basedow's disease" (exophthalmic goitre), and such an affliction might seriously depress a hellenic worshipper of physical beauty. But it seems hardly adequate to have made her seek death, without the added burden of emotional despair.

Her later poems record increasing misery and loneliness, restless travel, "loveless loves" and premonition of death. From the three posthumous volumes come such titles as "Solitude Nocturne," "Résurrection Mauvaise," "Déroute," "Vieillesse Commence," "Détronée," and "Cyprès de Purgatoire." Short quotations will suffice to convey their tone:

> L'amour dont je subis l'abominable loi
> M'attire vers ce que je crains le plus, vers toi![30]

or:

> Les êtres de la nuit et les êtres du jour
> Ont longtemps partagé mon âme, tour à tour . . .
> Les êtres de la nuit sont faibles et charmantes . . .
> On ne boit qu'un baiser décevant sur leur bouche . . .
> Et leur amour n'est qu'un mensonge de la nuit . . .[31]

or:

> Le monde inhospitable est pareil à l'auberge
> Où l'on vit mal, tout est mal, on dort mal.
> Et pendant que le cri des femmes se prolonge,
> Je cherche le Palais Impossible du Songe.[32]

The Dream here was not, of course, such as comes with sleep, but that illusion of Love which she had pursued all her life. The final volume, *Haillons,* is filled with cries of pain and horror, of foreseeing the end and wanting it to come swiftly.

The known facts of her last year are gleaned from Colette's *Ces Plaisirs* and from news notes following her death. She was living alone in her Paris residence, an "Arabian Nights dream" of luxury crowded with the trophies of her travels. Colette conveys vividly the macabre effect of rooms hung with gloomy colors and inadequately lighted by brown tapers; the exotic flowers and food and drink; and the unpredictable eccentricity of the hostess, dressed always in diaphanous black or violet, who might walk out in the middle of a dinner in response to mysterious summons from a nameless "Friend." This figure was so anonymous and so capriciously tyrannous that Colette surmises she may have been the figment of an imagination already clouded by intemperate habits. It is known that the unhappy poet was drinking to excess, an indulgence particularly dangerous in view of her thyroid imbalance.

A few weeks before her death she was to appear in a tableau as Lady Jane Grey on the executioner's scaffold, and wishing to enhance her effectiveness as the tragic heroine, Vivien put herself through a punishing regime of violent exercise, little food, and much alcohol. She made a brilliant appearance, but fainted on the stage and was carried home to bed. Soon afterwards, as the result of further drinking to escape black depression, she strangled while attempting to eat and was quickly stricken with pneumonia.[33]

It was at this point that, with the utmost secrecy, she joined the Church of Rome, as Violet Shilleto had done before her. Colette's matter-of-fact surmise is that a dour and disapproving elderly maid was responsible for summoning a priest while her mistress was delirious, and Natalie Clifford Barney in the longest of her memorial poems to the dead girl agrees with Colette in implying external pressure:

> Et pourtant ils ont pris ton âme splénétique
> Aux décevants espoirs du dogme catholique,
> Voulant ouvrir tes yeux avides de repos
> A leur éternité—mais tes yeux se clos . . .
> Tes esprits affaiblis, ils purent te changer,
> Mais l'oeuvre de ta vie est là pour te venger . . .[34]

But the consensus of popular opinion was that this was a deathbed repentance inspired by sheer panic.

It is possible, however, to trace in life and work hints which acquit the poet of mere faint-hearted apostasy from her devout paganism. The first is her friend Violet's similar step, marked upon her ineradicably by her own remorse. Then there are the many "violette" poems celebrating the beauty and innocence of that first love, which were written steadily, except during the brief happy period of her third affair. There is also the parallel theme of guilt when her ideal of love was violated, as during her second liaison and her last reckless extravagances. There are even one or two tenuous religious allusions in late poems—"Chapelle," "Chapelle de Marine," "Dura Lex Sed Lex," and there is *Le Christ, Aphrodite et M Pépin*, a bitter prose satire on an age of scientific materialism which was giving only lip service to its deity. But more significant is Germain's report of what was to him the most amazing aspect of her conversion—it was the concept of Mary the Virgin which drew her to the Roman Church. How little after all even her close friends comprehended the basic motivation of her life: a compulsive seeking for maternal tenderness.

To understand the odd finale to her story one must return to a phase of her life so far neglected—her many contacts with artistic and literary men of her day. The critics Charles, Droin, and Germain were her personal friends, Sansot, LeDantec and Brun her staunch allies. Her collector's interests had gained her the friendship of Ledrain, curator of oriental antiquities in the Louvre, and her passion for music—she was an accomplished interpreter of Chopin—had won that of Gauthier-Villars, music critic as well as novelist, and of Saloman Reinach. One must also return to the second portion of Barney's already partially quoted memorial poem:

> Ils ont caché ton corps sous une pierre
> Chrétienne, ton squelette émiette sa poussière
> Très respectablement dans un tombeau banal,
> Anonyme, et couvert du bloc familiale.
> Et craignant pour leur nom ce scandale: la Gloire,
> Ils offrent leur dernière insulte à ta mémoire . . .

"Ils" were her relatives, and it is true that she was buried at Passy beneath a slab bearing for identification only her father's name, John Tarn. Immediately upon her death the quick-witted and practical Reinach, foreseeing attempts on the part of church, family and even some friends to suppress evidence of her emotional history, took possession of letters and unpublished manuscripts and deposited them in the Bibliothèque Nationale, with the stipulation that they should not be made public until after the year 2000 A.D.[35] It will, therefore, rest with another generation to compile the definitive record of her work and her essentially tragic life.

Some years later in *Notes and Queries* Reinach wrote the following informal tribute in response to an inquiry:

> I could quote from those volumes at least two hundred verses which rank among the finest specimens of French poetry.

. . . I am aware that there are some objectionable elements in her books, and wish that they should not be dwelt upon; but her genius—for genius she had—is the more extraordinary as she wrote in a language not her own. I feel sure she will be famous some day, and think it desirable that we should try to know more about her before it gets too late.[36]

All the critics who grant her this superlative poetic quality agree that she has received nothing approaching her due recognition because of the lesbian element in her work. In view of the small number of persons in any generation who are tolerant of such love, it may be that she will never receive it.

There remains little to mention in the way of variant French poetry, though occasionally some isolated chance-encountered fragment—like a sonnet to Hermaphroditus by Marguérite Yourcenar—stimulates a fruitless search for more of an author's verse. The *Mercure de France* reported in 1902 Henry Rigal's *Sur le Mode Sapphique,* of which Pierre Quillard's review says that it was prefaced by a quotation from Pierre Louÿs: 'When a loving pair is composed of two women, then it is perfect.'[37] The slim volume was made up of a dozen brief episodes laid in a dimly distant Ionic island setting, and recounted in antiphonal stanzas the love between Chrysea and Mnais. It was apparently a close imitation of Louÿs's *Songs of Bilitis,* with Mnais in the more masculine role. It ends with a shepherd lad catching Chrysea's eye one evening and piquing her imagination by dreams of "a stronger and better love." Were it not for the title, says Quillard, one could well believe the amorous dialogue one between a girl and an *éphèbe*—an effeminate man.

The only other woman poet sufficiently variant to attract critical comment was Paule Reuss, noted by Clarissa Cooper in her *Women Poets of the Twentieth Century in France.* Reuss's volume *Le Génie de L'Amour* (1935) was dedicated to her fellow poet Anna de Noailles, and is said "to breathe a pure idealistic love like that of Dante for Beatrice." Cooper's only quotation is:

> Vous demandez d'aller vous voir!
> Mais serait-ce quitter ce soir
> Vos mains jointes dans la mienne?
> Sera-ce vous quitter au matin?
> J'ôterai ma robe blanche;
> Au clair de lune de la lampe,

> Sera-ce toi vers moi qui te penches?
> Je passerai dans les sentiers
> Déjà connus ou oubliés
> Et je dirai: Madame! alors
> Que j'avais dit mon trésor![38]

This suggests a proud and ironic restraint to equal Natalie Clifford Barney's.

Poetry—German

The first contemporary variant poetry in German was probably an item cited in Hirschfeld's *Jahrbuch* simply as: Plehn. *Lesbiacorum Liber.* 1896. As it is not listed in the German publishers' catalog during the 1890s, it must have appeared in a periodical or as a part of some longer volume. The only possible author is a Marianne Plehn who produced a long monograph on geology during the same decade. Her interest in a field cultivated chiefly by men supports the assumption that her literary outlook was also masculine, and her rather labored Latin adjective would imply that her "Book of Lesbians" celebrated women of similar temperament.

In 1898 considerable notoriety attended the publication of *Auf Kypros* by Marie Madeleine (Baroness von Puttkamer), an author included by a later literary historian among "exponents . . . of the right to unrestrained sexual freedom even if perverse," and described as "so brazenly pornographic [an adjective which the critic employed freely] that the less said the better."[39] The volume was later privately reissued in a de luxe edition with color plates by nine or ten established contemporary artists.[40] Though most of the poems in *Auf Kypros* are heterosexual, six or seven match Renée Vivien's in lesbian frankness, e.g. "Vergib" and "Greisenworte." "Sappho" too much resembles other imitations of that poet's most passionate ode or Louÿ's *Songs of Bilitis* to need special attention. Another, almost flippant in tone, is from a group entitled "Aus dem Tagebuch einer Demi-Vierge," and sketches with great economy what is evidently a tranvestist episode. The speaker has given her "Kätzerl" sweets, liqueurs, cigarets ("natürlich Kyriazi Frères!")—and kisses—and has kept up her "strenges incognito" so successfully that her Puss really believes her a Man-About-Town. Only the American "Götze" on the end-table (surely Billikin) grins wickedly to hear the impostor repeatedly promise the frustrated girl 'Everything!!—next time!'

The remaining three lesbian poems express tragic regret for initiating a younger girl. "Vagabunden" is a prophetic warning:

> Verlassen wirst du Haus und Herd
> um meiner dunklen Schein.
> Du wirst verachtet und entehrt
> und wie ein Bettler wirst du sein . . .
> Und um uns hier ist Hass und Hohn,
> und alle werden uns verdammen,
> und alle Pfaffen werden droh'n
> mit Strafen und mit Höllenflammen.
> Wir sind verflucht für alle Zeit!
> und wirst doch Haus und Herd verlassen
> um meiner Augen Müdigkeit.

"Crucifixa" pictures the innocence of a young girl before her initiation and her plight afterward:

> Ich sah an einem hohen Marterpfale
> an einem dunklen Kreuz dich festgebunden.
> Es glänzten meiner Küsse Sündenmale
> auf deinem weissen Leib wie Purpurwuden . . .
> Ich gab dir von dem Gift das in mir ist;
> ich gab dir meiner Leidenschaften Stärke,
> und nun, da du so ganz erlodert bist,
> graut meiner Seele vor dem eignen Werke.
> Ich möchte knie'n vor einem der Altäre
> die ich zerschlug in frevelhaftem Wagen—
> Madonna mit dem Augen der Hetäre,
> ich selber habe dich ans Kreuz geschlagen!

And a later untitled poem goes even farther, in wishing the beloved dead rather than as she has become:

> Ich wollte, es läge kühl und blass
> dein geschändeter Leib unterm Kirchhofsgrass,
> erlöst von Schmerzen und Sünd',
> und fleckenlos wärst du auf's Beue—
> ein Lilie im Morgenwind.

One cannot help wondering whether Vivien, who knew German well and doubtless read these poems at about the time she was writing her own impassioned elegies to Violet, may not have felt their influence.

During the 1890s the picturesque vagabond, Peter Hille, was roaming the country with his scribbled manuscripts in the pockets of his shabby jacket. He was so indifferent to publication that nothing was printed until after his death in 1904, when his friends assembled his *Collected Works*. Of these, the first volume is made up of poems, among them a long rhapsodic biography of Sappho,[41] representing her as devoted wholly to Beauty. She worships nature, women, and particularly youth as embodiments of beauty, and wants to remain young and free herself, leaving only her poems as offspring. But Hille hears premonitory echoes of "the thunder of Jove"—passion—which will presently overcome her. Therefore, his picture is that of an emotional adolescent; it evades her variant loves and stops short of her marriage, her childbearing, and of her hypothetical passion for Phaon. Among the prose "Aphorisms" in his second volume Hille includes a severe indictment of current lesbianism,[42] which he considers as depraved as any other illicit passion. He says that only women so dedicated to spiritual beauty as to forego all physical expression are entitled to call themselves disciples of Sappho. Thus he is a precursor of Rilke, who similarly idealized her emotional experience as nearer the "divine intent" even than happy heterosexual love. In short, both men are basically ascetic.

In the same year that Hille's work appeared in print a lesser lyrist, Ernst Stadler, then only twenty, published in *Der Magazin für Literatur* a poetic drama, "Freundinnen."[43] It presents the culmination of an ardent friendship between Sylvia and Bianca, one fifteen, the other eighteen, in their mutual awareness of passion under the spell of a full summer moon, but it does not have specific lesbian implications.

A second woman poet, more restrained than Madeleine, is Toni Schwabe, whose *Kom, Kühle Nacht* appeared in 1909. Its first group of "Lieder" celebrates the loss of a male lover remembered with bitterness, for his ruthless passion threatened the girl's life and destroyed her love. The poet sees ahead no feminine happiness, no home or children—a brief cradle song speaks of a child abandoned to others' care while the singer roams the world, a slave to desire—but only 'a mad riot of roses and dancing' and the brief ecstasy that comes with night and dies at dawn. (Dowson's *Cynara*, written in the nineties, "I have . . . gone with the wind, Flung roses, roses, riotously with the throng Dancing . . ." comes inevitably to mind.)

A later group of sonnets are like Louise Labé's in concealing the sex of the beloved, but are aggressive and masculine in mood. A "Lied der Bilitis an Mnasidika" borrows the most fervent of Louÿs's lesbian episodes, and some pages of "Translations from the Danish," said to be of Schwabe's own composition, begin with two "Songs to Lenore." The first poem in "Die Stadt mit Lichten Türmen" is a dream in which a young count bears the singer into a beech wood and tries futilely to possess her, never divining that only her 'smiling pity' prevents her from dealing him a death blow. Probably the most typical mood of the whole volume is represented in "Nie Traf Ich Einen," in which she says that

> 'no one has ever curbed me with the bridle of love. Where I was weaker I refused myself altogether. . . . I have caressed only those who craved my love and wanted my violence, and them I have contrived to satisfy and to make dependent upon me. Me—me alone no one can succor, for though I have known every kind of love, no one has ever truly possessed me, made me surrender.' "

This is exactly the mood of Rachilde's and Schreiner's heroines and of Barney's poems.

Only one variant poet has been traced in Germany subsequent to World War I, a woman who wrote under the pseudonym of Iris Ira. Her volume, *Lesbos* (1930), consists of free renderings of Sappho's and Anacreon's surviving fragments, and a similar rendering of the *Songs of Bilitis*, complete with introductory narrative. (Richard Dehmel had translated in the 1890s only two dozen of its prose-poems.) A translator's preface to the volume pleads the necessity of maintaining mood rather than literal accuracy, but while the verse displays skill and grace, its tone throughout is more charming than passionate. And passion, of course, was the very essence of Louÿs's own work.

Poetry—English

Poets in English offer nothing as explicitly lesbian as the work of Vivien or Madeleine, and they seldom equal Barney or Schwäbe in frankness of implication. Indeed, last century's "thick veil of ellipse and metaphor"[45] still shrouds most of our feminine variant lyrists, and even where it has thinned, critics in general have either failed or refused to penetrate it. Consequently some readers may incline to skepticism concerning already familiar material cited below, but in that case they are urged to re-examine it with open mind, not in anthologies but in the authors' original context, and not for overt lesbianism but for clearly variant significance.

In America, Amy Lowell was the first poet to venture at all openly upon variant ground. She was born three years earlier than Vivien and Barney, the grand-daughter of James Russell Lowell and sister of a president of Harvard. In spite of this formidably respectable heritage, she did not escape to Paris but lived out her life in the family mansion in Brookline, though she did create within it her own particular haven. As surely as Renée Vivien felt herself born in the wrong era, Miss Lowell was born in the wrong flesh for a worshipper of female beauty. Even in her adolescent journals she bemoans the excessive weight which robbed her of appeal. Living too early for endocrinology to aid her, she tried rigid dieting, but succeeded only in doing permanent damage to her health. Something of a tomboy in her younger days, as she matured she adopted also the male psychological role. Clement Wood has documented for her as thoroughly as did Moore and Wilson for Emily Brontë this consistent assumption of masculinity, and the reader must be referred to the final chapter of his biography for detailed evidence. He lists there all Lowell's poems written from a male viewpoint, but for the present purpose only such require mention as are love lyrics addressed to women and spoken as if by the poet in her own person, not through the lips of a fictitious man.

Miss Lowell published nothing until 1912, when she was nearly thirty, but then in *A Dome of Many-Colored Glass* she included a number of variant verses. "Hora Stellatrix," for instance, contains the following lines:

'Tis night and spring, Sweetheart, and spring!
Starfire lights your heart's blossoming.
In the intimate dark there's never an ear . . .
So give; ripe fruit must shrivel and fall.
As you are mine, Sweetheart, give all!

The poem entitled "Dipsa" is virtually an epithalamium fifty lines in length, among them:

I wonder can it really be that you
And I are here alone, and that the night
Is full of hours, and all the world asleep,
And none to call to you to come away;

> For you have given all yourself to me,
> Making me gentle by your willingness.

There is also a sequence of nine sonnets in slightly less specific vein,⁴⁶ as plainly written to a woman, and as plainly spoken by the poet herself.

In *Sword Blades and Poppy Seeds* (1914) five of the last poems—"Blue Scarf," "White Green," "Aubade," "A Lady," and "In a Garden"—are written to women and are full of passionate imagery. In *Pictures of the Floating World* (1919) there is a sixty-page sequence, "Planes of Personality: Two Speak Together," more extensive and unmistakably variant than anything found elsewhere in Lowell. In the first poem, "Vernal Equinox," one finds: "Why are you not here to overpower me with your tense and urgent love?" The second is the often quoted "The Letter," empty of variant suggestion when lifted from its context, but ending:

> I am tired, Beloved, of chafing my heart against
> The want of you;
> Of squeezing it into little ink drops
> And posting it.
> And I scald alone here under the fire
> Of the great moon.

In her final volume, *What's O'Clock,* there are thirty pages beginning with "Twenty-four Hokku on a Modern Theme" and ending with "Onlooker," which are comparable with, though less passionate than, the sequence above.

Charlotte Mew, a woman who by date of birth (1870) should precede Miss Lowell, took her own life in 1928. Virginia Moore describes her as definitely variant.⁴⁷ Unhappily for literature she destroyed all traces of that fact even more carefully than did Emily Brontë or Emily Dickinson—so completely that we have of her work only two thin volumes, scarcely fifty poems in all. This meager remainder is of high enough quality to gain her inclusion in the *Dictionary of National Biography* and in virtually every anthology of twentieth-century poetry. It does not, however, include a single poem of which one can say "this is more variant than otherwise," though two or three (especially "The Farmer's Wife") are poignantly successful in expressing a man's emotional viewpoint. Several (e.g., "Madeleine in Church") show a deep religious conviction of sin, and doubtless this, as well as a passion for privacy, led her to the wholesale winnowing which critics, being unaware of her emotional bent, laid to rigorous self-criticism of an esthetic sort. Certainly if what she destroyed was at all comparable to what remains, there has been no more tragic literary, as well as personal, suicide since Chatterton.

Writing undoubtedly at the same time as Amy Lowell, for she was born in the same year, was Rose O'Neill. This woman is likely to be recalled today as the creator of the Kewpies, those coy cherubs which became a national fad early in the century, rather than as a serious artist and writer. Nevertheless, she was poet, novelist, and illustrator, the income from her juvenile and humorous works enabling her to pursue her deeper interests. Her claim to inclusion here rests on her single volume of serious verse, which was not published until 1922. Of it, Clement Wood says in his *Poets of America:*

> Her poetry will lose a certain Puritan following because of her cryptic frankness on the theme of love. She does not write this across the sky; neither does she, as is the convention, make this creep into a hole and draw the hole in after it. It is here, in a few poems; those who are not offended by this note in the masters since the Greeks, will not be offended by it here.[48]

Its title, taken from Shakespeare's most debated sonnet, is *The Master Mistress,* and the title poem hymns "a lovely monster . . . seeming two in one, With dreadful beauty doomed," but the subsequent references to variance are comparatively few and almost equally vague. Only a dozen poems among some two hundred are unmistakably variant—ten written "To Kallista" (that notation appearing as sub-title) ; "Lee: A Portrait," and "A Dream of Sappho." None but the last alludes vividly to any physical expression of love, but all are passionate, and many are specific in their praise of feminine beauty. The third poem in the volume reads:

> The sonnet begs me like a bridegroom,
>   "Come within."
> "This palace! Not for me, the desert-born!"
> I turn me, as from some too lordly sin,
> And like a singing Hagar, pause and pass—
> To lift for night's sweet thieves my restless horn
> In broken rhythms of the windy grass.
> I will not be the measure-pacing bride,
> But where the flutes come faintly,

> Sing outside.
> Like drifting sand my love doth drift and change—
> I strangely sing because my love is strange.

From the lot of these variant poems the reader retains half-realized images of two different loves, one a delicate and feminine personality, "ceaselessly weeping," the other:

> Mimic, dancer, cavalier,
> Silky hand the proud horse loves to fear;
> Sailor and adventurer . . .
> She who lingers, loves, and goes alone."⁹

Though verses spoken through the lips of a fictitious man are much less frequent than in Amy Lowell's work, two such poems occur. And there are many to which a Celtic titanism—fancies of removing mountains or seizing the moon and stars for toys—lends a definitely masculine tone. Such phrases as "in your princely fashion" and "fitting for you who feast upon fierce things" indicate, moreover, that the poet glories in the masculinity of one of her woman-loves.

Since this volume, whose quality Wood compares to that of the Elizabethan Thomas Campion, is far superior to even the best of O'Neill's prose, the same question arises as in the case of Louise Labé: how is it that from so articulate a writer, one who rhymed as she breathed, we have no greater quantity of surviving verse? The answer may well be the same, in view of her history.

She was born in Pennsylvania, but lived in no state long enough to call it her own. Her father was a bookseller of more literary than practical gifts, and there is little doubt that the swarming, hilarious and penniless family in her first novel⁵⁰ is based on her own background. From infancy the gifted child was destined for a stage career, but it was discovered early that she was too high-strung to endure public appearances. She then chose illustrating as her métier, and although self-taught, was already selling drawings in her early teens. From Omaha, where she attended a convent day school, she went alone at fifteen to New York to seek a better market for her work, and lived there in another convent until her marriage three years later. When her husband died, she was twenty-three and already an established illustrator and the financial mainstay of her family.

The humorous magazine *Puck* soon became her chief outlet. She joined its staff, and in 1902 married its editor, Harry Leon Wilson, later famous as author of *Ruggles of Red Gap* and *Merton of the*

Movies. In 1904 O'Neill published *The Loves of Edwy,* which like two of her three subsequent novels, is written in the first person and from a man's viewpoint. It is significant that the narrator of this story spends his life in fruitless love of the bewitching heroine, a term in jail for an altruistic forgery being the somewhat strained device which deters him from marrying. The girl, who has returned his love since adolescence, finally accepts another man, but a total psychological block prevents her consummating the marriage.

In 1905 Wilson met Booth Tarkington and the two at once became intimate, going to winter on Capri at Elihu Vedder's "beautiful, unbelievable villa," and there collaborating on *The Man From Home.* O'Neill studied art in Rome and Paris from 1905 to 1907, and twice exhibited in the Paris Salon. She and her husband apparently did not return to America until 1912, living in the interim in their own Villa Narcissus on Capri, which is mentioned as one of her several residences later. Upon her return to the States she was separated from Wilson, and thereafter lived in the Ozarks, in Connecticut, and in New York on Washington Square, where she became a close friend (as was Millay) of Elinor Wylie. In 1929 and 1930 she produced her last novels, *The Goblin Woman* and *Garda,* in the latter of which the heroine and a twin brother, Narcissus, are "the two parts of a single whole," she, the pagan and undisciplined body; he, the sensitive poetic soul. In her first two novels (the second was a whimsical mystery) the central feminine figure embodied soul and conscience, the man being the pagan spirit.

One gains in the end the picture of a dual personality, whose loves may well have changed like the drifting sand, and who made her most profound effort toward sincerity in *The Master Mistress.* It is known that Capri early in the century was the home of an international homosexual colony, and O'Neill could scarcely have lived there for several years without being drawn into the circle, at least superficially. But her early religious training would have made it difficult for her to freely embrace or champion its way of life. Embodied in her novels are many charming light love lyrics, written by male characters to their loves, and in all probability her private notebooks contained a good bit of more personal variant poetry which will never be made public.

In 1906, at the age of thirteen, "E. Vincent Millay," as she then signed herself, saw her first verses printed in the young writers' section of *St. Nicholas Magazine,* and four years later her farewell poem— seventeen was the age limit for the "League"— won the year's cash prize. Entitled "Friends,"[51] this poem presents in two neatly balanced stanzas the incompatible temperaments of an adolescent boy and girl. The girl's rejection of the senseless brutality of football was the poet's own, as the hatred of all cruelty in her later work attests. The girl's occupation—embroidery—was unlikely to have been that of young "Vincent," who enjoyed a boy's outdoor activities as well as a boy's name.

From her debut in *St. Nicholas* to the end of her life, virtually all of Millay's work appeared first in periodicals, so that for tracing its chronology Yost's bibliography of 1937 is invaluable. From this we know that "Interim," her first poem of variant significance, was written in 1912 along with the better known "Renascence." "Interim" is a threnody which at least two critics[52] have meticulously insisted is the product of pure imagination, since no one intimately known to the poet had died when she wrote it. It is possible, however, to suffer tragic loss through separation, especially when young, and every homely and poignant detail of "Interim" speaks of immediate experience. One passage near the middle needs particular attention:

> . . . That day you picked the first sweet pea—
> I know, you held it up for me to see
> And flushed because I looked not at the flower
> But at your face; and when behind my look
> You saw such unmistakable intent
> You laughed and brushed your flower against my lips
> (You were the fairest thing God ever made
> I think). And then your hands above my heart
> Drew down its stem into a fastening
> And while your head was bent I kissed your hair.
> I wonder if you knew . . .
>   . . . If only God
> Had let us love—and show the world the way!
> Strange cancellings must ink th'eternal books
> When love-crossed-out will bring the answer right![53]

The experience described here obviously involved another woman, and remained unconsummated. Like Hille and Rilke, the poet feels such love to be potentially the most perfect in the world; but, unlike them, she sees perfection only in completion, not in abstinence. Furthermore, the last two quoted lines have a kind of classroom echo, as of discipline by some harsher agent than the deity of "God's World."

When Millay submitted this poem along with "Renascence" for

inclusion in *The Lyric Year* she herself so much preferred "Interim" that she ventured to plead by mail for its inclusion.[54] As it is inferior to "Renascence" in both profundity and restraint, her preference argues that it had been written too recently for her to gain perspective upon it. She was twenty at the time, three years out of high school, and living in a small Maine town of rather limited intellectual and personal opportunities, according to her sister Kathleen's later picture of it in *Against the Wall*. It is also clear from all her poetry and her correspondence that hers was a highly emotional temperament. All this suggests that for a considerable time in her late teens Millay was completely absorbed in a passionate variant attachment, which then suffered some abrupt termination. Out of her grief grew "Interim" and a number of other laments which trickled into print throughout the next two or three years. Examination of her first published volume (*Renascence,* 1917) shows that save for "God's World" and "Afternoon on a Hill," the whole collection sounds a note of personal loss and melancholy.

During her years at Vassar (1913-1917, her twenty-first to twenty-fifth) she admitted an attachment to another fair delicate girl, at least to the extent of her own "Memorial to D.C. (Vassar College, 1918)," which appeared in the volume *Second April*. Death actually terminated this friendship, but the group of "little elegies" assembled under the title above are merely slight and graceful by comparison with "Interim" and its aftermaths. It is probable that certain later laments, such as "Song of a Second April" and "To One Who Might Have Borne a Message," were truer expressions of this later loss. A third woman is pictured in a sonnet in *The Harp Weaver:*

> Love is not blind. I see with single eye
> Your ugliness and other women's grace.
> I know the imperfections of your face—
> The eyes too wide apart, the brow too high
> For beauty. Learned from earliest youth am I
> In loveliness, and cannot so erase
> Its letters from my mind, that I may trace
> You faultless, I must love until I die. . . .[55]

This is less passionate than many of her love lyrics, and it alone among them speaks of lifelong constancy. It might have been written to the poet's mother, to whom, as her letters testify, she was ardently devoted.

That variant emotion was at least an intermittent preoccupation with Millay until she was thirty is evident from examination of her total work before 1923, the year of her marriage. There are a number of sonnets and other verses in which the sex of the subject is uncertain, if not deliberately concealed, but which do not have the tone of those specifically written to men. Then there is her poetic drama, *The Lamp and The Bell,* written during a sojourn in Paris soon after graduation from Vassar, and presented at the college in 1921. Its theme is an undying devotion between two young women, and Elizabeth Atkins's description of it is so delightful that it must be borrowed:

> The kingdom of Fiori is Poughkeepsie-on-the-Hudson, and college students and faculty keep looking straight through their Italian veils, very much as Elizabethan Londoners keep lifting their masks in Shakespeare's Illyria and Verona and Messina.
>
> The theme is that one of burning concern in any girls' school—the theme of friendship; and the play takes up their endless arguments as to whether it will last. Octavia, the very mildly wicked stepmother in the play, supposedly a queen but essentially a dean of women, avers that the friendship of the princess and her own daughter is not healthy and will not last. Of course the girls prove her wrong. The princess, without a murmur, gives up her lover to her friend; and long afterwards she consents to violation by her most loathed enemy, in order to be permitted to reach her friend as she lies dying.
>
> The theme is surely Elizabethan. From Lyly to Beaumont and Fletcher, Elizabethan literature is filled with asseverations that friendship is a stronger thing than sexual love. . . . The only novelty is that this twentieth century play deals with the friendship of women instead of men. . . .[56]

Friendship, however, is much too cool a description for the love between the princesses. The relation is passionate, though as always in her variant verse Millay avoids any implication of physical intimacy.

By the time that this drama was written, however, Millay also had published a number of lyrics of heterosexual inspiration. Indeed, among the conventionally minded she had gained a quite shocking reputation on the strength of them, for they antedated the now notorious Twenties. Many of them are flippant or bitter in comparison to those inspired by women, and they flaunt inconstancy and promiscuity. See for instance the sonnets "Oh think not I am faithful to a vow," "I shall forget you presently, my dear,"[57] "What lips my lips have kissed . . . I have forgotten," and "I being born a woman. . . ."[58] In short, these betray conscious striving toward a masculine sexual standard to match that of her partners. They remind one that "Vincent" had concealed her sex at the date of her first publication. A critic, citing in an adult review the "phenomenal" quality of a *St. Nicholas* entry Millay wrote at fourteen, confessed uncertainty whether the poem was written by a boy or a girl.[59] Fellow poets reading "Renascence" thought it a man's work, and a Barnard professor during her brief months there (repairing entrance requirement deficiencies for Vassar) pronounced "Interim" to be written in the character of a man.[60] The same viewpoint marks her libretto for Deems Taylor's opera, *The King's Henchman.*

After her marriage in 1923 all of Millay's published verse was marked by greater emotional reticence, and if she wrote privately anything comparable to her earlier variant lyrics the chances are against its ever being made public. (There has been no providential Reinach to salvage her reliques for posterity, and it is rumored that censorship is being exercised. Letters have been admitted to the published volume of her correspondence which imply some early heterosexual indiscretion, while all variant traces have been eradicated save a proper name or two[61] in connection with which the published implications are unrevealing. To the student of variance, however, they are significant.) The one notable exception to this general reticence is *Fatal Interview* (1930), of which Atkins said in 1936 that she, herself,

> must be the first post-Victorian critic on record to state in cold print . . . that a still breathing married woman, name and dates given, has written a poem of extra-marital passion, not as a literary exercise in purple penmanship, but as an honest record of immediate experience.[62]

The experience did not occur very close to the date of the volume's publication, however, for many readers will remember individual sonnets coming out in this or that magazine over a considerable number of years, and not in the order in which they finally stand. The majority might, as far as verbal evidence goes, have been written to a person of either sex, and they differ so sharply among themselves that even allowing for the poet's mercurial temperament and the gamut of emotion she wished to record, one sometimes feels they cannot all have been inspired by the same individual. It may be brash to suggest that they could have grown out of more than one experience, and that the fifty-two were merely assembled into one matchless tracing of the birth, growth and decline of human passion. But one of them, numbered XXI, demands special attention:

> Gone in good sooth you are: not even in dream
> You come. As if the strictures of the light,
> Laid on our glances to their disesteem,
> Extended even to shadows and the night;
> Extended even beyond that drowsy sill
> Along whose galleries, open to the skies
> All maskers move unchallenged and at will,
> Visor in hand and hooded to the eyes.
> To that pavilion the green sea in flood
> Curves in, and the slow dancers dance in foam;
> I find again the pink camellia-bud
> On the wide step, beside a silver comb—
> But it is scentless; up the marble stair
> I mount with pain, knowing you are not there.

This verse was originally written either to a woman and fitted later into the artistic pattern of the whole, or the man who inspired it could appear (without incongruity in the dreamer's mind) to have lost a masquer's accessories—pink camellia-bud and silver comb—which are scarcely masculine. Was he one whom a woman's costume would have become? Did the dreamer at times secretly wish him a woman? Or was this sonnet (and just possibly others in the sequence also) written specifically to a woman?

It has been the critical fashion for some time to discount Millay's literary importance because of the sharp decline in the quality of her work after *The Buck in the Snow*. Her "Epitaph for the Race of Man" in that volume may be seen almost as her own poetic abdication. An artist whose gods were Life and Beauty and whose devil was Cruelty may well have found herself paralyzed by the horror of global and total war. If one predicates also the burden of a dual emotional nature, one half of which was in later years censored by the other—for no mature modern of her intelligence would lightly court the charge of arrested adolescence, no daughter of New England would willingly display what her generation considered emotional deformity—one has supplementary explanation of her creative paralysis.

Not all of this country's variant poetry has been written by women; at least two men have contributed narrative verse. Edgar Lee Masters's *Domesday Book* (1929) follows Browning's *Ring and the Book* in that it begins with a girl's death and traces the history which led up to it, through the memories of far more than Browning's dozen persons. In the end Elenor Murray is seen as a woman too passionate and open-hearted to live peacefully or to end her days in happiness. Within a decade she gave herself lavishly to several men but was self-defeating in her very generosity, and finally ended her life because her efforts to meet her lovers' need only brought suffering to others as well as herself.

One of the earlier reminiscences in the book comes from Alma Bell, a high-school teacher who knew Elenor at seventeen and loved her deeply. Recognizing the dangers ahead for one so susceptible to passion, she attempted to help the girl "to ripen to a rich maturity" unscathed. She had success in warding off certain unsavory male advances, but not in avoiding emotional involvement herself, since, as she observes, few persons are wholly either masculine or feminine in spirit.

> . . . the flesh's explanation
> Is not important, nor to tell whence comes
> A love in the heart—the thing is love at last . . .
> My love for Elenor Murray never had
> Other expression than the look of eyes,
> The spiritual thrill of listening to her voice,
> A hand to clasp, kiss upon the lips at best,
> Better to find her soul, as Plato says.[63]

Despite this conscientious restraint the town became aware of the intimacy, and Alma Bell was forced to resign her position and leave

> . . . under a cloud
> Because of love for Elenor Murray, yet
> Not lawless love, I write now to make clear.[64]

The exceptional small town coroner, tolerant and philosophical, who elicits the stories which compose the pattern, is an evident mouthpiece for the poet himself. His final estimate of the girl's character is one of human dignity and largeness of spirit surpassing that of her calumniators and even her lovers and friends. But the early suspicion of lesbianism cast one of the shadows which reached beyond the limits of her little Midwestern community and augmented the difficulties of her later life.

The single protesting voice in American poetry is that of George Stirling, whose *Strange Waters* is a brief narrative related to the work of Robinson Jeffers in both its Pacific coast setting and in grimness of theme. To a childless, but quite happy, poet and his Irish wife are sent the latter's eighteen-year-old twin nieces. They are the children of her much older brother, to whom she has alluded only once during her married life proclaiming him a monster. His deathbed letter implies some ironic justice in their being left to her. They are fiery-haired beauties, abnormally reticent except with one another, and their mutual devotion is marked. The more boyish twin exhibits a brilliant intellect which fascinates the poet, but he intuitively senses something amiss, and listens at the door of the bedroom where they sleep together. To his horror he hears evidence of active lesbianism, and in the morning he accuses them openly. Refusing to answer him, the two set out for their usual daylong roaming on cliffs and shore. However, they do not return. When their bodies are washed in from the Pacific, óne proves to be a boy. The subtle implication is that they are the incestuous off-spring of the poet's wife and her brother. Their relation, then, is not variant, but it gives Stirling opportunity to pass upon lesbianism a judgment quite as black as upon incest, for which in this case a hereditary etiology is implied.

From England the variant contribution is even thinner and more evasive than from America. Richard Aldington's *Loves of Myrrhine and Konallis* (1926) is yet another derivative from Louÿs's *Songs of Bilitis*. Its pair are the young goat-girl, Konallis, and the prosperous courtesan, Myrrhine, who bids her maid close her doors to male lovers, "for this is a sharper love."[65] The tenuous drama progresses through white nights, bacchic revels, momentary unfaithfulness, and philosophic communing, and ends with Myrrhine's death and Kon-allis's subsequent marriage. Though graced with felicitous phrasing and vivid evocation of passionate mood, it is the weakest of the echoes from Louÿs's original because the least direct in presentation of its theme.

Victoria Sackville-West's *King's Daughter* (1930) is very different but even more cryptic. Its echoes are wholly English and recall the Elizabethan lyrists from one of whom the poet is descended. The scant two-dozen pages, full of country images sharp and delicate as frost, conjure up the spirit—seldom the physical presence—of an elusive coquette and of the proud speaker, who

> Although the blackness of her heart torment
> Me and her whiteness make me turbulent,[66]

will commit neither pleas nor actions to paper. One early line disclaims intimacy: "How shall I haunt her separate sleep?" The only others nearly as explicit are:

> Estranged from all, and rapt, I only ask
> To be alone when I am not with you.[67]

It is not until reaching the final poem, "Envoi," that the poet indicates that anything has actually occurred outside of her haunted imagination.

> The catkin from the hazel swung
> When you and I and March were young . . .
> The harvest moon rose round and red
> When habit came and wonder fled . . .
> Snow lay on hedgerows of December
> Then, when we could no more remember.
> But the green flush was on the larch
> When other loves we found in March.[68]

Here, for a moment, is the flavor of Millay, but not the intensity, and to give evidence that the whole volume breathes subjective passion one would need to quote it entirely, which is scarcely practicable. The most vivid of the poems is also one of the best known:

> Cygnet and barnacle goose
> Follow her when she passes
> Barefoot through daisied grasses.
>
> Briars blown straying and loose
> Catch at her as she goes
> Down the path between woodbine and rose.
>
> Seeking to follow and hold her,
> The silly birds and the thorn.
> But her laughter is merry with scorn.

What would she say if I told her
That the goose, and the swan,
And the thorn, and my spirit, were one?"

A negative note, barely audible, is sounded in the *Scrapbook* of
Katherine Mansfield, published by her husband, Middleton Murry,
in 1940, a dozen years after her death. The poem is dated 1919, and
entitled "Friendship."

When we were charming Backfisch
    With curls and velvet bows
We shared a charming kitten
    With tiny velvet toes.

It was so gay and playful;
    It flew like a woolly ball
From my lap to your shoulder—
    And oh, it was so small,

So warm and so obedient,
    If·we cried: "That's enough!"
It lay and slept between us,
    A purring ball of fluff.

But now that I am thirty
    And she is thirty-one,
I shudder to discover
    How wild our cat has run.

It's bigger than a tiger,
    Its eyes are jets of flame,
Its claws are gleaming daggers;
    Could it have once been tame?

Take it away; I'm frightened!
    But she, with placid brow,
Cries: "This is our Kitty-witty!
    Why don't you love her now?""

Obviously Mansfield, unlike Millay, did not see perfection in the
fulfillment of variant love. Or at least not in this particular fulfillment. Passages scattered through the *Scrapbook* and the more
reticent *Journal* (1928) reveal a compulsive and abject devotion in

the lifelong friend alluded to in the poem above. (See, for example, "Toothache Sunday" in the *Scrapbook*.) The intensity of her friend's emotion troubled Mansfield, who sometimes felt herself "a callous brute" to be unable to return it in kind or to make its possessor happy. "I don't know why I always shrink ever so faintly from her touch. I could not kiss her lips."[71] But, however innocent of expression, the relationship was a problem she could never discuss with her husband, and she felt that it cast a permanent, if faint, shadow between her and "J." (Murry).

(From the recent sympathetic biography of Mansfield by her fellow New Zealander, Antony Alpers, several supplementary impressions emerge: 1) Ida Baker ("L.M.") was never abject, but rather a dedicated priestess most happy to be elected and given a direction in life. 2) It was not her shadow which fell between Mansfield and Murry so much as the former's compulsion to write. Katherine repeatedly blamed Murry's self-absorption for the difficulties in their relations (Nelia Gardner White takes the same view in her novelized biography *Daughter of Time*, 1941) but surely her own was quite as marked. 3) While she was in Queen's College, London, between fourteen and seventeen, there seems to have been some talk of her "unwholesome" friendships. Alpers uses the plural, but discusses only her domination of Ida Baker, unless her wooing of her feminine cousin Sidney Payne for a couple of years was also suspect. According to Alpers this courtship proceeded largely by letter, one of which he quotes to refute the charge. 4) From the picture of her two unhappy marriages (the first almost farcical) and her obviously ambivalent feeling for Ida Baker, it seems that she was a person unable to give herself completely to either man or woman. Was this because of her obsession with writing, or was that relentless creative urge the result rather than the cause of some deeper emotional block?)

The most notable feature of all these twentieth century lyrics is the women's relatively articulate confession of variant interests. Before 1900 only "Michael Field" and Matilda Betham-Edwards (to be mentioned later) admitted inclination toward their own sex. Now the Catholic O'Neill, the New England Lowell and Millay, the British Sackville-West reveal it without apology. Schwabe and Madeleine offer their testimony still more openly, and Barney and Vivien, with the independence of expatriates and women of fortune able to create their own milieu, proclaim it not only in writing but in their lives. Indeed Vivien at least promises in any long view of western literature to figure as a minor Sappho, the greater part of her work dedicated to this limited but seemingly imperishable theme.

CHAPTER VII.

FICTION IN FRANCE

Before 1914

If variant poetry burgeoned suddenly with the turn of the present century, new developments in fiction were equally apparent. Between 1900 and 1950, novels with female variance as either a central or a major theme averaged more than two per year. A rather larger additional group used variance as a minor motif or in a telling incident or two. Of this generous crop a good half was the work of English and American authors; an equal proportion was written by women; and although active championship of lesbianism or variance was comparatively rare, better than half the fictional presentations were either sympathetic or neutral. These counts are based upon a hundred-odd volumes available for examination, plus an additional score or so of unequivocal reviews.

The new century's characteristic changes were least evident in France, where for a couple of decades variant fiction had appeared in quantity, and where at least two or three women (Rachilde, Jane de LaVaudère, Camille Pert) had contributed. We have seen that Pierre Louÿs between 1896 and 1901 even struck a new note of cheerful insouciance, but his *Aphrodite* and *Bilitis* pictured courtesans of the classical era, and the adventures of his three girls in *King Pausole* were set in a zany fantasy well removed from reality.

From reviews and publishers' records we know that during the century's first decade fully as many inferior lesbian novels appeared as in the one preceeding, a few of which will be mentioned later. The outstanding work, however, was that done by the couple signing themselves Colette-Willy, who opened a new era by portraying their own times with both frankness and sympathy. Willy was the established music critic and light novelist Henry Gauthier-Villars. Sidonie Gabrielle Colette has since been recognized as the foremost French woman writer of her time, but in 1900 she was merely a piquant personality who, a decade earlier, at seventeen, had come to Paris from the provinces and married Gauthier-Villars. Consequently, when *Claudine à L'Ecole* appeared (1900), it was taken to be mainly a work of Willy based upon his wife's girlhood experiences. Critics have since established that it and its three successors, *Claudine à Paris* (1901), *Claudine en Ménage* (1902) and *Claudine s'en Va* (1903) were less his than Colette's own, and the fifth volume, *La Retraite Sentimentale* (1907) was recognized at the time of its appearance as hers, since by then she had separated from her husband. The first four of the series have been translated as *Claudine at School, Young Lady of Paris, The Indulgent Husband,* and *Innocent Wife,* and are fairly well-known.

This series presents the emotional history of the delightful Claudine between the ages of fifteen and thirty, and incidentally incorporates the authors' opinions upon many sorts of sexual relation. Claudine appears first as a day pupil in a provincial public school somewhere in the mountainous *départements* of southern France. Motherless, she is brought up after a fashion by a father so absorbed in his studies as to approach a caricature of the absent-minded professor, and by a free-tongued servant comparable to Proust's Françoise. She grows up a tomboy, free to climb trees, to roam alone over the wooded hills about her small town, and to read at will in her father's uncensored library.

Her emotional development begins with an attraction appropriate to her years (fifteen) but uncommonly intense, to a pretty assistant mistress, Mademoiselle Aimée. With Claudine's wily arrangement to be tutored in English at home, this affair promises to develop richly, but it is interrupted when the headmistress, a domineering redhead, also contracts a passion for her assistant. Knowing on which side her bread is buttered, Aimée abandons Claudine, to become the pampered darling of her superior. Two or three of the "big girls" understand perfectly what is going on, and Claudine even eavesdrops one day upon an intimate moment enjoyed by the two women in their dormitory quarters while their classes run wild in the schoolrooms below. Later, the headmistress implies to Claudine that had she not from the outset shown antagonism, her affection might have been bestowed on her rather than on the somewhat insipid junior mistress.

In the course of the year, Claudine discovers that she is becoming attractive to men, notably the school's visiting physician, a "wolf" at whom she laughs although he has an irritating power to move her. He uses his political influence to the end of enjoying Aimée's favors, an affair to which the older mistress appears indifferent, her jealousy being reserved for feminine rivals. A second diversion develops when Aimée's young sister, Luce, enters at mid-term as a charity pupil and is badly neglected by the two mistresses. A year Claudine's junior, this thin green-eyed youngster becomes her adoring slave, constantly manoeuvering for caresses, but receiving only blows, which she appears to find almost as satisfying. To herself, Claudine admits that, were the girl anyone but a sister to the fickle Aimée, the affair might go farther.

At the graduation dance—a neat bit of satire on provincial entertainment—Claudine is much sought after by local and visiting swains, and analyzes afterward why she found their attentions so unsatisfactory. She contemplates what she wants of love:

> I terribly needed Someone, and was humiliated by this lack, and because I could not give anything to anyone I did not love and know through and through—a dream which will never come true, eh?[1]

This précis of the feminine ideal marks the beginning of Colette's since-famous dissection of women's emotional psychology.

The second volume carries Claudine through the year—her seventeenth—which her father decides must be spent in Paris, ostensibly in the interests of his scientific work, but actually with an eye to widening her circle of acquaintance. Sick with nostalgia for her native Montigny and loathing every aspect of her urban imprisonment, Claudine succumbs to a long illness which has two important results. Her hair must be cropped, and her contacts are confined to her father's older sister and the latter's grandson, a pretty creature of her own age as effeminate as she is boyish. Very nearly disliking Marcel, Claudine still feels a physical attraction much like that which drew her to Luce. But Marcel's emotions are absorbed in an affair with a male schoolmate—an affair which has made trouble for both boys at their Lycée and evoked the wrath and contempt of Marcel's father. Evasive about his own experiences, Marcel is avidly curious about Claudine's relations with Luce (pride prevents her mentioning Aimée). It is Marcel who sees the modish possibilities in Claudine's cropped head, and takes her to an English tailor to be outfitted *en garçonne,* a style eminently suited to her both physically and psychologically.

During her illness Claudine has heard from Luce that her situation at the school has become intolerable and she is ready for desperate measures. Presently she meets Luce on a Paris street dressed more smartly than she is herself, and learns that the girl, who had sought help from an uncle (a gross sixty-year-old widower), is now being lavishly kept by him. Nevertheless, Luce manages to have a boy-friend from the Beaux-Arts on the side, and is also eager to resume relations with Claudine. The latter, too, feels the earlier attraction, but realizes she cannot tolerate intimacy with a little *grue* who is living with her own uncle. With humorous honesty she admits to herself that despite having "read everything—and understood it" before she was sixteen, when it comes to "real life" she is nothing but "an ordinary good girl."

In the course of her acquaintance with the pretty Marcel she meets Renaud, the latter's widowed father, and is drawn to him despite his intolerance of his son's homosexual affair. She thinks he is just the man she would have chosen for a father—urbane and witty, but with sombre emotional depths. Soon she is in love with him. The man, twenty years her senior, struggles against a reciprocal attraction, but Claudine's headlong infatuation wins, and the book ends with their engagement.

The first section of *Claudine en Ménage* analyzes with skill her as yet incomplete marital adjustment. She resents the memory of her elaborate wedding and her husband's continuing mixture of fatherly indulgence and experienced sensuality which shames her adoring naïveté. The couple have spent a year in continental travel uncongenial to the Montigny tomboy, and as she settles in Renaud's Paris apartment she is homesick for her native province and rebellious against the routine of sophisticated entertaining her husband wishes to resume.

Accepting life on his terms with what grace she can, she presently meets Rezi, a seductive Austrian, wife of a retired English officer, and soon they are mutually infatuated. Their emotion can find no outlet because the colonel's jealous surveillance and the unremitting social activity in her own household afford them no privacy. After a period of increasingly painful frustration Claudine appeals to her husband for aid. Renaud has all along shown the same excited interest in this affair that his son exhibited in her relations with Luce, and he readily agrees to find the pair a private haven. He insists, however, on retaining the key to their "nest" himself and on escorting them to it whenever they wish to go there. This complaisance bordering on voyeurism offends Claudine, who is at heart wounded by his lack of jealousy. Gradually she realizes that what she feels for Rezi is mere infatuation. She suspects that her partner has been intimate with other women about whom she is evasive, and she even finds reason to wonder whether before her marriage Renaud and Rezi might not have had an affair. Her brooding discontent increases during three weeks of illness when she can keep watch on neither husband nor friend, and comes to a head on the day when she pays a surprise visit to the "nest" and finds the two there together. In a fury of jealousy and disillusionment she goes home to Montigny.

There, healed by springtime in the country, she owns that she is still as much in love with Renaud as his letters show him to be with her. She finally writes him that he has been too indulgent, too like a doting father. 'I wanted Rezi and you gave her to me like a bonbon. You should have explained that there are sweets one cannot eat without becoming ill.'[2] She tells him that if they are to be happy she must be more his equal as he must be more her master. Life seems to her so much more sane and wholesome in the country that she is determined to stay there, and she hopes he will consent to make his permanent home there as well. When business or even pleasure call him to Paris, she will let him go, knowing that when he returns it will be from genuine inclination. The volume closes with this ultimatum without disclosing Renaud's response.

In *Claudine s'en Va* the viewpoint shifts to that of a very different young married woman, but Claudine, moving in and out of the picture, is still a dominant influence in the story. Its central figure, Annie, is a submissive creature who has been married four years to Alain, an autocratic cousin whom she has adored slavishly since childhood. While he is absent on a protracted business trip Annie discovers herself—her uninfluenced personality is very different from her husband's, and her married life has been a one-sided affair never affording her real satisfaction. The latter revelation is the fruit of long talks with Claudine, whose own marriage, now radiantly successful, becomes for Annie the embodiment of what mutual love should be. Her husband has forbidden her to associate with Renaud and Claudine, whom he considers too "fast" to be a good influence, but Annie learns that the sister to whose care he has entrusted her is involved in a sordid affair with an alcoholic journalist and that Alain himself has, since their marriage, carried on a long liaison with a woman who has always disgusted her. This painful enlightenment comes during a hectic season at an international spa. She turns more and more to the bohemian but wholesome Claudine, who convinces her that a middle course is possible between the looseness into which she has been so quickly plunged and the rigid conven-

tionality of her former life. As their intimacy grows it becomes apparent that Claudine is strongly drawn to her but is as strongly self-
disciplined. At one point when they have been exchanging confidences
and Annie rests her head on Claudine's shoulder, hungry for tenderness, Claudine springs up crying "Not too far! In another instant I
would—and I've promised Renaud——"[3]

Annie finally feels that further life with her husband is impossible, and she prepares to leave on a secret quest for emotional
orientation before his return. In bidding her goodbye and godspeed,
Claudine confesses that she could easily have become emotionally
involved, but dared not risk a second experience like the one with
Rezi. She must abide by her promise to her husband, even though
because of the different circumstances, she, herself, can see no
harm in giving what comfort she might to the suffering Annie. Her
final words are almost mystical—a confession of faith in Love as
something precious enough to seek at all costs, and when found, to
preserve at any price.

La Retraite Sentimentale, appearing in 1907 after Colette's divorce
from Willy, carries Claudine's story to its conclusion. At the outset
Renaud is in a Swiss sanitorium, exhausted by the hectic pace at
which he has lived, and Claudine is with the now-divorced Annie
on the latter's Burgundian estate, in order to spare Renaud the
jealous concern her life alone in Paris might occasion. The potential
attraction between Annie and herself is dormant, and Claudine,
wretchedly lonely without her husband, amuses herself by drawing
from her companion a full account of her *Wanderjahr*. She learns
that Annie has run the gamut of sexual experiment with men in
search of her romantic ideal, but has gained nothing beyond
momentary appeasement. More unwilling than ever to risk a further
barren experience with Annie, Claudine yields to a fantastic impulse.
Her woman-shy stepson, Marcel, arrives for a visit just as Annie
feels impelled to set out on another sexual quest, and Claudine
throws the two together in the hope that each may solve the other's
problem. The tragi-farcical outcome suggests that this episode may
have been plotted during Colette's collaboration with Willy, for
it echoes the most cynical note of the earlier volumes.

The concluding portion of *La Retraite Sentimentale* shows
Claudine, now thirty and widowed, once more entrenched in her
beloved country house in Montigny. Her father and the old servant
have died, and she is alone with her cherished dogs and cats, still
faithful in spirit to Renaud, and filled with tolerant pity for the
restless Parisians (Annie among them) who often motor down to

see her. This final volume has no place in a study of female variance save for its picture of Claudine's resolute refusal in maturity to become involved with Annie.

As has been said, all of the volumes are now recognized as chiefly the work of Colette, and also as more autobiographical than could be admitted at the time of their composition. They may, therefore, be trusted as giving a fairly accurate picture of a certain group of Parisian literati at the turn of the century. There is something of Willy in the idealized Renaud and also in the caricatured Maugis, alcoholic music critic and paramour of Annie's sister-in-law. Judging Willy's attitude from that found in his independent fiction, the complaisance of Renaud toward his wife's lesbian liaison was less improbable than certain contemporary critics—Rachilde among them —felt it to be. From passing references in Colette's much later volume of personal reminiscences, *Ces Plaisirs,*[4] it would appear that the group in which she moved during her early married years—that is, the middle and late Nineties—were tolerant of male as well as female homosexuality, and Marcel's affairs were probably drawn from life. Colette's divorce after twelve years of marriage, however, is said to have been due to heterosexual irregularities on her husband's part. A second marriage in 1914 to Henri de Jouvenel, by whom she had a daughter, seems to have brought her a more settled happiness. But it should be noted that Stella Browne, in a psychological study of some women authors with homosexual tendencies,[5] mentions Colette as having been involved herself before 1914 in two powerful variant attachments, one with the film star, Marguérite Moréno, whom she met while she was earning her living on the stage between her two marriages, and the other with an unnamed foreign noblewoman. Character sketches of both these women, naturally drawn with great discretion, appear in *Ces Plaisirs.* From them one gathers that Colette's relations with Moréno were intimate, but "the Chevalier" (the nickname perhaps an echo from Peladan's chaste lady) is presented as a romantic idealist unwilling or unable to cross the boundaries of physical intimacy with anyone.

To return to Claudine, she has some masculine secondary characteristics—she is proud of her boyish height and acrobatic abilities —and a personality in which unfeminine traits were emphasized by her freedom and independence while young. But she never rebels against the feminine role. She is also proud of her beautiful hair and eyes, and she never abandons skirts even on her strenuous cross-country rambles. She enjoys her power to attract men, though she scorns flirtation and breaks an umbrella on a boulevardier who risks the traditional continental pinch. Her reaction to the women who attract her is definitely male—primarily physical, roused by beauty and passivity, and manifesting itself in a desire to conquer and dominate. It contrasts sharply with the clinging adoration of Luce, Aimée, and Annie. It is most often stirred, after the initial "crush" on Aimée, by girls younger than herself, those who recall her own youth or the masochistic devotion of young Luce. This is particularly stressed in the early pages of *Claudine en Ménage,* when, taking Renaud on a visit to her old school, she finds there a handful of delicious adolescents spending their holidays in the dormitory, and plays recklessly with them. It appears again in *Claudine s'en Va,* when she encounters at the spa an impudent comedienne so much like herself a few years earlier as to provoke universal comment on the resemblance. This young woman, Polaire, was a real not a fictional character who had acted in a dramatic version of *Claudine à Paris* in 1903, and who appears in the story under her own name, as do various other contemporary personalities in the course of the five volumes. (A particularly malicious sketch of Mme Dieulafoy, whose opera *Sémiramis* had just been presented, figures in *Claudine s'en Va* in a letter from the music critic Maugis.) *

Taken together, the five *Claudine* novels present a complete sexual philosophy. It is Claudine's progressive maturing under the influence of Renaud which weans her away from her variant leanings, but the influence is not one-sided. As their marital relationship deepens and mellows, Renaud is led to "love Love," to be, as Claudine puts it, more "chaste," less fond of sensual virtuosity *"qui s'aide d'une combinaison de miroirs . . . et de mots fait pour le chuchotement et qu'on se force à crier à haute voix, tout crus."*[7] In short, he has acquired a more feminine outlook. Here, in brief, is the distilled wisdom of the woman pronounced a genius in portraying the nuances of feminine psychology. Lesbian attractions are legitimate but they belong to youth. Mature love is neither uninhibited sophistication nor romantic idealism, but a mutual devotion in whose interest each sex must sacrifice something and must attempt to acquire some part of the other's outlook. It has taken four decades of Freud and his successors to produce the almost identical wisdom which appears in all the better marriage manuals one reads today. One might say that although France did not contribute so much as Germany and England to the scientific study of sex, her long years of frank attention to it from the personal and literary angles bore fruit before the scientists' harvest.

The *Claudine* series spanned seven years, but they were not the only works of their genre to appear in France. In the matter of public acclaim, perhaps the most important item was an opera, *Astarte,* presented by the Académie Nationale de Musique on February 15, 1901, with a score by Xavier Leroux, which critics characterized as Wagnerian, and a five-act libretto by Louis de Gramont. (It is cited in Martens's *Book of Operas* as *Omphale,* and was apparently composed in 1891, though there is no record of a dramatic performance before 1901.) The libretto has not been available, and the following account is drawn from the review by Breville in the *Mercure de France* for April 1901, and the summary in Hirschfeld's *Jahrbuch*[8] of an article in *Le Temps* for February 20, by Pierre Lalo. The drama combines two episodes from the mythological cycle of Hercules: his bewitched assumption of woman's dress and his death caused by the shirt of Nessus. Hercules is represented as going to Lydia to stamp out the infamous lesbian cult of Astarte by slaying Omphale, its high priestess. Instead, he is reduced by her seduction to abject slavery, forgetting all his previous triumphs and the purpose of his quest. Shedding his warlike accoutrements and 'using the skin of the Nemean lion for a bedside carpet,' he watches with fascination a lesbian ceremony which Breville pronounces one of the most beautiful ballets ever presented on the stage, 'consecrated not so much to those *amours animales* of which Verlaine speaks as to the harmonious disposition of groups and colors,' its erotic climax being veiled in 'suddenly imposed shadows.'

At the ballet's end Hercules is willing to abjure Vesta, adopt the religion of Astarte, and enter into the marriage with Omphale urged by the high priest. But Omphale, at last enamoured of a man, demurs because she knows that the sequel to the nuptials must be the sacrifice of Hercules on Astarte's altar. At this point, the maiden Iole appears bringing the miraculous tunic of Nessus from Hercules's wife, Dejanira. This tunic supposedly will save him from the power of Astarte and rekindle the flame of legitimate love. The charms of Iole so transcend those of Hercules in the eyes of Omphale that she offers to release him and his warriors if she may keep the girl. Hercules, "toujours naïf," accepts the bargain, dons the tunic, and bursts into flame, igniting temple and palace as well. Omphale, undisturbed either by his dying cries or the general conflagration, embarks for Lesbos with the enraptured Iole amid the ritual chants and dancing of all the women.

Breville, who finds Leroux's score worthy of serious attention, is fairly scornful of Gramont's book. Here, he says, Hercules is not a mythical hero but a robust swashbuckler who stalks about like the professional wrestler paid to let an amateur win the bout. Amorous psychology, he feels, has given way to mere physiology; Omphale's sudden preference for Iole is unconvincing, and moralists have no real case against a work which ends in barren triumph for the purely sensual. Despite this negative judgment the opera must have survived at least from February till April, which suggests that Breville's opinion was prejudiced.

In the same year a popular star of music hall and demi-monde, Liane de Pougy, published a novel, *Idylle Saphique*. Rachilde in the *Mercure* pronounced it well-written but omitted comment on its theme, evidently thinking the title sufficiently obvious. She confined herself to lamenting that the author seemed on her way to becoming a respectable woman (*honnête*), 'and what is worse, a bluestocking.'[9] The *Jahrbuch*, which repeatedly deplored the French tendency to regard homosexuality as an experience possible for anyone, rather than the innate tendency which that journal's sponsors championed, considered the *Idylle* psychologically sound, and gave an extensive résumé of the plot,[10] which seems representative enough of the sensational variant novels of the time to merit review here. Annhine de Lys, famous Parisian *courtisane*, differs from most of her class in dreaming of a great love. Her profitable life with a millionaire or two has sickened her of both luxury and sex, so that when a twenty-year-old American falls in love with her she is moved by the girl's intense worship. She herself has hitherto avoided 'lesbian degeneracy,' and continues to resist it in its completeness, having been warned by a colleague that it wrecks the nerves.

Florence, the American, is engaged to a fellow countryman, who, like Claudine's husband, has not objected to several variant experiments on her part, but of her passion for Annhine he is jealous for the first time. He purchases Annhine's favors at a fabulous price, thinking thus to disgust his fiancée with her adored, but instead she turns against him. When a previous love of Florence's, realizing that she too has lost the girl, stabs herself in the presence of the current pair, Annhine falls ill from shock and leaves Paris. But some months in Italy and Spain and a romantic interlude with a young man do not serve to eradicate her memories of Florence, and the two are finally reunited. Annhine sells her Paris mansion because it has been the scene of professional liaisons which now seem shameful to her, and she and Florence plan a "marriage" and a future of constancy and happiness. But the other courtesan's prediction proves correct: Annhine suffers a breakdown, and Florence plans to marry the ever-devoted American suitor in order to support her love. Annhine, knowing herself doomed, begs the girl to enter the marriage seriously and give up lesbian practices, but after her death Florence merely cancels her engagement a second time and goes her way alone. Interestingly enough, the reviewer in the *Jahrbuch* finds the suitor a wholly incredible character, and believes only an American could be so casually tolerant. Yet the review of *Claudine en Ménage* follows immediately in the same number of the journal, with no editorial comment on the parallel situations in the two.

In the following year (1902) a novel of less artistry voiced strong disapproval of lesbianism. Charles Montfont's *Journal d'une Saphiste* is an autobiography which follows Aline from her first boarding school initiation at the age of ten into her middle twenties. Her second love, beginning in adolescence, is for the delicate and feminine Mirette, an orphan who spends vacations in her home. Since Aline is motherless and her father without suspicion, the two girls enjoy a protracted affair until the father arranges a marriage for Aline. Her husband, alerted by her docile frigidity and by watching her with her friend, tells her she must choose between them. She chooses Mirette. Her father dies financially ruined, and as her ex-husband will understandably enough contribute nothing to her support, she is obliged to keep herself and her love by selling herself secretly to one of her husband's friends. Mirette senses the truth, and, already weakened by passionate excesses, dies in raving delirium. Aline ends her diary with an exhortation: 'Women, seek only the love that all mankind honors, the healthy and honorable, because fertile, love of men,' and leaves the document to a friend as a warning to all girls and schoolmistresses against 'the extravagant madness of lesbian love.' The implication is that she then commits suicide. The entire book, while using moral tags at beginning and end to placate the censor, is written with detail bordering on pornography, and Mirette's death is as much medical nonsense as was Annhine's mentioned above, or Mlle Giraud's from meningitis.

As was said earlier, the dozen years before World War I produced as many variant novels of diverse quality as appeared in the 1890s. These ranged from Morel's *Sapho de Lesbos* and Faure's *La Derniere Journée de Sapho*, both of which whitewashed their classical heroine; through Willy's *La Môme Picrate*, in which the lesbian motif is incidental, and de Régnier's *L'Amour et le Plaisir*, a clever imitation

of eighteenth century farce; to LePage's *Les Fausse Vierges* and
Hoche's *Le Vice Mortel,* melodramas holding lesbianism responsible
for murder and suicide in improbable circumstances.[11] The only
novel to rate serious consideration in both the *Mercure* and the
Jahrbuch was Daniel Borys's *Carlotta Noll, Amoureuse et Femme de
Lettres* (1905).[12] In this book, the heroine's passion for a famous
male literary colleague is supplanted by infatuation for the homosexual Myrtil, who lures her into active lesbianism and introduces
her to the fatal habit of inhaling ether as well. (Annie in *Claudine
s'en Va* had a similar fondness for chloroform. *Sic transeunt* modes
in drugs!) When Carlotta is finally abandoned by Myrtil she suffers
general paralysis and ends in an institution. The book's chief claim
to critical attention seems to have been its prose style, which notably
resembled that of Louÿs.

Post-War Trends

War, as always, checked the flow of fiction on any exotic themes.
But Marcel Proust in his invalid's ivory tower was steadily working
on *À La Recherche du Temps Perdu,* which emerged intermittently
from 1918 to 1926. (*Swann's Way* had appeared in 1913, but it and
The Guermantes Way are least pertinent to the present study,
variance in the latter being confined to the male liaisons of the Baron
Charlus.) One of the major factors in Proust's long narrative is
the lesbianism of its narrator's mistress, Albertine. This is strongly
foreshadowed in *Within a Budding Grove;* its development provides
much of the narrative suspense in *The Captive,* and it reaches a
climax in *The Sweet Cheat Gone.* Proust weaves the lesbian strand
skillfully through his complex but controlled pattern. A sadistic
episode between Mlle Vintueil and a friend figures briefly in the
Combray-childhood section of Marcel's history (which in the completed cycle precedes *Swann's Way*), but this ties into the later
pattern when Marcel learns that Albertine had, during adolescence,
been associated with this pair of women.[13] Then comes Marcel's
obsession with the group of bold and athletic girls at the seaside
resort of Balbec and his final fixation upon Albertine who was one of
them;[14] his temporary separation from her while he is absorbed
with the Duchesse de Guermantes and his military cousin, Robert;
his later living with Albertine alone in the family town house and
attempting to cut her off from all her previous feminine associates
save the trusted Andrée,[15] whom he later ironically discovers to have
been her lover;[16] and his final awareness that even his first love,

Gilberte Swann, was associated with a nameless girl transvestist whom he had imagined to be a boy; and that Gilberte had also known Albertine's circle.[17]

Critics are now agreed that the tapestry of female variance which Proust wove with such art was in part a transposition of the male homosexuality he did not dare to treat so openly. Perceptive readers detected this at once. Colette in *Ces Plaisirs* pronounced his lesbians unconvincing little monsters, and Natalie Clifford Barney in *Aventures de L'Esprit* writes of warning him when his early volumes appeared of the difficulty of translating the experience of one sex into terms of the other.[18] Even quite naïve readers of his work in English have been sceptical of Albertine's freedom to visit Marcel in his hotel room late at night whenever he sent the servant Françoise to fetch her, and one could cite many similar inconsistencies with any known code of etiquette for "respectable" and marriageable girls in France or elsewhere. Thus Proust's whole lesbian canvas is in part invalidated as a social document. But still the types he portrays, their various interconnections, and most of their psychology, ring perfectly true for any group of young female sophisticates. He was certainly well acquainted with many variants of both sexes, and one need discount his feminine data very little.

In 1922 Romain Rolland, already famous for his greatest novel, *Jean Christophe,* published *Annette and Sylvie,* the first volume of his second series, *A Soul Enchanted.* As *Jean Christophe* was the life story of a man, so the later novel presents the emotional history of a passionate woman, with her ultimate fulfillment in motherhood and devotion to a son. The first episode is an attachment between the heroine, Annette, and her illegitimate half-sister, Sylvie. The former is the daughter of a puritanic and intellectual wife, the latter of a less cultivated but more charming mistress. The progress of the girls' intimacy after both are orphaned in their twenties is unfolded with keen insight into their contrasting natures, one serious and violent, the other self-contained and gracefully wise.

> Sylvie's affection was perfectly unrestrained, laughing, gamin-like, impudent, but at bottom extremely sensible. . . . In Annette there dwelt a strange demon of love . . . she suppressed it . . . for she was afraid of it; her instinct told her that others would not understand it. . . .[19]

The two are drawn to one another with an intensity which Annette does not suspect as unusual. Just before its climax their love is endangered by the passing infatuation of both girls for a summer-resort Adonis, for Sylvie a mere flirtation, stimulated largely by rivalry, but for Annette a dangerous flare of passion alight for the first time in her twenty-five years. Up to this point the girls' devotion has expressed itself only in constant companionship, endless confidences, and free but innocent caresses. In Annette's town house they have occupied adjoining rooms. Occasionally Sylvie, a light sleeper,

> . . . would get up and go over to the bed where Annette lay prostrate, with the sheets thrust up in a mountain by her crossed knees; and . . . would fascinatedly watch the dull, heavy but strangely passionate face of the sleeper who was drowning in the ocean of her dreams. . . . She wanted to waken her abruptly and put her arms about her neck. "Wolf, are you there?" But she was too sure the wolf was there to try the experiment. Less pure and more normal than her elder sister, she played with fire, but she was not burned by it.[20]

After Annette's stormy introduction to heterosexual passion, how-ever— ("That is love? . . . I don't want any more. I'm not made for it!") —they spend some weeks together, and now

> they were ruminating on their fever, their transports . . . all that they had acquired and learned from each other during the preceding days. For this time they had given themselves completely, eager to take all and give all.[21]

Their passion fights its way successfully through the phase of their desiring to dominate and possess one another:

> Their intimacy became so necessary to them that they wondered how they had ever done without it . . . but the two little Rivières felt another, stronger need, that went deeper, to the very sources of their being: the need of in-dependence.[22]

The episode ends with Sylvie set up as a modiste, and Annette returning to social life in the intellectual circles her father had frequented, the two seeing one another less and less often.

The second portion of the book records Annette's experience with a highly eligible and attractive man whom she loves deeply. He and his family, however, hold the conventional view that a wife should be completely absorbed into her husband's life and milieu, and as this threatens her independence she breaks the engagement, though she is so moved by her lover's desolation that she gives herself to him before parting. Unable to yield completely either to man or woman, she would today be branded as a narcissist by psychoanalysts, but in the 1920s a major artist could still present with sympathy such a quest for individual integrity.

Written in the same year and treating the same theme more obliquely was Victor Margueritte's *La Garçonne* (issued in a considerably expurgated English translation in 1923 as *The Bachelor Girl*).[23] Monique Lerbier, a true child of her decade, gives herself to her fiancé a fortnight before her wedding, not only in token of loving trust but in an effort to be more his equal in experience and courage. Then almost on the eve of the ceremony she learns that she is merely a pawn in a business deal between her father and Lucien, and also that her fiancé has not given up a mistress of long standing nor does he intend to do so. Outraged, she breaks with both him and her family, launches herself as a decorator, and after some years of struggle achieves conspicuous success. Along with her business career she leads a complicated personal life with three or four lovers, one of them a woman, and only after much travail attains emotional stability and a happy marriage. Among the omissions from the English translation are the most explicit heterosexual scenes and all homosexual passages.

In the original French version the latter are of considerable importance. The first involves Monique and her chum Elizabeth, both sixteen. "Zabeth" has adored Monique for three years without daring to reveal her desires, which Monique for her part has never suspected. Then on a sweltering afternoon the girls slip off their blouses—one is reminded of Mlle Tantale—and fall to comparing breasts. Now Monique senses her friend's excitement and responds, and only a chance interruption prevents her immediate initiation into the life of the senses. Nearly a decade later, when Monique has plunged feverishly into the bohemian life of Paris in the effort to forget Lucien, she and Zabeth (now married) participate in a fashionable opium party and at last consummate their long-deferred caresses.[24] Monique's important lesbian affair, however, involves a music-hall star who is still bewitching at fifty, with whom she enjoys some months' intimacy. It is this woman's tactful and knowing

advances which release her emotions from the ice in which the
wreck of her engagement has frozen them. The two often dance
together in public, are recognized at once as intimate by the male
and female homosexuals who throng the dancing clubs, and suffer
neither personally nor professionally from the association. It fades
to a predictable end when Monique discovers that men no longer
repel her. Both women then return to heterosexual associations.[25]

As in pre-war years, during this third decade variant novels of
all qualities swarmed from the presses: Proust's *Sodome et Gomorrhe*
(1921-22), *La Prisonnière* (1924), and *Albertine Disparue* (1925);
in 1925 also, Jacques Lacretelle's *La Bonifas* and Edward Bourdet's
La Prisonnière; and scattered over the same and later years, a shower
from the pen of one Charles-Etienne (an inferior disciple of Willy),
and a blast from Max DesVignons as hypocritical as Montfort's and
La Vaudère's prototypes of twenty years earlier.

Lacretelle's novel, translated into English as *Marie Bonifas* in
1927, is worth special note. Its central figure is a motherless child
of four or five, stocky and ugly, when her father settles in the decaying
Picard hamlet of Vermont. Once thriving, the town has declined
into a dreary aggregate of men like the retired Major Bonifas,
unmarriageable girls, and acid gossips who spy upon each other
behind half-closed shutters. This country backwater, so different
from the urban setting of most variant fiction, is Marie's lifelong
home. The story covers the half century preceding World War I.

Brought up roughly by her hard drinking parent and an ill-
tempered servant, Marie's life is uneventful until a gentle country
girl replaces the old shrew and becomes at once mother, playmate,
and tutor. Marie blossoms as her adoring satellite, experiencing
(as early as her tenth year) a sensation she thinks of as "melting"
when Reine caresses her. She develops an antipathy to her father's
drunken coarseness, and resents both his attentions to Reine and
the bold admiration of soldiers and country louts whom the girl
attracts. This childhood idyll has a shocking end when Reine,
pregnant by the Major, throws herself from a window and dies
within a few hours. The curses of her peasant mother convey the
essence of the tragedy, though no understanding of its details, to
the terrified and prostrated child. A stronger conditioning against
men could hardly be devised.

In the boarding school to which her father consigns her for the
next half dozen years Marie develops her second passion for the
older girl appointed as her "shepherdess." She remains at school

during vacations in order to wander the halls and garden paths she has walked with Geneviève; she violently hates the latter's fiancé; and for another of Geneviève's young charges she conceives such jealousy that she attacks and beats her rival and is consequently expelled. The following years from sixteen to nineteen she spends in a progressive school near the Swiss frontier. Its principal, a Parisian, has studied at Lausanne and taught abroad, and her advanced practice is to allow her girls complete freedom outside the classroom. Marie's delight is carpentry in a shop where she spends all the hours not given to outdoor sports with her English, American and Scandinavian mates. Conscious now of her masculine build and lack of charm, she cultivates cynical indifference to romance, but her instinct rejects the feminism preached by the headmistress and her friends. Marie's brief visits to her father are boresome, and it is only at his death that she realizes the loss of her one tie on earth.

Nostalgia recalls her to Vermont, where she establishes herself as mistress of the house, refuses the attentions of the physician who attended her father, and attempts to become a part of the town's life. But although the soft femininity of a local aesthete makes a certain appeal, she is impatient of the woman's affectations, and she has too many traits in common with a dowager philanthropist to make that old aristocrat congenial. Because of her financial contributions to a charity school, however, Marie is at least tolerated, and she puts her carpentry to good use in renovating the school's quarters unassisted.

Claire, the sewing mistress of the new school, a penniless, timorous and fragile young woman of twenty, appeals instantly to Marie's emotions. Within a matter of weeks they are inseparable. Marie frightens off a tentative suitor of Claire's in a fashion which sows the seeds of town gossip. When Claire succumbs to pneumonia Marie nurses her through the illness and later takes the girl into her house as companion. As Marie herself has by now refused a second proposal, slander runs rife. The isolation in which the two live is delightful to Marie, but it palls upon Claire so much that when a previous swain returns from his regiment she welcomes him. Marie is seized with a jealousy she cannot conceal. The man taunts her with her reputation, but since she is innocent, even ignorant of its implications, her reaction is merely one of defiance.

When Claire contracts tuberculosis, Marie takes her to the Mediterranean coast and acts as housekeeper and nurse to her socially-inferior beloved. Far from being grateful, the girl puts her bene-

factrice through some bitter hours, although she does soften before
dying. Returning alone to Vermont, Marie discovers that her eccentric
benevolence has only fed the ugly legends about her until the
girl's death is credited to their intimacy, and she is completely
ostracized. She responds with contempt, buying strong tobacco
at the village shop, riding astride as no other Vermont woman has
ever done, and laughing in the faces of those who cut her. This
blatant defiance ultimately provokes retaliation from the town's
riff-raff, friends of Claire's soldier-suitor, so that her property and
person are no longer safe and she is forced into complete seclusion
with only books for company.

   Now, for the first time, she learns the nature of her own difference.
She recognizes that from earliest childhood she has found men
ridiculous and revolting; that women have provided the only interest
in her life; moreover, that

> there was a certain resemblance between all the faces that
> had attracted her; it was the same shade of melancholy, the
> same emotion of a disappointed soul. . . . Whenever she saw
> on a woman's face . . . a certain regret, a yearning look . . .
> she felt a tug at her heart; she wanted to rise up and offer
> herself as if she had been created to be the guardian of a
> plant too fragile. . . ."

Made conscious also of possible physical intimacy between women,
and knowing herself already branded in the town's eyes as guilty
of it, she goes through a period of acute temptation, and is restrained
from making advances to a shopgirl only by the latter's murmuring
at a critical moment a phrase that Claire had often used.

   It is only when World War I breaks out and Vermont is invaded
by German troops that La Bonifas comes into her own. Then the
disorganized community, abandoned by its craven officials, turns
to the emerging recluse whose administrative ability, dauntless
courage, and considerable cunning save it from complete ruin.
Thereafter, Marie enjoys a position of honor. Her older enemies
have died or fled, her younger persecutors have been drawn off into
the army. Indeed, old enough by then to be the mother of the
younger troops, and having won their respect, she feels only warm
admiration for their strength. "Marie Bonifas had made her peace
with men." She is not, however, essentially altered even by this
change in one of her basic attitudes. Her interest still centers about
young girls and women. A daughter of her one-time "shepherdess"

is now her own goddaughter, and Marie frequently visits her old school at the edge of town. The final scene in her drama occurs at a prize-giving fête at that institution when Marie, occupying a seat of honor, watches a dance-pageant presented by the students. At the sight of all this young beauty costumed with the freedom of the Twenties, and at the sound of a girl soloist rendering with fervor the lament from Gluck's *Orpheus,* the famous woman dissolves in a passion of tears. It is the final irony of her life that one sympathetic observer should whisper to another that she must be thinking of a dead lover.

Exclusively variant women are rare in French fiction, and this long and careful study of one is easily the best of its sort the country has produced. Lacretelle has neither romanticized his heroine nor taken sides in the heredity-environment dispute. Both innate masculine traits and early conditioning start Marie on her variant way, and her later social persecution is due equally to her own temperament and to the town's spiteful prejudice. This same temperament saves her from succumbing intellectually to feminism or to the specious medical lore on variance which she reads. She finds outlet for its strength only as the war provides her with a man's job to do. As far as simple realism and dispassionate tolerance are concerned, *La Bonifas* has scarcely been bettered in any language.

Nothing could offer a sharper contrast than Bourdet's drama, *La Prisonnière* (1925), which borrowed its title straight from Proust's novel of the preceding year. Within eight months of its presentation at the Théâtre Fémina in Paris it was playing also in Berlin, Vienna, Budapest, and New York. The germ of the play is said to have been its author's encounter during the war with a fellow officer who was deliberately seeking death as escape from domestic tragedy,[17] and the key character is this man's wife, a lesbian who never appears on the stage. The heroine is a girl of twenty whom the older woman has captivated. As the play opens young Irene is struggling to remain in Paris against her father's efforts to take her with him to Rome, where he is assigned to a diplomatic post. A widower, he has been accompanied on other missions by his mistress, as both his daughters know, but discretion dictates a more conventional ménage in Rome. When in desperation Irene pleads an impending betrothal as reason for her wishing not to leave Paris, her dictatorial parent takes matters in hand and in short order has made the pretended excuse a reality. So Irene must cope also with Jacques, the hitherto unsuccessful suitor (at that time happy with a mistress who hoped one day to be his wife). Jacques suspects that an old school friend, d'Aiguines, is

Irene's lover and the real reason for her staying in Paris, but when he approaches the latter, now married, he learns that it is Mme d'Aiguines who is the object of Irene's absorbing passion. His first reaction is one of relief, but the unhappy husband assures him that the case is much more serious than if it were a matter of another man.

> Understand this: they are not for us. . . . Under cover of friendship a woman can enter any household . . . she can poison and pillage everything before the man whose home she destroys is even aware of what's happening to him. When he finally realizes . . . it's too late—he is alone! Alone in the face of a secret alliance of two beings who understand one another because they're alike . . . because they're of a different planet than he, the stranger, the enemy! . . . *Get out* while you still have strength to do it![28]

At this point Irene begs Jacques to marry her or even to take her as mistress. She has been invited on a long cruise with Mme d'Aiguines and knows that to go will mean her complete ruin. Whether her adored is cruel, or whether Irene fears social ostracism, is never clear—she merely implores her fiancé to "save" her. "It's like a prison to which I must return captive, despite myself." As a result Jacques makes her his wife, in spite of his friend's warning and his own recognition of the other man's wretchedness and premature aging. The couple spend a year away from Paris, but with their return the struggle begins anew. Irene has been a devoted wife and has severed all connections with her former love, but she has been able to feel no passion for her husband, and when an appeal comes from Mme d'Aiguines, who is ill, Irene returns helplessly to the old bondage. As for Jacques, he is fortunate enough to discover his former mistress still unattached, and as she responds to his kisses he says merely, "How beautiful!! A *woman!*"

Despite the hints above that Irene's captivity is purely physical and that she would like to escape it, all her symptoms throughout the play are those of romantic and imaginative love. Every moment apart from her friend is misery, and the violets she constantly receives become a romantic fetish. Bourdet has been skillful in portraying the effect on a number of persons of the conflict engendered in Irene by a love she feels to be guilty. But her own actual feeling for and relation with Mme d'Aiguines are never made clear. It is, of course, easy to see why this play, even with such evasion of a major psychological issue, swept the western world while the superior efforts of Rolland and Lacretelle raised only slight critical ripples. Chiefly, it condemned lesbianism. But also Bourdet exhibited sheer inspiration in avoiding the direct presentation of a lesbian on the stage. For it is difficult to find an artistic middle ground between the unconvincing monster of hack writers and a character perhaps too sympathetic to please the strait-laced. Later his results will be compared with other plays appearing on the American stage.

A very few words will do justice to the inferior novels referred to above. Charles-Etienne's *Les Désexuées* is concerned chiefly with male homosexuality, but a subsidiary plot is woven about Josette, childhood companion of one of the men, who, through acting in a lesbian drama, is drawn into an affair with the much younger ingenue. This 'pitiful child' adores her brilliant colleague until Josette gives way to passion, whereupon the girl feels she is being merely used as emotional outlet, and leaves the cast. Subsequent volumes, *Notre Dame de Lesbos* and *Léon dit Léonie*,[29] include liaisons between Josette and women attracted to her by her success in the dramatic role of Sappho, as well as a variety of other lesbians' affairs. *La Bouche Fardée* centers about Gisèle, who enjoys a brief affair with her uncle and is pursued by both his son and his daughter, but her secret love is the nephew Claude, like herself an orphan, whom her uncle has brought home from Jamaica and to whom he is closely bound. In the end it appears that Claude is actually a girl, and she and Gisèle have one ecstatic night together, (though both are under suspicion of having murdered the uncle), before Claude is forced to flee back to the West Indies alone. Gisèle drifts through subsequent volumes picturesquely inconsolable. The situation here constitutes a triumph for lesbianism—a girl with satisfactory heterosexual experience still prefers to all other men the one who proves a woman in disguise. Of *Inassouvie* the main figure is a dominating woman ruthlessly bent upon an operatic career. Idol of the day school where she teaches singing, she holds "orgies" in her luxurious apartment with favorite pupils. The one girl who genuinely loves her is a fifteen-year-old with a tragic family background. The violence of this child's affair with Adriane wrecks her fragile health, whereupon her brother and a friend use stolen snapshots of an orgy to break up Adriane's engagement and injure her musical career. In the end, however, Adriane triumphs by trapping the two boys in a situation which compromises them as homosexuals, and she also takes violent revenge upon the elderly fiancé and his son who have repudiated her. In temperament she is related to Rachilde's masculine heroines, and even more closely to the central figure of James Gibbons Huneker's *Painted Veils,* first privately printed in English seven years earlier. The variety of Charles-Etienne's lesbians and their experiences are reminiscent of Peladan, but he pretends to no high purpose, and indeed, the echoes in his work from known predecessors (Rachilde, Willy etc.) are sufficient to make one suspect synthetic inspiration from still others less familiar.

The nadir of quality was touched in Des Vignon's *Plaisirs Troublants,* which like *Le Journal d'une Saphiste* pretended to attack lesbianism while including more scandalous detail than novels which tolerated it. This tale pictures the encounter in their middle-twenties of two friends who have known each other in public school, without dormitory intimacies. The more masculine is happily married, save that her husband is too absorbed in business to satisfy her. The other is a typist and the mistress of one of her employers whom she hopes to marry. The chance meeting ignites an infatuation which circumstances allow to flame for a week unchecked, and the consequences are disastrous. Erotic reveries leave Marceline unable to work and estrange her from her lover. Germaine is roused to make such excessive sexual demands on her husband and her maid that both fall ill. Marceline dies of tuberculosis; Germaine is saved by a cliterectomy and then childbearing. The ostensible theme of the book is the criminal waste in any sexual exercise save for the purpose of procreation, but the author's real interest, quite as obviously as Montfort's, is in sales, not reform.

This wave of homosexual fiction during the Twenties was heavy enough that a new periodical, *Marges,* circulated a questionnaire on the subject in 1926, soliciting 'a certain number' of current authors' opinions on the social significance and moral effects of the abundant crop. If such established writers as Proust, Rolland and Colette were approached, they failed to reply. The thirty-odd answers varied from a Catholic's terse quotation of St. Paul: "Let not the word be spoken among you," to essays of several pages defending homosexuality as a recognized segment of human experience and a legitimate subject for literature. Everything from war, Freud, and athletics to decadence, avarice, and original sin, was blamed for the fictional epidemic. Suggested methods of combating it ranged from ignoring variant fiction in all review sheets to imprisoning and whipping its authors or committing them to asylums. The summarizing editor, throwing up his hands, suggested that some other magazine might like to attack the prevalence of heterosexual activity in current literature and devise some means of combating that![20]

While chance and not the *Marges'* effort was probably responsible, review sheets actually did soon feature less variant fiction than before. For reasons quite unrelated to the dispute, Rachilde retired from the staff of the *Mercure de France* and Hirschfeld's *Jahrbuch* died, both before the end of the decade, and no equally serviceable records of variant titles replaced them. Therefore, most of the dozen French novels of the 1930s cited here or there as significant must pass without comment, since neither the volumes themselves nor adequate notes upon them have been accessible. Since the end of World War I much French fiction has appeared in English translation almost simultaneously with its home publication, and such titles will be left for consideration along with our own contemporary products. Two titles, however, must be mentioned here, for one, Suzanne Roland-Manuel's *Le Trille du Diable,* has not been translated, and the other, André Gide's *Geneviève,* though published in France in 1936, did not come out in English until 1950.

In 1929 Gide's *School for Wives* showed the effect upon a submissive but intelligent girl of a love match with a man incapable of the least selflessness or intellectual honesty. A first sequel, *Robert* (1930), presented the husband's view of the marriage and of his own undeserved suffering. The second, *Geneviève,* gave the daughter's autobiography through adolescence. Geneviève begins her story at about fifteen with her infatuation for a schoolmate. Sara is the daughter of an artist and aspires to a stage career for which she appears well fitted. Geneviève's father sharply opposes the friendship because of Sara's bohemian background. Her mother, as always, stands between her daughter and her husband's dictatorial harshness, although her own approval of Sara's influence is not unqualified. Sara herself is emotionally unmoved, enjoying chiefly her domination of Geneviève and another girl whom she includes in a "secret society," bound by distinctly feministic vows. The affair reaches its climax when Sara's father exhibits a nude study, the face concealed by a hand mirror, for which the journals announce that his daughter was the model. Geneviève's already half-wakened senses catch fire from this revelation of her beloved's beauty, and she becomes ill with excitement and fury when her younger brother steals from her a magazine reproduction of the canvas.

Both mother and father are for once agreed that the association with Sara must be terminated, and Geneviève is withdrawn from her school and tutored by friends of the family. In the woman tutor she takes an intellectual interest only, for she is too closely bound to her mother to feel emotion for another woman of the same age.

Her reaction to the man, a married physician, is more complex. She is not conscious of sexual attraction, is in fact repelled by the idea of sex and marriage, largely from observing her parents' experience. She has also absorbed from Sara (an illegitimate child) a contempt for the conventions. As a feministic declaration of independence—on the conscious level—she asks her mentor to give her a child by him which will then be wholly hers to bring up. The good doctor, recognizing the immaturity and relative impersonality of her feeling for him, contrives to remain detached, fatherly, and helpful. Geneviève's mother confesses to her later that she herself at a particularly trying stage of her unhappy marriage, was for a time in love with the doctor, and one infers the profundity of the daughter's identification with her from the fact that the girl subconsciously turned to the same man.

Roland-Manuel's *Le Trille du Diable* (1946) is reminiscent of Lacretelle's *La Bonifas* in that its setting is a declining village and its heroine's history is traced from about 1870 until after the first World War. But Florence Benoit, unlike Marie Bonifas, is a ruthless egotist who never serves anyone's interest but her own. Spoiled daughter of a pretentious speculator, she anticipates wealth and a brilliant marriage as her due, and when M Benoit dies impoverished she makes life a veritable hell for her mother and younger brother. She then steals a mediocre but kindly man from his fiancée and leads him much the same sort of life, later attempting also to dominate and possess her only child, a son sufficiently like her to defy her in the end.

Her earliest conquest is Augustine Virot, daughter of her father's bookkeeper, a tall not too attractive girl with whom her association is innocent until after their hearing a charity concert in the neighboring city of Santerre. On this occasion Florence, then about fourteen, conceives a romantic infatuation for the violinist Soline, largely under the spell of his spectacularly brilliant encore, *Le Trille du Diable*. Although Florence does not see Soline again until she is past middle age, she nurses an undying passion for him which leads her into all manner of absurdities and against which all subsequent emotion seems pallid. As the title of the novel indicates, the author intends the meretricious musical number and its aftermath to epitomize an unwholesome flight from reality.

For several years after this fateful concert the two girls divert themselves by enacting love scenes between Florence and Soline, the latter impersonated by Augustine. Their caresses, progressively more intimate, finally become so necessary to both that, when Augustine enters normal school in Santerre, Florence fabricates excuses for visit-

ing her there every week. To achieve privacy for their clandestine
meetings she also invents elaborate lies which enable them to engage
a succession of cheap hotel rooms for the afternoon, and so to play
out their erotic 'Soline' improvisations without hindrance. The game
loses interest for Florence as soon as she begins her conscienceless
gamble for a husband, but she cannot let Augustine escape her, and
she spoils the unhappy girl's first engagement to a rather passive man
by writing him slanderous anonymous letters, the same device as
she has already employed to capture her own husband.

As for Augustine, the early playing of a male role plus the
humiliation of her engagement's unexplained ending turn her from
any thought of marriage until middle age, when after a dreary stretch
of elementary teaching, she finally accepts, *faute de mieux*, one of the
town's eccentrics at whom she had laughed as a girl.

As has been stated, the three or four subsequent variant French
titles, all of which appeared in English within a year after their
original publication, will be discussed with fiction in English.

CHAPTER VIII.

FICTION IN GERMANY

Before 1914

Insofar as secondhand information is to be trusted, it appears that female variance figured but twice in German fiction before the late 1890s. Lewandowski's *Sexualprobleme in der Modernen Literatur und Kunst . . . seit 1800* lists Johannes Flach's *Sappho: Greichische Novelle* (1886) under the heading of homosexual literature without further comment. The *Jahrbuch* during 1907 cited a passage from a romantic novel of the 1820's, Ernst Wagner's *Isidora,* which describes the same sort of innocent play between a princess and her maid-in-waiting as Lamartine pictured in "Regina," with the difference that the bond between Wagner's two girls appears wholly physical.[1] As Lewandowski's criterion for inclusion seems to have been overt sexual action, he may have omitted subtler studies of variance; and Hirschfeld's frankly biased journal was not too much concerned with discreditable bisexual records. Therefore it is possible that nineteenth-century German novels comparable to Balzac's *Seraphitus-Seraphita* or *Cousine Bette* were passed over as negligible. But when one recalls the emptiness of the record in English during the same period, and remembers that in the matter of feminine mores Germany resembled Victorian England rather than France, any exhaustive reading of German fiction promises rewards incommensurate with the labor involved.

Interest in female variance was, however, already alive when Hirschfeld's efforts in 1896 began to encourage its literary expression, as evidenced by the sudden outburst of fiction as well as poetry during the following decade. In 1897, Gabriele Reuter, a writer of ability, published a novel of autobiographical pattern, *Aus Guter Familie,*[2] which included among its heroine's early experiences a variant, possibly lesbian, attachment—the *Jahrbuch's* note does not specify. In 1900 Elisabeth Dauthendy produced *Vom Neuen Weib und Seiner Sittlichkeit*,[3] semi-narrative sketches like Colette's in *Ces Plaisirs*. The "New Woman's" ideal is a life of quiet intimacy with other women, free of the "brutal" relations with men which dull appreciation of more delicate emotional nuances. An interlude with a tribade, a 'confident, wise, almost manly' individual, at first promises fulfillment of all the writer's hopes. But a few amorous nights force her to recognize that, like a man, this woman cannot distinguish between crude sex and love. In the same year von Seydlitz used a case history from the 1840s—possibly from the same source as Kaspar's *Klinische Novellen* —as the basis for *Pierre's Ehe: Psychologisches Probleme*.[4] Its hero is unfortunate enough to love an odd, hard, masculine girl who finally succumbs to his persistence, but is unable to cooperate sexually, and presently the partners find themselves in love with the same woman. In the course of a jealous brawl Pierre believes he has killed his wife; he makes a successful escape into the merchant marine and dies in Saigon without learning that he is innocent of manslaughter. The wife, now a confirmed transvestist, lives out her life as a valet without further emotional complication.

In 1900 also, Alfred Meebold included a tragic variant novelette, "Dr. Erna Redens Thorheit und Erkentniss,"[5] in the volume *Allerhand Volk*. The larger portion of the tale presents Dr. Erna's unhappy heterosexual affair with a fellow medical student. To recover from her consequent depression she travels in Italy with an artist, Lucie, who has been her particularly warm and eager confidante. The latter is a homosexual, but she manages to conceal the nature of her feelings until the two meet another woman, an artist long acquainted with Lucie. In the course of a quarrel this woman reveals Lucie's secret. Although Dr. Erna has now recovered from her heterosexual disappointment and exhibits a sympathetic understanding of Lucie's emotion, she is unable to return it in kind, and in despondency Lucie kills herself. Dr. Erna then returns to Germany full of crusading zeal against those who persecute homosexuals. This bears slight but sufficient resemblance to Borys's later *Carlotta Noll* in French to suggest that both may have been based on a single known episode, or that the one influenced the other. The German version, be it noted, is by far the more sympathetic.

In 1901 a Danish novel by O. W. Moller was translated under the German title *Wer Kann Dafur?*[6] This traces the efforts of a German officer's daughter to overcome a lesbian attraction and marry a young astronomer in the Heidelberg Observatory. She becomes deeply attached to her suitor but cannot respond physically; and so they part, although because of her masculine temperament and interests they are much closer in spirit than most married couples. Involving little dramatic action, this psychological study seems to have been of as high quality as Reuter's *Aus Guter Familie*. In contrast, August Niemann's *Zwei Frauen*[7] involves an infatuation between a married woman and the brilliant music student whom her husband, head of a conservatory, has accepted as a pupil despite her apprehensive protests. The danger she foresaw materializes, and from there on the story becomes what the reviewer calls 'an imitation of Belot's *Mlle Giraud* which is hardly a credit to German letters.'

Much more interesting, in view of its author's subsequent reputation, was Jacob Wassermann's *Geschichte der Junge Renate Fuchs* (1900), and it is a matter of regret that this volume, though it ran to several editions, has proved inaccessible. The *Jahrbuch's* review mentions a lesbian affair between two minor characters, a university student of political economy and the daughter of 'one of Europe's most famous courtesans.'[8] A puritanic critic later describes the heroine herself as "wading through all manner of filth,"[9] but makes no reference to homosexual experience either on her part or anyone's else.

The year 1903 saw the publication of three lesbian titles. In Maria Eichhorn's *Fraülein Don Juan*[10] the heroine's strong and domineering sensual nature is roused in adolescence by homosexual affairs, but she later knows many men and never returns to her lesbian practices. Maria Janitschek's "Neue Erziehung und Alte Moral"[11] in *Die Neue Eva* is the story of an orphan girl raised among seven foster brothers as one of them and without much supervision, so that she is enlightened early about matters of sex. At puberty she is abruptly cautioned by her foster mother against looseness with men and given a fearful picture of the fate of the unmarried mother. The resulting emotional conflict is severe, but at sixteen, when she shares her room and bed with a charming feminine guest, 'at last in Agathe's arms Seffi found a lovely peace.' Upon being harshly berated for this innocent-seeming play, she defies authority. 'It is your own upbringing that has driven me into the arms of my friend—now leave me there!'

An inferior *Sind Es Frauen?*[12] by Aimée Duc pictures a large group of openly lesbian women in a German university town. Most of them are past the teens and slightly reminiscent of Peladan's group centered about the Russian Simzerla, especially in that they spend much time discussing all aspects of sexual psychology. Most of them are foreigners—there seems to be a tendency in second-rate homosexual fiction to saddle some other country than the author's own with the origin of lesbian characters. The leader of this group is Minotschka Fernandoff, a Russian 'just released from three years of marriage,' after having discovered that in sexual relations she needs to play the man. There is also Annie who has "escaped" marriage after only six months, Bertha Cohn whose beloved "Fritz" has moved in the other direction, getting engaged and finding she prefers a male lover, and Dr. Tatjana, mature and wise in the new medical psychology. And last, living with Minotschka, is a Polish music student, Countess Marta Kinzey, on whose account the Russian girl has come to Germany. The plot proceeds through a separation between Marta and Minotschka, during which the latter resists the advances of an actress and the former enters into a marriage of diplomatic necessity with a man who 'knows all about her' and is her husband in name only. In the end after much painful misunderstanding the two are reunited, to find that each has been faithful to the other. This is one of the volumes about which the *Jahrbuch's* reviewer was most enthusiastic from a psychological viewpoint.

In 1901 *Weiberbeute*[18] was published in Budapest over the ambiguous pseudonym, Luz Frauman, and later it was considered worthy of a 4,000-word summary in Magnus Hirschfeld's *Die Transvestiten*. Here transvestism plays a significant role for the first time since Rachilde's novels, to the first of which this bears considerable resemblance. As in *Monsieur Vénus,* double inversion of sexual roles somewhat blurs the homosexual aspect; however, the period during which both significant characters are living as women justifies its inclusion here. Nana, an athletic but seductive girl reminiscent of Maupin, marries from cool expedience the wealthiest and most enslaved of her admirers. Thereby she incurs the implacable hatred of his son, a delicate boy 'with the face of a Japanese girl,' who lays an idolized mother's death to his father's dalliance with Nana. The father would ship his son to Australia, but Nana offers an alternative. She is skilled in hypnotism; she will throw the boy into a trance, and by suggestion will eradicate all memory, not only of his hatred but of his sex, leaving him convinced that he is a girl. 'Conviction is the very essence of a human being,' she says, 'and so shapes growth that after this the boy's male development will be arrested and he will be virtually a woman.'

This fantastic plan is carried through, and for three years the changeling, dressed as a girl, is Nana's passionate adorer. In the meantime Nana has borne her husband a son who will be his heir unless the older boy is restored to his proper status. This dilemma naturally troubles the father and when in addition his wife's charming 'companion' is demanded in marriage, he decides the mummery has gone far enough. But he reckons without Nana. Exerting her hypnotic powers now upon him, she moves him to shoot himself, inherits his fortune, consigns her own son to a boarding school, and sets out upon a world tour with her 'girl companion.' In love with the latter from the outset, she now considers releasing him from the hypnotic spell so that they can marry, but she fears a return of his former antagonism, and, in view of her own seniority, she decides to assume the man's role herself. Always with the aid of hypnotism she achieves this end, marries her stepson, and sets up a household. Presently the desire for a child seizes the couple. Nana is for adoption but the 'wife' objects. And now, as Hirschfeld says, 'comes a climax of fantasy so grotesque that the imagination conceiving it must really have been warped.' Through her convenient powers Nana induces illusory pregnancy in the "wife," bears the child herself, and contrives to get it into the "mother's" arms at the correct psychological and physical moment.

But now an unforeseen complication develops. The "wife" hails the son as a girl. The necessity for concealing the child's sex from everyone throughout its childhood puts a grave strain on Nana, but her ingenuity is equal to the task, and the family enjoys an uncommonly happy life for a matter of twenty years. When illness overtakes Nana she refuses a physician, and only on her deathbed pours out the truth to her "wife." Though the hypnotic spell is now broken, the latter's mental "set" is so completely established that he takes the story for mere delirious babbling. The author, Hirschfeld assures us, solves the two survivors' problem as ingeniously as he contrived it, though it is difficult to imagine how. Aside from the stepson's years of subjective lesbianism before marriage, the novel's most noteworthy point is its presentation of hypnotism as able to effect complete endocrine change, an exaggerated foreshadowing of modern psychosomatic theory, and quite opposed to the then-popular hereditary hypothesis.

The remaining handful of minor novels before 1910 are of the sort which invariably appear upon a theme already proved profitable. *Urningsliebe,* by "O. Liebetreu"[14] is a masochistic tale of a girl who gives herself, her strength, and her money to a succession of five or six loves, and ends in prison serving a three year sentence for an offense committed by the last of them, in order to save her friend's good name. Erich Muhsam's *Psychologie der Erbtante*[15] is a half-satiric tragedy of a masculine woman of middle age, rather like Bonifas, who commits suicide because of a mysterious 'unlucky love' (supposedly heterosexual), in order to leave all her property to the girl

with whom she had no luck. 'Theodor' (probably Anna) Ruling's
"Ratzelhaft,"[16] one of three novelettes in her *Welcher unter Euch
ohne Sünde Ist,* also ends with a suicide. It is the story of a girl whose
family has discovered her lesbian relations with a beloved friend
and has separated the pair. *Dreiunddreissig Scheusale,*[17] published
first in Leningrad (then, of course, St. Petersburg), was the work
of a Russian actress, Annibal Sinowjewa. In it, a lesbian woman
has lived for some time with a younger girl in a relation so perfect
that she never doubts its permanence, and from sheer pride in her
beloved's beauty she encourages the girl to model for a life class
of thirty-three men. The girl, as thoroughly schooled in erotic
virtuousity as was the *Girl with the Golden Eyes,* becomes the common mistress of the artist group and never returns to her feminine
lover. (This was not the sole, or even the first, Russian notice of
feminine variance. Tolstoi had skirted it earlier in *Anna Karenina*
with the brief emotional flame lit in Kitty by Varenka, and Dostoievsky
came a step closer in *A Friend of the Family,* with the mutual
attraction between Nyelochka and her friend. Both of these incidents
occurred in late adolescence.)

During this same decade two major artists produced a series of
works all of which are still freely available in German, and one,
at least, in English. The symbolists in France did not touch upon
female variance, unless one thinks of *Monsieur Vénus, Méphistophéla,*
or *La Gynandre* as distantly related to symbolism, but these two men
included the theme in spreading canvases of definitely symbolic
style.

The first is the work of Heinrich Mann, older brother of the more
famous Thomas. His *Die Göttinnen* (1902-03) is trilogy within whose
epic sweep he attempts to include every experience open to a woman
of his time. Its subtitle is "Die Drei Romane der Herzogin von Assy:
Diana; Minerva; Venus." But it is not under the aegis of Diana, as one
might imagine, that the countess meets lesbian experience. The first
volume (the only one available in English) is concerned with her
devotion to the cause of Freedom, not for women, but political freedom for all oppressed people. Under the spell of Minerva in the
second book her interest is turned to the arts, including letters.
Though these two works are far from empty of dramatic emotional
episodes, it is Venus who leads the countess at last to seek every
possible form of love. After experience with several widely different
male lovers, the most satisfying of whom is a younger man who 'thinks
like her,' she returns to her mansion in Naples and takes 'the one
lover not yet tried—the crowd.'

She fills her house with beautiful young people in lieu of canvases and statues.

> 'An unbroken stream of bodies which promised pleasure passed through her bedroom—slim delicate bodies and athletic, well-trained ones; the yielding firmness of girls and the delicate bones and melting flesh of children. The fisherman from Santa Lucia followed the clubman. The warm golden peasant girl with coarse heavy brows above her quiet eyes left the impress of her robust figure on the cushions where [a titled beauty] had lain; and she with her cold perfection interrupted the convulsive ecstacy of [another girl's] first passion of surrender and abandon.'[18]

When this comparatively tame promiscuity palls, the countess turns to sadism. Though never indulging actively herself, she provokes frenzied jealousy among her own and others' lovers, and the resulting violence would equal, were it not merely suggested rather than amplified, any recorded by "the divine marquis." After all this, by way of final experiment, the countess has staged for herself alone, and at enormous cost, a lesbian bout between two expert performers, girls already so spent with depravity that their flesh is 'like a no longer fresh glove over a masterfully sculptured hand.' At the end of their act they collapse, deeply unconscious, but the countess merely gazes down at them with weary disillusion.

> ' "Is this all? Or have these sweet cheats, ripest of the lot, withheld some final sweetness? Alas, this fruit is like all the others. I myself shall never pluck it, and I would its taste were already gone from my lips." '[19]

The chief significance of this episode is its serving as climax to all that has gone before, evidently representing for the author the ultimate depths of sexual depravity.

The second major German author is Frank Wedekind, who, like Balzac, presents three sharply contrasting pictures of female variance. Comparable in innocence to *Seraphitus-Seraphita* is the devotion in *Mine-ha-ha* (1909) of a child dancer to her ballet mistress, a woman in the late twenties, oriental in coloring, boyish of build, and military in the ruthlessness of her discipline. For sheer magic in imparting the illusion of reality to fantastic circumstances this novelette has few equals, but attention must be confined here to its variant aspects. For a half-dozen years, between seven and fourteen, Hidalla lives only for her fortnightly ballet lessons, and the intervening days pass in a maze of gruelling practice and bemused reverie. The latter, however, is not sexual. When Hidalla reaches the age—about eleven—for nightly appearance with the ballet troupe, objective self-expression partially relieves the intensity of her introverted emotion. As soon as she leaves the conventual rigors of the school for life as an élite demi-mondaine her outlook is completely altered. Although she feels no love for her wealthy male protector, she watches—at the age of perhaps sixteen—from his loge in the great municipal opera house while her former idol dances starring roles, and feels only a reminiscent warmth, as much for her own remembered obsession as for its one-time object.

She skirts the edge of two other experiences which serve to define the stringent ban upon lesbian intimacies in the training school. In pre-adolescence she feels a transient tenderness for a companion, but the latter is terrified at a half-proferred kiss during a twilight stroll. Does Hidalla not know the penalty for "going with" another girl? The sour and hideous servants who do the dormitory housework are there because in their training days they "went with" girls, thereby ruining forever their chances in that mysterious but alluring world beyond the gates into which the school's finished products are released—though neither of the children has any idea what their place in it is to be. Hidalla's second attraction is to one of the younger children whom she sees enter the school at seven as she did, shy and bewildered, and (like Claudine) she feels for this reflection of her earlier self a maternal as well as passionate love. She is barely adolescent at the time, but the love-starved life of these orphans whose existence is bounded by the Spartan walls of the school makes some such overflow of the heart inevitable. The small hours of a night that she spends crouched at the foot of the little girl's bed, struggling with the hunger to go closer, restrained only by the knowledge that to do so may mean the child's ruin, make a scene of delicate intensity equalling any in literature.

Wedekind's second variant woman is the tailored and monocled English countess slavishly bound to Lulu, central figure of his symbolic dramas, *Earth Spirit* and *Pandora's Box*. Lulu represents amoral, or, one might say, purely biological Woman. She is irresistable to the male, and knowledge of her brings brief ecstasy and lasting devastation. But she is as much victim of the force within her as are the men she enslaves. She is driven to murder in self-defense; then, fleeing the law in more and more desperate circumstances, she herself is murdered by an underworld wretch modeled upon Jack

the Ripper. The English woman alone of all her lovers goes unre-
warded throughout years of abject devotion, for Lulu is too completely Woman to feel any response save to Man. The countess not
only exhausts her fortune in the service of her beloved, but at one
point voluntarily contracts cholera so that she can enter the hospital
where Lulu is hiding from justice; thus permitting Lulu to escape
by assuming her clothing and identity. (It could be that the plot of
the later *Urningsliebe* had its germ in this devotion.) In the end,
realizing that Lulu has always wilfully used her, the countess attempts
suicide, but Lulu feels neither pity nor compunction. She tells Jack—
the man who finally kills them both—that the countess is her sister
and insane, but his sophisticated intuition suggests the truth. He
strokes the Englishwoman's head and mutters 'Poor creature,' quite
the only sympathy she has ever received. It does not, however, prevent
Jack's knifing her when she attempts to defend Lulu against him.
Just before this happens, in a solitary monologue, the countess says:

> 'I am not a man, my body has nothing in common with
> those of men. Is it that I have a man's soul? But tormented
> men have small and narrow souls, and I know that is not my
> case, when I have given up everything, made every sacrifice.'[29]

She resolves to leave Lulu, who, she realizes, has from the beginning
felt an uncontrollable antipathy to her. She will study law and
implication being, of women like herself rather than the *Ewig-
devote the rest of her life to fighting for the rights of women—the
Weibliche*. It is at this point that the apache's knife ends her
unhappy existence.

In 1911 Wedekind published the satiric and still more symbolic
drama, *Franziska: A Modern Mystery*, in which the primary theme
is a woman's struggle for individual independence. The protagonist
Franziska, a girl just under twenty when the play opens, has been
irrevocably prejudiced against the traditional feminine lot by childhood circumstances. She has also refused marriage with two men,
one a physician who assumed that her surrender to him meant abject
adoration, the other an elderly nobleman from whom she accepted
an insurance policy securing the future of any child her free life
might produce. She is bent upon living with all the independence
of a man. Opportunity offers when she meets Veit Kunz, a theatrical
manager whose sudden bursting into her drawing room out of a
thunderstorm marks him as Mephistopheles to her Faust. He sees
in her boyish bravura the possibility of exploiting her in the world

of entertainment. Until lately, he says, audiences wanted women with lovely breasts, shoulders and arms. But his hunch is that taste is changing, and his business is to keep one jump ahead of the mode. Interestingly enough, it is as a singer he means to feature her, indicating a taste for feminine tenors a good decade earlier in Europe than in the United States, where they were not fashionable until the Twenties.

While studying voice and posing as a man, 'Franz' has a tavern affair with a young prostitute which is cut off at its zenith when the girl is shot by a jealous lover. Her next adventure is as the husband of a middle-class heiress, who wants, not a romantic hero, but a respectable husband and *pater familias*. When children fail to appear, the woman blames her husband's fondness for a young dancer, and threatens to kill the girl unless she lets "Franz" alone. From a scene between Franziska and Veit Kunz, however, it appears that he and she have been intimate for a year, and a child is on the way. Franziska is resentful. Marriage has proved irksome because of her wife's desire for a family, and has limited her freedom with both sexes. A child will be the final handicap. Kunz tells her that her wife is a much worthier soul than she, and that motherhood will bring more maturity than multiple adventures or his own dramatic training. However, he says that if she persists on her chosen path, vanity, selfishness and ambition such as hers are the drives that produce successful artists. An enemy informs her wife that Franziska is a woman, and the shock of the revelation causes the wife to commit suicide, setting Franziska free.

The third act of the drama moves to the estate of a wealthy nobleman, amateur playwright and owner of a private theatre, who has applied to Kunz for the services of his intriguing "male" star. Most pertinent to the present study is an interlude in which Franziska, in eighteenth-century man's costume, appears to the count in a species of symbolic vision as the wish-fulfillment of his most secret dreams. She tells him she is neither boy nor woman, but the ideal of all those incapable of real passion; for love of another cannot go beyond love of self in these "Wunchlosen." This technical description of narcissism (along with the drastic effect upon Franziska of early hatred of her father) shows Wedekind's familiarity with the then very new doctrines of psychoanalysis.

The remaining acts show Franziska first sufficiently feminized by early pregnancy to play the part of Delilah on the stage, and to become infatuated and run off with the actor cast as Samson, who treats her with rough and contemptuous masculine superiority. Veit

Kunz is prostrated. At fifty he sees his lifelong conviction controverted that happy sexual and professional association on a footing of equality must guarantee a permanent union. His brilliant intellectual acumen is outplayed by female biology—Woman beats the devil!—and he is barely saved from suicide. Finally Franziska, persuaded to abandon her career for the sake of her son's health, is shown living in rural poverty with him. She refuses support from either Kunz or "Samson," each of whom is sure her child is his, and accepts the protection of an ascetic artist who paints her as the madonna. Here Wedekind hits the narcissist complex dead center. It is proof against both homosexual and heterosexual experience and only partially resolved by maternity, since she can tolerate only a man weaker than herself and one romantically deluded about her.

Because of the Eulenberg scandal in 1907 literary reference to homosexuality was checked for a time in Germany, and no doubt only Wedekind's established reputation and his disparaging treatment of the theme made the theatrical production of *Franziska* possible in 1911. By 1914 Dr. Kurt Heller was asking in the *Jahrbuch:* "Wo bleibt der homoerotik Roman?"[21] He was referring to male homosexuality, and he deprecated the moralistic tone of Thomas Mann's *Death in Venice,* considering it disappointing from the author of *Buddenbrooks.* His answer to his own rhetorical question was that no sympathetic work could clear the hurdle of state censorship, for even a wholly "spiritual" treatment must be defined by some contrast with the sensual. Only true literary freedom could provide incentive for creative writing of first quality.

Until the post-war change in government no such freedom prevailed. In 1917 Sophie Hochstetter's *Selbstanzeige: Die letzte Flamme*[22] had to be printed privately. When it was attacked by a reviewer in *Der Tag,* the author defended the criticized "urnische Beanlagt" as an essential stage in the self-comprehension which was the theme of the whole novel. She also offered to supply the volume gratis to any interested reader, an indication that it had been excluded from public sale. With 1918, however, the ban was relaxed, and during the 1920s Germany shared with the rest of the western world a period of sexual freedom which ended only with the growing influence of Hitler in the 1930s. Even so, post-war sentiment in the English-speaking countries made German material unwelcome there, and the homosexual novels and magazines which abounded in Germany for a decade gained little circulation abroad.

With Hitler's ascendancy these titles were so soon obliterated that it is difficult now to find more than the mere record in German trade bibliographies of their original publication. This is especially true because in 1921 Hirschfeld's *Jahrbuch* (by then a *Vierteljahrschaft*) ceased publication. All efforts of the Humanitären Wissenschaftliche Komittee for repeal of the anti-homosexual Paragraph 175 of the Prussian criminal code had failed, and the organization was disheartened by the failure. Moreover, the fields of history and biography had been well covered in factual articles during the twenty-two years of the journal's existence. And as for its function of re porting current homosexual belles-lettres, that was abandoned even before its own death because such literature was regularly reviewed in 'other journals,' (e.g., *Die Freundin, Die Freundschaft, Freundschaft und Freiheit*—later *Eros—Junggesellen: mit die Beiblättern "Frauenliebe,"* and *Transvestit.*) These are now almost completely lost, so that even descriptive notes on the literature in question are not accessible today.

Post-War Gleanings

Of the few lesbian novels to reach the United States one of the best was Anna Elisabet Weirauch's three-volume *Scorpion,* which appeared in Germany between 1919 and 1921. It was translated a dozen years later in an abridged edition as two separate titles, *The Scorpion* (1932) and *The Outcast* (1933). Though slightly inferior in literary quality to *Marie Bonifas,* it shows equal mastery in accounting for and tracing the full history of an exclusively variant woman. The scene of Metta Rudloff's childhood is a dreary city household consisting of her ineffectual father and a spiteful puritanic spinster aunt. Her care is entrusted to a nursery governess hired for no sounder reason than that the child takes an instant fancy to her. The young woman exhibits a facile affection which quickly enslaves her little charge, but her emotions are wholly bound to a cashiered military officer, who controls her completely and who alternately neglects her and lives on her bounty. To supply him with funds, she more than once pawns the Rudloff's seldom-used family silver, employing Metta to secure it from its cupboard and taking her along on visits to the pawnbroker. When the misdemeanor is detected, the child is seriously involved, and the uncomprehended scandal, plus the loss of her beloved Fräulein, leaves a lasting scar.

During puberty and adolescence Metta attends a public school, but her father's snobbery discourages friendships with her mates, and she grows up a bored and lonely introvert. Nearing twenty, she meets, at the home of relatives, a handsome and enigmatic woman

a decade her senior and falls violently in love with her. Soon she is
spending most of her time in her new friend's rooms in a pension, and
she is spurred for the first time to real intellectual effort in order
to keep up with Olga's wide interests. (Among these is the life and
work of Karoline von Günderode, for whom Olga has come to feel an
almost mystic affinity which stirs Metta to jealous fury.) At the
pension Metta also meets a Dr. Petermann, musical aesthete and
cripple, who frequently plays his violin for the two young women.

Discovering that Olga is financially embarrassed, Metta contrives
to take foreign language lessons from her, but the two spend most
of the funds so earned on concerts, opera, and long country excursions. On one of the latter, Metta notices that they are followed
by a man. Her friend becomes distraught at the discovery and
betrays that she has suffered the same experience before. The mystified
younger girl on arriving at home is forbidden by her father to see
Olga again or to leave the house, and presently she is visited by a
psychiatrist. Under his questioning, she suddenly recalls that she
has pawned the silver, following her childhood pattern, in order to
redeem a gold cigarette case Olga was forced to sacrifice to momentary
need. This object, a gift from an earlier beloved friend of Olga's,
is decorated with a jeweled scorpion, the zodiacal symbol of passion
and death under which Olga was born. The psychiatrist delivers
a subtle lecture on the destructive effects of emotional friendships
between women. The mysterious man, he explains, was a detective
employed by Metta's father, who for some time has had the two
girls under surveillance, and to gain legal power over Olga, has bought
up her not-inconsiderable debts. Metta is to be sent to an uncle's in
the country so that separation may cure her of her unhealthy infatuation. Eventually, she is assured, she will thank her family and the
doctor for having saved her from ruin. She is forced to leave Berlin
without either explaining her departure or saying goodbye to Olga.

At her uncle's she sets herself one goal: to escape and return to
Olga. Before long she has so ingratiated herself with the household
that it is not too difficult to obtain money secretly from her uncle's
desk and to reach the railroad station. In Berlin, Olga meets her,
but instead of the warm welcome Metta anticipated, she merely
remonstrates against the madness of Metta's flight and refuses to
harbor her, knowing the girl will at once be tracked to her rooms.
After a very bad quarter-hour, however, Metta succeeds in persuading
Olga to accompany her in an impulsive flight. The two take the
next train scheduled for departure and get off at a station elected

by chance. In the modest hamlet so discovered they spend a few ecstatic days of veritable honeymoon.

Hitherto they have exchanged no caresses—indeed, Metta has often been deeply hurt by Olga's show of brusque coldness. Now at last she learns the true significance of her own feelings and of the older girl's previous restraint. Though Olga felt a reciprocal passion, she has had previous difficulties because of an affair with a woman, and she dreaded risking another such ordeal. She declares that never again can she endure "to be stripped naked in public." Once enlightened, Metta determines that they shall never be separated. Within six months she will attain her majority and be mistress of a large maternal inheritance. She writes her father of her whereabouts and her intentions, asking for temporary funds, but assuring Olga that if they are refused she will raise money on her expectations.

Her answer is a telegram from the aunt telling her that her father has had a stroke occasioned by the shock of her "robbing" her uncle, and that he is dying. Metta suspects a trap, but returns to find the news true, and lives through several hideous days before her father's death ends the nightmare. During the subsequent night, half-delirious from exhaustion and her aunt's vicious reproaches, she slips away to Olga's rooms for solace. Here she is found at dawn by the aunt, the wronged uncle, and detectives. She declares her intention of never leaving her friend, but Olga, in the face of public denunciation, fails to come to her support, merely insisting that she is without responsibility in the whole matter.

Confined at home and half-ill, Metta finds herself suddenly surrounded by medical books and pamphlets on homosexuality, all condemnatory or scandalmongering. Despite the bitter blow dealt her love and pride by her friend's defection, she writes Olga repeatedly, but receives no answer. After a time, sickened by her reading and wounded by Olga's silence to the point of apathy, she allows herself, under pressure from her aunt, to become engaged. The socially noteworthy match is featured in the news, and on the eve of her marriage she has word from Petermann of Olga's suicide. Olga had, of course, had none of her letters, but had received many scurrilous anonymous threats in which Metta recognizes the hand of her hated aunt, and Olga had, moreover, been prosecuted by the Rudloff estate which held her debts. Shocked into sudden hard maturity, Metta sells the family house, settles an allowance on her aunt, and leaves Berlin, her only mementos Olga's "scorpion" cigaret case and the revolver with which she shot herself.

The first German volume ends here, and the second opens in an
unspecified large city, which in all probability actually represented
another aspect of Berlin. There Metta, completely on her own,
attempts to adjust to independent life. She plunges resolutely into
solitary study, but without the incentive of discussion with Olga she
finds the effort empty. Consequently she determines to "learn by
living," and allows herself to be drawn into a bohemian group,
several members of which room in her own pension. Among these
artists, journalists, and entertainers she finds a sexual freedom which
profoundly shocks her, but laying the shock to her hitherto sheltered
life, she refuses to withdraw, and shrugs off the half-maternal admoni-
tions of a "respectable" coterie in the house. She is presently involved
with a night club singer, Gisela, to whom she is drawn by learning
that the girl's obvious physical wasting and reputed drug addiction
are the results of hopeless love for a woman. Their affair is essentially
a matter of mutual physical assuagement, each girl being still in
love with someone else. It is developed slightly more in the German
volume than in the English *Scorpion* of which it forms the second
part, but is not seriously expurgated in the latter.

A much more vital attachment begins between Metta and a
handsome sculptress, Sophie, but is broken off by the latter because
she has lived for years with an invalid who is completely dependent
on her. This woman was Sophie's salvation in a desperate period
of her youth, and would give up the struggle to live if she felt
herself no longer needed by her partner. Left essentially friendless
by Sophie's withdrawal, Metta drifts into a restless quest for diversion
among the group of professional entertainers and homosexuals of
whom Gisela is one. In the course of making a round of night clubs
Metta becomes wretchedly ill from experimenting with cocaine, and
recognizing amused contempt in the eyes of attractive strangers of
the social class in which she was raised, she goes home filled with
self-loathing to employ Olga's cherished revolver and rejoin her lost
love. She is checked by the ministrations of one of the "respectable"
older women in the house, who confesses to a deep (though entirely
innocent) affection for her, tells her she is too young to be knocking
about alone, and sends her to stay with a sister in Hamburg whose
husband is an alderman and whose daughter is a sheltered adolescent.

In this new milieu Metta is at first terrified lest she be followed
by Gisela, but her fears prove groundless, and she is soon acting
the model young lady, though she has need to guard her allusions
to places recently frequented and uncensored books she read with
Olga. She soon discovers that the daughter of the house is, beneath

a seraphic exterior, as sophisticated as any of her late associates. The girl is carrying on an affair with a man twice her age whose charm briefly touches even Metta. She also constantly presses Metta to confess to lesbian tastes and experience, declaring that she "can always recognize the type," and doing her best to seduce Metta by skillful caresses. This Hamburg interlude ends with a weekend trip on which Metta is supposedly Gwen's chaperone. The fascinating man joins the expedition secretly, and proves a connoisseur of liquors and an adept at clandestine contrivance. In the girls' room, Gwen, spurred by alcohol and the spring night, makes an unusually insistent play for Metta, but just as the latter is about to yield, the connecting door opens to admit the man, and she recognizes the whole trip as "a put up job" to seduce her into a party à trois. Utterly revolted, she makes a clean break with this life also, and searches further for some emotional stability and peace.

The third German volume (of which *The Outcast*, in English, is a literal and complete translation) shows Metta in a mountain town where she has made no personal contacts and has told no one anything of herself or her past. Falling in love with the beauty of the region, she buys land and decides to build; consequently, she must go to Berlin for legal and architectural advice. There, renewing connections with the crippled Petermann, she meets in his pension a woman who reminds her strongly of Olga and who produces almost as instantaneous an emotional impact. Metta soon learns that this is the friend who originally gave Olga the scorpion cigaret case, and that it was Corona who terminated the association because she believes it is always better to end love while it is still beautiful than to let it die. Corona has not even known of Olga's death until she sees the scorpion in Metta's hands.

Instead of returning to the mountains to watch her hitherto thrilling new house take form, Metta lingers in Berlin in Corona's toils. She finds this woman less intellectual and harder than Olga, and dislikes intensely the exhibitionistic group of lesbians, some tailored, some merely histrionic, with whom her new flame associates. When she finally discovers that Corona is still half-involved in an old affair with a married woman, and is also encouraging the advances of a Russian girl in the pension, Metta flees to her mountains and lives quite alone in her new house, save for visits from Petermann and another man of tragic history met at Sophie's before the end of that association. A passionately-anticipated visit from Corona, which Metta hopes may result in the latter's taking up residence with her away from urban distractions, proves a bitter

disappointment. Corona finally confesses that she is incurably restless
and empty, a huntress who is free of an actual pain of physical
need only while she is in process of snaring a new victim. She asks
the privilege of using Metta's mountaintop as an occasional sanctuary.
Thereafter Metta settles in, not happy but at least relatively serene,
to live alone and provide temporary peace for such of her friends as
care to seek her out.

Comparison of this novel with *La Bonifas* is interesting because,
despite their similarity in basic theme and the influence of initial
traumatic incident, they are so widely different. Even the first incidents illustrate the difference: in *La Bonifas,* the physical violence
of suicide enacted before the child's very eyes; in *The Scorpion,*
a psycho-social teapot-tempest involving the child only through her
cross-questioning by a children's psychiatrist, which she meets with
passive resistance. In the one novel a female creature is endowed
with all the extroverted tastes, interests, and abilities usually considered male. In the other the female creature is wholly feminine
save for her sexual inclinations. Accordingly, Weirauch stresses the
influence of environment. None of her lesbians are really masculine
in appearance, and only one male homosexual looks born to the
role. On the other hand, biographical vignettes are adroitly introduced
to account for almost every variant in the story, and these are even
more effective because they are not notably Freudian in pattern.
Indeed, this novel's quality lies in its verisimilitude, an effect naturally
easier for a woman writer in this field than for a man. The inevitable conclusion drawn from these two novels together is that
sexual variance is not so much an inborn factor in a life pattern
as it is a concomitant result of other aspects of personality and
experience.

A second German lesbian item, *Die Schwester,* is a drama of 1924
which in style shows the influence of Wedekind. The author, Hans
Kaltneker, takes care to present in a foreword his convictions about
homosexuality: it represents the height of egotism, the antithesis of
the Christian spirit, for to love one's own sex is to withdraw from
the common life of humanity and imprison oneself in a futile
sterility. He doubtless felt it necessary to voice this reassurance
because in the first act of the play his attitude to the heroine appears
wholly sympathetic. The homosexual Ruth loves her young stepsister, Lo, but controls her feelings until chance throws them together for a night. She is subsequently cast out by her stepfather,
and his daughter is hastily married to the first available man. Ruth
then lives with a lesbian artist, whose 'eyes and mouth were shadowed

by black melancholy,' and who tells her that lasting love is impossible for their sort—they can gain satisfaction only through debauchery. The two visit a homosexual tavern—presented symbolically after the fashion of Wedekind—and Ruth chooses among the commercial dancing partners a girl who resembles her lost stepsister. As she is very drunk, she imagines this is her sister's spirit, and she "receives a message" that Lo really loves her, but advises her to abandon her vicious way of life and devote herself to helping other lost women. She later learns that Lo had died but a few moments before she received this mystic communication, and takes it for a supernatural revelation. Accordingly she becomes a nurse in a women's hospital for veneral disease, but her unconcealable preference for the gentler, slim, young patients breeds antagonism, and when she herself becomes infected she is discharged. Too ill to work, she is violated by men and robbed even of her clothing. She ends in a woman's prison where her dying act is to give her one remaining garment to an ungrateful drunken prostitute. Thus, she is redeemed through having sacrificed herself for others.

In 1927 Frank Theiss, in *Interlude*, employed a lesbian episode to explain the failure of his hero's first marriage. The wife had, at eighteen, been "entrapped" by an older woman highly esteemed in the community. "The enticements and snares must have been cunningly laid, for it was always unthinkable to Kurt . . . that Sabina could have been in love with her."[23] When, after six months or so, the affair came to light, "the furious father would certainly have called on the police authorities if any power of police or judiciaries could have helped," a subtle thrust at the injustice of legal penalty for homosexual men as compared to none for women.

The parents then married their daughter off to the first available man, but the affair had left a scar. This was not the frigidity one might expect. On the contrary, it was "an alert and conscious, a more than mature . . . an erotic atmosphere"[24] which made the girl unusually "beguiling" to men. Still, she was not happy in her marriage, and the explanation given is that she had been physically awakened without knowing love. Thus, she was drawn to her husband also without love, and their marriage was the "exchange of a conventional form of excitement." Once she had obtained a divorce and married someone whose appeal for her was complete, not merely physical, she "became another person. This voluptuous glitter was all gone, she was just sweet and charming."[25] While the handling of the episode is somewhat hasty and superficial, the argument it presents against pre-marital lesbian experience is more

subtle and rather more convincing than many one meets in anti-
variant fiction.

A sterner condemnation of lesbianism came from Herbert Eulenberg in "Der Maler Rayski," a novelette in the volume *Casanova's
Letzte Abenteuer* (1929), in which he presents a domineering lesbian
woman of almost sadistic ruthlessness. This titled landowner has
long kept a younger cousin-companion in lesbian bondage. She
loathes men, but must have an heir to inherit her properties, and
hits upon the device of inducing her beloved to bear a child whom she
can then adopt. Since the sire must be of good stock, she selects
a contemporary artist whose qualifications please her, summons him
to paint portraits of her and her companion, and contrives to get
the latter married to him by stressing the excellence of the girl's
financial prospects. The couple fall genuinely in love, and, under the
influence of normal love, the girl blooms from strained pallor into
perfect health and loveliness. As soon as a child is expected, however,
the older woman secures a series of such advantageous commissions
for the artist that he must be absent until after his child's birth.
She then denies him access to the infant—what right has any man
to the child in whose begetting he has played but a momentary
part, while the woman has carried it for nine months and must
nurse it for as many more? To clinch the matter she tells him of
the long years of intimacy between herself and his wife. Now he
feels that his bride's innocence was all pretence, and that anyone
who could have deceived him about so black a past can never
be trusted. He makes off, proudly refusing any monetary settlement
then or later, and deteriorates into a worthless drifter because of
this devastating blow to his self-respect. The two women remain
together, apparently happy, since motherhood provides the girl with
some normal interest.

Since the film *Mädchen in Uniform* had fairly wide circulation
in this country, Christa Winsloe's corresponding novel *The Child
Manuela* will need but a brief résumé. The motion picture was
released in 1932 and reached this country in the latter part of
the same year, but the novel did not appear even in Germany until
1933, and so must have been one of the last variant publications
launched before Nazi ascendancy wiped out homosexual literature.
Those fortunate enough to have seen this remarkably sympathetic
picture or any of several good amateur productions of the play on
the legitimate stage here are unlikely to have forgotten it. The
motherless Manuela, at fourteen, enters a boarding school for the
daughters of officers where the headmistress, herself descended from

a military line, imposes barracks discipline upon her young charges. One mistress alone contrives to preserve some human warmth despite the severity she is obliged to maintain, and the girls worship her.

Manuela, accustomed to maternal tenderness throughout childhood, is made almost ill by the harsh regime until her emotions fix themselves upon the general favorite, Fräulein von Bernberg. It is soon evident that her feelings are more profound and violent than the average. The mistress, moved by the pathetic and neglected girl, befriends her and becomes warmly attached to her, even confessing that she prefers her to the other students, but she warns Manuela that such emotions are not countenanced among soldiers' daughters and admonishes her to learn self-control. The knowledge that she is loved raises Manuela to a dizzy ecstasy which she manages to conceal for a time. But the excitement of playing male lead in an amateur theatrical, plus a party afterward with heavily "spiked" punch and abandoned dancing, prove too much for her high-strung temperament, and, slightly hysterical as well as literally drunk, she proclaims her secret to the entire school. The relation between pupil and teacher, though passionate, has been wholly innocent, and Manuela is unaware of its further potentialities. The adamant headmistress puts the worst construction on her hysterial outburst, sentences her to solitary confinement for the remainder of the term— diplomacy prevents her expulsion—and forbids her to see Fräulein von Bernberg again. Now genuinely ill from shock and emotional frustration, the girl contrives to reach her idol's room, but the older woman, aware of the danger to them both and afraid of her own emotions, maintains a frigid composure. Beside herself, Manuela climbs to the top floor of the tall school building and leaps to her death at the foot of an open stairwell.

This school interlude comprises only the last third of the novel, the previous sections portraying Manuela's development from her earliest memories to the time of her entering the institution. The family has moved from one army post to another, the necessity for maintaining her father's military prestige taking precedence over all other family needs. The girl was first passionately devoted to her mother. During pre-adolescence she falls in love with a public schoolmate, Eva, who is also the choice of her older brother. Manuela spins fantasies of being a male acrobat or dramatically winning the notice of her adored in other ways, but it is only as Berti's sister that she is of interest to Eva. After her mother's death, at thirteen, she has a brief and stimulating friendship with a boy violinist, but it is his mother who appeals to her emotionally and to whom she sends flowers. When the woman embraces her, she experiences the first stirrings of unrecognized passion. Aware of her obvious blossoming, her father's prim housekeeper assumes it is young Fritz who has roused her emotions, and the woman persuades her father and aunt that she must be separated from him. Hence the boarding school.

Here one has an uncommonly high-strung child with a strong mother-fixation, without friends of her own age up to the time of her mother's death. She often mentally assumes a boy's role because only men and boys seem to count in the life about her. At puberty she is deprived of both mother and mother-substitute and shut into a virtual military prison, the opposite of her hitherto relatively free existence. Both the inevitable emotional explosion at school and the careful preparation for it owe a debt to Freudian theory.

In a second novel, translated in 1936 as *Girl Alone,* Winsloe includes variance only in passing. The heroine is Eva-Maria, whose name skillfully forecasts the mixture of sensuality and romantic mysticism in her later experience. As a struggling art student, she first loves a handsome boy whom she does not succeed in winning. She is next seduced by one of her instructors, an established sculptor and Don Juan for whom she poses nude, and as an aftermath of this bitter affair she gives herself recklessly to a stranger on a night when otherwise she might have leaped into the river. The variant element is introduced in the person of Fax, a tailored and gauche fellow student with whom she shares an apartment. This girl loves Eva passionately, but receiving no response, she is satisfied to look after her with almost maternal solicitude. The two enjoy sundry revels with a bohemian group including one inseparable lesbian couple and a number of unattached homosexual women. When Fax, though still in love with Eva, engages in a flirtation with one of these, an alluring actress, jealousy spurs Eva toward giving Fax what she craves. Eva waits in her roommate's bed for her return from a studio party, but Fax does not come home until daybreak—she has succumbed to the actress's blandishments—and Eva never confesses what she had intended. Eva herself remains unmoved by genuine passion throughout the crisis.

This is apparently the final variant episode in German fiction before the Nazi purge began, and three years later authors who had dealt with the subject, however mildly, were eager only for general oblivion of that fact. Thus far, there has been no evidence of a subsequent variant renascence.

One feature of these foreign twentieth-century novels which must strike even a casual observer is the high incidence of suicide among variant women. Physical or mental illness is also often attributed to lesbian practices. Both reflect the extent to which variant fiction was based on clinical reading. Both, too, are facile means of producing dramatic effect, and tend to placate the strait-laced by suggesting that, though man may tolerate aberration, nature will not. Such devices are avoided by writers of first rank—Colette, Rolland, Proust, Lacretelle and Mann—while in Wedekind the melodramatic is seasoned by satire. A second conspicuous motif is the struggle for personal independence which leads women to eschew marriage and motherhood or to achieve self-realization at the expense of family responsibilities. This reflects the progress of the women's movement and the influence of Ibsen, Ellen Key and others. Discernible also is a slight decrease in the proportion of bisexual experience, due undoubtedly to the prevalence of hereditary theory. And last, there appears in more than a few novels a background of shifting homosexual groups, far above the underworld level, such as Peladan alone pictured earlier and then only as small private closed circles. It will be interesting to see how many of these continental features appear in English and American fiction.

CHAPTER IX.

FICTION IN ENGLISH

Introduction

The variant novels still to be surveyed in English number well over a hundred. In part this surprising count reflects the general growth of interest in sexual psychology and the increase in the number of feminine authors, both of which trends developed slightly later in the English-speaking countries than elsewhere. But beyond doubt it is also due in some measure simply to the greater accessibility of material in our own language. Book reviews in English and the indexes locating them have multiplied enormously since 1900, and, noncommital though reviews may be with regard to variance, a practiced reader grows sensitive to significant evasion. Even more fruitful, of course, is the wide, if superficial, skimming of each year's output, a habit which nets not only unreviewed trivia but minor variant incidents in better novels as well. Had titles in French and German been equally ready to hand, the score here would certainly be more equitable.

In rapid survey of this century's English fiction certain rough divisions emerge. The first fifteen years might be called the age of innocence, in that no published work referred to overt lesbianism, variance was not a subject of dispute, and no particular school of psychological thought had come to the fore. After 1915 more sophistication was apparent and variance became a controversial issue, particularly in England where the struggle for suffrage exacerbated any reference to women's departure from the feminine and domestic role. Thereafter, for a decade or so partisan shots echoed intermittently back and forth as they had in France a quarter-century earlier, with the difference, however, that now the attack frequently employed the batteries of Freud. During the first of these decades World War I exerted a perceptible influence, quickening cross-fertilization between continental and Anglo-American attitudes in general, and, in particular, leading to the translation after 1920 of enough French fiction so that occasionally specific influences could be detected in our own novels. Another aftermath of war was that relaxing of all sexual strictures which characterized the Twenties, and, in line with the growing freedom, literary treatments of variance multiplied rapidly, reaching a first peak in 1928.

In that year Radclyffe Hall's *Well of Loneliness* incurred legal prosecution for its explicit defense of a lesbian woman.[1] The restrictive effect of this action was no more than local and temporary, and as usual in cases of censorship the long range result was wide publicity for the banned title and for others on related themes. Consequently, the number of novels giving attention to variance swelled to a second peak in the middle Thirties, but the general tone was altered. Authors were now more self-conscious. The best, if at all sympathetic, dealt more gingerly with the delicate subject than before the attack. The majority, of intermediate popular quality, were careful to sound a disparaging note. And there sprang up also for the first time in English the wave of mediocre work which always follows profitable publication of better material in any field. Some of these inferior tales were censorious, some defensive, but all were so unrestrained that in this country, at least, certain pressure groups, notably the Catholic League for Decency, were roused to crusade for wholesale suppression.

A less obvious influence was also at work. The "flaming youth" of the Twenties, product of war and of general rebellion against Victorian inhibitions, had reached a point of disillusionment with sexual freedom, and now, as the "lost generation", were groping toward emotional stability. This quest for adjustment called forth a quantity of popular psychology and sociology, stemming largely from Freud, which deprecated irregular attachments, especially the homosexual, and exalted marriage and family life. Thus, some decline in variant fiction was evident before the end of the Thirties. Then, in 1939 the second World War exerted initial pressure in the same direction, for, as always, the younger generation's urge to perpetuate itself before too late threw added emphasis upon heterosexual relations and parenthood. And finally, in the publishing business, to usual wartime handicaps was added the new military requisition of cellulose for explosives, which resulted in an unprecedented shortage of paper and stringent selectivity in published fiction. Altogether it was inevitable that during the early Forties the variant literary stream should run low.

It did not, however, cease entirely, and since the end of World War II, trends in fiction suggest that variance is on its way to becoming a recognized if not accepted segment of human experience. The probable underlying reasons for this change are varied. One is the usual aftermath of war. Besides regularly producing a bumper crop of infants, war has, since the days of Sappho, swelled the number of variants by segrating the young to some extent during just those years when sexual interest is at its height. More conscious effort was made to combat this tendency during World War II than ever before, both in the armed forces and on the home front. Preventive measures this time were as much educational as disciplinary, so that the war generation emerged with some grounding in "psychiatry at the fox-hole level." One result is that among women there was no such deliberate post-war affectation of masculinity as occurred in the Twenties. Another is that many incipient authors were prepared to write of variance with some balance and perspective.

A further possible reason for the relaxing of at least the American attitude toward variance is the publication of the Kinsey reports on sexual behavior.[2] The appearance of the male volume in 1948 encouraged the production of several serious novels featuring male homosexuality, a subject hitherto stringently banned from English fiction. It is not safe to say that this lifting of taboo significantly affected the feminine picture, since female variance was never so rigorously outlawed, and the count of pertinent titles was as large in 1943 and 1944, for instance, as in 1949 and 1950. For this same reason Kinsey's second volume on the female (1953) seems unlikely to produce an effect comparable to his first. But one fact is certain —the inclusion of incidential variant and even lesbian episodes and characters is on the increase in popular current fiction.

This statement leads to consideration of a third and purely practical reason for the increase—post-war innovations in the publishing business. Before 1941 experiments in producing books of high readability and low cost had not achieved financial success, but four years of government subsidy to the end of providing the armed forces with reading matter put the venture on a paying basis. At present, fiction available at magazine cost and from all magazine outlets has become a commonplace of daily life. While these paper-covered novels were at first reprints of titles notably successful in other editions, since 1950 a number of companies have issued originals in the same format. Quite naturally one sure-fire selling feature on the newsstands is frankness with regard to sex, and the multiplication of both reprints and originals dealing with female variance provides objective evidence of interest in that subject. Another requisite for fast sales is a not-too-exalted literary level, and the combination of sex latitude and popular quality has alerted would-be censors. For some years these self-appointed groups have sought to control the paper-backed market and have here and there succeeded. Variant titles have been conspicuous in all lists under fire from moral vigilantes, and the current question is whether censoring agencies will succeed in once again checking quantity circulation of such material.

The Age of Innocence

The last mentioned variant narrative in English was Henry James's novelette *The Turn of the Screw* (1898). Treating as it did the seduction of a girl of eight by a depraved governess, it was considered along with French titles of its decade which it resembled more closely than did any of the novels soon to appear in English. Of these last, none offered more contrast to French sophistication or could more fittingly have ushered in twentieth-century fiction in our own tongue than the innocuous tale published in 1900 by a now-forgotten British novelist, Ellen Thorneycroft Fowler.

Within the first quarter of *The Farringdons* Mrs. Fowler includes a series of three passionate attachments experienced by the motherless heroine. These occur before Elisabeth is twenty, but they are noteworthy because of the author's peculiar stress upon them.

There are two things which are absolutely necessary to the well-being of the normal feminine mind—namely, one romantic attachment and one comfortable friendship. Elisabeth was perfectly normal and extremely feminine, and consequently she provided herself early with these two aids to happiness.[3]

Despite this insistence on normal femininity, the object of the girl's comfortable friendship is a boy neighbor; that of her passionate attachment a tall, handsome and witty Cousin Anne, a decade older than she is.

All the romance of Elisabeth's nature—and there was a great deal of it—was lavished upon Anne Farringdon. . . .

The mere sound of Anne's voice vibrated through the child's whole being, and every little trifle connected with her cousin became a sacred relic.[4]

Deep in the reading of mythology, Elisabeth sees her cousin as Diana, builds a shrine to her in the garden, and practices a ritual of burnt offerings before it. She also takes great interest in the Book of Ruth, sensing "a parallelism to herself and Cousin Anne (in feeling at least)."

> People sometimes smile at the adoration of a young girl for a woman, and there is no doubt but that the feeling savours slightly of school days and bread and butter. But there is also no doubt that a girl who has once felt it has learned what real love is, and that is no small lesson in the book of life.[5]

This devotion occupies Elisabeth from twelve to sixteen, when the cousin's death plunges her into melancholy which threatens her health. She is accordingly hurried off to boarding school, where during the next four years she experiences a case of passionate hero-worship for the headmistress, and a "devoted friendship" with a schoolmate who became for a time "the very mainspring of Elisabeth's life. She was a beautiful girl . . . and Elisabeth adored her with the adoration . . . freely given to the girl who has beauty by the girl who has not." Upon this girl Elisabeth lavishes

> that passionate and thrilling friendship . . . so satisfying to the immature female soul, but which is never again experienced by the woman who has once been taught by a man the nature of real love.[6]

The latter experience she meets at twenty. All these careful statements indicate the author's full awareness of the nature of variance and her taking a deliberate stand with regard to it. Equally definite is the implication that none of these early adorations involved physical intimacy.

Two years later (1902) a Canadian-American girl of twenty-one published *The Story of Mary MacLane,* written as a journal covering three months during her nineteenth year and purporting to be literal autobiography. Like the comparable "Story of Opal," printed as authentic by the *Atlantic Monthly* in 1920, but partially "debunked" by discerning critics, it wās probably laced with more than a dash of fiction. In its day it created sufficient sensation to be burlesqued in Weber and Field's revue of that year, and sold well enough to allow its author a half-dozen years in Boston and New York.

Conspicuous in its self-revelation is undying hatred of the father whom Mary lost at the age of eight.

> Apart from feeding and clothing me . . . and sending me to school—which was no more than was due me—I cannot see that he ever gave me a single thought. Certainly he did not love me, for he was quite incapable of loving anyone but himself. . . .[7]

Of her mother she says later,

> How can one bring a child into the world and not wrap it round with a certain wondrous tenderness that will stay with it always! . . . My mother has some fondness for me—for my body because it came out of hers. That is nothing—nothing. A hen loves its egg.[8]

Mary feels herself unloved also by the rest of her family—older sister, older and younger brothers, and stepfather—all of whom are "strictly practical and material, seeing close human relations as the stuff of literature, not real life. . . ." She is herself a genius, infinitely apart from the crude barrenness of Butte, Montana, though she owns to keen sympathy for women there who are "outside the moral pale." All this, of course, is once again the "dark hero complex," that sense of being outcast but superior, which has since been so well analyzed by Romer Wilson in Emily Brontë and others. For 1902, three decades *before* the era when parents could do no right, it was fairly strong meat.

As for men, MacLane is certain none can ever rouse or possess her except the Devil. "He will be incarnate, but he will not be a man." He will hurt her, and passion for him will free her from herself, but it will last only three days, and "there must be no falling in love about it."

> My shy and sensitive soul would be irretrievably poisoned and polluted. The defilement of so sacred and beautiful a thing

as marriage is surely the darkest evil that can come to a life. And so everything in me that had turned toward that too bright light would then drink deep of the lees of death.[9]

It was this devil fantasy upon which Weber and Fields seized, and on the stage the Dark Gentleman, played by William Collier, fled in terror before the *enfant terrible*.

The pertinent point to which all the foregoing leads is an attachment to a high school teacher of literature first encountered when Mary was eighteen, "the first person on earth who ever looked at me tenderly," to whom she refers with adolescent sentimentality as the "Anemone Lady." About this woman she spins passionate reveries, wishing they might live together high on a mountainside away from the world. With the beginning of this friendship "I felt a snapping of tense-drawn cords, a breaking away of flood gates— and a strange new pain . . . a convulsion and a melting within."[10] Nevertheless, carresses went no farther than "your hand in mine," and the association seems to have lasted but a year. Still Mary says:

> Sometimes I am seized with nearer, vivider sensations for my friend the Anemone Lady . . . I feel a strange attraction of sex. There is in me a masculine element that when I am thinking of her arises and overshadows all the others. . . . So then it is not the woman-love but the man-love set in the mysterious sensibilities of my woman-nature. It brings me pain and pleasure mixed. . . . Do you think a man is the only creature with whom one may fall in love?[11]

This pseudo-naïveté wakes a suspicion of literary influence which is strengthened by her second volume, *My Friend Annabel Lee* (1903). Here she proclaims her few early literary loves to have been Poe, the juvenile books for boys of J. T. Trowbridge, and " 'Three Grains of Corn,' by a woman named Edwards," and she voices acute loathing for Archibald Clavering Gunter without citing reasons. Mathilda Betham-Edwards was an Englishwoman who lived in France during the late nineteenth century, and the *Oxford Book of Victorian Verse* includes a sonnet of hers, "A Valentine: The Pansy and the Prayer Book," ending with the following sestet:

> The while I knelt, I let a pansy glide
> Between her grave sweet face and open book
> And whispered as she turned with chiding look—

"Heaven has not willed, dear heart, that aught divide
Love pure as ours, nor blames if thought of me
Come like this flower between thy God and thee."[12]

This MacLane would have loved, as she would have hated the farcical treatment of variance in *A Florida Enchantment,* and to assume her acquaintance with both would explain her otherwise unaccountable singling out of these two authors alone for special mention. Both of MacLane's volumes betray a disingenuous effort to present herself as a child genius springing as it were by parthenogenesis from the intellectual wasteland of Montana. It is probable that her reading had been more extensive and had influenced her more than she admitted.

As to the volume of 1903, it is not only less startling than the first but seems more youthful. The "friend" of the title is a Japanese statuette in which her fantasy sees "a woman of fourteen" who has known love for a week, after which "the strong stranger went away," leaving life drab. Here is the Devil again, and "Annabel" is obviously no more than Mary's own *persona,* hard, experienced and self-contained even before adolescence. One wonders whether MacLane may have suffered some early traumatic experience with a man which produced this recurrent fantasy and prompted her sympathy for the déclassées of Butte. As for women, "Annabel" is her only admitted friend. The volume records nothing beyond Mary's roaming alone in Boston, falling in love momentarily with Minnie Maddern Fiske as the Magdalen, and adoring the Puvis de Chavannes murals in the Public Library—those delicate wraiths so remote from reality. Of human contacts there is no mention; she is solitary and bitterly nostalgic for the Anemone Lady, or, rather, for their mountainside eyrie of her own imagining. Passages in her third volume, *I, Mary MacLane* (1917) shed some light on her actual experiences at this time, but must await discussion in proper order because the later volume reflects the comparative emotional sophistication which had permeated this country in the intervening years.

The next variant item was an historical novel by John Breckenridge Ellis (1902), but precedence will be given to the recently published *Things As They Are* (1951), written in 1903 by Gertrude Stein, because of its closer similarity to MacLane's autobiographical volumes. This earliest effort of Miss Stein's, written when she was twenty-nine, is recognized as very near to her own experience by Edmund Wilson, a long-time student of her total work.[13] It records the emotional entanglements among three young American women

over a period of two years, and opens on a transatlantic liner
carrying them to Europe. Adele, the central figure from whose
viewpoint the whole story is written, is oppressed by exhaustion and
"the disillusion of recent failures" in Baltimore, and as Mr. Wilson
points out, Miss Stein herself went abroad in the summer of 1902
after having abandoned hope of a degree from Johns Hopkins where
she had pursued the medical course for five years.

The three girls are characterized at length. Helen is

> the American version of the English handsome girl. In her
> ideal completeness she would have been unaggressively de-
> termined, a trifle brutal and entirely impersonal; a woman
> of passions but not of emotions, . . . incapable of regrets,[14]

that is, definitely a masculine personality; but actually she is no more
than "a brave bluff." Sophie is a New Englander with "the angular
body of a spinster but . . . a face that would have belonged to the
decadent days of Italian greatness," and with "the unobtrusive good
manners of a gentleman." Events prove her, however, to be both
feminine and feline. Adele has "the freedom of movement and the
simple instinct for comfort that suggests a land of laziness and sunshine." Very early in the narrative she exclaims, "I always did thank
God I wasn't born a woman,"[15]—this surprising statement is neither
then nor later elaborated in any way—but everything about her save
her intellect is passive to the point of inertia, and she struggles against
being drawn into the "turgid and complex world" of passionate intimacy.

She finds it impossible, however, to remain indifferent to Helen's
subtle courtship, which includes "fluttering" caresses as the three
lie on the deck under the stars. Her familiarity with attraction between women is evident from some early self-searching:

> As for me is it another little indulgence of my superficial
> emotions or is there any possibility of my really learning to
> realize stronger feelings. If it's the first I will call a halt
> promptly.[16]

At one point Helen charges her with "middle-class morality," to
which Adele retorts:

> I simply contend that the middle class ideal which demands
> that people be affectionate, respectable, honest and content,

that they avoid excitements and cultivate serenity is the ideal
that appeals to me, it is in short the ideal of affectionate family
life.[17]

But that (says Helen) means cutting passion quite out of your
scheme of things. Adele replies:

> Not simple moral passions, they are distinctly of it but
> really my chief point is a protest against this tendency . . . to
> go in for things simply for the sake of experience. . . . [That]
> is to me both trivial and immoral. As for passion, it has no
> reality for me except as two varieties, affectionate comradeship
> . . . and physical passion in greater or less complexity . . . and
> against the cultivation of the latter I have an almost puritanic
> horror and that includes an objection to it in any of its many
> disguised forms.[18]

In accordance with these principles Adele spends her summer in
Spain, happy in the mere "family" comradeship of a cousin. But
during the subsequent winter she plays a divided game. She cannot
resist going repeatedly from Baltimore to New York to see Helen,
though once there she is not only passive but resistant to the other
girl's wooing. She even says explicitly that they have few interests in
common, but still it is she who does all the traveling to make their
growing intimacy possible, for Helen's resources are sharply curtailed
by unsympathetic parents.

Thus far, the third girl, Sophie, has remained surprisingly passive
in view of her long-established intimacy with Helen, but in the course
of this winter she enlightens Adele as to the precise nature of that
intimacy. Adele is so shocked that it is implied clearly that the relation is physical and, up until then, wholly outside her own acquaintance. Not even this revelation, however, can detach her from Helen,
although she deliberately elects a second summer abroad alone and
suffers when Helen's letters are stopped by a visit from Sophie. During
the subsequent winter her own relations with Helen reach the stage
of physical expression, but the change is not a happy one.

> Their pulses were differently timed. She could not go so fast
> and Helen's exhausted nerves could no longer wait. Adele
> found herself constantly forced on by Helen's pain. It was a
> false position . . . her attitude was misunderstood and Helen
> interpreted her slowness as deficiency . . . and the greater her

affection for Helen became the more irritable became her
discontent.[19]

This is trite enough to readers of modern sexual psychology as set
forth in marriage manuals. It was not trite coming from an unmarried American girl in 1903.

At this juncture Sophie invites Helen to accompany her on another
European trip. (As Mr. Wilson drily remarks, for the more prosperous American college graduate, Europe was then an imperative.)
Helen accepts, and although Adele is certain that Sophie is financing
the trip she dares not put the question directly. Or perhaps she does
not want to, for Helen has urged her to spend the summer abroad
also, not with them, but within easy reach.

And so the lover of serenity travels for her third summer as a kind
of semi-detached appendage to the other pair, and the remainder of
the action is almost as tedious and confusing to the reader as to Adele
herself. Because of the physical incompatibility so well described
above, Helen has now cooled considerably in that respect, but her
emotional dependence upon Adele increases with Sophie's balking of
private communication between them—one more testimonial to the
soundness of "Proust's law": the inverse proportion between "love"
and accessibility. Because Adele, on the other hand, is now rather
more than less physically attracted, her health and peace of mind
suffer noticeably during her frustrating periods with the other two.
But she is bound not only by her genuine love for Helen but by her
confidence that the other girl really loves her. When she reads Helen's
final desperate letter promising that she will never again allow such a
situation to develop, Adele exclaims with impatience:

> Hasn't she learned yet that things do happen and she isn't
> big enough to stave them off? Can't she see things as they are
> and not as she would make them if she were strong enough . . ?
> I am afraid it comes very near to being a dead-lock.[20]

This sentence concludes the book, to which Miss Stein originally
gave the title *Quod Erat Demonstrandum,* the implied proposition
being that such an emotional game could never be worth the candle.
The current title, chosen by the editor, throws the emphasis upon
Helen's inability to be honest with herself or others, in contrast to
Adele's ruthless clarity. If Adele acted against her own middle-class
convictions, it was at least without self-deception at any stage of the
game. Mr. Wilson suggests that continued preoccupation with women,

and her unwillingness to abandon herself again or to write openly about it, was responsible for the increasing obscurity of Miss Stein's work and the lofty emotional detachment of her viewpoint.[20]

John Breckenridge Ellis's *The Holland Wolves*, published late in 1902, was largely in the cape-and-sword tradition of the time, but he inserted a variant touch by making its central figure a transvestist and treating the emotional consequences seriously. Rosamunda, daughter of a Spanish leader in the war with the Netherlands, has been bred in a convent where flagellation was a common practice. When, at nineteen, she must choose between becoming a nun there or accompanying her father to the Low Countries, she elects the latter course. Disguised as her father's squire, she engages in espionage and from expediency pays court to Anna, a Dutch girl in her teens. The latter falls deeply in love with her and abandons family and reputation to follow her. But Rosamunda's fancy has been caught by an officer in the Dutch forces, to whom she confesses that she is a woman. When he pronounces Anna no better than a camp follower, Rosamunda challenges him to a duel, worsts him, and consequently is cured of her passion for him. Thereafter she becomes one of the most cruel of the inquisitionary soldiers.

Since she has never been in love with Anna, and the latter throughout much of the story believes her to be a man, the variant issue is as confused as always in a romance of sex disguise. Like Gunter's farce, however, the tale bears witness to interest in intersexual types even among superficial American readers, for Rosamunda has no feminine characteristics. It also indicates the author's belief that such types result from environment rather than heredity. Rosamunda, despite her Spanish coloring, is revealed at the end as Anna's sister (stolen from Holland in infancy), and not related at all to the Spaniards upon whom she has modeled herself. The blood kinship between the two girls, moreover, is evidently meant to account for Anna's spontaneous attraction, which after the revelation of Rosamunda's sex becomes a profound sisterly devotion. Readers were thus provided with a spicy morsel but spared the slightest moral indigestion. (If this account makes the tale seem one of mere sex disguise, comparison with Compton Mackenzie's *Sylvia Scarlett* of a few decades later will make the difference apparent.)

The first of the century's openly published titles by a major writer was John Masefield's *Multitude and Solitude* (1909), its author's least-esteemed novel to judge from the neglect accorded it by literary historians, libraries, and secondhand catalogs. It is true that from the standpoint of artistry it falls into two almost unrelated halves; but it is, nevertheless, a convincing study of a young dramatist in search of his soul—that is, of the "high and austere" character he feels essential to a great artist. He does achieve his end via some gruelling years with a medical unit in South Africa, but he is driven to this heroic measure by a series of major and minor frustrations reminiscent of the tricks of Fate in Thomas Hardy's work. Among the major tragedies is the death of the woman he has long loved, and this calamity is the end of a chain of trivial mischances in which the detonating factor is jealousy on the part of his beloved's woman friend. There is an artistic preliminary sounding of the variant note early in the book when, depressed at failing to find Ottalie in her London apartment, he stops at a café where he sees

> a red-haired fierce little poet who sat close by reading and eating cake. The yellow back of *Les Fleurs du Mal* was propped against his teapot. Something of the fierceness and passion of the Femmes Damnées . . . was wreaked upon the cake.[21]

After Ottalie is drowned while crossing to Ireland, her friend Agatha tells the lover what he had already guessed: Ottalie's visit to her Irish relatives was partially the result of his not having definitely proposed marriage. And his failure to do so was (again in part) due to Agatha's jealously interrupting a tête-à-tête between the lovers, and later delaying a letter from Ottalie to him. Agatha confesses all this during her prostration after her friend's death.

> "I was jealous. I was wicked. I think the devil was in me."
> . . . He would have asked to look upon Ottalie; but he refrained in the presence of that passion. Agatha had enough to bear. He would not flick her jealousies.[22]

There is no suggestion that Ottalie reciprocated Agatha's love, nor any implication of lesbian intimacy. Ottalie's brother, however, tells the hero that although she loved him she thought him "too ready to surrender to immediate and perhaps wayward emotion"—an obvious hint at the heroine's physical coldness or Victorian repression in the heterosexual field.

Two years later and half a world away the Australian woman known to letters as Henry Handel Richardson recorded the emotional development of an adolescent girl in *The Getting of Wisdom*

(1910). At fourteen Laura is already too hard and independent to feel close to her emotional widowed mother, and at boarding school she is subjected to refined cruelty by her mates because she is so "different"—partly in her precocious literary interests but most of all in her dislike of boys. To gain face among them she invents a romance with a curate; the exposure of this fiction brings more ridicule which hardens her further. Her inner withdrawal becomes complete after the expulsion of an adoring younger girl who stole in order to buy her a keepsake.

In the midst of her bitter isolation she is chosen as roommate by a popular girl a few years her senior, and at once succumbs emotionally to the first kindness and championship she has ever known. It is clear, however, that no physical intimacy ensues—Laura kisses Evelyn only once, and then impulsively when the latter, in a fit of pique, remarks that all men are fools. The friendship is slowly blighted by Laura's passionate jealousy if the older girl goes out with men or shows attention to other girls, a "tyranny" to which the senior will not submit. The school gossips about this conspicuous attachment, but without censure or apparent awareness of questionable possibilities even on the part of the mistresses. After a brief and abortive religious "conversion" Laura sets herself to cultivate her literary talent by way of emotional outlet, for there are hints that she will never feel attracted to men. The wisdom gained during this difficult adolescence is summarized at the end by the author, who says that though the girl returned home feeling that she "fitted no hole," she could not yet know that

> just those mortals who feel cramped and unsure in the conduct of everyday life will find themselves . . . in that freer world where no practical considerations hamper, and where the creatures that inhabit dance to their tune.[23]

That is, in the somewhat narcissistic world which they, as writers, create. This is a penetrating recognition of authorship as sublimation, written as it was several decades before psychiatrists began to take the writing fraternity apart.

Another novel with rather stronger variant overtones appeared in England in 1914, Ethel Sidgwick's *A Lady of Leisure*. This pleasant social romance had for its main theme a muted echo from the Women's Movement: the wealthy and idle girl's need of a routine occupation. Violet Ashwin, daughter of a frivolous social belle and a Harley Street physician, is driven by a sense of utter futility to

fly in the face of convention—and her mother's prejudices—and ap-
prentice herself to a modiste. Her co-worker, Alice Eccles, is an
enterprising cockney who supports a neurotic mother, preferring
this burden to marriage with a suitor whom she suspects of engaging
in illegal enterprises. Alice is tall, handsome, high-spirited, and
infinitely more self-reliant than the sheltered upper-class girl, whom
at first she assists and patronizes with a kind of affectionate raillery.
Soon, however, the two are close personal friends, to the horror of
Violet's snobbish mother. Between Violet and her father, though, a
close alliance has always existed, and he applauds both her job
and her new friendship, seeing at once the solid quality beneath
Alice's unpolished surface.

When Violet works herself into a collapse and is sent to the
country for the summer,

> Alice longed to have news of her—but she was not going to
> ask for it. . . . Her adoration for Violet, violently repressed,
> since its torrential force made her almost ashamed, was a
> thing unique, unheard of, as Miss Eccles believed, in the
> world before. The revelation of woman to woman is often
> just as remarkable, for all the truisms on the subject, as the
> revelation of woman to man.[24]

Somewhat later, Mrs. Eccles' mental condition having become a
danger to her daughter, Dr. Ashwin copes with the mother and
engages Alice as lady's maid to his wife, hoping that her companionship may restore his still convalescent daughter's interest in living.
When he tells Violet that Alice is in the house she colors visibly
and runs upstairs, "her face still pink and her heart thumping."

> Alice dropped her hands and coloured gloriously, far more
> gloriously than Violet at her best could have accomplished.
> Her work slipped from her knees and she spread her splendid
> arms. . . . [Violet] went straight to her and fell upon her
> breast.[25]

The only further detail mentioned is Alice's kissing the other girl's
hands. The friendship survives Alice's marriage and the birth of her
first child, and she is the only person save Violet's parents to attend
the latter's subsequent wedding. Here, then, is an unmistakably
passionate relationship between adults—both girls are in their middle
twenties—presented with complete sympathy and approval, and en-

couraged by an established physician. It is, of course, quite innocent of lesbian implications.

Since Miss Stein's novelette remained unpublished for half a century, MacLane and Ellis would be America's only representatives in this early period but for short stories which appeared sporadically. One of Josephine Dodge Dascom's *Smith College Stories* (1900), "A Case of Interference," just skirted the variant field. A junior, prominent because of her literary ability, enters the despised arena of campus politics to save an unpopular gifted freshman who worships her from leaving college. A little later the *Ladies' Home Journal* published a slighter college story, "The Cat and the King," by Jennette Lee, in which a freshman shams illness in order to join her senior idol in the infirmary, and is extricated from ensuing complications by a wholly sympathetic woman physician. These were both written on an adult level. The only known variant juvenile, *The Lass of the Silver Sword* by Mary Constance DuBois, ran in *St. Nicolas Magazine* during 1909 and was published in book form later.[16] Centered about the adoration of a fourteen-year-old girl for a senior of nineteen in her boarding school, it was sympathetic but so circumspect as to lack full vitality. Catherine Wells's "The Beautiful House" (*Harpers Magazine*, 1912) pictures an idyllic relation between two adult artists, for the older and less feminine of whom the connection ends tragically with the marriage of the younger woman. Helen R. Hull's "The Fire" (1918) will be discussed later with its author's longer narratives.

It is noteworthy that none of this early fiction records disapproval of variant experience on the part of either the authors or society. It is seen as educative and beneficial during the teens, or even in the following decade for the single woman, and it provides the only happiness during adolescence for several girls more gifted than their peers. If in Masefield's novel its sequel is tragic, jealousy rather than variance per se is responsible, and Miss Stein condemns the experience she describes, not as lesbian, but as generally spineless and unintelligent. In the cases (Miss Stein's and Miss Richardson's) where antipathy or indifference to men is noted, women's attraction to their own sex is not responsible, but is rather a concomitant product of unspecified factors.

Sophistication and Dispute

In 1915 D. H. Lawrence, with *The Rainbow*, hit the first ringing blow upon the anvil of controversy. As the messiah of robust heterosexual passion, Lawrence needs no introduction, and in this early novel he attacked right and left all factors which militate against it in modern society—unhealthy urban and industrial life, sterile intellectuality (especially among women), and lesbianism. It is in the final portion of his three-generation panorama that the current representative of the Brangwyn clan, sixteen-year-old Ursula, contracts a passion for a schoolmistress. She has just had a brief but complete heterosexual experience, and Lawrence implies that the tide of emotion which overflows toward Winifred Inger is little more than an aftermath of that physical awakening. A ten-page chapter significantly entitled "Shame" gives the history of their affair, which reaches its first climax at Winifred's river cottage when the two bathe nude at night. Immediately after this episode the girl's one desire is to get away. Over a period of months, however, "the two women became intimate. Their lives seemed suddenly to fuse into one." During the long vacation, Ursula, as always when away from the older woman, is desolate and afire for her, but with their reunion

> a heavy clogged sense of deadness began to gather upon her, from the other woman's contact. Her female hips seemed big and earthy, her ankles and her arms too thick.[27] [The last touch is a highly original bit of anthropometry.]

Winifred, deeply in love with the younger girl, wishes to leave the school and live with Ursula in London where they can mingle in literary circles and participate in the Women's Movement. Ursula repudiates the suggestion and goes on to other heterosexual adventures, but—possibly as a result of her lesbian experience?—she is always too much concerned with her own emotions to become a satisfactory partner for men. Her leaving a lover and going out to steep herself in the light of a full moon is offered as symbolic of her narcissistic self-absorption.

This novel was published by the solid firm of Methuen, but was withdrawn after a police court verdict of indecency which was based on attacks by three or four reviewers. The charge was general, only one (Robert Lynd) making an oblique allusion to its lesbian aspect. Lawrence was not notified directly of the court order, and since he had neither funds nor influence to launch a legal protest,[28] this act of censorship raised few echoes in comparison with some cases to be noted later. It did, however, postpone general circulation of the novel, and undoubtedly focussed some attention on lesbianism.

A year later the American Henry Kitchell Webster touched briefly but scathingly on the subject of variance in *The Great Adventure* (1916). In this history of a marriage the girl who has looked forward to motherhood is frustrated by the birth of twins, the implication being that she desired merely an object upon which to project her own personality, and the self-abnegation demanded by two young entities, boy and girl, is beyond her. Accordingly while the children can still be cared for by nurses, Rose leaves her home and seeks self-realization on the stage. In the course of her first year she takes an artist's interest in a beautiful but inferior colleague in the chorus of a revue, whom she coaches in diction and for whom, among others, she designs flattering costumes. But when her Galatea becomes infatuated with her she is disgusted.

> Rose understood this better than Olga did, having had to evade one or two "crushes" while at the University. It was a sort of thing that went utterly against her instincts."

Olga's efforts to persuade and caress her into intimacy are worse than futile, and in retaliation for Rose's contempt Olga spreads gossip of an affair with the director which does Rose grave professional injury. After some further experiment, Rose returns to her family a more mature and humble woman. Olga is presented as a strongly antipathetic personality, and Rose's quest for self-expression proves sterile and unrewarding for all concerned. Learning unselfish adjustment in marriage is "The Great Adventure."

In January 1917 the first British novel appeared which was devoted wholly to variance, and the first in English since James's *The Bostonians* of 1855—Clemence Dane's *Regiment of Women*. Its attitude is as bitter as Lawrence's in *The Rainbow*, but any question of influence is excluded by the author's indication that it was written before the latter was published. Title and initial quotation announce the theme as "the monstrous empire of a cruel woman," and its four-hundred-page plot revolves about a subtle sadist, outstanding mistress in a girls' day school. Clare Hartill (the surname is surely symbolic), brilliant, sardonic, and never attractive to men, has colleagues and pupils alike well under her domination. The other mistresses stand in awe of her superior intellect, her uncanny success as a teacher, and her mordant tongue. The girls—she is really interested only in the higher secondary classes—are emotionally subjugated by her alternation of warm praise and stinging raillery, the praise intensified by "sudden brilliant smiles" and the discreet laying on of hands.

Clare is a woman of feverish friendships and sudden ruptures, "unmaternal" to the core

> and pitiless after victory: not till then did she examine the nature thus enslaved, seldom did she find it worth the trouble of the skirmish. . . . To the few that pleased her fastidious taste she gave of her best, lavishly . . . to them she was inspiration incarnate.[30]

But her interest even in these favorites "required their physical nearness" and died with their departure from school. Just as Clare has reached the "dangerous age" of thirty-five a new teacher of nineteen enters upon the scene:

> . . . vehement Alwynne—no schoolgirl—yet more youthful and ingenuous than any mistress had right to be, loving with all the discrimination of a fine mind and all the ardour of an affectionate child. Here was no . . . fleeting devotion that must end as the schooldays ended. Here was love for Clare at last, a widow's cruse to last her for all time. Clare . . . relaxing all effort, settled herself to enjoy to the full the cushioning sense of security.

But even so, Alwynne was "too obviously subject through her own free impulse to entirely satisfy. Clare's love of power had its morbid moments, when a struggling victim pleased her."[31]

So great is the older woman's magnetism that Alwynne, wholesome and spirited enough to hold her own at first, does not detect the other's egotistical cruelty until it is exercised upon a student. This hypersensitive child of thirteen, Louise, whose precocity approaches genius, Clare has forced intellectually beyond her strength and reduced emotionally to half-hysterical subservience. Alwynne's strong maternal instinct moves her to intervene on Louise's behalf, and a dangerous triangle develops. When, ill from tension, Louise fails in an important interscholastic competition, Clare turns suddenly hostile and excoriates her, not only for the failure, but for her interpretation of a dramatic role rehearsed in addition to her schoolroom load. Playing the tragic child Prince Arthur in *King John* has already driven Louise past the limits of stability, and after this

double humiliation at the hands of her idolized persecutor, she leaps
to death from an attic window. (This antedated by fifteen years
Winsloe's *Mädchen in Uniform,* of which the denouement and certain
other details are so similar that some influence seems beyond
question.)

The tragedy and its aftermath—Clare, crowding her own guilt
below the threshold of consciousness, persuades herself and Alwynne
that the latter is in part to blame—brings Alwynne to the verge
of breakdown, and so she goes on leave to relatives in the country. A
sympathetic cousin who is something of an amateur psychiatrist
gradually probes to the root of her trouble and offers an impersonal
estimate of Clare, whom he has never met and has reconstructed
solely from the girl's still loyal accounts. His opinion gives her
pause, and subsequent encounters with Clare, so shaken by the
suicide and by Alwynne's long absence that she lacks her usual
finesse, complete the girl's disillusionment. She finally marries the
cousin.

This overlong narrative carries psychological conviction but suffers
from blurred focus. Clare's heartlessness once her victims are en-
thralled supports the initial claim that sadism is its thesis, but the
spell she casts is variant passion no less intense for being subjectively
induced and never allowed expression (the one real caress in four-
hundred pages figures early in her conquest of Alwynne). This
passionate element assumes primary importance during her final
struggle against a male rival. Close to the end a woman who has
known Clare all her life tells her:

> When you allow [a girl] to attach herself passionately
> to you, you are feeding and at the same time deflecting from
> its natural channel the strongest impulse of her life. . . .
> Alwynne needs a good concrete husband to love, not a
> fantastic ideal that she calls friendship and clothes in your
> face and figure. You are doing her a deep injury. . . . I tell
> you, it's vampirism. And when she is squeezed dry and flung
> aside, who will the next victim be? One day you'll grow
> old. What will you do when your glamour's gone? I tell you,
> Clare Hartill, you'll die of hunger in the end.[32]

Egotism is implied here, but the main issue is variant seduction, and
Clare's retort is a long boast as to her prowess in that line amply
justified by earlier incidents. She concludes defiantly that she and
Alwynne "suffice each other. Thank God there are some women who

can do without marriage." The reply is: "Poor Clare! Are the grapes very sour?"

Surprisingly, this "final triumphant insult" touches the quick.

> The insult could cut through her defenses and strike at her very self, because it was true. Her pride agonized. She had thought herself shrouded, invulnerable. . . . She sat and shuddered at the wound dealt; . . . at the arrow-tip rankling in it still.[22]

Clare's reaction is not prepared for in advance. Moreover, this episode is so placed and treated as to make it the supreme climax of the plot, and the implication is clear: it is the sex starvation of spinsterhood which produces variance, a barren substitute for married love. If the spinster is brilliant and proud, a sadistic egotism constantly requiring fresh victims will be a concomitant. Clare's spinsterhood is involuntary; she is, then, a potentially tragic figure, and the novel would have gained in power had she been so presented throughout. But she is shown only as momentarily pathetic, and after such moments her recoveries are too ready and her retaliations too mean to permit of sustained sympathy. One is left with a sense that the author had known a Clare Hartill all too well, had emerged hating her, and had not yet achieved the detachment necessary for producing artistic unity.

Later in 1917 *I, Mary MacLane* provided an autobiographical sequel to the author's volumes of fifteen years earlier. Like her first book, it is an impressionistic journal of the preceding year which includes considerable retrospective information. Once more Mary is in Butte, convalescing from a grave illness induced by a half-dozen hectic years in Boston and New York. She still hates men, who have never stirred any emotion in her, and with whom in their "crude sex-rapacity" she has been careless as no "regular woman" would dare to be. One gathers, then, that the heartbreak from which she has suffered for a year is not the work of a man.

> It is one thing I do not dwell upon in this book of Me. Much of Me had nothing to do with my heart when it broke: though I loved with all of Me . . . one who lives in New York —and I lost and lost, all the way. There was mere human ordinariness, about which I built up a strangely sincere temple of grace which I looked to see shed light on my life like the eternal beauty of a Daybreak. I gave the best

I knew to it, from a distance, and I lost. . . . All was broken without so much as a clasp of hands.[34]

That Mary is now well aware of all potentialities between women is clear from other comments; for example, that she "wasted" several years in the two eastern cities on friendships (with women) from whose ill effects she will never recover, having given too much of herself in the "headlong newness of knowing and owning friendship after long young loneliness."[35] Elsewhere, she mentions translating Sappho, and says:

> I am some way the Lesbian woman, . . . [but] there is no vice in my Lesbian vein, . . . [though] I have lightly kissed and been kissed by Lesbian lips. I am too personally fastidious, too temperamentally dishonest . . . to walk in direct repellent roads of vice even in freest moods.[36]

She believes lesbianism to be subjectively induced, as against those who consider it due to "pre-natal influence." Some women are lesbian because they are born aggressive, some feel themselves challenged by the limitations imposed on women, some are merely so lonely that the first understanding person "wins a passionate adoration the deeper for being unrealized." She believes that all women "except two breeds, the stupid and the narrowly feline," have a lesbian strain; that is, there is always some "poignant flair" of sex in their close friendships, though all "good non-analytic creatures" would deny it with horror. (This last suggests at least an acquaintance with Freud.)

She has now returned to cultivate in solitude the *Me* neglected during her preceding distracted years. There are evidences that she has more than dabbled in oriental philosophy and believes in reincarnation, which, she says, gives her many buried selves to delve for —surely Valhalla for a narcissist. Mild as this volume is in its condemnation by comparison with the preceding two, its stress upon the suffering and "waste" in variant friendships, and its reference to lesbianism as "repellent vice," align it with them as opposed to variance.

Such pointed attacks as those of Lawrence and Miss Dane were bound to stimulate counterattack. The first appeared in A. T. Fitzroy's *Despised and Rejected* (1918), though women's variance was of secondary importance in a novel whose main issue was the tragic wartime persecution of Conscientious Objectors; particularly of male homosexuals who took refuge in that camp. Because both "Conchies" and homosexuals were anathema in 1918, the publisher was prosecuted and fined some £160.[37] The author, wife of the composer Cyril Scott, apparently weathered the storm without major consequences, though she wrote nothing more under the same name.

The feminine incidents in the novel concern an actress who, at thirteen, had adored a boarding school teacher; however, she cooled when the latter responded, because she hated to be caressed. Her teens included similar attractions, and she had several unpleasant experiences with men during her years of becoming established in the theatre. These experiences precede the opening of the story. The action begins with amateur theatrical activities at a summer hotel, in the course of which Antoinette falls in love with a taciturn dark woman reminiscent of her first idol, and, on the other hand, rouses emotional interest in an effeminate young man in the cast. The summer interlude ends without resolving either affair. Both amours are continued by letter, a medium which frees Antoinette of her physical inhibitions. Thus, she learns that Dennis has previously been much drawn to men; and on her part, she becomes so attached to the dark Hester that she visits her in Birmingham. She is as yet unaware of any "abnormality" in her feeling, knowing only that Hester represents the promise of some imperative emotional release. When she discovers that Hester has had a liaison with a man, her love is instantly chilled, although it had reached the verge of overt expression.

Meanwhile, Dennis, obtaining no response from her, has become involved with a poet in desperate circumstances for whom he feels a maternal tenderness. From this point on, the long narrative is concerned chiefly with its male cast, but it includes Antoinette's finally considering herself in love with Dennis. He has now, however, irrevocably elected the homosexual path; he tells her that he recognized her at first meeting as another homosexual and that that was the reason for his instant attraction. Despite his immediate detection of her proclivities, Antoinette is presented as feminine in both appearance and temperament. The cause of her narcissistic failure in either normal or variant adjustment is that throughout adolescence she was always awaiting the charmed age of eighteen, when the thrilling business of Real Life would begin. That is, she nursed a romantic ideal impossible of realistic achievement (Cf. Gourmont's *Songe d'une Femme*). At the end she complains:

> Everybody seems to think you're abnormal because you
> *like* to be. . . . As if being different from other people weren't
> curse enough in itself. . . . People judge the fine by the sensual,
> of whom there are plenty also among the "normal."[38]

This is a fair enough statement of a variant argument which will
be encountered again later.

A more oblique and much more artistic species of defense is
incorporated in Arnold Bennett's *The Pretty Lady* (1918), of which
the main theme is the relation between a wealthy London bachelor
and a Parisian courtesan war-bound in London. Despite the outcry
the book raised among reviewers, the sexual aspects of this affair
are subordinated to the soothing effect of the French woman's simple
and cosy subjective complaisance, in contrast to the hectic wartime
mood of the Englishwomen with whom Hoape is thrown. One of
these, Concepçion Smith, is the daughter of a British financial
magnate who operated in Lima, and it is not wholly clear whether
her mother or merely her given name and her upbringing were
Latin-American. Orphaned at eighteen, she returned to London
and kept house for her bachelor uncle, a cabinet minister, earning
a reputation as hostess and wit. Having married for love, and lost
her husband within the first few weeks of World War I, she leaves
for Glasgow early in the story to dull her sorrow through canteen
work in a munitions plant. She is described as having a masculine
mentality, being relatively indifferent to feminine graces, and lacking
somewhat in obvious sex appeal. She is at this time about thirty.

Her closest friend has been Lady Queenie Lechford, perhaps a
decade younger, a spoiled only child, capricious, flippant, the type
of hectic and brittle "flapper" who was to become so common a figure
in the fiction of the 1920s. That the two quarrelled bitterly over
Concepçion's leaving London one learns only when they are reunited
late in 1916, after Concepçion has broken under the strain of overwork
and the shock of a horrifying accident to a factory girl. The two
women's reunion is delineated with the subtlest indirect touches, but
it is clearly passionate. Of the two, Concepçion seems the more deeply
involved. Though there are hints that she herself is not uninterested
in Hoape, she tells him Queenie is in love with him and urges him
to marry the girl in spite of the considerable difference in their
ages. She would do anything in the world, she declares, to win even
a few weeks' happiness for her young friend. Even while Hoape is
evading her suggestion, Lady Queenie, given to reckless watching

of air-raids from the roof of her parents' town house, is killed by falling anti-aircraft shrapnel. Concepçion, with nothing now to live for, plans suicide, but is dissuaded by Hoape's concern for her, and one foresees that these two will eventually marry. Bennett thus appears to diagnose variant (possibly lesbian) connections as one phase of war-time hysteria, induced mainly by the shortage of eligible men. Though there is a shade of satire in his picture, there is certainly no disapproval.

The next two novels, both American and both published in 1920, made relatively brief but quite significant additions to variant literature. By a count of lines, Kate Chancellor occupies little space in Sherwood Anderson's *Poor White*, story of a shanty-town boy's rise to prosperity and a good marriage. But she supplies the most vivid thread in the pattern of his wife's emotional development. When Clara leaves her father's farm for the state university she is wholly uniformed in matters of sex. From 'some bungling early experience she is wary of men, though conscious of a certain power over them. The relatives with whom she lives while in college play little part in her life save to repeat her father's misunderstanding of trivial "petting" incidents which are unsought and distasteful to her.

Clara finds her college courses no help toward the practical conduct of life in any field, and her one fruitful contact is with a girl two or three years her senior who plans to study medicine. Kate Chancellor, as masculine as her musical brother is effeminate, is quite frank in admitting her homosexual nature (thus implied to be innate), though she never mentions lesbianism. For three years the girls are constantly together. Their avid discussions range through politics, religion, and philosophy, but center most often on sex differences in temperament, and the problem facing all women in marriage: how to continue as individuals and not become mere colorless stereotypes like most housewives of their acquaintence. Kate is more drawn to Clara than to any other woman she has met, dreads marriage for the girl, and yearns to take her along as companion in the free and purposeful life she means to live. But she is honest enough to admit that her own pattern is not Clara's, and that to bind her emotionally would only increase the groping girl's confusion. Her closest approach to physical expression occurs during one of their customary walks together, when to drive some point home she stops and takes Clara by the shoulders.

> For a moment they stood thus close together, and a strange gentle and yet hungry look came into Kate's eyes.

It lasted only a moment and when it happened both women were somewhat embarrassed. Kate laughed and taking hold of Clara's arm pulled her along the sidewalk. "Let's walk like the devil," she said, "come on, let's get up some speed."³⁹

On her return from college Clara becomes involved at once in the business of getting married. She manages to resist her father's pressure toward a match profitable to him, but soon is plunged by circumstance into marriage with the book's main character—the union is emotionally a premature step for both of them. Throughout this troubled period Clara tests all that happens against her memory of Kate's honesty and gentleness, and on her wedding night itself, offended by the crude "surprise party" sprung by the farm hands, she thinks of Kate, "who had known how to love in silence."

> Clara put her hands to her eyes as though to shut out the scene in the room. "If I could have been with Kate this evening I could have come to a man believing in the possible sweetness of marriage," she thought.⁴⁰

In the end, however, her marriage proves no worse than the average in understanding and happiness. There have been few such sympathetic and unexaggerated pictures of a variant woman in our literature; and none of the others was written by a man.

The year's total balance of sentiment was evened by James Gibbons Huneker's *Painted Veils*. This picture of musical and literary New York was so continental in its cynical frankness that it was first issued privately, though it soon found regular publication and is now available in paper covers. As its epilogue states, its hero Ulick is a young man whose favorite authors are Thomas à Kempis and Petronius, and whose experience reflects this duality of taste. Heroine of the Petronian chapters is a dynamic girl, Easter, who rises by her own efforts—in more fields than one—to the status of world-famed prima donna. Early in her career she considers sources of revenue for European study. To accept support from her lover would give the man too much claim upon her. So her thoughts turn to a fellow student of voice, a dilettante with whom already "an intimacy had developed."

> She began thinking of Allie Wentworth and her set. Allie was an heiress . . . a masculine creature who affected a mannish cut of clothes. She wore her hair closely cut and sported a

walking stick. Her stride and bearing intrigued [Easter],
who had never seen that sort before. . . . Allie was always
hugging her when alone."[41]

Although Allie makes relatively few appearances, it is clear that
she financed and accompanied Easter for a number of years. It is also
implied that the cause of Easter's duel with Mary Garden in Paris
was not, as the newspapers claimed, a man. "When Allie Wentworth,
who was Easter's second, read this in *Le Soir* she burst into laughter."
(When the book appeared, gossip claimed that Mary Garden was
the model for Easter, and that this duel naming her as opposite was
inserted for camouflage.)

Upon Easter's return to New York she says to Ulick, who is
jealous of Allie:

> That girl helped me over some rough places in Europe. I
> shall never give her up, never. . . . I love sumptuous characters.
> That's why I love to read *Mlle Maupin*. Also about that
> perverse puss Satin in *Nana*. She reminds me of Allie and her
> pranks—simply adorable, I tell you! Toujours fidèle."[42]

Later, Easter, now the pursuer because Ulick has turned cool, follows
him to the apartment of his current mistress, a vulgar little creature
who is transported at

> being treated as a social equal by the greatest living lady
> opera singer. . . . Emboldened by her success Dora persuaded
> Easter to go with her into the dressing room, from which
> much later they emerged wearing night draperies. A queer go,
> this sudden intimacy, ruminated the young man."[43] [*A queer go*
> is a bit of *double entendre* worthy of Spanish comedy.]

Finally, there is a party in Easter's quarters including a handful
of lesbians, one or two smoking cigars, and Allie Wentworth, whose
jealous rage is so childish that she must be publicly reproved. With
this Zolaesque portrait of a lesbian woman who is unscrupulous,
ruthless, and promiscuous, there is no need for Huneker to articulate
his opinion of variance.

Few contrasts could be sharper than that between the continental
sophistication of Huneker and the midwestern simplicity of Helen R.
Hull. As early as 1918 she had published in *Century Magazine* a
short-story ("The Fire") of a small-town girl's love for the middle-

aged spinster who gives her not only art lessons but her first contact with a mellow and cultured personality—a benign reverse of the destructive relationship in *Regiment of Women*. The innocent friendship is broken off by the girl's jealous mother on the grounds that "it's not healthy or natural for a girl to be hanging around an old maid." Miss Hull's *Quest* (1922) records the effect upon a growing girl of constant tension between her parents. As precocious as Miss Dane's Louise, Jean falls in love at twelve with a high-school teacher, and simultaneously forms a feverish alliance with a classmate considerably older and less naïve who adores the same woman. Because the other girl is so much more accessible than the teacher, it is the former who draws the mother's fire here, and she terminates the connection with a touch of melodrama which leaves her daughter wary of variant emotion, in the same way that the family situation has affected her with regard to heterosexual love. Jean's subsequent relations with men are inhibited, and her two or three very warm friendships with girls and women during college and her early years of teaching never approach the intensity of her first love.

In *Labyrinth* (1923) Miss Hull attacked from a feminine angle the problem posed in *The Great Adventure:* the frustration of a versatile woman cut off from personal and intellectual contacts by housework and the care of children. After a decade of marriage Catherine returns to a challenging position which she held during World War I, though her husband, a professor, disapproves of the venture. A series of domestic crises plus the professor's calculated move from New York to a small midwestern campus finally thwart his wife's efforts to escape unrelieved domesticity. No variance complicates Catherine's problems, but through minor characters three other emotional adjustments are presented, one involving two women.

The ménage of a professor whose wife is nothing but a *Hausfrau* is dull beyond endurance for all concerned. A woman physician and her husband appear happy, but the man privately mourns his wife's sacrifice of maternity to her professional career. Catherine's younger sister, a social worker and unmarried, has broken away from her mother because "I can't be babied all my life—all sorts of infantile traits sticking to me," and is living with an older fellow-worker. When her sister advises marriage, she retorts:

> Husband! Me? I'm fixed for life right now. . . . Anybody needs someone loving 'em, smoothing 'em down, setting 'em up, brushing off the dust . . . I know a little thing or two

about love. But [this way] you can do that . . . through and around whatever else you're doing . . . I know lots of women who prefer to set up an establishment with another woman. Then you go fifty-fifty on everything. Work and feeling and all the rest, and no King waiting around for his humble servant."

This is Miss Hull's nearest allusion to physical intimacy, and while not explicitly implied, neither is it repudiated. Sympathically as the variant pair are portrayed, they are no more romanticized than the heterosexual couples. The older woman has been a fanatic in many causes and a hunger-striker for suffrage, is moody and violent, and quarrels with any critical male at sight. The younger is cool, practical, and a bit hard. But the alliance apparently stands as good a chance of survival as any in the book, and the author accepts it as a matter of course. The only dissenting voice is the professor's; he is bitter in his animosity and contempt.

Publishing simultaneously with Miss Hull but more nearly in the vein of Huneker was England's Ronald Firbank, whose delightful absurdities began to flower with *Vainglory* in 1918. Firbank was particularly fascinated by all aspects of homosexuality, and not one of his brief novels is without some reference to it. To render these allusions delicate he cultivated a frivolous obscurity, but it was no more designed to conceal that are a dancer's veils to hide the form beneath. Probably the most significant in our field is *The Flower Beneath the Foot* (1923) .⁴⁵ Its setting is a principality the approximate size and importance of Monaco, with a court circle madly international. Here, as always, the lesbian glimpses are oblique, but there are three of them. A visiting Queen Thleeanouhee of the Land of Dates becomes so openly enamoured of the blonde and bovine English ambassadress that the whole court fears an "incident." A lady in waiting in love with the Prince, after her romance is shattered by his diplomatic marriage, flees to an adored Sister in the convent where she was educated, dreaming of a return to earlier delights. She is a bit chilled at being invited, as an adult now, to wield a whip. And last, two of the queen's ladies are becalmed for a summer afternoon alone in a small sailboat. One (she reminds her colleagues of Anthony Hamilton's Miss Hobart) is a girl of "delicate sexless silhouette, whose exotic attraction had aroused not a few heart-burnings (and even feuds) among several of the *grandes dames* about the court."⁴⁶ Her companion is a ripe and languishing widow.

The exiled count upon whom they intended to call catches sight
of their motionless craft and trains his telescope upon it.

> Oh poignant moments when the heart stops still! Not since
> the hours of his exile had the count's been so arrested. Caught
> in the scarlet radiance of the afterglow the becalmed boat,
> for one brief and most memorable second, was his to gaze on.
> In certain lands with what diplomacy falls the night. . . .
> Those dimmer-and-dimmer twilights of the North were un-
> known in Pisuerga. There Night pursues Day as if she meant
> it. "Oh, why was I not *sooner?*" he murmured distractedly
> aloud."

Needless to say, no judgments are even hinted in Firbank's tales.
If his paired ladies are rather ridiculous, so are his pretty gentlemen
and his mixed couples young and old, his kings and social climbers
and mad old ladies. Since all life is clearly so absurd, he seems to
say, what to do save sit back (with all possible grace) and titter at
the spectacle? Edmund Wilson's diagnosis of Gertrude Stein might
apply also in some measure to Firbank, though he did not retreat so
far into literary obscurity.

Post-War Crescendo

These novels of Firbank's, shot through with allusions to both
male and female homosexuality, remind one that two-thirds of the
volumes of Proust's *Recherche du Temps Perdu* had been published
in France by 1923, and were, of course, known to many English and
American writers before being translated. It is easy to overrate the
influence of Proust, especially as both James Joyce and Dorothy
Richardson had anticipated him in "stream of consciousness" technique, the one with *Portrait of the Artist as a Young Man* (1915),
the other with *Pointed Roofs* (1917). But in no one else of Proust's
quality was homosexuality so integral a part of the narrative fabric.
Translations of Proust's most significant volumes appeared in English
between 1924 and 1930. It might also be noted that Margueritte's
La Garçonne was translated in 1923.

A second increasingly important influence was that of Freud,
already discernible in *Regiment of Women* (though a good case
could be made there for Adlerian overtones also), and becoming
more and more obvious in other novels of the same calibre. A striking

example was Harvey O'Higgin's "Story of Julie Kane," which ran
serially in *Harper's Magazine* during 1924, and was as much a
dramatized psychiatric case-record as the earlier work of Dubut de
LaForest in France. Its main emotional themes are a virtually incestuous devotion between the male protagonist and his mother,
and the passion of a spinster school mistress for the young heroine,
her ward. The author, who delivers a good many brief lectures along
the way, labels this last emotion thwarted maternity, but by the
time Julie has reached late adolescence he is describing Martha
Perrin's feeling for her as follows:

> It had come to this, that Martha put herself to sleep at
> night imagining that Julie was in her arms. . . . She kissed
> the undergarments that were to touch the beloved young
> body; and when she had made a dress she caressed it and
> hugged it to her breast so that it might by proxy be her
> arms around Julie. . . . When she had Julie in the sewing
> room to try on the clothes she had made, her hands shook,
> her heart suffocated, and she turned away and wept while
> she fumbled over some pretense of taking up a tuck in the
> back of the garment. . . . After Julie had gone she sat with
> her face in her hands, her cheeks burning against her cold
> fingers, her mouth aching, seeing still the dimples in Julie's
> shoulders, kissing them in her imagination and crying weakly,
> starved.[48]

Few passages have been so explicit since Sappho's famous Ode,
which was less extended.

When Julie is about to leave for college, Martha suffers complete
collapse, one symptom of her illness being that, though starving,
she cannot touch food. A new physician, in the act of taking her
pulse as Julie enters the room, at once prescribes Julie as nurse.
During the period of sickroom intimacy the two fall into each
others' arms and have some weeks "as happy as a honeymoon," though
O'Higgins is careful to repeat that the rapture is essentially that
of mother and daughter. If the sensations described above are
offered as maternal, one can only say that the author was convinced
of an incestuous element in all parent-child relationships. One rather
remarkable aspect of the whole is that though patently psychiatric,
the book does not express that condemnation of the emotions
described which was common to later disciples of Freud. Indeed,

a physician encourages the intimacy of Julie and Martha, as did Violet Ashwin's father in *Lady of Leisure*, though, of course, without advocating lesbian activity. In the situation as presented by O'Higgins, however, some physical release would have been inevitable.

In the same year there appeared in England a much subtler treatment of variance in Radclyffe Hall's early novel *The Unlit Lamp*. Unlike her better known *Well of Loneliness*, this narrative relegates love between women to secondary importance, its focus being the forced martyrdom of unmarried daughters in the name of filial duty. Joan Ogden is the one competent and unselfish member of a neurotic family bent on maintaining social position in their country village. Elizabeth Rodney, a dozen years older, has won a degree from Cambridge before coming, under pressure, to keep house for a bachelor brother in the same community. Her one interest is tutoring Joan, whom she hopes to see achieve a college education and some sort of life beyond small-town domesticity. Mrs. Ogden believes herself bent upon a successful marriage for her daughter, but her actual purpose is to hold her beloved child at any cost; her chief weapon is hypochondria. Joan wants to become a doctor, and Elizabeth offers to provide joint living quarters in Cambridge and to help finance the medical course, but the two girls' long struggle ends with the mother victorious. Elizabeth, unable to endure repeated frustration, leaves the town, eventually marries, and settles in South Africa, refusing to return or to communicate with Joan.

Beneath this drama of parental tyranny runs a strong current of variant emotion. Mrs. Ogden is fragile, jealous, hysterical and over-demonstrative. Both younger women are unfeminine in appearance, cool and fearless in temperament, both affect a masculine simplicity in dress, and Joan crops her hair decades before fashion sanctions that mode. Elizabeth has a masculine distaste for easy caresses and meticulously conceals the depth of her feeling, so that Joan's shy reciprocal emotion never finds outlet (the "unlit lamp" is the passion Elizabeth refuses to set alight). The basic situation, then, is a variant triangle in which the clinging and helpless mother wins against a rival who will employ none of the tactics of seduction, and the result is the virtual ruin of both girls' lives. There are intimations here of what was to become open championship of lesbian love four years later in *Well of Loneliness*. But they are only implicit.

Also in 1924 Arnold Bennett contributed a short draught of his cool common sense in *Elsie and the Child*. With customary realism

and irony he presents a London physician's household centered about
Miss Eva, aged twelve, an only child. The doctor, busy day and
night earning every advantage for his daughter, sees little of
her. His wife is a domestic perfectionist and strict disciplinarian.
The emotional center of the child's life is Elsie, the wholesome but
rather dull servant who was hired originally because Eva (like Metta
in *The Scorpion*) took an instant fancy to her. Elsie is all heart, quick
only in her intuitions, humbly devoted to the aristocratic young
mistress whose care falls largely upon her. A crisis is precipitated
when the parents, aware of their daughter's too-great dependence
upon Elsie, attempt to send the girl to boarding school. She is
acquainted with the headmistress, a hearty tweedy friend of her
mother's, quite the type to captivate some schoolgirls, but not Eva.
Having shot up like a weed to Elsie's considerable stature, the
child is all nerves, and when crossed by her mother she breaks out
with the hysterical declaration that it is not her parents but Elsie
whom she loves and from whom she will not be parted.

Elsie realizes at once that the outcome will be the dismissal
of her and her husband. The latter, a victim of shell shock in World
War I, is a bemused introvert given to dangerous fits of temper.
It is he who turns upon Eva with the charge that her feeling for his
wife is not love, since she does not care if her stubborn whim brings
ruin on Elsie and himself. Made aware for the first time of the
problems of others, the girl gives in and goes off to school. Bennett
contrives with great skill to imply strong emotional undercurrents
in Eva's childish demands for personal service and caresses, and
in Elsie's doting ministrations. He also makes clear that the husband's
violence is actually aroused not by fear of losing his place but by
jealousy, though none of the three persons involved are aware of
this.

Concerning as it does a girl of twelve, this story might not be
classed as variant by psychologists, but one cannot help feeling that
Bennett contributed it to the rapidly swelling count of variant fiction
as testimony to his own stand in the matter. Despite Eva's unusual
height and her susceptibility to Elsie's spontaneous warmth, she is not
conceived as a prospective homosexual. Stimulated one summer
night by watching a sophisticated garden party from her window,
she slips down to the servants' quarters to practice a nascent coquetry
on Joe as well as Elsie. There could hardly be a clearer statement
of Bennett's opinion that variant emotion is as natural to puberty as
growing pains, particularly where maternal affection is wanting, but
that its natural span runs out with early adolescence.

In 1925 four novels dealing with variance reached the English reading public—the translation of Rolland's *Annette and Sylvie* and Virginia Woolf's *Mrs. Dalloway,* both treating it briefly and with sympathy, Sherwood Anderson's *Dark Laughter,* touching upon it even more casually and with disfavor, and Naomi Royde-Smith's *Tortoiseshell Cat,* devoted wholly to the theme and wholly condemnatory. Rolland's lesbian interlude between the half-sisters Rivière has already been described. Anderson's heroine, a married woman on the verge of taking a lover, recalls privately her first trip abroad under the guidance of a couple whose sophistication she did not suspect until on shipboard. The woman had made skillfully veiled lesbian advances which she recognized for what they were and resisted with equal skill. Anderson clearly condemns this deliberate attempt at seduction, but no more severely than he condemns the woman's ruses to snare wealthy subjects for her portrait-painting husband. The episode is slighter than the one in *Poor White* and of little weight in its chief actor's life.

Mrs. Woolf's passages are much more subtle, though most of them, like Anderson's, are incorporated in Clarissa Dalloway's reminiscences of her girlhood. Even preliminary to these, however, we learn that Mrs. Dalloway is happy that her husband insists on her sleeping in a separate room after an illness.

> She could not dispel a virginity preserved through childbirth which clung to her like a sheet; . . . through some contraction of this cold spirit she had failed him again and again. She could see what she lacked. . . . It was something warm which broke up surfaces and rippled the cold contact of man and woman, or of women together. For *that* she could dimly perceive. She resented it, had a scruple picked up Heaven knows where, or, as she felt, sent by Nature (who is invariably wise) ; yet she could not resist sometimes yielding to the charm of a woman, not a girl . . . like a faint scent or a violin next door. She did undoubtedly feel then what men felt. It was a sudden revelation which one tried to check and then yielded to, and felt the world come closer, swollen with some astonishing significance, some pressure of rapture, which split its thin skin and gushed and poured with an extraordinary alleviation.[49]

Her first experience of this sort came to her in her late teens or early twenties in connection with the delightful madcap Sally Seton.

Had that not after all been love? . . . At some party she
had a distinct recollection of saying to the man she was with,
"Who is *that?*" And all that evening she could not take her
eyes off Sally. . . . The strange thing, on looking back, was
the purity, the integrity, of her feeling for Sally. It was not
like one's feeling for a man. It was protective on her side;
sprang from a sense of being in league together, a presentiment
of something that was bound to part them (they always spoke
of marriage as a catastrophe), which led to this chivalry. . . .
She could remember going cold with excitement, and doing
her hair in a kind of ecstasy . . . and dressing and going
downstairs, feeling as she crossed the hall "if it were now to
die 'twere now to be most happy." That was her feeling—
all because she was coming down to dinner in a white frock
to meet Sally Seton!

[Sally] stood by the fireplace talking, in that beautiful
voice which made everything she said sound like a caress . . .
when suddenly she said, "What a shame to sit indoors!" and
they all went out on to the terrace and walked up and down.
She and Sally fell a little behind. Then came the most
exquisite moment of her whole life passing a stone urn
with flowers in it. Sally stopped; picked a flower; kissed her
on the lips. The whole world might have turned upside
down![50]

When the men of the party (one of them in love with her) return
and make casual, half-teasing conversation,

It was like running one's face against a granite wall in the
darkness! It was shocking; it was horrible. Not for herself.
She felt only how Sally was being mauled already, maltreated;
she felt his hostility; his jealousy; his determination to break
their companionship. "Oh this horror!" she said to herself,
as if she had known all along that something would interrupt,
would embitter her moment of happiness.[51]

There is no further reference in the novel to Sally, and Clarissa
Dalloway lives on for us into her mid-fifties, wife and mother, never
again in such intimate touch with life, unless it is in her relation to
her daughter. For although above she has said that the charm of a
girl never moves her, her love for the eighteen-year-old Elizabeth

is the most vital element in her current existence. The girl is undergoing a spell of inexplicable devotion to a shabby, unkempt, embittered woman tutor, for whom Mrs. Dalloway finds it difficult to
repress a burning hatred, and one realizes that this hatred is but
the obverse of the emotion she will not recognize for the beautiful
daughter so different from herself and so aloof.

The reader will remember that in the other strand of the dual
narrative Septimus Smith, shell-shock case from World War I, fails
to regain his mental balance or to respond to his devoted wife
because he cannot admit to consciousness the love he felt for a fellow-
officer who was killed. In her preface, the author says that Smith
is intended to be Clarissa Dalloway's "double," and that in its
first conception the story, lacking him, ended with Mrs. Dalloway's
death. It would seem that her contribution here to the problem of
variance is the possibility of its being a happy experience where
innocence is easy—as for a woman; but for a man too scrupulous to
accept the almost inevitable outcome in the male, it may be fatal.

It is a radical step from *Mrs. Dalloway* to the forthright *Tortoiseshell Cat,* in which a lesbian woman plays a sinister part. The central
figure, a motherless girl in her late twenties, is still a pristine innocent,
thanks to her exclusive devotion to a scholarly father lost a short
time before. Gillian is baffled by her worldly-wise younger sister's
hold upon men, and by the quixotic devotion of a girl who leaves
her private school in protest when Gillian (a teacher there) is
dismissed. It is this innocence which cost her her teaching position—
she chose French poetry to read aloud on the basis of its beauty alone,
genuinely unaware of its sexual connotations—and presently it leads
her into even more serious danger.

After her sister's marriage, left alone in a dreary residence club
and bored with a part-time secretaryship, she meets a fellow resident,
half American and completely bohemian and fascinating. The initial
encounter is significant:

> But as V.V. came with a swift steady stride, the free rapid
> movement of a woman who had been much with horses, who
> had ridden from childhood, Gillian knew, with a thrill of
> recognition so strange, so new to her experience that the
> shock of it took away all sense of every other consideration,
> that she beheld in the flesh the very image of a perfection
> wrought by her own imaginings in the secret places of her
> dreaming mind. This was not a beautiful creature for all

the world to gape at, it was the figure—unique of its kind—
for which the shrine of her spirit had stood empty and waiting
until now.[52]

A definitely masculine figure, as the passage goes on to emphasize, and
a masterly analysis of romantic love-at-first-sight. The woman's voice
is flat and unlovely, but Gillian, for all her musical ear, is too en-
thralled to care. All that she is aware of for some time are the lavish
personal ministrations and caresses with which she is showered.
She learns without grasping the implications that V.V. has lived
with a long succession of women, many of them minor actresses.
Early in her life there was one, mentioned seldom and cryptically,
on whose account she was evidently disowned by her family and incurred debts not yet paid.

Before long, Gillian's emotional preoccupation evokes remon-
strance from her sister, the once-adoring student, and the latter's
recently acquired sculptor-husband; but to her their warnings are
absurd. The sculptor lived before his marriage with a faunlike
musician whom he loved and protected from fortune-hunting women.
This elfin Heinrich is as bewitched as Gillian by V.V.'s physical
beauty, and as V.V. has an eye to the main chance, she inveigles him
into an engagement. As soon as he becomes importunate and "boring,"
however, instinct conquers interest and she shakes him off, clinching
the matter one evening by refusing an invitation because she must
bathe Gillian and put her to bed. With a stolen key, V.V. manages to
enter the apartment where Gillian is actually bathing in a meager
British "portable" before an open fire, and attempts to embrace her.
Gillian, though excited by the caresses, fights her off in sudden horrified realization of what their long ambiguous dalliance has been
leading to. For the first time in her life she comprehends the passion
she has observed in others, and her revulsion is violent. Heinrich, however, reads quite another meaning into the shadow-struggle he sees
silhouetted on her drawn blind, and goes home to shoot himself.

Gillian falls gravely ill from shock, but finally, safe in her sister's
comfortable home, regains her balance.

The only person who had escaped unhurt was V.V. But she
was unhurt because long ago she had been so maimed, her
soul had been so warped and stunted by the influence she
could still recall though she was too vitiated to resent it, that
nothing now would make very much difference. V.V. had
gone her own way and Gillian could not follow her. She had

taken the first steps on the road down which V.V. was dis-
appearing, and had come back to the place where it started.
And now that road was closed.[53]

However marred it is by such expository passages and by its sudden
melodramatic suicide, the story carries more conviction than *Regiment of Women* through coming to grips with the physical issue
and through its more sympathetic presentation of the lesbian woman.

In 1926, drama for the first time took precedence over fiction,
of which the year's sole example was the translation of Louis
Couperus's *The Comedians*. This historical novel laid in the reign
of Domitian includes a pair of lesbians, the emperor's cousin and
his wife's niece, who frequent the inns of Rome disguised respectively
as gladiator and street wench. Life at court is such a nightmare of
intrigue and surveillance that only their mutual passion and their
secret adventures make existence tolerable. The "gladiator" is shortly
killed in a street brawl, and the other girl, though her interests
have seemed bisexual, fades into melancholia.

As to the theatre, the international success of Bourdet's *La Prisonnière* has already been cited. Its New York run as *The Captive* began
in September, and its drawing power very likely led to the presentation of two related plays later in the season. Thomas Hurlbut's
lesbian *Hymn to Venus* opened in Atlantic City in late November
and was scheduled for further trial in Chicago before appearing on
Broadway. Its initial performance rated a single brief review in the
New York Times,[54] chilly and vague, saying of the play only that
its theme was that of *The Captive* and that it ended with a suicide.
There was no indication whether the treatment was sympathetic
or otherwise, and the text of the play has not been available. It was
withdrawn after a second performance and reached neither Chicago
nor New York.

The second effort, *The Drag* by one "Jane Mast," made its
debut in Boston in February 1927 with Mae West among the cast.
Because, as the title indicates, it dealt with the stringently tabooed
subject of male homosexuality, it was at once suppressed, and sufficient adverse sentiment was aroused to bring about the closing
of *The Captive* after a successful run of five months,[55] especially
interesting in view of the strong condemnation of lesbianism in the
French play. This official action seems to have had only local
effects, for no difficulties attended the publication in England of the
translation of Lacretelle's *La Bonifas,* or of Rosamund Lehmann's

Dusty Answer, in which the middle section is a study of variance. There were also oblique variant allusions in Mrs. Woolf's *To the Lighthouse* (1927).

Lacretelle's stout championship of Marie Bonifas needs no further comment. *To the Lighthouse* was Mrs. Woolf's most subtle study of the contrast between masculine and feminine personality. Here Mrs. Ramsey personifies the selfless unifying influence of woman's intuition in her dealings with an intellectual husband, a diverse brood of six children, and a swarm of family friends of all ages and temperaments. The individual most devoted to her is an artist of thirty-three, who "with her little Chinese eyes and puckered up face . . . would never marry. . . . She was an independent little creature."[56] With masculine honesty Lily Briscoe recognizes that she is not so much in love with Mrs. Ramsey as with the mysterious force, intuitive and emotional, which she radiates and which Lily herself must always lack. And so she masters her own emotions in moments when Mrs. Ramsey is maternally tender, and quivers with uncontrollable laughter at the older woman's failure to understand the situation when she urges marriage upon her. Still, nearly a decade after Mrs. Ramsey's death, she weeps for her loss when she returns to paint again at the site of their earlier association, "feeling the old horror come back—to want and want and not to have."[57]

Miss Lehmann's *Dusty Answer,* like many first novels written before their authors are wholly mature, was autobiographical in structure, following its heroine from childhood to her early twenties. Daughter of a scholarly father who tutors her at home and a frivolous mother who lives much abroad, Judith grows up in virtual solitude, her only acquaintances a group of children who occasionally visit an adjoining country house. These exotic cousins, four boys and a girl, fascinate the lonely child, who looks forward to their infrequent appearances and does her best to achieve some personal relation with one or the other, but they continually elude her. The object of her secret first love is Roddy, most elusive of all; at the moment when some mutual spark seems about to leap between them, his friend Tony comes for a weekend, a jealous effeminate boy who at once absorbs Roddy completely.

During Judith's course at Cambridge she and a very beautiful classmate are mutually attracted and spend two rapturous but innocent years scarcely out of one another's sight. When Judith returns after her last "long vac," however, she senses a profound change in her friend, who spent her own free time in residence making up delinquencies. From a gossiping classmate Judith learns that Jennifer had a guest for much of the period, and that the two indulged in "wrestling matches" on the lawn which many of the girls found in doubtful taste. This dark Geraldine, a deep-voiced older woman of powerful physique and personality, presently reappears. Though Judith pointedly avoids the pair, Geraldine seeks her out and commands her to "let Jennifer alone," since the latter is "beginning to find herself" and Geraldine plans to take her abroad. This scene is a triumph of subtlety; presented from the viewpoint of the innocent Judith, it still conveys the exact nature of Geraldine's feeling for and hold upon Jennifer. Judith withdraws completely, leaving Jennifer so torn between her old love and her new passion that even after Geraldine's departure she cannot regain nervous stability, and is forced to leave college.

After a melancholy last term, Judith goes home to a single passionate summer night with Roddy, but upon discovering that what to her was a pledge of lasting love was to him but a casual episode, she breaks with him forever. In the course of the next year or so she wins from each of the remaining cousins just such personal responses as she once craved, but these are now empty. Her only vivid moment comes with a letter from Jennifer, incoherently half-explaining their broken friendship (which Judith has long since comprehended) and begging for a meeting in Cambridge. But when Judith keeps the appointment, Jennifer fails either to appear or to send a message, and the final flick of irony is a distant sight of Roddy and his friend Tony strolling past in intimate absorption. While Miss Lehmann takes artistic pains to point no moral, first Roddy's and then Judith's absorption in a variant friendship seem deterrents to happy emotional resolution through other channels.

First Peak: 1928

In contrast to the two preceding years, 1928 offered a harvest as rich and varied as any single season until then: Radclyffe's Hall's *Well of Loneliness,* Compton Mackenzie's *Extraordinary Women,* Elizabeth Bowen's *The Hotel,* and Virginia Woolf's *Orlando.* Not foremost in literary rank but certainly best known is *The Well of Loneliness,* for its censorship became a *cause célèbre* in the publishing world. Issued in January by the solidly established firm of Jonathan Cape, with an introduction by Havelock Ellis, the work was reviewed favorably in reputable literary periodicals. Shortly, however, it was attacked in the sensational London newspaper, *The Express,* with the result that it was banned in England and its

publisher sued. Forty-five leading British authors, from Lascelles
Abercrombie and Arnold Bennett to Leonard and Virginia Woolf,
signed a letter of indignant protest, and a half dozen physicians and
legal authorities volunteered to testify at the publisher's trial, but
their testimony was not allowed.[58] The reason for its condemnation
while so many other variant novels were passed without action was
its explicit defense of lesbian experience.

Although for a decade or so the novel has been freely available
in inexpensive editions, a brief summary may be offered. Stephen
Gordon, only child of solid county parents whose dearest desire is
a son, receives the name and upbringing that would have been his.
From infancy she is the image of her father, masculine in build,
mannerisms, abilities and tastes. At eight she experiences unmistakable passion for a housemaid; throughout adolescence she
despises feminine garments and amusements; in her late teens she
rejects a first suitor, long her good friend, whose sudden amorousness
seems to her unnatural. The death of her father leaves her without
an ally and bitterly solitary. At twenty she becomes infatuated with
a new neighbor's wife, a former American chorus girl, who plays the
coquette and accepts lavish gifts but evades caresses by pleading
her husband's jealousy. Stephen's discovery that a male rival has been
successful drives her to frenzy, and the American, fearful that the
girl may inform her husband of her infidelity, forestalls the possibility
by showing him Stephen's last letter. This outpouring of naked
passion, at once passed on to her mother, leads to Stephen's being
turned out of her home and virtually driven from England. Soon
she achieves a literary reputation of sorts, but her lack of passionate
experience proves an artistic handicap. In London and Paris she
meets both male and female homosexuals but shuns them, hating
their immediate interest in her because she hates her own "difference"
and wants only to be accepted as a normal human being.

Then World War I gives her, along with others of her sort,
the chance to do a man's job in an ambulance unit. She falls deeply
in love with a younger co-worker, innocent and feminine, whom she
struggles to protect from danger. After their release by the armistice,
a holiday together forces both to admit the nature of their love—
an interlude less specifically detailed than Lawrence's lesbian passage
in *The Rainbow*, but, of course, presented with complete sympathy.
Now united, the two girls attempt to make a life for themselves in
Paris, but neither find tolerable the bohemian existence which is
open to them, and both suffer under the slights which exclude them
from conventional society. Eventually, Stephen's early suitor seeks

them out and falls in love with Mary, who responds but will not consider disloyalty to Stephen. The latter, realizing that Mary can never be happy with her outside the social pale, makes the dramatic gesture of pretending intimacy with a distinguished lesbian she has known superficially for years. She achieves her purpose—Mary accepts the man, and Stephen is left once more to loneliness.

The story is more engrossing than *The Unlit Lamp* because of swifter pace and greater intensity, but inferior in literary art, since it is often over-emotional and occasionally lapses into bald special pleading. Moreover, there is a blur in the explanation of Stephen's variance. Emphasis on her physical masculinity indicates hereditary causes, as does her father's early recognition of her anomaly. But his consequent indulgence of her proclivities, and the stress laid on both parents' desire for a male child, hint at belief in prenatal as well as childhood conditioning. Miss Hall's evident purpose was to absolve Stephen of the slightest responsibility for her temperament, and inevitably one is reminded of Lacretelle's *Marie Bonifas,* translated in the preceding year but probably known to Miss Hall in French upon its appearance in 1925. The two differ in that Lacretelle lays Freudian stress on negative childhood conditioning, while Miss Hall's comparative hereditary emphasis marks her a disciple of the older school of Ellis and Hirschfeld. Despite its shortcomings, *The Well of Loneliness* made a heroic gesture for tolerance of lesbian relations among persons of integrity, and the author had the satisfaction before her death of seeing it widely accepted.

Compton Mackenzie entered the variant lists armed with gentle satire. *Extraordinary Women,* like Norman Douglas's *South Wind* to which its foreword pays respect, is laid on the island of Capri, here called Sirene. It includes almost as many lesbian individuals as Peladan's *La Gynandre* of forty years earlier, and considering its author's Catholic affiliation, it may have been written with some similar, though milder, intent. Every nationality is represented and every age, from Lulu de Randan, sent vacationing with her governess to break off a flirtation with a tradesman's son, to a fading Roman wife given to tearful sentimentality over the boyish young beauty she adores. Roughly there are two generations of lesbian women, among the older a poet who poses as a modern Sappho, a tailored Englishwoman who has bred bulldogs and supported *boxeuses* in Paris for a few decades, and Lulu's Anglo-French mother. The younger group includes a stormy and self-defeating Greek concert pianist, an American hypochondriac, millionaire's daughter, and the picturesque and irresistable poseuse, Rosalba Donsante, child of the third

of her Swiss mother's five international marriages. What plot there
is centers about Rosalba and Aurora Freemantle, the Englishwoman,
who finds the girl an incarnation of the boyish ideal she has celebrated
in her lesbian verse for years. "Rory," dreaming of permanence at
last, remodels a villa halfway up to Anasirene at reckless expense,
but her beloved is of no mind to be caged there, and leads practically
every woman in the cast a hectic chase before the curtain falls upon
her unheralded departure in pursuit of a last inamorata, leaving
poor Rory in tears in her empty paradise.

The tale offers a potpourri of sophisticated intrigue fertilized by
idleness and wealth. Its various types are superficially convincing
enough, but they are largely unaccounted for beyond the influence
of their frivolous environment. Many of the older women have been
married at least once, and even young Lulu has narrowly missed
a heterosexual entanglement before succumbing to Rosalba's glamor-
ous seduction. Few men enter upon the scene save hotel servants
and one or two twittering homosexuals and eccentrics. Rory alone
(physically as masculine as Stephen Gordon) is treated with some
gentleness as a victim of hereditary forces, although even she is more
ridiculous than appealing, and the total effect of the novel is one
of cool detachment, the report of a witty and superior observer.

Among these outspoken narratives Miss Bowen's quiet social
comedy, *The Hotel,* is conspicuous for a sexual reticence as absolute
as any before 1915. The hotel of her title, a conservative Riviera
establishment frequented by professors, clergymen, retired officers
and their families, provides a lively background for her understated
central drama. In this, the actors are two: a British girl of twenty
and a cosmopolitan widow twice her age with a son at school in
Germany. (The action antedates World War I.) Sydney is ostensibly
recuperating from overstudy for a recent university degree, and
acting as companion to a married cousin. Actually, as she is wretchedly
aware, her relatives have financed her holiday in the the expectation
of her capturing a husband. But Sydney is wholly absorbed in
Mrs. Kerr. This exquisite worldling, of whom the other guests stand
a bit in awe, accepts the girl's small services and gifts with just
enough warmth to keep her enslaved and the onlookers socially
envious. Malicious gossip naturally flourishes over the bridge tables,
and though it stops just short of slander, Sydney finds the association
all in all more wearing than rewarding.

When the son arrives on holiday it is clear that he is held captive
on a similar emotional leash, and Sydney's intelligence recognizes

that their charmer is playing one against the other and battening on their mutual jealousy. But not until, piqued at a black mood of Sydney's, Mrs. Kerr accuses her of playing for a passionate response, and voices disdain for "emotions so unbalanced," is she moved to rebellion. The injustice of the charge, when she has all but broken under the strain of emotional control, finally dissolves the spell. On the rebound Sydney tries being engaged to an estimable but rather colorless clergyman, but Mrs. Kerr's brilliant subtlety has spoiled her for finding happiness in a commonplace association. Her final saddened conclusion is that the whole Hotel interlude has been a kind of lotus-eater's dream bred of idleness in an artificial environment, and her only hope is that all its cloying preoccupations will fade with return to "reality" in England.

This study of heartless egotism may owe something to *Regiment of Women,* but it achieves the unity and detachment which Miss Dane's study lacked. The problem here is simpler, of course; Mrs. Kerr's beauty and assurance lead to conquest without effort, and aside from her vanity her own emotions are little involved. Of the pair, then, Sydney alone is variant, a telling example of that protracted adolescence which is common among the intellectually precocious. Her attaining adult perspective without benefit of a happy heterosexual romance marks Miss Bowen's independence of current Freudian theory, a point of artistry in her favor. Another is her humorous vignette of a pair of elderly spinsters whose one-time variant devotion has withered into querulous possessiveness. All in all, pale aquarelle though *The Hotel* is among the year's more positive canvases, its quiet statement carries authority.

Any cursory treatment of Mrs. Woolf's *Orlando* must do it grave injustice, but here the emotional thread must be drawn from the rich fabric and examined as nearly as may be alone. No one yet has analyzed *Orlando* fully, and such critics as have not slighted it in discussing Mrs. Woolf's work have tended to find it uneven and confusing. Complex it is indeed, but a part of the critical confusion has come from failure or refusal to recognize as perhaps its main theme the relation of intersexual traits to creative ability. It attempts in fact to sustain four parallel motifs. The most obvious is the biography of a timeless individual who enters as a boy of sixteen acquainted with Shakespeare and Queen Elizabeth, and is still living in October 1928 as an English woman of thirty-six. A second is the changing social roles of the two sexes from century to century and their consequently shifting relations to one another.

A third is the corresponding fluctuation—perhaps resultant, perhaps only concomitant—in the emotional "Spirit of the Age" in English literature. This is least coherently traced and may be ignored here. The fourth and most cryptic is a parallel between the history of Orlando and the literary and perhaps personal biography of Mrs. Woolf's colleague and friend, Victoria Sackville-West, more than one of whose photographs illustrate Orlando's later career, and whose family estate of Knole is clearly pictured in the descriptions of Orlando's ancestral house. (For judicious comment on this last motif and on Mrs. Woolf's other variant references, the reader is referred to David Daiches's laudatory study of her work published in 1942.[59])

In the sixteenth century Orlando is a budding poetic dramatist (as was Thomas Sackville, of the family living even than at Knole). As a debonair boy he lives the sexual life of a lusty age, and is far from innocent when in his late teens profound passion overtakes him. With a Russian girl-princess, niece of the ambassador from St. Petersburg, he lives out a burning romance worthy of the period, which ends tragically when Sasha sails for home without adieu. The Russian girl is no innocent either; she is secretive, older than he emotionally, though younger in years; he suspects her of dalliance with a muscovite sailor and even, after her desertion, of being the ambassador's mistress rather than his niece. Though anything but masculine, she is robust and by spells cruel in temperament; she wears Russian trousers against the cold, and skates, rides and loves with the zest and endurance of another boy. But her desertion has a woman's cruelty, and it throws Orlando presently into a state of delayed shock which produces a seven-day trance.

He emerges a melancholy seventeenth-century philosophic poet, ridden by a passion for fame. Soon he is stalked by a ridiculous and masculine Roumanian bluestocking who—perhaps because she is six-feet-two—plays the man's role in the game of hearts. For a moment "Orlando heard . . . far off the beating of love's wings." But at the point of becoming ensnared, suddenly "it was Lust the vulture, not Love the bird of paradise, that flopped foully and disgustingly upon his shoulders. Hence he ran. . . ."[60]

He escapes by accepting a diplomatic post in Constantinople, where he achieves brilliant success until a local uprising terminates his mission. He lives in the ornate luxury befitting an emissary of Charles II to the Sultan, and becomes "the adored of many women and some men," but only from a distance. In private he is still melancholy, and escapes to write poetry in the hills by day, by night to roam the city streets, where he meets a gypsy dancer, Pepita. With her he contracts a marriage of sorts and, rumor hints, has a trio of offspring. This episode is sketched so briefly that one can only guess at its significance. It cannot well have repeated the early romance with Sasha, since she was a court lady of brilliant culture and Pepita is a daughter of the streets. But neither can it have echoed the passage with the Archduchess Harriet. Honest passion for an illiterate woman does not inspire the self-loathing bred of an itch for an otherwise hateful social and intellectual peer. Whatever it meant to Orlando, after the uprising ends his official services, he bestows a farewell embrace upon the gypsy and falls into his second seven-day trance. It may be that this one registered inability to endure an emotional impasse any longer.

From it he awakes a woman, but Mrs. Woolf lays stress on the fact that the change is merely one of physical sex and not at all of temperament.

> The sound of trumpets died away and Orlando stood stark naked. No human being since the world began has ever looked more ravishing. His form combined in one the strength of a man and a woman's grace.[61]

With the gypsies (not apparently Pepita's clan) to whom Orlando escapes, she still lives a man's life, for among nomads, temperament and daily duties are much the same in both sexes. After some seasons of successful adaptation to this barbaric simplicity, nostalgia for England and for literary pursuits turns Orlando toward home. And now she faces the difficult business of learning to act the lady. High comedy attends her efforts, particularly in connection with a renewed pursuit by her former *bête noire,* the bluestocking, who now through a transformation corresponding to her own is an absurd and lachrymose Roumanian nobleman. Amid the relaxed proprieties of the eighteenth century, Orlando often roams London in man's dress, more at home in the honest company of daughters of joy than in the artificial salons of her peers.

> There were many stories told at the time, as, that she fought a duel, served on one of the King's ships as a captain, was seen to dance naked on a balcony, and fled with a certain lady to the Low Countries where the lady's husband followed

them. . . . She enjoyed the love of both sexes . . . for her sex
changed far more frequently than those who have worn only
one set of clothing can conceive.[62]

The neatness with which fantasy here dodges any scandalous implications may well account for the difficult *tour de force* which
the whole volume is.

With the advent of Queen Victoria, a depressing social change
occurs: humankind is rigorously divided into Men, whose role is to
lead, protect, support; and Women, who must submit, be timorous,
and cling. The results, both personal and literary, Mrs. Woolf
plainly considers lamentable. Orlando's history turns emotionally
barren and housewifely, and neither reading nor writing afford
her any relief. Though she suffers from personal loneliness and social
disapprobation, she refuses to consider marriage under such a regime.
She waits instead for the twentieth century:

> There was something definite and distinct about the age,
> which reminded her of the eighteenth century, except that
> there was a distinction, a desperation. . . .[63]

In this century she meets a man with the spirit of a poet—he knows
Shelley by heart—but who has also been "a soldier and a sailor and
. . . explored the east." Mutual love is instantaneous, and complete
union follows swiftly upon the intuitive moment when both cry
out together: "You're a woman, Shel!" "You're a man, Orlando!"

> For each was so surprised at the quickness of the other's
> sympathy, and it was to each such a revelation that a woman
> could be as tolerant and free-spoken as a man, and a man as
> strange and subtle as a woman, that they had to put the mat-
> ter to the proof at once.[64]

The natural and happy results are marriage and a son, but not a
Victorian ménage. "Shel" is gone the greater part of the time on his
adventurous voyages, and Orlando is free to "write and write and
write" and win literary prizes.

Clearly Mrs. Woolf felt that to be an integrated, and above all,
a creative personality, one needs freedom from the Procrustes' bed of
sex. She was not preaching license in the name of some bohemian
deity of Bloomsbury or Greenwich Village. She was begging psycho-

logical *Lebensraum* for the creative artist. Nevertheless, the total sum of Orlando's experience is, beyond question, bisexual.

Among these four novels of 1928, Mackenzie's satire was mild rather than sharp; Miss Bowen pictured variance as an unhappy state but treated her variant girl with entire sympathy; and Mrs. Woolf pled as it were in the abstract, Miss Hall in passionate particular, for the variant, even the lesbian woman of personal integrity. The annual balance was, therefore, on the whole positive, and it is clear that the verdict early in the year against *Well of Loneliness* restrained British publishers only from issuing lesbian propaganda.

CHAPTER X.

FICTION IN ENGLISH (continued)

Sequel to Censorship

Just how specifically the skirmish of censorship and its attendant publicity affected subsequent work is difficult to say. The next few years saw in print nothing more outspoken than translations of Rachilde's *Monsieur Vénus* and Colette's *Claudine at School*. This can probably be attributed to caution on the part of both publishers and authors. That antagonistic voices, first largely women's and then men's, swelled into a full chorus by 1933, might similarly seem a protracted echo of official disapproval. On the other hand, some tolerant treatments of variance were finding publication, and in 1934 it was these which constituted eight out of that year's ten offerings. As to how much the rapidly augmenting flood—a total of over thirty variant titles in six years—was attributable to 1928's focusing of attention on the controversial subject, how much merely to an inevitably growing preoccupation with it, no armchair theorizing can safely decide. But that it owed something to the former seems beyond question.

Among this six-years' crop a handful of more or less negative contributions, all by American women, probably stemmed from Miss Lehmann's *Dusty Answer,* whatever impetus they gained from later developments. All were novels of boarding school or women's college life, all autobiographical in pattern, and none were confined to variant experience. In the first, Wanda Fraiken Neff's *We Sing Diana,* the variant passages would seem a deliberate counterattack upon *Well of Loneliness* except that the two appeared almost simultaneously in 1928. Mrs. Neff's heroine, an orphan brought up by a passionless spinster, is already conditioned against heterosexual romance by her rearing and adolescent experiences before reaching college. There, during her freshman year, Nora is an inadvertent witness of an emotional scene between two brilliant and respected upperclassmen.

> She was conscious of the drooping narrowness of Gwendolyn's shoulders, the slenderness of her neck, as she threw herself against Minna's bulky frame. . . . Nora had a sick memory of the fungi she had studied in botany, the rank growth, forms of life springing up in unhealthy places, feeding on rot. . . .

And of a girl who suddenly embraces Nora, the author says:

> There was something about Emily which brought back . . . her earliest childhood terror [a quite irrelevant incident involving a cat]. She detached herself violently and avoided the sight of Emily's darkly flushing face. . . . Only instinct, like the swift revulsion of a young animal sniffing a poisonous weed . . . held her back.[2]

(In reality the terror here is of her own response, and the whole picture, if the author faced it honestly, is that of the potential variant who will suffer infinitely rather than admit her own inclination.) She, like most of her friends, can achieve no adequate relations with men in their limited environment, and Nora herself, after a later somewhat unconvincing fortnight's liaison terminated by her lover's sudden death, drifts back via graduate study abroad to be dean in just such a college as she left.

A milder reaction is registered in *Against the Wall* (1929) by Kathleen Millay, sister of Edna St. Vincent, whose variant publications were by then several years old. The younger Millay's theme is mainly protest against the restricted position of women, including an arraignment of the women's college, which should educate its students to be adult, but, while doing so, treats them as children. Her references to variance are belittling. The phenomenon seems confined to a handful of girls on the campus, one of whom is threatened with dismissal by the student president. But the heroine, Rebecca, has overheard during her freshman year that same president sob out her love for a boyish upperclassman, and she now threatens the disciplinarian with exposure unless her present harsh fiat is rescinded. In the course of an inevitable "bull session" after this incident, Rebecca expresses her opinion to timidly questioning fellow students.

"Is anything that doesn't end in—babies—abnormal, per-
verted?"

"I suppose so, if you come right down to it."

"If there's so much of it I don't see why it's abnormal."

"No," said Rebecca, "neither do I. Only like a lot of other
things, the word has come to be more important than what it
stands for. Anyway, I think most women would be more happy
with a man for a—best friend—than with a woman. What do
you think?"³

To this Socratic question there is a chorus of affirmatives from everyone save a member of the suspect group who chances to be present.

Marion Patton-Waldron's *Dance on the Tortoise* (1930) is set in
a boarding school. A girl just out of college, feeling herself emotionally unready for marriage, seeks greater maturity through a year of
teaching, and inauspicious though the chosen milieu might seem, she
achieves her goal. She is drawn early into emotional friendship with
a French colleague, Helene. A similar bond exists between the headmistress and an older teacher, a pair unseparated since their college
days, and Lydia learns that they have been seen passionately kissing;
however, she shrinks from similar expression with her friend. Helene
becomes involved in an affair with a countryman which ends with
her death from induced miscarriage. It is only after this tragedy, the
precise cause of which the innocent Lydia only half-guesses, that she
wonders whether Helene might not have resisted seduction had she
herself been able to give her friend the emotional release so badly
needed. But she knows she could never have done so. In her distress
she turns to the headmistress, only to find the latter growing over-
fond of her. In the end she accepts her deferred suitor eagerly:

"These bunches of women living together, falling in love
with each other because they haven't anyone else to fall in
love with! It's obscene! Oh, take me away!"⁴

Apparently she is alone in feeling so. Students and teachers consider
the relation between the headmistress and her friend admirable and
touching. Like those in Henry Handel Richardson's Australian school
two decades earlier, they are not only without immediate suspicion,
but ignorant of any discreditable possibilities. This is very nearly the
last work of fiction to claim such innocence for its characters.

In the same year Elisabeth Wilkins Thomas, in *Ella*, touched on
variance so gingerly as to be almost ambiguous. Ella knows but two

real drives throughout—one a love of poetry, the other a compulsion comparable to Mary MacLane's "not to give up my me-ness." In college she derives an intellectual thrill so keen as to carry strong emotional overtones in the philosophy classes of a casual, tailored, and sardonic woman professor. However, their relation is confined to the classroom. Later as a private-school teacher Ella is closely attached to an older colleague, and though the two speak frankly of loving one another, no passion is admitted between them. Madge has, in her youth, been deeply attached to a younger girl whom she helped and protected when both were students in Germany. When this ex-protégée, now married and a mother, pays a visit to the cottage where Madge and Ella are summering together, Ella finds herself dreading the visit. Her dread grows with Madge's minute, feverishly excited preparations for her old love's advent, and unconscious jealousy is clearly at its root. But the young mother and her closeknit little family barely pause for a meal, unaware, in their happy self-absorption, of the disappointment dealt by their refusal to accept further hospitality. Madge, long afflicted with a heart condition, has over-exerted herself in preparation, and hidden grief at its futility brings on a fatal attack. Only the depth of Ella's loneliness after her friend's death brings home to her how much of her "me-ness" has been jeopardized in this relationship, and she determines to depend thereafter only upon herself and the solacing beauty of poetry. Her solitary orphaned childhood is the apparent explanation of her narcissistic fear of personal involvement.

Mary Lapsley's *Parable of the Virgins* (1931) devotes rather more space to variance than its predecessors. Its theme, like theirs, is the failure of women's colleges to deal adequately with the emotional fevers bred of segregation during late adolescence. Along with a few grave heterosexual crises—one, an abortion which its subject faces without remorse because of the wholesome first-hand knowledge of life she has gained—there are variant entanglements involving half a dozen or more girls, though none of the relations are admitted to be lesbian. Mary, antagonistic to men, is obsessed by passion for Jessica, whom she induces to break a lukewarm engagement. Then Bob, a boarding school product "like a nice athletic boy," precipitates tragedy by flirting with her adored. Mary's furious jealousy moves an unsympathetic dean (had the author perhaps known one like Mrs. Neff's "Nora"?) to separate her from Jessica by telling Mary that the latter is her victim, fearing and hating her but unable to break the unwholesome spell without help. In consequence, Mary hangs herself. Jessica then collapses, and her state is so aggravated by the

harshness of the college's woman physician that an understanding
faculty member interferes and introduces a psychiatrist. Like Millay,
the author puts her own comment into the mouth of a brilliant
student:

> If the college had known more about human nature it
> would . . . have said to Mary, "Fight out your own salvation,
> you have as much right to it as Jessica." But the college did
> not believe that, and Mary herself did not believe it. . . . What-
> ever one may think of the [homosexual] relation . . . one thing
> is worse: to permit a human being to live in an atmosphere
> of constant disapproval. . . . When the moment to resist
> [suicide] came she was too weakened, too convinced that she
> had sinned.[5]

The second variant constellation centers about Crosby, "the college poet," a senior of twenty-four who has already published some
volumes of verse. (As Mrs. Lapsley's college was Vassar, it is impossible not to identify Crosby with Edna St. Vincent Millay.) This
histrionic aesthete has had experience with more than one man, but
her chief interest is in cultivating "crushes" to bolster her ego. Her
favorite, an idealistic freshman, is saved from grave harm by over-
hearing her cruelty to one or two other victims, and emerges with
enough maturity to retain independence and yet not to hate her
fallen idol.

Turning to items outside the college category, the briefest of
1929's comments on variance was the bitter passage in Theiss's translated *Interlude,* in which lesbianism is excoriated and held responsible for the failure of its victim's first marriage. Equally hostile was
Wyndham Lewis's *Apes of God* (1930). In substance Lewis's sophisticated satire is related to those of Firbank in its concern with male
homosexuals, and his writing about them has something of Firbank's
zany touch. But his references to a mannish middle-aged spinster are
contemptuous, and his chapter "The Lesbian Ape," in which an
equally mannish sculptress keeps a male nude model posing until he
faints, and then stands above his prostrate six-feet-two of Greek
magnificence and leers asininely with her silly inamorata, is written
with undiluted hate.[6]

In the single novel of these two years wholly devoted to variance,
Naomi Royde-Smith's *The Island* (1929), implicit censure is more
impersonal but equally harsh, and the influence of Freud is obvious.

In the same author's *Tortoiseshell Cat,* it will be remembered, an intellectual London girl narrowly escapes a lesbian attachment. Here the gauche and provincial Myfanwy Hughes succumbs, with distressing consequences. An orphan brought up by a prudish spinster aunt, the girl at nineteen is sent to a farm in Wales for her health. Because she is timid, awkward, and painfully shocked by talk of animal breeding, her uncle dubs her Goosey, a nickname she later tries to shed but never outlives.

> Believing herself to be without the power to attract, she substituted a horror of the physical triumphs of sex for a regret that she could not hope to take her part in them.' [The classic refusal to compete.]

In the spring a combination of sunshine and physical well-being produces a momentary emotional release which the author equates explicitly with mystical religious experience. The transient mood crystallizes upon a handsome farmer riding by on a stallion, but he is too occupied with his restive mount to give her a second glance, and this failure to attract even when aglow with new physical awareness plunges Goosey back into complete heterosexual frustration.

Now all her thwarted impulses center upon a female summer boarder from Liverpool, an egomaniac of twenty-four who poses as petite and helpless. Goosey's enslavement dates from her chance glimpse of the girl nude to the waist, but their association stays within an early-teen pattern of endless confidences and sentimental endearments. After Almond's departure Goosey lives only for her letters. The country couple who saw no harm in the active friendship regards this preoccupation as so "morbid" that they ship the girl back to her Liverpool aunt to remove her influence from their daughter. In the city, Almond's snobbishness and Goosey's jealousy of her impending marriage separate the two for a few years, during which Goosey loses her aunt and is driven by loneliness to consider the suit of a widower many years her senior. She covets the prestige of marriage, and one gathers that her physical distaste for the idea might wane but for her occasional distant glimpses of Almond. She has reached the point of betrothal when Almond bursts into her life again, begging sanctuary from a cruel husband, whereupon Goosey dismisses her suitor and arranges a future *à deux* with her adored in the huge ugly house she has inherited. However, at the "cruel" spouse's first summons Almond is off again, and there follow decades of periodic returns made only when she wishes to spite her husband or, years later, an independent daughter. Goosey's life is spent in waiting.

Early in this intermittent association the two women became intimate. For Goosey at first,

> Here were no reluctances, no shame, no abashment. This was love without conditions, maternal in tenderness, marital in strength, but equal and unfettering.[8]

But as the relation progresses she has misgivings, never more specifically accounted for than that "now there was something else. They never spoke to one another about it—even at night. And in the daytime Goosey pretended it wasn't true."[9] Soon tensions and quarrels develop, and eventually, being left alone for long stretches, Goosey feels occasional attractions to other women. The strongest attraction is inspired by a new milliner from London, a charming and competent woman who, out of pity for her outmoded rival, considers taking Goosey into partnership. But she is regaled on all sides with well-founded gossip of Goosey's long "queerness," and while her decision is hanging fire, Almond once more appears and buys a hat in the new shop. Goosey sees this as not only black disloyalty to herself but as a move to captivate the new proprietress, and her jealous hysteria alienates both women permanently.

Now completely solitary, Goosey falls captive to a male evangelist's magnetism. This maladjusted celibate labors for social as well as spiritual reform; his immediate goal is the suburb's beautification, which has been hampered by reactionaries. Among them, Goosey had been one of the most stubborn, but now her religious near-conversion wakes a sense of guilt concerning her relations with Almond, and she resolves to give up the hideous house she has kept as a sanctuary for her friend. She makes an appointment with the revivalist, planning full confession and the sacrifice of her property, but before this occurs, Almond meets the man and so ensnares him that he marries her almost at once. Henceforth, Goosey shuts herself into her dreadful house, willfully defying love, beauty, and goodness, and ends as a mad old woman.

In *The Tortoiseshell Cat* the lesbian aggressor was somewhat masculine, and had herself been seduced when young. In *The Island* no hereditary traits are apparent in either woman, nor has either any variant history. Conditioning is over-labored in Goosey's case, while Almond is an almost incredible monster of egotism. Whereas the earlier novel created the illusion of being drawn from life, this one smacks too strongly of a case history to come off well artistically.

A milder but scarcely happy picture is painted in *That Other Love* (1930) by Geoffrey Moss (on internal evidence probably a woman). Phillida, daughter of a well-born Englishman (who dies while she is an infant) and a joyously vulgar actress, enjoys ten years of bohemia before her father's relatives claim her. The widowed aunt who then assumes her upbringing is a perfectionist and very possessive. At sixteen, overprotected, a recluse, and too suddenly launched in the social life of the Twenties, Phillida is violently revolted by the advances of a professional seducer. In her panic she clings to a cool and serene sculptress who rescues her from the drunken party where she was molested. After some years in art school and an abortive romance with a man old enough to be her father, she again meets the sculptress at a seaside resort, is again drawn to her, and wants to paint her portrait. The older woman will not permit this until they have returned to the anonymity of London. There they become intimate (though this is not explicitly admitted), and subsequently live together for four years in an isolated cottage in Normandy.

Then Phillida becomes convinced of her need for children—"not a man—I could never love a man as I love you"—and she determines to marry one of her suitors, all of whom appear either naïve or indifferent to her variant interlude. The older woman, reluctant from the first to sacrifice her detached serenity but now as dependent on her young companion as the girl is on her, stoically accepts the inevitable and sets about readjusting herself to a life alone.

In addition to the translation of Colette's second Claudine volume as *Young Lady of Paris* (and Mrs. Lapsley's college story), 1931 produced an interesting contrast: one novel of highest quality, Dorothy Richardson's *Dawn's Left Hand*, and one, the first of its kind in our immediate field, which was cheaply sensational. This last, Sheila Donisthorpe's *Loveliest of Friends*, may be left for discussion with others of its ilk. Miss Richardson's title was tenth in the dozen comprising *Pilgrimage*, her Proustian chronicle of an English girl's development from childhood to maturity. This particular volume contrasts Miriam's two simultaneous love affairs, one with a younger woman, one with a scientific-minded novelist-reformer, Hypo, whom literary gossip has identified as H. G. Wells. Though chronology is vague in this stream of consciousness record, Miriam must at this time have reached her middle or late twenties. By virtue of education and background she moves among the Bloomsbury literati, but since she supports herself as a dentist's receptionist, she must live in an ordinary London boarding house; and it is against the latter background that the emotional drama with Amabel unfolds. This charming girl, half-Parisian, half-Irish, is also involved in a liaison with an Englishman of distinction. A beauty, and ultra-feminine, it is nevertheless she who takes the initiative in the rapidly flowering friendship. The quality of the relation is conveyed in such passages as the following:

> . . . the Sunday following the evening at Mrs. Bellamy's, where we were separated and mingling in various groups . . . and suddenly met and were filled with the same longing, to get away and lie side by side in the darkness . . . talking it all over until sleep should come without any interval of going off into the seclusion of our separate minds . . . [then] waking and seeing with the same eyes at the same moment . . . the wet gray roofs across the way.[10]

There is no suggestion of physical relations, and in another place the author describes as their most intimate moments the silences in which they were

> suddenly and intensely aware of each other and the flow of their wordless communion, making the smallest possible movements of the head now this way now that, like birds in a thicket intensely watching and listening; but without bird-anxiety.[11]

In recording the affair with Hypo, on the other hand, considerable physical detail is given, as for example the first time the two saw one another unclothed:

> This mutual nakedness was appeasing rather than stimulating. And austere. His body was not beautiful. She could find nothing to adore, no ground for response. . . . The manly structure, the smooth, satiny sheen in place of her own velvety glow was interesting as partner and foil, but not desirable. . . . It had no power to stir her as often she had been stirred by the sudden sight of him walking down a garden or entering a room.[12]

The climax of this affair occurs while Miriam is house guest of Hypo and his wife, a woman so selfless that she pretends blindness to his infidelities because they benefit his work. Miriam wakes in the night to find her host at her bedside, and suffers his possession in

> an immense fathomless black darkness through which, after an instant's sudden descent into her clenched and rigid form, she was now traveling alone on and on, without thought or memory or any emotion save the strangeness of this journeying.[13]

At another time

> she demanded of herself whether she cared for him in the slightest degree or for anyone or anything so much as the certainty of being in communion with something always there, something in which and through which people could meet and whose absence, felt with people who did not acknowledge it, made life at once impossible, made it a death worse than dying. . . .
> There was a woman, not this thinking self who talked with men in their own language, but one whose words could be spoken only from the heart's knowledge, waiting to be born in her. . . . Men want recognition of their work to help them believe in themselves. . . . Unless in some form they get it, all but the very few are miserable. Women . . . want recognition of themselves . . . before they can come fully to birth. Homage for what they are and represent.
> He was incapable of homage. . . . It was his constricted, biological way of seeing sex that kept him blind.[14]

So specific a contrast between the psychology of the two sexes suggests that the whole volume may have been written as a contribution to the current dispute over the value of variant love. During Miriam's total history (recorded in subsequent volumes) she loves two other men, but without physical intimacy. Neither is conspicuously male in appearance and both are preoccupied with subjective aspects of personal relations. Plainly Miss Richardson, like Mrs. Woolf, feels that between the most sharply differentiated members of the two sexes, the biological act can be the only bond.

Miss Richardson's novel was sexually frank but took care to imply the absence of physical intimacy between its variant women. In the one acceptable sympathetic study of 1932 Naomi Mitchison employed other means of avoiding offense. "The Delicate Fire" is the title story in a collection of short narratives of ancient Greece. Miss Mitchison, daughter of a schoolmaster, wrote several volumes recapturing the life of the past, possibly designed for her father's older students, but on an adult level with regard to historic mores. This particular tale covers some months in the late adolescence of Brocheo, daughter of the favorite of Sappho. Since her widowed mother cannot leave the country estate which supports them, Brocheo is sent to an aunt in Mitylene to be prepared for a fitting marriage. Sappho's open quarrel over her brother's alliance with the courtesan, Doricha, has inclined conservative mothers to entrust their daughters' training to the conventional Andromeda, but a passionate friendship between Brocheo's young cousin and Sappho's daughter Kleis draws the older girl into contact with the famous poet. The precocious Kleis analyzes as the key to her mother's temperament a desire to possess utterly anyone she loves, estranging her from one after another of her beloved friends when they marry, and making it difficult for Kleis to have either suitors or close friends. But Brocheo senses genius in Sappho's intensity as compared to Andromeda's polite talent, and becomes the great poet's willing pupil. The story ends discreetly with the beginning of Brocheo's tutelage, for some given details of a scene between Kleis and her young friend suggest that had it continued into the relation between Sappho and Brocheo it would have sailed in dangerous waters.

This was the year in which the German motion picture *Mädchen in Uniform* was released and Weirauch's *Scorpion* translated. (The latter's sequel, *The Outcast*, followed in 1933.) Except for these, 1932 boasted only a pair of titles on a level with Miss Donisthorpe's mentioned above, which must wait for later consideration. After this season in which everything published, no matter what the quality, was relatively tolerant of variance, the pendulum swung back in 1933, when but one of five authors had even a moderate word to say for it.

The most nearly sympathetic was Thomas Beer, whose volume of short stories, *Mrs. Egg and Other Barbarians*, included "Hallowe'en," written in 1927 but not, like the others, previously published in magazines. In this tale the monumental but endearing Mrs. Egg, inveterate eater of sweets and worshipper of her tall son, Adam, encounters on Hallowe'en night the striking Bill Sloan, village tomboy, whom she had known before her marriage and removal to New York some years earlier. Now divorced, Bill has come back to visit her girlhood chum, wife of a friend of Adam's. Mrs. Egg elicits from Adam that Jane's husband is "out of luck nights," and they agree that the fault lies in the girl's upbringing—"Jane's mama was too much of a lady to say drawers in a King's Daughters meetin'. I bet the darn truth is Janie's scared of men yet." Anent Bill's divorce, they recall that

> "Dr. Sloan raised Bill peculiar. He believed folks are just —s'perior kind of animals. No souls or nothin'. I never can get shocked any about sensible people's morals. . . . I just want to say this for Bill. I bet she don't do any harm."[15]

This was written at the height of that psychological season when parents could do no right; but Beer concedes to the hereditary camp Bill's height and absence of hips, and both girls' tenor speaking voices. Mrs. Egg is called out from her grandson's hilarious party for a farewell from Jane and Bill, who because they admire the wholesome woman profoundly, want her to be first to know they are leaving—"for good." Jane begs Mrs. Egg to look after her husband, against whom she has nothing save that she cannot endure marriage and "loves someone else more." Without protest Mrs. Egg busies herself with lunch for the night travelers—they are driving—and sends them off, perhaps significantly just before midnight of the witches' holiday. But after they have gone she can say only

> "They're human beings, Dammy. [But] if they'd stayed a minute longer I'd ha' screamed. Oh, Dammy, ain't things peculiar!"[16]

She is consoled by learning that Adam thinks this the only solution for all concerned and has foreseen tragedy from the moment of Jane's marriage.

The next episode, narrowly skirting the sensational level, was included in *Orient Express* by the British Graham Green,[17] who in 1933 was writing only psychological thrillers. A lesbian journalist, after supporting for four years a beautiful countrywoman picked up in a cinema, realizes she is about to lose her love to a man ("How could one hold her, with only a mouth?") Philosophically cutting her losses, Mabel decides to capture Carol, a dancer traveling alone on the Express, and immediately begins to plan the redecoration of her London apartment in honor of her new conquest. The plot develops otherwise, however, and Mabel goes on alone.

In *Entertaining the Islanders*, Struthers Burt's most sophisticated effort, he treats the modish theme less gently. After a three-year liaison with a rather hard woman journalist, the hero falls genuinely in love during a winter in the Bahamas, and returns to New York to break with his old flame. Even during their intimacy Marian "had made no pretense of faithfulness," but what frees him of any remorse at severing the connection is his discovery that she is now involved with a married woman,

> a small beautiful bronze young woman with square-cut yellow hair. Taut, condensed, masterful, engraved. . . . Her brilliant tawny eyes looked David up and down without interest. In the jacket of her dark suit was a white camellia. . . . Marian was nothing if not up to date, was she?[18]

He wonders how husbands put up with "childlike little ghosts. . . . Children making childlike little substitutions for reality . . . and always so proud of their substitutions."[19] This, of course, is close to quotation from Freud.

Sinclair Lewis hit even harder in *Ann Vickers*. The chief figure in his briefly sketched tragedy, Eleanor Crevecoeur, was in an early section of the novel devoted to the battle for suffrage, and was humorous, fearless, and intelligent, though "looking all the time like an anemic Bourbon princess." Later during World War I she has one serious liaison with a man and an exhausting list of casual affairs. Then she meets a sleekly tailored woman executive of a department store with a Ph.D. in psychology. Dr. Herringdean frightens off the heterogeneous swarm of males and appropriates Eleanor for herself. But once her prey is caught, she loses interest, turns pettily cruel, and pursues other women. Eleanor wastes to a neurotic wraith and finally commits suicide. The whole episode occupies only ten pages, but is mordant and damning.

The final blow of the year was struck by George Jean Nathan, dramatic critic for the *American Statesman,* in a slapstick parody offered as a critique of the current British drama. Nathan had commented earlier (without special reference to England) on "the increasing number of women players who are of the sexual disposition of the Aeolian Greek colonizers," and on their "freezing" presence on the stage—"all their emotional scenes are dead."[20] In this skit, "Design for Loving," (the title a jibe at Noel Coward's *Design for Living*) , the cast includes:

> Lord Derek, a hermaphrodite; his father, an onanist; his mother, a lesbian; his sister, a flagellant; Lady Vi Twining,

his sister's friend, an auto-erotist with tribade tendencies; his
servant, a homosexual and transvestist;[21]

et cetera. Though the dialogue is so caricatured as to mar the wit,
it mentions the many one-sexed couples to be seen in any large hotel
or restaurant, and the negligible action includes "significant" glances
and caresses among the three women. Plays other than Coward's (if
any) that might have inspired this effort have not been discovered.
If Nathan hoped to purge the current theatre by ridicule, he was
doomed to prompt disappointment. In 1934 a translation of *Mädchen
in Uniform* adapted to the legitimate stage was produced by high-
grade amateur groups in more than one large American city and
played to crowded houses, and late in the year Lillian Hellman's
The Children's Hour began its successful run on Broadway. This
was subsequently taken over by Hollywood, and readers who saw only
the film will wonder at its inclusion here. The mainspring of the
plot was the same in both versions—the ruin of a thriving boarding
school and of the two young women who own it through vicious
slander circulated by a pupil, already a well-developed paranoiac at
the age of twelve. In the film one of the women is accused of intimacy
with her fiancé, the school physician.

In the play as Miss Hellman wrote it the charge is lesbianism
between the two mistresses. This fabrication, fairly sophisticated for
a twelve-year-old, is the fruit in part of surreptitious reading of *Mlle
Maupin,* in part of an overheard quarrel between one of the young
women and an aunt who taunts her with jealousy of her friend's
fiancé. The dreadful child's garbled exaggerations galvanize her
grandmother into hasty action. Over-night the school is emptied by
horrified parents. The young women lose their suit for slander
through the cowardly flight of the aunt, their chief witness. The
younger woman breaks her engagement when she sees that her fiancé
will never be sure but that a grain of truth underlay the slander.
The other woman is tortured into realizing for the first time that
she has never cared for men, and that unadmitted passion has in
fact underlain her restrained love for her friend. Feeling irremediably
soiled, she shoots herself. As its easy Hollywood transmutation proves,
the core of this tragedy is not the persecution of variance. It is the
destruction of two blameless individuals through hysterical prejudice,
and the lesbian issue is only a super-explosive detonator of that hysteria. But is the older woman's suicide a tragic waste chargeable to the
social mores which made her feel so soiled? Or is it tragic merely
because she is physically innocent—that is, does Miss Hellman, like

Mendès, distinguish between light and darkness here on the strength of technicalities alone? The text provides no answer.

The rest of the year's offerings were fiction ranging in quality from that of Henry Handel Richardson, Victoria Sackville-West and Isak Dinesen to the now frequent sensational penny-catchers. Probably most of the book of short stories, *The End of a Childhood,* which Miss Richardson gave to the public in 1934, were written earlier. The title group consists of fragments related to her *Richard Mahoney* novels (1917-1929) which seem rather discards than sequels (as were those in Galsworthy's *On Forsyte 'Change*). Another group entitled "Growing Pains" is more reminiscent of her *Getting of Wisdom* of 1910. Indeed, of these eight sketches, six present so integrated an emotional sequence that although their girls bear different names one wonders whether they are not bits from a trial flight toward another novel centered about a woman. A noteworthy feature in all these sketches, as also in *The Getting of Wisdom,* is the absence of a father and the relative insignificance or incompatibility of the mother.

In "The Bathe" a beautiful child of six is sickened by the physical ugliness of two obsese middle-aged women who strip and bathe nude, with self-conscious tittering, on an isolated beach. Until this moment the child has been eager for adult status, but now "oh never—never—no, not ever now did she want to grow up." In "Preliminary Canter" one twelve-year-old girl adores another and is baffled and furious when the latter "flirts" with a farm hand. "Conversation in a Pantry" presents the uneasy efforts of a girl of fourteen to learn from one three years older what it is one must "take care about" when out with boys. She gets evasive answers, but they are sufficient to recall her disgust upon first realizing that married couples sleep in the same bed. On the other hand, as her informant speaks of her own love, "she had never known before that Alice was so pretty, with dimples round her mouth and her eyes all shady. Oh, could it mean that—yes, it must: Alice simply didn't *mind*." "The Wrong Turning" pictures the violent shock to another fourteen-year-old, invited to go rowing by an interesting new schoolfellow (male), when the pair blunder on a swimming hole where naked soldiers are indulging in harmless but rough horseplay, and the men shout suggestively after the embarrassed youngsters.

"And Women Must Weep" is the aftermath of an eighteen-year-old's long-anticipated first ball. She has been a wallflower, and afterwards, locked in her room,

Oh the shame of it! . . . not to have "taken," to have failed

to "attract the gentlemen"—this was a slur that would rest on
her all her life. And yet a small voice that wouldn't be silenced
kept on saying "It wasn't my *fault!*" . . . She had tried her
hardest, done everything she was told to . . . [but] really,
truly, right deep down in her, she hadn't wanted "the gentlemen" any more than they'd wanted her: she had only had to
pretend to. . . . She cried till she could cry no more."

The final and longest sketch, "Two Hanged Women," gives as it
were the cumulative result of such experiences. The word "hanged,"
it should be noted, is merely a mild and dated Australian expletive
equivalent to the American "darned," and is applied to a pair of
young women by a couple who find the two in their own favorite
spot for petting, but its use in the title lends a telling *double
entendre*. The older girl, nearing thirty, is tall and thin with
straight bobbed hair and a man's gait. The other, in her middle twenties, has been urged to marry by a dominating mother,
but is nauseated by physical contact with her beau, Fred. Even
if he sits too close she must "screw herself up" to bear it. On
the other hand, she craves the social status of a regularly courted
girl, and indulges in a brief fantasy of being escorted by the handsome and devoted man. People are sympathetic to that, she says,
and "let us into the dark corner seats at the pictures as if we'd
a right to them. And they never laugh. Oh, I can't *stick* being laughed
at!"²³ After the bitter retort, "Gawd! Why not make a song of it?"
her companion claims that it is the mother who has put these romantic notions into her daughter's head. Whenever the two girls
are out together the mother is furious, and "does she need to open
her mouth? Not she! She's only got to let it hang at the corners
and you reek, you drip with guilt."²⁴ The sketch ends with the
younger girl shuddering and crying out that she would "rather die
twice over" than submit to Fred's passion. She clings to her friend,
who holds her in a gentle and maternal embrace. Taken all together,
these half-dozen vignettes present a most convincing etiology for
a homosexual woman.

In Victoria Sackville-West's *Dark Island* (1934) the reserved and
elusive Shirin, oldest child in a family best described as philistine,
cultivates defensive reticence. She desires "quietly to remain un-
guessed, unknown, and thus to protect oneself from the pain of
life." During summers on the southwest coast of England she falls in
love with a rocky island a mile offshore, tree-covered and crowned by
the romantic pile of LeBreton castle, because it seems the embodi-

ment of her dreams of privacy. After a successful decade in London society which includes marriage and children, she finds her life so pointlessly harried that she escapes it by a quixotic sacrifice of maternal ties and reputation. In her thirties she enters upon a second marriage with Sir Venn LeBreton, owner and virtual over-lord of the island of Storn. It is largely for the sake of his island that she marries him, for to her it is still the remote and secret sanctuary for which she has hungered all her life. When, with the intuition of the fiercely proud, Sir Venn divines her motive, he makes clear at once that the property descends in the male line, wives are mere consorts and heir-bearers, and Storn is no more hers than any servant's. Thus, she has merely involved herself in a barren and humiliating life imprisonment. Soon she discovers that her husband is at times a physical as well as a mental sadist, and her misery reaches desperation unrelieved by the bearing of two children.

Since her teens she has had one constant friend, Cristina, a tall, powerful and competent woman, but their relation has been so reserved, so impersonal, that only its persistence has raised it above mere acquaintance. In her loneliness Shirin turns, though without unburdening herself, to Cristina; and after his male secretary suddenly dies, she prevails upon her husband to engage her friend. The latter perceives at once that Shirin's life is wretched, but she is vouchsafed no more explanation than becomes slowly evident to her loving eyes. More and more as time passes, however, Shirin comes to depend upon her for just such wordless but complete communion as that between Miriam and Amabel in *Dawn's Left Hand*. Sir Venn presently becomes aware of this bond, and unable to move his wife from her determination that her friend shall stay with her or she herself will leave, he takes Cristina sailing on a day of squalls and returns alone with a story of her accidental drowning. Shirin accepts this story impassively and continues to live with him, outwardly composed but inwardly in torment. When, some years later, he taunts her with his having deliberately eliminated Cristina, she soon contrives his death in return by a long kiss after she is sure that she is stricken with diphtheria. He dies and she sur-vives, but since Storn is now his son's and the son is a replica of the father, she soon declines to a willful death.

Two points should be noted here: first, the stress laid on the impersonality of the two women's relationship until Shirin's mar-riage becomes a torture justifying any human solace; and second, the ingenuity employed to contrive her ominous situation. Sir Venn and his feudal domain are the stuff of post-Elizabethan tragedy or gothic romance, difficult of assimiliation into a twentieth-century pattern. But the island's isolation sets it apart from the present, just as Shirin's withdrawn spirit separates her a little from current reality. Thus the tenuous variant union can flower without reference to society, and the triangular drama can be enacted beyond the world's reach. This latter portion of the novel is in miniature as much of a *tour de force* as Mrs. Woolf's *Orlando*, and the similarity is particularly interesting in that the elusive Shirin is hauntingly reminiscent of Clarissa Dalloway in Mrs. Woolf's book which her own preface proclaims to be tinged with autobiography.

As distinguished as the work of these two British women was *Seven Gothic Tales* (1934) by the Danish Isak Dinesen (Baroness Karen Blixen), whose artistry in English is as remarkable as Conrad's. She is also adroit in maintaining a continental outlook without offending her adopted audience, a feat she achieves by setting her tales in a day when the Romantic Period had the freshness of youth, and recounting them with a serene detachment which precludes "reader participation." No more than discreet hints of male homosexuality lend flavor to "The Monkey," and in "The Roads Around Pisa" the two feminine romances contributing to the involved plot are seen in retrospect, only one member of each pair actually appearing in the narrative. The younger of these two women, Agnese, is a transvestist who has traveled for a year as a man. Her reasons are disclosed gradually. Her beloved friend, like Lamartine's Clothilde, was obliged to marry an elderly Croesus though she was in love with a young cousin. Afterward, when she occasionally slipped out to meet her love, her bosom friend, Agnese, allayed suspicion by occupying her bed, a safe enough favor since the husband was impotent and took his pleasure in toying with his "lovely pet" by day; at night merely inspecting her room to know she was there. To keep the world from guessing his humiliating secret he required a child, and sent a surrogate of his own choosing to effect that end one night when Agnese had taken his wife's place. Already indifferent to men, Agnese was goaded by this violation to abandon the feminine role altogether and roam the country as a Byronic gentleman.

The very old lady whom a highroad accident leads to unburden herself to a fellow traveler while expecting death, has, like Agnese, been averse to men all her life, but social necessity has made her wife, mother, and now grandmother. The fact that her daughter died in childbirth has increased her animus against the male sex, and her granddaughter's marrying in the face of her prohibition has estranged them. She tells her confidant, a melancholy Hamlet, that in her long life she has known but two passions, one for a girlhood friend from Denmark, the other for her beautiful grandchild. She cannot die without sending her forgiveness to the girl, and she extracts from the young Danish listener a promise to deliver her message. Contrary to her expectations, however, she lives, is happily reunited with her granddaughter, and through love for the latter's infant son at last achieves tolerance for the opposite sex (cf. *Marie Bonifas*). She also discovers that her Danish messenger is nephew of her first beloved, who died a spinster. Since both these loves are recounted by one of their actors, they do not appear on the surface to have been lesbian, but there are certainly no implications to the contrary. The two women, young and old, appearing in the story are both somewhat masculine; of each pair of loving women, one never married; and for three of the four, the early variant love seems to have been the most vivid of their lives, surviving marriage or other liaisons.

Another contribution from the continent was the translation of Colette's *Claudine s'en Va* as *The Innocent Wife*. Properly it is fourth in its series, but it lacks the outright lesbian element of the third, which awaited publication in the following year. All the Claudine novels, it should be noted, were issued in the United States, while England risked no sympathetic treatments more overt than those of Geoffrey Moss, the two Richardsons, and Miss Sackville-West.

The remainder of the year's crop were also American, two of good quality. One was Anthony Thorne's heartening idyll, *Delay in the Sun*, in which forty-eight hours' suspension of bus service in Spain resolves a variety of emotional conflicts in its English passengers' lives. The variant couple are mannish Jean Porteous, daughter of a titled British family and a rebel against the social existence expected of her, and Betty Sale-Jones, blonde, helpless and fluttering, from "the plastery gentility of Kensington." Thus far their common bond has been the determination to escape family strictures and win personal freedom. They are merely good companions with some tentative notions of sharing a flat in London on returning from their trip. Then their visit to an empty bull ring moves Jean to mimic with startling verisimilitude the Spanish performers both have seen.

> In the hot Spanish sunlight she played at bull fighting for the sake of a pretty girl in a yellow dress who sat in the *barrera*. Playing together, they mocked a dangerous game. And dangerously they entered a secret world in which they had so great a need of each other.[25]

Later in the moonlight they visit the flower-drenched public gardens and lie on the warm grass, "fingers still linked as they lay looking upwards into the sparkling sky." When they come back to lights and crowds they fall paralyzingly shy and dare not share their common room and bed. After a restless night apart, each comes to much the same conclusion:

> What had happened to them last night was something beyond their control. Then let this strange force follow its own law—let it part them forever or join them forever. It was something too big for their reason, and too delicate. . . . Of no use to fight, reason, or wonder.[26]

And it is without further resolution of their problem that they let the suddenly-restored bus service carry them away from the scene of their inarticulate romance. The author has cannily left each reader to supply what sequel best satisfies his own philosophy, but the lingering mood is distinctly one of warm tolerance and sympathy rather than disapproval.

In *After Such Pleasures,* on the other hand, Dorothy Parker grazes the surface of variance with flippant malice. The final story, "Glory in the Daytime," sketches the tentative advances of a New York sophisticate to a newly arrived and naïve little wife with a passion for stage celebrities. Using the long-famed Lily Wynton as bait, the Gothamite invites the provincial to tea—to the disgust of the latter's husband, who always refers to the predatory Hallie as "Hank" and declares that all "those women" make him sick. Starry-eyed with anticipation, little Mrs. Murdock finds her hostess alone, clad in trousers and silk shirt. She is welcomed with a long kiss and the admonition, "Don't tell Lily!" But the famous star on arrival proves to be middle-aged, withered, and brassy-haired. She is already too drunk to follow the conversation, demands brandy, and soon dozes off. Mrs. Murdock leaves in sad disillusion, with a new appreciation of her astringent mate, only to find that he has gone out in a temper for the first time to pursue his own ends.

The Worm's Turning

Since the total count of variant titles in 1934, including the sensational items not yet touched upon, mounted to ten, it is not surprising that some public reaction should set in. It will be even less so after a rapid consideration of those omitted trivia, of which within as many years some half-dozen accumulated. Because the first

was a fairly obvious rebuttal of *Well of Loneliness,* it deserves more
attention than some others. It was *Loveliest of Friends* (1931) by
Sheila Donisthorpe, who was reputedly an English actress with a
number of other romances to her credit, but its verbal idiom is not
British and it was published only in New York.

Written with intense sentimentality, it pictures the ruin of
Audrey, introduced as the happy wife of a doting but pedestrian
husband whose hobby of gentleman-farming takes him often out of
London. The couple's intimate life is described in some detail as
ideal, yet Audrey is given to playing Chopin in the dusk to relieve
her unspent emotion. Presently she is assiduously courted by boyish,
impudent and exquisitely-tailored Kim, similarly blessed with a
husband who dotes upon her and allows her every freedom. Kim's
showers of gifts and passionate telephone calls intoxicate the inexperienced Audrey. Although the first attempted caress and Kim's
confession that she is a lover of women are profoundly shocking,
Audrey soon succumbs without reservation. Then she discovers that
there is a former beloved for whose daily letters Kim watches avidly;
next, she learns that several of her own London circle have been
loved and discarded by Kim; finally, a current rival is flaunted to
rouse her jealousy. This cheap blonde American flirt is a transparent
copy of the ex-chorus girl in *Well of Loneliness,* just as a vivid
phrase applied to Kim—"a head so fiercely alive it seemed delicately
to light the air around it"[27]—is lifted verbatim from the description
of Jennifer in Miss Lehmann's *Dusty Answer.*

Audrey spends several delirious weeks at a shore resort with
Kim (described in detail) of an intensity impossible to support for
long, and when immediately afterward the blonde recaptures Kim
by the classic device of parading a rival—a repulsive caricature of the
mannish and profane lesbian—Audrey's overstrained nerves give way.
A period in a sanatorium restores her temporarily, but, back in
London again, she is helpless against her passion. After melodramatic
incidents involving all four women, Audrey attempts suicide, and
failing to achieve her end, she leaves home and husband to wander,
derelict and outcast, for the rest of her days. Close to the end the
author breaks out in vituperation against

> those who clamor for recognition of the sinister group who
> practice . . . these sadistic habits . . . crooked, twisted freaks
> of Nature who stagnate in dark and muddy waters, and are so
> choked with the weeds of viciousness and selfish lust that,
> drained of all pity, they regard their victims as mere stepping

stones to their further pleasure. With flower-sweet finger-
tips they crush the grape of evil till it is exquisite, smooth
and luscious to the taste, stirring up subconscious responsive-
ness, intensifying all that has been, all that follows, leaving
their prey gibbering, writhing, sex-sodden shadows of their
former selves, conscious of only one desire in mind and body,
which, ever festering, ever destroying, slowly saps them of
health and sanity.[28]

This effusion is an obvious retort to Miss Hall's relatively controlled
plea for tolerance at the end of *Well of Loneliness,* and the volume
gives every evidence of being written hastily to profit by whatever
conservative reaction there was against the sympathy aroused among
the literati by Miss Hall's effort.

The next exhibit was from the pen of the American Tiffany
Thayer, writer of near-erotica, and comprises one chapter in his
Thirteen Women (1932). A fragile beauty in whom puritanic sex-
repression has induced tuberculosis is quickly cured by an affair
with her Denver physician's lesbian wife. The two have in common
a hatred of men. The younger believes their love unique and
blessedly free of the uncleanness of sex, and when, back in New
York, she is bawdily enlightened by an old schoolmate who is now a
vaudeville performer, she wastes swiftly to the death her abortive
romance postponed.

Of the same calibre was *The Establishment of Madame Antonia*
(1932) by one Leyla Georgie, comprising life sketches of the inmates
of Hamburg's most élite bordello, and supposedly recorded by one
of the group. Nearly all the women are titled or from the top level
of European society, but have been reduced by malign chance. The
variant pair are a Russian princess and a new recruit whom she
protects and cherishes. Discovering that though her protégée loves
her, she is unable to return her passion, the princess introduces the
girl to a nobleman who marries her. Natacha then commits suicide.
The whole volume is little more than a romanticizing of earlier
foreign erotica which celebrated more fleshly relations among prostitutes.

The title of Idabel Williams's *Hellcat* (1934) accurately describes
its heroine, who expends her efforts only on such persons as she can
steal from someone else or can live upon without sacrifice on her part.
One of the latter is a lesbian whom she scorns as long as men are
handy, but whose hospitality she finally exploits for a long season,
keeping her victim in a constant fever by pretending an innocence

which sees in lesbians only fit subjects for police court or madhouse.

Gerald Foster's *Strange Marriage* (1934) deserves an extra word because here transvestism basically affects the plot for the first time since the fantastic German *Weiberbeute* of 1906. A girl, expelled from college just before graduation, hides out in a lonely beach shack until she can go home without revealing her disgrace. Shingled and accustomed to trousers she lives as a boy for safety, but finds that even boys are not safe from the lifeguard who seeks her out at night. He is, however, delighted on discovering her real sex. His masterful possession of her, outrages her pride, but her body registers traitorous complaisance. In a fury of rebellion against a woman's double disadvantage, she resolves to live as a man. By putting the width of the continent between her and her past life she contrives to get a college degree on the west coast and a job in a law office, continuing her studies at night. When the senior partner's daughter falls in love with her she reciprocates with warmth, marries the girl (who is innocent to a degree), and lives as her husband for several years. Then the coincidental reappearance of the beach guard not only makes her apprehensive of recognition but revives the response he was the first to stir. A quick disappearance leaves her wife an apparent widow, and she marries the man. The bisexual experience here seems more indebted to earlier French trivia than to current psychological theory, which taxes unwilling defloration with negative rather than happy heterosexual results.

As Lilyan Brock's *Queer Patterns* (1935) has been revived in two different paperbound editions since 1950 and is thus easily available, a short description will suffice. A musical-comedy star tries marriage to one of those perfect husbands so useful in accentuating indelible variant leanings. She comes fully to life, however, only under the hands of a dynamic woman director of serious drama, with whom she enjoys two perfect years before gossip obliges them to part or face professional ruin. A long illness induced by the separation and by a subsequent wealthy husband's drug-crazed violence provides opportunity for a trained nurse to fall in love with her. The nurse is driven to suicide from jealousy of the other woman. The drug-addict husband finally strangles the star. This is offered as an example of ineradicable inborn variance.

Quite the most melodramatic of the lot was *Male and Female* by Jack Woodford (1935), in which a girl about to be married realizes that her comparative physical coolness to her fiancé stems from a hitherto unadmitted attraction to a girl friend. The latter, a brooding introvert afflicted with frequent migraine, is quite aware of her own feelings, and thrusts herself between the pair, after they marry, with incredible temerity. The young couple have a stormy year which would have wrecked their union—since the wife prefers feminine gentleness to masculine "brutality" in lovemaking—but for their occasional periods of ecstasy when the interloper is laid low by her chronic ailment. It finally appears that this "friend" is virtually a witch (a fictional throwback of a full millennium). In modern terms, she exercises some hypnotic power over the wife even at great distances. Since, however, she is not evil at heart, she finally commits suicide in a burning house by way of ending her own unhappiness and effectively terminating her fateful influence.

Virtually the last item of this sort from the point of date was Gawen Brownrigg's *Star Against Star* (1936), pretending to British authorship, but, like *Loveliest of Friends,* written in American idiom. It apes *Well of Loneliness* closely in its dependence upon inheritance and childhood conditioning, but in this case Dorcas resembles a hot-blooded mother who has had many male lovers and who virtually seduces her own daughter at the age of nine or ten. A year in a Swiss boarding school when she is sixteen ends with the expulsion of Dorcas and her bisexual American roommate for lesbian intimacy. Two efforts at affairs with men leave Dorcas cold, and from one man she parts because he speaks with contempt of "Lezzies." Later, in Paris, she meets a beautiful novelist already renowned at twenty-six, and within twenty-four hours the infatuated pair achieve complete intimacy. They return to live for a time in England; however, they encounter at once the same social disapprobation they had met among the British contingent even on the *rive gauche.* A literary critic warns Dorcas, moreover, that she will be jealous of Consuelo's work, and that emotional release may have an adverse effect upon the latter's creative powers—an interesting inversion of Miss Hall's attributing Stephen Gordon's sterility to lack of such release. Both predictions prove all too accurate, and the union goes completely on the rocks within a matter of months. Worthless as it is artistically, the novel stresses a detail previously hinted only in *That Other Love:* it is the younger girl who disrupts an older woman's well adjusted and successful life. Also evil fruit from even completely happy physical expression is at odds with the Freudian theory which the author elsewhere makes show of accepting.

The final pair of tales have been left until last because of their direct bearing on censorship efforts which got under way during 1934 and 1935. One was *Love Like a Shadow,* which, although written under the name of Lois Lodge, exhibits many of the characteristics of male authorship listed earlier in discussing erotic writing. Of the college in which it begins, it reports "bull sessions" of crass vulgarity, raw petting parties and assignations after dances, and lesbian alliances kept only slightly undercover. In a New York residence club a burgeoning lesbian coterie includes a cigar-smoking physician who spouts variant biology and philosophy at every chance, a feminist poet with two girls—children under ten—whom she has already started on the path to Lesbos, and a variety of free-living artists, entertainers, and Park Avenue sensation-seekers. The heroine, Jean, is antagonistic towards men because of her father's flaunted infidelities; another girl, because she was raped at twelve by her uncle. Jean is an idealist in search of a lasting alliance, but her first love (a college roommate) marries to scotch "queer" gossip in a midwestern home town; and her second proves compulsively promiscuous to the point of seducing Jean's teen-age sister. Jean finally becomes the wife of her millionaire employer "in name only" because his fifteen-year-old daughter needs a mother, but she finds her stepdaughter already bisexually experienced, and the two are soon united in the Great Love of both their lives—approximately the fourth affair for each. The father conveniently dies (of extra-marital excesses) and leaves the pair free to roam the world at will and live happily ever after. This précis suggests but feebly the hundred-proof distillate of promiscuity, exhibitionism, hard drinking, wild lesbian propagandizing, and bad poetry which comprises the original.

Cut from the same cloth was *Mardigras Madness* (1934) by Davis Dresser, a gentleman revealed by the Library of Congress catalog as writing under six pseudonyms, one of them feminine. It is a racy tale of Barbara from the country, whose aunt is a prude and whose "steady" is too puritanic to satisfy her ardent needs. The Mardigras season, which she spends with a girl friend in New Orleans, is a salacious riot including a midnight ritual orgy worthy of Peladan, but the variant episode occurs during the day when masquers roam the streets at will. She and her friend are picked up by two women, a tall harlequin, and a shingled pirate who says, "I'll take you captive—before some nasty man beats me to it." The women call each other Frankie and Johnny, and even before the party reaches their modest apartment Barbara senses a mystery, "an indefinable *something* which set them apart from anyone she had ever known."[39] In the apartment alcohol flows freely, and since Barbara has never before tasted so much as wine, her confused exaltation discreetly blurs her impressions of first a "sentimentality" which vaguely bothers her, then a crescendo of caresses until "the world faded into blackness under Frankie's soothing touch."[31] The whole incident occupies a half-dozen pages.

This title had a significant publishing history. In 1938 the same firm issued *One Reckless Night* by Peter Shelley, one of Dresser's many tags. Except that in this later volume the heroine and her friend bear different names, its text is that of the 1934 narrative verbatim, save for one alteration and a scant two percent deletions. The latter comprise vivid and specific bits of heterosexual detail. But the important change is the transmutation of the lesbians into a pair of men, "a striking couple, both extremely tall, and they carried their costumes with a swagger."[31] They pick the girls up in a magnificent foreign roadster, the scene of the drinking party is a patio of corresponding grandeur, and as the heroine lapses from consciousness she dreams that it is her fiancé who possesses her. The obvious purpose of both versions, as of *Love Like a Shadow* and the same grade of purely heterosexual writing, is to convince the callow reader that "everybody's doing it, it's smart in the Big Cities." No matter how much one may deplore censorship in principle, one can hardly deny its justice in such cases as these. Actually, the second version of Dresser's tale is no better than the first in moral impact, and the fact that the only change in plot required to make it acceptable for publication was the alteration of the lesbian episode, throws light upon the chief target of the snipers.

To be sure, variant fiction was not alone in its flamboyance, nor was it alone under attack. The heterosexual frankness in works of high quality during the twenties had been followed by lesser and lesser efforts, and finally by pseudonymous volumes such as *Naked Escape, Innocent Adulteress,* and *Born to be Bad.* Male homosexuality, as well, was represented in a handful of dubious volumes culminating in *Scarlet Pansy.* Non-fiction also took advantage of the open market with hastily penned volumes on sexual psychology and perversions, and revivals or new translations of Krafft-Ebing, Stekel, and lesser lights of the preceding half-century. A crop of short-lived presses— "Eugenic," "Anthropological" and "Physicians"—sprang up to profit by the open season. Reaction was inevitable. Since earlier battles to prevent publication had, as we have seen, been lost in this country, censoring groups now trained their guns upon sales agencies wherever they had sufficient influence. In one city a single sale of a blacklisted item might lay a bookseller open to prosecution and seizure of all contraband stock. In another, supplying a title specifically requested by a patron might be safe, but having the same volume visible even on inconspicuous shelves within the shop was penalized. In a third it might be that no restrictions were imposed, as for example Atlantic City, where the excursionist from Boston or Philadelphia was apt to find all the books banished from his own city lavishly displayed in boardwalk windows. This uneven but increasing restraint was soon sufficient to make the production of sensational items a gamble instead of a sure profit; the fly-by-night presses withered as suddenly as they had grown, and what little trash was issued had to seek vanity publishing.

Above Reproach

Variant fiction of quality, however, suffered no very great check. In 1935, for instance, this country saw the publication of two sympathetic translations, Christa Winsloe's *Girl Alone* and Colette's *The Indulgent Husband,* and also of Gale Wilhelm's *We Too Are Drifting.* This last was a brief first novel by a young woman pictured frankly on the dust jacket as shingled and tailored, who was a stylistic disciple of Ernest Hemingway, (by then a major influence). Her prose had a lean economy worthy of her master, and the grudging acclaim her novel received would certainly have been warmer and more voluminous except for her subject.

Her central figure is Jan Morale, an artist of thirty whose woodcuts have already merited a one-man showing. Jan's childhood was pinched and sordid; the brother who always hid behind her skirts ended by being hanged; and she herself might have starved as a printer's devil but for a helping hand from the established sculptor Kletkin. He would like to marry her, but recognizes that no man can hope to possess her. For she is the model for his prize-winning *Hermaphroditus,* and is more convincingly masculine in temperament than even Miss Hall's Stephen Gordon. The disgraced brother was her twin, and effeminate, which implies heredity as the cause of her variance. At the opening of the story Jan is entangled with a society beauty who has raised marital deception to a fine art in the interests of her predatory lesbian habits. Jan has been no more than physically captivated; she is already restive, and tension increases when she falls romantically in love with the serene innocence of Victoria, just out of college and living with her conventional suburban family. Jan's meticulous restraint in refusing to sweep the younger girl off her feet, and the slow development of their complete intimacy, are presented delicately but without evasion. The relationship survives the married woman's jealous efforts to destroy it and persists for a time, but with increasing strain. For Jan holds to a lifelong rule against intruding her bohemian eccentricity upon conventional households, and Victoria finds frequent absences hard to explain at home. Victoria is an only child not only loved but loving, with all the pliant passivity of Verena Tarrant in *The Bostonians*. In her placid life the need for evasion or struggle has never before arisen, and they are alien to her now. Therefore the two girls' long-nursed plans for a holiday together go down before a suddenly projected family trip. Jan, furtively hidden, must watch a transcontinental train pull out bearing her beloved, accompanied by her parents and the "nice boy" they wish her to marry. Here again, as in *Star Against Star*, the older and well-established woman is the one to suffer from a consuming intimacy.

The British contribution of the year was a brief section of Francis Brett Young's *White Ladies*, in which the now familiar pattern of *Regiment of Women* is discernible. Bella, descended from two generations of independent and passionate women and virtually orphaned, is sent to boarding school at sixteen because she is too much the tomboy to be manageable by her grandparents or the mistresses of her private day-school. The "first passionate devotion of her life" for a music mistress she outgrows upon discovering that the woman is a facile sentimentalist, but she falls at once into "instinctive adoration" of a crisp and ironic headmistress, who seems the antithesis of her former love. On closer acquaintance the contained Miss Cash reveals a "protean" range of mood, from childlike gaiety to "spiritual incandescence," but her astringent scorn of admitted love preserves Bella's illusion of emotional detachment through five years as pupil, teacher and secretary-companion. Then Miss Cash offers hysterical opposition to Bella's associating with men, and this brings the girl to see her at last as

> a faded middle aged woman of imperious and uncertain temper, pathetically nursing an illusion of emancipated youth and freedom and daring in what was really the arid life of a confirmed old maid.[32]

Later, in the company of a man she loves, Bella meets Miss Cash on the street with another worshipful young girl and recognizes a sinister element in these consuming attachments. When the man observes that though the schoolmistress has the face of an old woman she still moves like a girl, Bella replies that she is ageless because she is a vampire, living on young blood. Neither of the women here appears at all masculine, though Miss Cash is a feminist and a man-hater and Bella has a man's practical intelligence and drive. Bella's loves are substitutes for family ties, and the older woman is again the egotist in need of constant adulation.

In 1936 Rosamond Lehmann skimmed variance fleetingly in *Weather in the Streets* with a dialogue between a divorcee of boyish appearance and her one-time schoolmate who plainly has suspicions about the cause of her marital difficulties;[33] the suspicions are, however, unfounded. Marcia Davenport gave her prima donna in *Of Lena Geyer* just such a faithful adorer as Allie Wentworth in Hunekers' satiric *Painted Veils,* but she is careful to specify that though gossip attributed a lesbian color to the relationship it was actually blameless.[34] (One suspects that there may have been living models for both authors' couples of singer and satellite in the New York musical world of the early century.)

The year's most important item was the British edition (the American followed in 1937) of *Nightwood* by Djuna Barnes, a young American of the Paris group of expatriates following more or less in the literary footsteps of Gertrude Stein and James Joyce. Fortunately Miss Barnes's work is intelligible without a key, her kinship being perhaps closer with T. S. Eliot, who wrote the preface for this, her first full-length narrative. On initial reading, the first hundred pages of *Nightwood* may seem only a crowded canvas of figures romantic in their eccentricity and linked by little save Left Bank geography. Gradually one perceives that their dual axis is a pair of young women, one an American. Nora Flood owns a decaying homestead near enough New York to be crowded, whenever she is there, with the gifted bohemians her hospitality welcomes. The scene of *Nightwood,* however, is mainly Paris, where Nora acts as publicity agent for a small circus. Of the enigmatic Robin Vote, who moves through the story in a kind of somnambulism, one learns little save that sometimes she breaks absently into fragments of debased song in any of a half-dozen languages, and exhibits a compulsive lesbian promiscuity, the two together suggesting a dubious background. At twenty she drifts into marriage with a wealthy Jew, but childbirth wakes her violently to the knowledge that neither marriage nor motherhood is tolerable to her.

She and Nora are drawn to one another on sight, wander about the continent happily together, and settle for some years in Paris. But Robin is increasingly involved in transient contacts, though she suffers them without volition and is happy only on return to Nora. Then a fading and greedy widow captures and attempts to hold her, and Robin is so torn between her two emotional poles that her always precarious stability is destroyed. The occasion of Nora's first meeting her was a circus performance from which the girl fled in inarticulate panic because the animals were magnetically drawn to her side of their cages, and a lioness stretched paws through the bars and fixed her "with brimming eyes of love." The book ends with Nora's tracing Robin's final headlong flight from Paris to her own American country place, where she finds the deranged girl engaged in poetically beautiful but spine-chilling play with Nora's great dog. The volume *in toto* is a tragic prose poem of the lost—all those whose sole métier is instinct and emotion, misfit and outcast in a culture whose law is social regimentation.

Perceptibly related in style, although far inferior in artistry, is Helen Anderson's *Pity for Women* (1937). In this story, an over-sensitive motherless girl attempts to make her way alone in New York, living in a residence club more sinister in its inbred hysteria than any woman's college dormitory. The hysterical manifestations are not only variance but the reckless struggles of older girls to capture men. The "blind dates" to which Ann submits, the drinking and promiscuity and aftermaths of abortion and suicide which she sees among her housemates, so sicken her that when she acquires a room-mate to assuage her loneliness, she clings to the cool and serene Elizabeth as a savior. The two girls enjoy a period of innocent friend-ship precious to both, but it is jeopardized when an older woman galvanizes Elizabeth into passionate tension. This imperious Judith soon brings Ann also under her spell. She then drops the more con-tained Elizabeth, and takes Ann as her housemate outside the club. This move estranges the two girls and also terminates a promising acquaintance between Ann and the one man whose company she has been able to enjoy.

There is at first the usual period of honeymoon ecstasy between the two housemates but then bit by bit Ann pieces together Judith's crowded history, one only to have been expected, but prostrating to the naïve Ann. She is particularly shaken by the story of Judith's dearest love, a girl as young as herself, whose marriage for the sake of a child drove Judith to attempt suicide. She also suffers from their social isolation, which is complete save for Judith's still adoring older friends. No new contacts on Ann's part are permitted. From an agony of jealousy Ann wastes so alarmingly that Judith, to reassure her, goes through a species of marriage ceremony, using the familiar passage from the *Book of Ruth*. But this gesture is worse than futile. Ann's state has been induced not by need of permanence but by unconscious terror of it, which warred with her passion. As she feels the fetters closing, her mind gives way. Of the three women depicted, Judith is an innate homosexual and the two younger girls are diverted from normal orbits by contact with her. Elizabeth has stamina enough to regain her balance, although had she remained Judith's choice the outcome must have been dubious. The immature and unstable Ann is wrecked beyond hope of recovery.

After these two studies, ultra-modern in manner and somewhat morbid in substance, to read Elisabeth Craigin's *Either is Love* (1937) is to step back into another century. The almost expository narrative moves against a background in which horses still provide the means of transportation, and there is little to indicate that it is not the discreetly disguised autobiography which it claims to be. Indeed its prose style suggests an already established reputation in fields of non-fiction. It covers a decade in the life of its author, beginning with her late twenties. An employee of the federal government, she is singled out by a younger colleague who shows her the small attentions normally proffered by a man. As the acquaintance develops, its emotional tone disturbs Elisabeth, who recognizes it as what would ordinarily be called "falling in love." (However, as she explains, in the United States at that time the only available literature on psychology was written by William James; Krafft-Ebing and Havelock Ellis were barely heard of, and even the feminism of Olive Schreiner and Ellen Key was "only for the very emancipated.") For two years the pair struggle against circumstance, the need for secrecy, and their own increasing passion. To the young Rachel, the experience of variant (if not lesbian) love is not wholly new. Heretofore her friends have been attracted by her boyishness, but now Elisabeth is averse to any travesty of a heterosexual relation. Theirs must be an honest love between two women. Finally some months together abroad give them a typical interlude of complete and perfect union.

Then family complications separate them, and the brief periods they can snatch together are fevered by the effort to crowd too much ardor into too little time. During a long stretch with the width of the Atlantic between them, Rachel falls back into her youthful pattern of responding to the dynamic reaction she involuntarily rouses in other women. This infidelity to what is still her great love induces loss of faith in herself, and finally she suffers so acute a sense of guilt that she turns against all physical expression and follows the lead of a new friend (a mystic enamored of self-abnegation) into the church. Elisabeth could have foregone intimacy if that was required to preserve their friendship; but Rachel's retroactive conviction that their whole association was wrong seems to her sheer sacrilege. She feels that the Rachel known to her is dead, and a decade passes before she is able to enter upon another emotional relationship.

This second love is heterosexual, and the other half of the volume records its course, terminating in marriage. The two experiences, though different in detail, are subjectively identical and quite justify the title, *Either is Love.* The author's final comment upon variance is well-considered enough to warrant quotation:

> I do not even now understand the expression "sinful" as I hear it in connection with love between women. . . . I should think sin was something that did harm in some form, to other people or, of course, to oneself. . . . Lust demoralizes both participants. . . . Married life does not preclude it, God knows, and there are great numbers of extra-marital forms. I can understand how lust might develop between women, and if that exists it is deplorable enough. But because incest occurs, is all family life vicious? Because there are brothels, is all sexual life unclean? A so-called Lesbian alliance can be of the most rarified purity, and those who do not believe it are merely judging in ignorance of the facts.[35]

This special pleading, more philosophic than Miss Hall's, is so much of a piece with the rest of the text that it is not obtrusive, and the volume raised no outcry in our press.

Nevertheless, in the same year the imported French film *Club de Femmes*, its story by Jacques Deval, was drastically cut for New York showing. The review in *Time* said:

> Manhattan censors promptly spotted Sapphic overtones . . . in the character played by beauteous Else Argall, Deval's wife. Censorship deleted her best scene, which shows her successfully fighting the urge to join the girl of her desire.[36]

This latter is the central figure, who is seduced by a man and bears his illegitimate child. "Considered fit for Manhattan cinema-goers was the shot in which [the lesbian] poisons the procuress telephone operator." If, as Ernst and Lindey claim in *The Censor Marches On*, the deletion of the "best" scene left an implication that the lesbian yielded to her desires, then as revived in 1948 the film must have been

still further cut (as indeed a certain incoherence suggests), for all
that it then showed was the older woman's maternal solicitude for the
naïve newcomer.

In 1938 the important contributions came from Gale Wilhelm and
Kay Boyle. To be sure, Dorothy Baker in *Young Man with a Horn*
hinted, in passing, at an alliance between a light-skinned Harlem
beauty and the white graduate student who later proves so unsatisfactory a wife to the hero. Ernest Hemingway also, in "Sea Change,"
one of the briefest pieces in *The Fifth Column* and the First Forty-
nine Stories, shows a lesbian interlude breaking in upon a satisfactory
heterosexual affair. The man tells his errant partner, "It's a vice."
The girl, promising to return to him, denies the charge. "We're made
up of all sorts of things. You've known that. You've used it well
enough." But neither of these treatments was very important, and
there seem not to have been others.

Miss Wilhelm's second novelette, *Torchlight to Valhalla,* resembles
her first in length and style, but differs in that both its girls are
masculine in little more than attire, and variant largely through conditioning. The older is even more closely bound to her father than
was Gillian in *The Tortoiseshell Cat.* In her desperate loneliness after
his death, she yields to a young musician (male) who seems an ideal
partner, but finds herself frozen and shamed by the experiment. The
younger girl has been forced since the age of fifteen to assume a
man's responsibility for herself and her once distinguished aunt, now
a bemused alcoholic. The two girls immediately find in one another
the answer to their needs and achieve a union which promises lasting
happiness. There is nothing here like Jan's bohemian existence in *We
Too Are Drifting* or her barren entanglement with the married
woman. Despite these seeming efforts to placate the prejudiced, Miss
Wilhelm's second title fared no better at the hands of reviewers than
her first.

Kay Boyle, then another of the American literary expatriates in
France, was already a writer of established reputation when she
entered the variant field in 1938 with two titles. Earlier, in *Gentlemen, I Address You Privately* there had been hints of male homosexuality. Incorporated in *Monday Night* there is a much more explicit lesbian episode, seen in part through the eyes of an eight-
year-old boy whose father is serving a life sentence for a crime of
which he is innocent. The rather pathetic wife and mother enjoys
a summer interlude with a *soi-disant* Russian princess, fugitive from
the Revolution of 1917. This Baya, world-vagabond, automobile racer

and aviator, even masquerades on occasion in the father's World
War I uniform,

> the visored cap . . . tipped on the side of her head, even the
> boots seeming to fit exactly, and the crop stuck under her arm-
> pit, and the face small, tough and reckless . . . "His uniform,
> his wife, his kid, the life he can't live handed me like a
> present," she said scarcely aloud, the casual rakish smile neat
> as a boy's."

Then the other woman shows interest in a man, and after some
stubborn haunting of the apartment, Baya slams out, "banging the
hall-door behind her so that the pictures jumped on the walls."

Miss Boyle's second narrative, "The Bridegroom's Body," did
not appear in book form until 1940 when it was included in the
volume *The Crazy Hunter*, but the *Southern Quarterly* printed it
in 1938. Here Lady Glourie, thirty-five but emotionally naïve as a
child, is mistress of an isolated manor with a swannery dating from
the sixteenth century, and wife to a man whose only interest is sport.
He and his cronies spend their days with rod and gun and their
nights in carousal from which she is excluded, so that she feels herself
isolated in a world of men given over to nothing but killing. When
illness in the swanherd's family makes it necessary to import a nurse,
Lady Glourie anticipates the company of another woman with pathetic eagerness. The arrival of a young and beautiful Irish girl is a
blow, the more bitter because Lord Glourie is instantly smitten. There
is also a handsome farmer on the place, reputed to be irresistible to
women; so when Lady Glourie learns that Miss Cafferty is given to
long walks by night as well as by day she infers the worst. The Irish
girl's shyly professed admiration for herself she takes as a studied
attempt at ingratiation.

It is the swans' mating season and the perennial battle is on
between old warriors and young cobs. On a night when the nurse is
neither in her room nor with her patient, Lady Glourie is called from
her bed to deal with a battle to the death between a young "bridegroom" and the fiercest of the old cobs. Thinking she may be in time
to save the young swan, she wades out waist deep to the rescue and
narrowly escapes dangerous attack by the old one. She emerges from
the icy water with the dead swan to find Miss Cafferty there, softly
hysterical, pouring out a torrent of endearment. She learns that from
the first the girl has been interested in her alone, fighting off the men

because she too hates their predatory cruelty. Her long walks she has taken

> "to think about you here, alone where there might be something left of you . . . some mark of you on the ground. I couldn't sleep in the room, I couldn't bear closing the door after I'd left you. . . . I've walked the country alone . . . talking out loud to you night and day, asking you to give me everything I haven't, peace and strength and that look in your eyes . . . one hint of what it is you have that nobody else has, just one weapon to fight the others . . ."[38]

Lady Glourie quiets her,

> but these were things she had heard once or once imagined. . . . She stood waiting, scarcely breathing, waiting for the words to start again. The chill she had not yet felt on her flesh entered her heart for the instant that the words abandoned this anonymous but exact description of love.[39]

When the girl does speak again it is to beg Lady Glourie to come away with her, escape from the manor, continue to "lend me what you can spare." The surcharged moment is interrupted by the noisy arrival of Lord Glourie with a lantern, demanding "What's up?" and annoyed to find them both drenched to the skin. "Lady Glourie looked down at her own strange flesh and suddenly she began shaking with the cold." Here the narrative ends, and as in *Delay in the Sun,* the reader must supply for himself the ultimate outcome.

Nineteen-thirty-nine saw the publication of two dissimilar novels, the American and anonymous *Diana,*[40] and *Promise of Love* by a new English author, Mary Renault. Of the latter, the main theme is the struggle of a nurse and a laboratory pathologist to work out satisfactory heterosexual relations against the odds of hospital discipline and of their individual homosexual interests. Vivian closely resembles a brother of uncommon charm, irresistible to both sexes but disinclined to take his relations with either seriously. Thus Mic, who has enjoyed a transient intimacy with the brother and seen his interest fade, is wary of allowing Vivian any hold upon him. She, for her part, is being gracefully courted by a fellow nurse, tall, tailored and debonair, and there are discreet intimations of her momentarily succumbing. One of the factors inclining Vivian toward Mic is Colonna's sudden and much deeper attachment to a new supervisor of nurses, and the completeness of this connection and the perilous professional risks it entails are left in no doubt. Vivian's growing intimacy with Mic narrowly escapes disaster when, in a spirit of deviltry, she dresses in men's clothes and gets the abrupt and brutal reaction the experiment invites. In the end, the two weather all storms and marry. The supervisor also accepts a male suitor, and Colonna is left to face the fact that as she grows older her Maupin pose will be less becoming and her conquests fewer.

Diana is an autobiography almost of the "true confession" type, though it carried a preface by Dr. Victor Robinson endorsing at least its subjective authenticity. Diana grows up the only girl in a household of brothers and she is very close to her father until his death. When in early adolescence she falls in love with a high school chum and recognizes her feelings as those of a boy, her reaction is one of shame not alleviated by an older brother's introducing her to the works of Havelock Ellis. In college she avoids friendships with women and evades one girl's advances by pretending ignorance. Delighted to find the attentions of a male graduate student acceptable, she is engaged to him for a couple of years, but an unsuccessful trial of intimacy eliminates marriage from her future plans.

During a year of study abroad, initiation by another American girl shows her where her fulfillment lies; this contact, however, is broken at once by the reappearance of an earlier flame of her new friend. Wounded and angry, Diana is ripe for a less sophisticated alliance with a girl who is shocked by lesbianism and refuses to recognize anything of it in their love. When intimacy finally develops, it is not too satisfactory, since Jane's scruples preclude any intelligent effort on her part to meet Diana's needs. Nevertheless, the two attempt for a year to live together after their return to the States. In the women's college where Diana teaches, their rooming off-campus stirs so much gossip that for the next year Diana must choose between Jane and her position.

Diana's second conscientious effort, in a coeducational college, to become interested in men is unsuccessful. Somewhat later she finds a young woman graduate student with whom she achieves happiness after a period of meticulous restraint reminiscent of *We Too Are Drifting*. Suspense is supplied by Leslie's mother's denouncing the pair and disowning her daughter, and by the reappearance of Jane, who attempts to capture Leslie out of wanton spite. Diana and Leslie are so eminently suited to one another, however, that they finally come through even more closely united. This narrative is certainly no literary masterpiece, and perhaps its strongest point is Diana's honest analysis along the way of the arguments against, rather than for, her chosen way of life. Since homosexuals need not fear pregnancy or assume responsibility for a home and family, they are free to make and break connections lightly.⁴¹ Only true sympathy, loyalty, and dedication to their unions can restrain them from snatching at facile satisfaction, and human nature being what it is, no lesbian alliance has more strength than the weaker of its two partners. These observations are not particularly original, of course, having often enough been demonstrated by example in a half century's fiction. Even the precepts themselves had appeared by 1939 in a good many hortatory manuals of sex psychology. Heretofore, however, they were voiced by strenuous opponents of homosexual intimacy. For a defender to present them with cool logic, and, in spite of them, to justify the calculated risk, marks an advance in psychological perspective since Radclyffe Hall's wholly emotional plea for tolerance a decade earlier.

Another War's Shadow

For the next threè years the preoccupations of war—plus the paper shortage—crowded variant fiction almost completely from the market, and even after readers and publishers once more hit a modified stride, the bulk of such fiction remained condemnatory for the rest of the decade. Angela DuMaurier's *The Little Less* (1941) reports effects as devastating as those in *The Island* from a long variant enslavement, even though in this case there is no physical intimacy. Toward the end of the book a spasm of lesbian debauchery marks one woman's repudiation of her Catholic faith in defiance of a deity who permitted her child to die. The orgy is followed by her suicide. In Fanny Hurst's *Lonely Parade* (1942), the picturesque trio of bachelor girls are solaced by mutual devotion of a variant cast, though never actually lesbian; but their unwedded lives are not especially happy.

The inexplicable burst of five titles in 1943 was largely damning, the minority report being Dorothy Cowlin's in *Winter Solstice*, a thinly disguised case history of a paralytic whose eight years' invalidism, of hysterical origin, is cured by a sudden emotional interest in a woman aviator. The relationship is brief and innocent, and is followed by marriage for both women. Craig Rice used the lesbian advances of an eccentric heiress to a Greenwich Village "poet" as a neat red herring in her murder mystery *Having a Wonderful Crime*, in which the heiress is the victim. In Jane Bowles's *Two Serious Ladies*, an inhibited Brooklyn housewife finds her first experience outside the States so inebriating that she defies her husband and lingers in the prostitutes' quarters of Colon, determined to "learn all the things she didn't know," even though she realizes they will not make her happy.

On a level to be taken seriously, Arthur Koestler in *Arrival and Departure* conveyed, through his hero's contact with a woman psychoanalyst, his estimate of both the good and the bad in an all-tolerant psychiatric viewpoint. Peter, heroic political refugee shattered by his ordeal in the hands of the enemy, is taken in and cared for in a neutral European city by his countrywoman, Dr. Bolgar. He falls in love and has a restoring liaison with a young girl who frequents the doctor's apartment, and he plans to follow Odette to the United States when a passport can be secured. His relapse into neurosis upon her leaving him without notice or farewell Dr. Bolgar repairs by a swift and skillful analysis of his lifelong martyr complex. Chance, however, reveals to Peter that the doctor is Odette's real love and he but a passing fancy. So, instead of following the girl, he returns to his perilous but "real" underground activities. The doctor is described as tall, full-blown, and masterful; Odette, as childishly slender, with a "boyish" unpainted mouth. In the end,

> Above all he felt a sadness . . . and pity for Odette, with her vacant look, her slimness and vulnerability—Odette the victim, drowned in the carnivorous flower's embrace.[42]

Certainly best-known of the year's titles is Dorothy Baker's *Trio*, on which a play was based, since its stage history virtually duplicated that of *The Captive* seventeen years earlier. Its opening in Philadelphia was well attended and reviewed, and the play ran on Broadway for a little more than a month before being closed through pressure from a combination of religious interests. One of the *New Yorker* staff interviewed various signers of the petition for its withdrawal, and found that several had neither seen the play nor read the novel from which it was made before lending their names to the protest.

The story presents the struggle between a Frenchwoman on an American university faculty and a young art photographer for possession of a girl who is departmental assistant to the former. Pauline Maury has just published a brilliant study of the *fin de siècle* French decadents, notably Verlaine and Rimbaud. Like them, she is an advocate of exploring the limits of sensibility under all possible stimuli from alcohol to sexual passion, with veiled hints at drugs and flagellation, but naturally this aspect of her life is well concealed. The girl Janet, at first a passionate intellectual and emotional devotee, has been reduced by intimacy with Pauline to the limit of stability when a whirlwind courtship by Ray Mackenzie and a wholesome heterosexual liaison with him save her from further exploitation. Though Ray reacts with blind rage and contempt to her confession of her past relations with Pauline, there is at least a chance that he will come around enough to marry her when he has cooled. The defeated and frustrated Frenchwoman shoots herself.

This is the essence of the drama, artistically in need of no accessories, but probably to avoid elaboration of its morbid emotional elements Mrs. Baker added an offense more permissible of stress. The substance of Pauline's monograph was stolen from the dissertation of a married friend to whose premature death her own relations with the woman contributed, and the widowed husband retaliates by exposing her plagiarism. This disgrace provides adequate motivation for the suicide which makes so effective a dramatic climax, but it lessens the power of the whole. Pauline as a self-defeating decadent is an unsavory but convincing personality. With the added onus of literary theft she too nearly degenerates into mere villain. Of this century's four widely circulated dramas, then—*The Captive, Mädchen in Uniform, The Children's Hour,* and *Trio*—only the German film succeeded in being good theatre without blurring in some way the variant theme.

Two passing references in 1944 were Erskine Caldwell's single flippant paragraph in *Tragic Ground:* a bartender's account of discovering his wife at play in the back room of her beauty salon with two of her young patrons,[43] and Jean Stafford's vignette in *Boston Adventure* of a Back Bay dowager who fawns upon each seasons' debutantes without once suspecting her own motivation. The heroine, however, bearing scars still unhealed from her childhood under the spell of a neurotic mother now in a sanatorium, is literally sickened by the woman's fulsome caresses.[44]

In 1945 Nora Lofts inserted in her historical novel *Jassy* a disparaging middle section, "Complaint from Lesbia," involving a triangle of two middle-aged school mistresses and the romanticized title figure, then a kitchen maid of thirteen. From girlhood the now-widowed Mrs. Twysdale has worshipped her intellectual cousin, Katherine, and in youth chose as husband the suitor who most resembled her. The two women have jogged along undramatically enough for twenty years in their joint school enterprise when the advent of the remarkable Jassy moves Katherine to unadmitted passion and Mrs. Twysdale to vengeful jealousy. It is the precocious Jassy herself, now a favored student through Katherine's efforts, who at fifteen accepts unjust dismissal without protest because she recognizes that Katherine will ultimately be better off keeping her lifelong business partner. Here Mrs. Twysdale, pettily feminine and feline, is alone identified with "Lesbia," (semantically unrelated to Catullus), while the other two exhibit traits implied by Miss Lofts to be masculine.

In the same year Mary Renault in *The Middle Mist* provided a tonic relief with a variant portrait as piquant as any since *Mlle de Maupin*. Leo (christened Leonora) can, at twenty-five, be mistaken for a teen-age boy even by her own sister after a long separation. She makes a good living by writing "westerns," lives on a houseboat within commuting distance of London, and avoids situations requiring feminine costume. For seven years she has maintained a comfortable domestic ménage with a nurse who once saved her life. Neither girl's single brief experiment with a man was happy, and both find their common life wholly satisfying. Still they do not avoid the company of men, and a good part of the story is concerned with the growth of Leo's friendship with a fellow author into a love which leads finally to marriage. Her difficult choice between her two very real loves, determined largely by her desire for children, is movingly presented.

Her initial attempt at masculine independence was occasioned by intolerable friction between her parents, and her own temperament made it a success. When her younger sister, kept feminine and helpless by a doting mother, follows Leo's pattern of flight, she simply presents herself on Leo's doorstep and stays for a long season without realistic thought of who is paying for her keep. Her own adolescent means of escape from family tension has been a steady diet of cheap fiction, and she can see her future only in its sugary terms. When real heartbreak ends a stupid little romance built on nothing more than wishful dreaming, she creeps back to the parental nest, where one imagines her withering into bathetic spinsterhood, haunting rental libraries in search of more stories with happy endings. The parallel development of the two sisters' lives constitutes a strong argument in favor of lesbian intimacy as against inhibited Victorian romancing. One of the most vivid features of *The Middle Mist* is its humor, a quality hitherto conspicuously lacking in variant fiction. (Gautier, Gunter, Bennett and Mackenzie are the exceptions.) Leo's taking a conceited young doctor down a notch by flirting

successfully with the nurse he brings to a party and then neglects for
other women would be hilarious in any setting. In a variant novel it
gleams as an unmatched gem.

Second Crescendo

The end of the war produced no such immediate effect on variant
fiction as did the beginning, but gradually quantity increased with
the accelerating speed of a geometric progression. Consequently,
many of the thirty-odd novels which appeared from 1946 through
1954—all still relatively accessible—must receive short shrift. Brief
and disparaging variant or lesbian passages were included in Remarque's *Arch of Triumph* (1945 in English), Edmund Wilson's
Memoirs of Hecate County (1946), Felix Forrest's *Carola* (1948),
Philip Wylie's *Opus 21* (1949) and *Disappearance* (1951), Theodora
Keogh's *Meg* (1950), Robert Wilder's *Wait for Tomorrow* (1952),
Joan Henry's *Women in Prison* (1952) and Maurice Druon's *Rise of
Silas Lachaume* (1951; in English, 1952). Characters varied from
prostitutes to socialites; action, from sentimental philandering to
a jealous knifing.

Longer derogatory treatments were presented by an equal number
of authors. In 1946 Jean Paul Sartre's *No Exit* (a translation of *Huis
Clos,* 1945) had a brief but unchallenged run in New York. Its
three characters, impounded in a small room in hell, are: a cowardly
political traitor who has also heaped every humiliation on a devoted
wife; a woman who has broken several men for her own amusement
and killed her unwanted child; and a manhating lesbian who has
stolen her cousin's wife and then talked her victim into a joint
suicide pact. Since the lesbian's sins seem less heinous than those
of the other two, her emotional anomaly must be viewed as evening
the balance.

Christopher LaFarge's *The Sudden Guest* (1946) is concerned with
a colossal egotist who closes her doors against victims of a New
England hurricane. Desperation emboldens them to enter despite
her, but she is untouched by their several stark tragedies. Only one
handsome and cultured woman is welcome, for reasons half snobbish,
half emotional. This Mrs. Cleever has with her an infant son, but is
indifferent to his welfare because of her grief at the drowning of
his nursemaid, with whom she was obviously infatuated. The last
waifs to arrive are a low-class boy and a girl of fifteen whom he has
saved from drowning and carries naked in his arms. Galvanized from
her stupor, Mrs. Cleever snatches the beautiful figure from him and,

unassisted, carries the girl off to her room. Later the spinster-hostess finds the two sleeping nude in each other's arms, and this alone has the power to move her—but only to jealousy and self-pity for her own loneliness.

Three comparatively mediocre works of 1947 were equally severe. George Willis's *Little Boy Blues* recounts the machinations of a lesbian to achieve marriage and motherhood as a "front" to protect her reputation and as a means of securing her future. She then deserts her victim and uses the child as a financial hold upon him while pursuing her own inclinations, until he is goaded into killing her. Ethel Wilson in *Hetty Dorval* pictures the near-capture of a Canadian girl of eighteen by a courtesan on vacation from her profession and posing as a respectable woman in Vancouver. In *Not Now but NOW*, Mary F. K. Fisher's chief figure is a woman as ageless as Orlando and a ruthless egomaniac in all eras and settings. It is in a small Ohio town during the Twenties that she involves a college girl in a lesbian scandal.

The title figure in James Ronald's *The Angry Woman* (1948) externally resembles Sinclair Lewis's Dr. Herringdean, and, like her, is a successful business executive. Her hold upon Fern Oliphant dates from a bedridden year in the latter's teens and continues till her suicide a decade later. Lesley uses every means to increase Fern's dependence upon her, and tries first to prevent and then to break up a marriage arranged by the girl's mother. Unlike Lewis's unalloyed monster, however, this woman insists she has never been a lesbian. Her own marriage failed on its first night (cf. the French *Méphistophéla*), and her passion for the girl has also gone unfulfilled. She sees her own fondness as the only truly maternal devotion Fern has ever known. To everyone else it wears the aspect of subjective cannibalism.

A more complex case appears in Margaret Landon's *Never Dies the Dream* (1949). But for its expressed horror of variant passion this novel would belong among the favorable studies, for its mainspring is a love as constructive and as delicately presented as that in the *Book of Ruth*. Like its author's now famous *Anna and the King of Siam*, it is laid in Siam, but in this work the heroine is an unmarried American missionary. India gives sanctuary in her mission school to a countrywoman a decade her junior, widow of a Siamese of high rank, because the girl is in danger of violence from her husband's relatives and of sexual molestation by a European. When India isolates herself with the girl to nurse her through an attack of typhoid, she is accused by a rival mission teacher of being "enamored" of her patient. Agonized soul-searching forces her to admit she feels Angela to be "bone of her bone, flesh of her flesh," but she can find nothing blameworthy in her love. The maternal element is further stressed when Angela, upon returning to America, leaves her most treasured possession as a parting gift to "my mother-in-love." It should be admitted that passion of any sort is regarded darkly in the volume—quite justifiably in view of its uglier recorded manifestations—but one can only regret an astigmatism which sees so vividly the beauty of a selfless passion (for its incandescent intensity is undeniably passionate) and is still blind to its essential nature.

Hugh Wheeler's *The Crippled Muse* (1952) does not condemn lesbianism per se so much as one of the personalities involved. This is another sparkling comedy of Capri. The three figures significant here are all Americans. Liz Lewis is a wealthy and domineering shrew of apparently innate masculinity, whose record as a finishing school teacher was as technically immaculate as Clare Hartill's in *Regiment of Women,* until her dismissal at perhaps thirty. This was occasioned by the conspicuous infatuation of a student in her late teens after the girl was violently orphaned. At the time of this story these two have lived together for a decade and the younger, Loretta, is more than tired of the arrangement; yet she stays because she feels responsible for their plight. A sympathetic young professor induces her to break away and marry him. He is not shocked by her history but is hotly antagonistic to the woman who has so long exploited her sense of guilt to hold her captive. (Incidentally, Liz had used Christina Rossetti's *Goblin Market* in her original capture of Loretta by stressing their parallelism—unconvincing—to Lizzie and Laura).

Less tolerance of lesbianism marks Sara Harris's *The Wayward Ones* (1952), a social worker's study of homosexuality in a reform school. Termed "the racket" by the adolescent inmates, it at first terrifies and repels a sixteen-year-old girl committed to the institution for unmarried motherhood. She sees, however, that the pairing of "moms" and "pops" brings solace and a sense of belonging to many of the girls involved, and that the authorities make no effort to check the practice, to which they remain questionably blind. When at last she "marries" one of the "pops" to gain protection from an unbalanced housemate who has attempted to kill her, her assumption of the new status marks the beginning of rapid deterioration. She becomes a ruthless liar and schemer, and makes plans to become a "call girl" for both men and women when she is released from the school.

Perhaps the most virulent attack was launched by Simon Eisner in *Naked Storm*, another paper-backed original of the same year. A predatory woman novelist, on the eve of departing for California, first seduces a young art student whom she leaves ill with self-loathing. On the transcontinental train she repeats the experiment with an older woman, who is highly intelligent but emotionally starved. This woman is also courted by a shy and unhappy man, but his rival's expert sophistication rapidly reduces his chances. At this point an ex-war correspondent decides to play *deus ex machina*. Moved by savage hatred of all lesbians and this arrogant specimen in particular, he takes advantage of a sixty-below-zero blizzard which stalls the train for some thirty hours in the Donner Pass, goads the self-sufficient lesbian into going out into the night for snow to ice her liquor, and furthermore, manages so to confuse her that she loses her bearings in the arctic blackness and freezes to death. The author plainly enjoys this dénouement as much as Belot enjoyed killing off Mme Blangy.

The latest condemnation is incorporated in *Strange Sisters* (1954), a pot-boiling murder story by a writer who calls himself "Fletcher Flora." Opening with the knifing of a man by a girl who has led him to embrace her but then finds her sexual revulsion unconquerable, it flashes back to the causes of her inhibition. The earliest was childhood idolatry of the more or less innocently seductive aunt who raised her (cf. the mother-daughter relation in *Star Against Star*). The second was deliberate seduction by a women's college instructor when the girl was a lonely and maladjusted freshman; the third a repetition with a department store personnel manager as agent. Each of these older women, in increasing degrees, was interested only in her own emotional needs and not at all in her victim's welfare. The girl ends with complete mental breakdown and suicide.

All these condemnatory treatments were balanced by as many mildly or strongly sympathetic studies. The briefest of these are two short stories, one "Orestes" in Rhys Davies's *A Trip to London* (1946), in which a lesbian waitress frees a middle-aged bachelor from his paralyzing mother fixation precisely because her attitude toward him is so free of feminine seduction. The other is Isabel Bolton's "Ruth and Irma" (1947), a reminiscent and gently ironic sketch of an infatuated pair of girls roaming the Riviera during the Twenties, which lays their histrionics directly to their saturation with that decade's fiction. A more important role is assigned to lesbianism in Lucie Marchal's prize-winning French novel of 1948 translated in 1949 as *The Mesh*, a Freudian study of a domineering woman's influence on the lives of her son and daughter. The son's marriage to a timid widow proves a fruitless gesture of defiance. The daughter, always jealous of the mother's preference for her brother, is gradually liberated from her own fixation by an increasing interest in the pitiful and helpless young wife. In the end her protective impulses become passionate and she takes the girl away to live with her. It is plain, however, that she, like her mother, will soon tyrannize over her captive as stringently as she herself has been dominated.

Another paper-backed original was *Women's Barracks* (1950) by Toreska Torres (according to *Publishers Weekly* the pseudonym of an established author). This purports to be a description of life in the London headquarters for women recruits of the Free French forces; however, it is not a translation. An important thread in the meandering plot is the love of a shy girl of seventeen for a much older woman, wholesome and maternal though vulgar, who has consoled herself while married to a "pansy" by intimacies with both men and women. One or two completely lesbian couples in the house refuse to recognize Claude as one of themselves—"She's a pervert, a curiosity seeker." Nevertheless her influence on Ursula is beneficent. Soon the girl turns to men, the lesbian interlude having cracked the shell of her naïve reserve and matured her for other experience.

Easily the eeriest of all references to variance is Shirley Jackson's in her remarkable study of late adolescence, *Hangsaman* (1951). Here a girl, as precariously balanced as Ann in *Pity for Women,* is inhibited by a father fixation, and driven farther from normal experience by a cryptically-described incident, perhaps actual assault, but more likely only heavy petting, by an older man at a cocktail party in her own home. In a "progressive" college, quite unsupervised, she becomes more and more solitary and withdrawn until her sudden friendship with an ideally sympathetic girl companion. This alter ego, whose allure she finally recognizes as physical and fights off, proves actually to be only the other half of her own split personality. In other words, the drama in *Hangsaman* is that of an abnormally sensitive girl's narrow escape from schizophrenia.

In the same year Whit and Hallie Burnett included in *Sextet: Six Story Discoveries* John Eichrodt's "Nadia Devereux," which its author describes as a feminine "parody" of Thomas Mann's *Death in Venice*. It need not, then, be further discussed than to say that it treats understandingly the secret infatuation of an internationally-renowned woman lecturer on international law for an exquisite girl on the clerical staff of the United Nations. Like its model, it follows the older woman's gradual disintegration and death from the violence of her inhibited yet undisciplined passion.

Appearing also in 1951 was a sensational trifle reminiscent of the worst of the 1930s, *Strange Fires* by Jack Woodford. This is a sexual riot with lesbian action prominent, in which, as in *Love Like a Shadow*, one girl is essentially "monogamous" in spirit. Rhoda and her finishing-school roommate, both initiated by their physcial education teacher, "marry" one another and are briefly happy. But the discovery that her partner and Miss Pat are continuing their relation wounds Rhoda deeply, and their taking her to an "orgy" in a Park Avenue socialite's apartment completes her disillusion. She finally marries a man (implying that she is still "normal"), and the two other young women continue in a mutually free alliance.

A sympathetic treatment which bows to orthodox standards by ending tragically is presented in *Spring Fire* (1952), paper-backed original by Vin Packer, admitted pseudonym of an established male author. Here a lonely boyish co-ed in a midwestern university is willingly seduced by her sorority-house roommate and finds the lesbian relation a happy one as long as it remains secret. It is the seducer, neurotic daughter of a promiscuous widow, who feels guilt and carries on simultaneously an excessive affair with a man to prove herself normal. The unsophisticated Mitch is urged to do likewise, but she cannot follow through her two squeamish efforts, and she reacts with loathing to drunken violation by a fraternity man. When suspicion of lesbianism falls on the two girls the neurotic accuses her victim of having been the seducer. Mitch is expelled from the sorority, and only the understanding dean of girls and the college physician avert disaster. In his naturalistic picture of campus sex life in general the author treats the lesbian aspect with comparative sympathy and attributes its destructive effects to the neurotic girl's sense of guilt. This is induced by her mother's influence and ripens into a full-blown psychosis. She ends in a mental institution.

Two much happier episodes were featured in novels of 1952. In Fay Adams's paper-backed original, *Appointment in Paris*, an American orphan in her teens is matured sufficiently to weaken a spinster aunt's dominance through her intimacy with a wholesome, if irresponsible, French courtesan living in a neighboring apartment. She then enjoys a liaison with a Frenchman and later happily marries an American. Both men know her history. May Sarton's infinitely superior novel, *A Shower of Summer Days*, includes the brief infatuation of an American girl, half-through college, for her Anglo-Irish aunt. Sent abroad by her mother to terminate an undesirable

romance at home, she at first truculently resists her aunt's overtures
and her own impulses toward friendliness. The aunt, once a great
beauty, childless, and still bound to her husband by mutual passion
which has survived two decades of marriage, is an irresistible personality and comes to exert great influence on the girl. As with
Lily Briscoe in *To the Lighthouse*, it is partly the relation between
wife and husband which fascinates the girl; however, her emotions
crystallize upon the woman. Her aunt recognizes the unmistakable
signs of passion, and far from being shocked, even wishes it were
possible for her to respond. By the end of the summer the girl is
cured, not only of her callow heterosexual obsession, but of the
variant love also, and emerges with adult appreciation of what
married love can be.

There remain a half-dozen novels in which variance plays so
large a part that they should not be ticked off too briefly. The first
is *Ladders to Fire* (1946) by Anais Nin, a stylistic disciple (in some
measure) of Gertrude Stein. There is a minimum of action, the
work being not so much a plotted narrative as a series of character
analyses in poetic prose. The author states her theme in a prologue:
woman's struggle to understand her own nature. Hitherto, she says,

> Action and creation, for woman, was . . . an imitation of
> man. In this imitation . . . she lost contact with her nature
> and her relation to man. Man appears only partially in this
> volume, because for the woman at war with herself he can
> only appear thus. . . . Woman at war with herself has not
> yet been related to man, only to the child in man, being
> capable only of maternity.[45]

Of such "incomplete" women there are five in the novel. One, a
cinema star with heterosexual experience, is still subjectively im-
prisoned within herself. A second, Lillian, is successively involved
with three others. This woman drifts on the current of conventional
existence into marriage and motherhood without once finding emotional fulfillment for her passionate temperament. Her first true
outlet is her friendship with Djuna, whose difficult youth has disciplined and matured her but left no time or strength for emotional
experience. Each personality finds its complement in the other, and
their relationship is fruitful for a time, but it achieves no expression
because in Lillian "sensuality was paralyzed. . . . She was impaled
on a rigid pole of puritanism." Soon Lillian becomes so jealous of

any woman Djuna looks at that the friendship perishes of its own intensity. At one point Djuna sees that

> she wants something of me that only a man can give her. . . . She has lost her ways of communicating with man. She is doing it through me.[46]

The association with Djuna so alters Lillian's perspective that she separates from her family and finds a man sufficiently immature to call out her maternal instincts. She humors and bears with him through all manner of vicissitudes, including his many transient affairs with other women. Cured now of her fear of sensuality, she plays the man with one of his flames whose influence she fears may be lasting, in order to distract her rival's attention from him. She succeeds only too well, and must finally terminate the affair to free herself of a second emotional dependent.

> Once again she had worn the man's costume . . . to protect a core of love. [The man] had not made her woman, but the husband and mother of his weakness.[47]

To one of his later fancies, a woman who "lived according to her caprices" and, like a man, refused to be "in bondage to the one," Lillian falls captive also, again, as with Djuna, loving in the other the opposite of all she is herself. This affair reaches physical completeness; even so, it does not bring the pair the unity both crave. Instead it makes them aware that they are lovers of the same man, and their one night together, though more satisfying than either has known with him, ends in a jealous quarrel. Thus the author diagnoses four degrees of emotional incompleteness: lowest is the inability to escape from self; next, the capacity for subjective but not overt abandon; third, the power only to imitate man's role, whether with man or woman; and last, freedom to play the woman but only with another woman. Just this relative rating of maturity appears original with Miss Nin.

A little later Josephine Tey, who with Dorothy Sayers and Ngaio Marsh raised British psychological mysteries to the level of serious fiction, made variance the key to two successive plots. In *Miss Pym Disposes* (1948) the title figure goes as visiting lecturer to a college of physical education where a formerly worshipped school friend is principal. Her interest is caught at once by an inseparable pair of seniors who lead their class, of whom an older foreign classmate says:

> That David and Jonathan relationship—it is a very happy one, no doubt, but it *excludes* so much. *Nice,* of course, quite irreproachable. But normal, no.[48]

"Beau," tall, beautiful and boyish, is the headstrong darling of wealthy parents. Mary is a reserved and sensitive introvert, only child of a struggling country physician. She is the logical recipient of the best position open for the following year, but the principal arbitrarily assigns the post to a fawning satellite of her own.

While practicing for a gymnastic exhibit, this favored candidate is fatally injured by the collapse of some heavy apparatus. Police investigation indicates accidental death, but a bit of circumstantial evidence discovered by Miss Pym points to Mary as being responsible for the accident. Her knowledge of Mary precludes such an idea, so she calls Mary in for an explanation. This interview is a masterpiece of reticent indirection. However, Miss Pym gets a seeming admission of guilt—though she is assured that death was never conceived as a possibility—and a promise that Mary will spend her life in self-sacrificing atonement. Since a conviction of manslaughter would not only destroy Mary but shatter her friend, her family, and the school, Miss Pym shoulders the heavy responsibility for keeping her secret and so becomes an accessory after the fact.

A bit later she discovers that it was not Mary but "Beau" who had tampered with the apparatus, and "Beau" is apparently little disturbed by the dire consequences. Mary has therefore sacrificed her life plans to save her friend. But she terminates the friendship. Murder or sudden death resulting from variance is not new in fiction. Miss Pym's and her author's circumventing its melodramatic consequences is distinctly original.

The same author's *To Love and Be Wise* (1950) again connects variant passion with murder, although this time the crime is unachieved. A disturbingly beautiful young American, Leslie Searle, inveigles his way into a literary household near London for the announced purpose of meeting England's best-loved radio broadcaster. Almost everyone in the book—and the cast is large—finds this young man irresistible, but they also sense that he is, in some way, uncanny. To one, he recalls certain milder legends of demonology; another is certain that "he must have been something very wicked in ancient Greece."⁴⁹ His presence breeds complications in both house-hold and community.

Shortly Searle disappears, and Scotland Yard suspects murder. In the end it turns out that the young Searle is a woman, who for years has lived intermittently as a man, and for many of those years nursed an obsessive passion for her cousin, a British actress whom she saw only sporadically. The latter, once a fiancée of the broadcaster, committed suicide after he jilted her, and Leslie has come tó England with a well-laid plan for eliminating him in re-venge. In the course of her association with his friends, however, and in particular with one who had opportunity to know her cousin better than she did, she discovers that her adored idol was largely a figment of her own imagination, the real woman having been ruthless and destructive.

In consequence, Leslie has abandoned her purpose, and merely escaped into her alternate feminine role. Despite the intuitive ques-tions Leslie Searle raises in everyone's mind (somewhat overstressed in aid of the plot), she is presented as a wholly sympathetic character, and can take her place with the medieval Ide and Mlle de Maupin as a successful transvestist and charmer. It is Miss Tey's engaging Inspector who brings home to her the basic immaturity of her protracted disguise, and, one infers, converts her to a more adult pattern of life.

In the year between Miss Tey's two volumes an anonymous *Olivia* (1949) was so reminiscent in style of *Either Is Love* as almost to suggest identical authorship. It too is an autobiographical record of experience long past, that of a Victorian adolescent suddenly transplanted to a finishing school on the outskirts of Paris. The Gallic freedom and gaiety of her new life release the girl's nascent emotions, and she falls deeply in love with one of the two French headmistresses. The book's value lies in the fidelity and vividness with which it pictures this first innocent passion. Narrative interest is supplied by tension between the two mistresses, who have lived happily together for fifteen years until a scheming newcomer on the staff turns one against the other for her own ends. Mlle Julie, Olivia's beloved, has always had favorites among the students whom Mlle Cara has somewhat resented, but only now, while Olivia is Julie's chosen, does Cara's jealousy reach the point of hysteria. After an accumulation of petty grievances magnified by the newcomer, Cara dies of a overdose of sedative almost certainly self-administered. Beside her deathbed Julie cries out, "She is the only one I have ever

loved!"—a cry prostrating to Olivia, who has had reason to believe
herself also cherished. Later Julie provides some comfort by telling
the girl that she has always been "victorious" over the emotional
temptations presented by students, but that now she wishes she
had yielded. This shows her cry to have meant that with Cara alone
she was physically intimate. She predicts that Olivia will not be
victorious under similar circumstances, and as at the outset of the
story Olivia has said, "I don't pretend that this experience was not
succeeded by others . . . but at that time I was innocent," it is
obvious that Mlle Julie's understanding of her nature was accurate.

A less innocent adolescent record written by Françoise Mallet,
a married woman of twenty, was published in Paris (1951) as *Le
Rempart des Béguines,* in New York (1952) as *The Illusionist,* and
in paper-covers (1953) as *The Loving and Daring.* This evidence of
wide popularity makes it necessary to say little here save that it
describes the initiation of a French girl of fifteen by her father's
mistress, a Russian woman twenty years older with a certain masculine
hardness sometimes approaching sadism. The latter is captivated by
Helene's resemblance to a young English girl whom she once
adored and whose defection left an unhealed wound. As long
as Tamara is independent and masculine, Helene is her slave, cutting
school, deceiving her father, even reluctantly accompanying her
adored to a lesbian night club. Then Tamara becomes Helene's
step-mother, and, relaxing at last under the influence of security,
she becomes much more feminine. Consequently, Helene ceases to
worship and looks forward to taking the dominant role herself, her
weapon the lesbian relationship which her preoccupied father has
believed merely an innocent "good influence." Though the experience
is hardly constructive *in toto,* both Helene and her author consider
it beneficial inasmuch as it brings the lonely adolescent out of a
phase of erotic reverie into wholesome contact with reality, and so
has a maturing effect.

A last sensational and ill-written item of the penny-dreadful type
was Carol Hales's *Wind Woman* (1953). Here a psychoanalyst treats
incipient neurosis induced in a young composer by her passion
for a woman who will permit no caresses, and her resultant frustrated
longing for an ideal lesbian relationship. In Laurel's history, as
revealed to Dr. Frances Garner, the author heaps Pelion upon Ossa
in the matter of anti-male conditioning, not without purpose. For
in the end the beautiful young analyst proves more than understanding; she makes no effort either to dispel her patient's prejudice
or to terminate her transference, and on the final page of the

volume she comes as near to open proposal of intimacy as an author could risk without being sued by the psychiatric profession.

The final tale to be considered, Claire Morgan's *The Price of Salt* (1951), while occasionally understated, still gives a convincing account of love between a married woman approaching thirty and a girl a decade younger. At eight Therese was consigned to an orphanage when her widowed mother remarried; she has since felt more alone than a true orphan. Ambitious to become a stage designer, she earns her keep in New York by temporary jobs and studies art at night. When the book opens, she is involved in a physically complete but unsatisfactory affair with a male art student whom she will not marry. She has had other male attention, and refuses a second offer of marriage before the story closes. Carol Aird is in process of divorcing an incompatible husband (and his domineering family), and negotiations are dragging over the custody of a seven-year-old daughter now with his family. The two women meet in a department store where Therese is employed as a seasonal "extra," and across an unromantic toy counter they are smitten with an infatuation as sudden as Gillian's in *Tortoiseshell Cat*. The older woman's reaction is less obvious, but within a day or two she has taken the girl to lunch and invited her to spend Christmas in her suburban house. Presently she suggests a motor trip to her family home on the west coast. Therese without hesitation closes the doors on her own life and accompanies her.

Intimacy develops perhaps a week after they set out and a month after their first encounter. Another week of happiness ensues before they discover a detective trailing them. Through pique at her leaving him, Carol's husband is bent on evidence which will give him full custody of the child. Even so, in their new intoxication the two women find amusement at first in eluding their shadow, and make a game of searching each new room for recording devices. When Carol finally attempts to buy the detective off, she is told that several incriminating records have already been sent to New York and that she had best get back to protect her interests. Promising to return in a fortnight, she leaves Therese in South Dakota to wait for her. But Carol's return is repeatedly postponed, and she finally writes that in order to see anything of her child hereafter she must promise to break with Therese entirely. She begs the girl to give her up and start afresh. "I would be underestimating you to think you could not."

In reaction to the shock, Therese feels not only abandoned but betrayed, as though Carol's picking her up and dropping her had

been a coldly deliberate game. Stunned and adrift she stops to
work for a time in Chicago until circumstances necessitate her return
to New York. She means not to see Carol again, and though news
that Carol has been ill moves her, it does not weaken her resolve.
Her immediate efforts toward employment in stage designing now
meet with prompt, if modest, success, for even her brief association
with the more cultured woman has increased her savoir-faire, and
the emotional experience has given her self-confidence such as none
of her contacts with men had ever done. She finally goes to an
unavoidable meeting with Carol, dreading the strain but unafraid of
yielding, and even when she learns that Carol has repudiated her
husband's humiliating list of conditions and thus forfeited all hold
upon her child, Therese still refuses her offer of a shared apartment.

Therese has placed a design for a stage set and is on her way
to a theatrical cocktail party to celebrate. She meets a British actress
there in whose eyes she sees a swift flash of interest comparable to her
own reaction on meeting Carol. Invited at once by the star to
an ensuing private party she accepts, feeling herself now quite able
to handle any foreseeable developments. But in the moment of its
birth this new sense of adequacy precipitates its own sequel. Knowing
herself no longer helplessly subject to Carol, she feels free to rejoin
her at will. She slips away without a word to her potential conquest
and returns to her early love.

Featuring as it does two women who have both had heterosexual
experience, and ultimately bringing them through many more tensions
than are indicated here, this narrative offers as strong an argument
for the validity of variant love as *Diana*. In a letter to Therese
after a legal session, Carol summarizes the essence of the argument:

> The rapport between two men or two women can be
> absolute and perfect, as it can never be between man and
> woman, and perhaps some people want just this, as others
> want that more shifting and uncertain thing that happens
> between men and women. It was implied yesterday that my
> present course would bring me to the depths of human vice
> and degradation. . . . It is true, if I were to go on like this
> and be spied upon, attacked, never possessing one person
> long enough so that the knowledge of the person . . . [could
> be more than superficial]—that is degradation. Or to live
> against one's grain, that is degeneration. . . .[50]

This takes no account of the Freudian charge of immaturity against the easier unisexual rapport, and its failure to do so cannot be laid in this day and time to ignorance of Freud. It has rather the sound of indifference, if not defiance.

The majority of favorable treatments of variance since the beginning of World War II have been little concerned with avoiding overt lesbianism, just as other fiction over an even longer period has been tolerant of a certain amount of heterosexual freedom. This fact, along with the rapid quantitative increase of variance in current fiction, may point, as has been suggested, to its gradual acceptance as a legitimate area of human experience. On the other hand it is precisely toward such casual acceptance that censoring groups have directed their fire. Prize-winning or widely acclaimed works with foreign settings such as *The Mesh* and *The Illusionist* have not been heavily attacked; neither have condemnatory treatments even of such low calibre as *Naked Storm* and the reprint of *Queer Patterns*. But blacklists have lumped *Spring Fire, Appointment in Paris,* and *Women's Barracks* with the heterosexual excesses of Mickey Spillane for censure (justified, if at all, only in the case of the first book), and these titles seem to have been withdrawn from sales-racks. Even if the pendulum swings back to greater conservatism, however, as it has done periodically in the course of literary history, its new position will not be identical with any earlier one. The overworked metaphor of spiral progress may apply here as to all other historical trends. To those who have witnessed changing attitudes toward homosexuality since 1900, it is a matter of regret that the ultimate swing of the new cycle must extend beyond our ken.

CONCLUSION

Periodic fluctuations in quantity, substance and style of variant writing have already been summarized in the sections sketching its history. It is now time to review certain more subjective aspects of the long record. For example, does variant literature lend support to hereditary theories of variance? At first glance, one recurrent physical type seems to do so: the woman fitted by nature to play the man. Tall, long of limb, narrow-hipped, wide-shouldered, direct-eyed, this figure has persisted from the dim era in which the Greeks conceived Artemis to 1950 when an Englishwoman created Leslie Searle. But the figure appears also in many settings other than variant literature. We meet it in the pages of romance and on the walls of galleries, on the silver screen and in élite advertisements. And, of course, many knights-errant, courtiers, dandies, athletes, matinée idols and swift-shooting cowboys are built on a similar pattern. Here the militant feminist will observe bitterly that in this man's world even our ideal of beauty is male. But the figure is not so much male as intermediate, and above all youthful. Many of the attributes catalogued above are those of adolescence just arrived at adult stature. In combination with adult savoir-faire they are appealing enough in the young man whose advantage is merely aesthetic. In a young woman, for whom the statistical norm of height and strength falls short of her brother's, they represent also superiority to her own kind in power and, therefore, in independence.

Because this type so captivates the general imagination, its appearances in variant literature are impressive out of proportion to their frequency. A complete count, from the valiant Ide to the undaunted Leo or Leslie, numbers roughly a score, and when one has subtracted those like Bradamante and Rosalind to whom lesbianism was never really attributed, the tally is reduced to a round dozen—hardly three percent of the variant total. Among the remainder, of whom a good many played a comparatively positive emotional role, no marked type recurs often enough to have any significance. A few figures are stocky and strong, but others may cast "a shadow thin as a blade;" some are voluptuously feminine. Nor does any one physical trait—except possibly height—accompany variance with any regularity. In fact, beyond the skeletal proportions already noted, the only somatic attributes mentioned in describing boyish women (and these not often) are deep voices and underdeveloped breasts. Other unfeminine details such as a striding gait or a brusque address, though they may owe something to hip articulation or vocal register, are usually mere mannerisms; that is, they are imitative rather than inborn. Of course these fictional data will not support conclusions as valid as those based on scientific observation, since beside the license natural to creative writing one must allow also for the reluctance of disapproving authors to provide their *mauvais sujets* with any hereditary excuses. Still, the long procession comprises variants individually convincing enough to give weight to their physical diversity. It is clear that the majority of variant or lesbian women observed by the writing fraternity are not masculine in physique.

Does sexual behavior, then, fall into patterns which might argue for some uniformities in endocrine balance? Again, it is impossible to classify the majority honestly, even by the simplest divisions into active and passive, homosexual and bisexual, and feel confident that the operative factors are innate. One may separate those whose passion is masculine in violence from the cool, the gentle, the maternally tender; but among the last may fall such conspicuously masculine figures as Stephen Gordon and Jan Morale. Or the aggressive Maupins or Leos may prove bisexual, the gentle Mettas and Miss Caffertys immutably set upon their own kind, and a petite and delicate Flordespine or Almond may be bold in her sexual advances. It is, however, possible to detect certain rough patterns not in physique or in sex behavior but in psychological attitude. There are masterful spirits who need to prove themselves the equal of any man, or to dominate rather than follow. There are rebels and lone wolves who defy authority or public opinion and are usually jealously possessive of the few they love. There are the more detached egotists and narcissists who see others only in terms of their own advantage and abandon themselves to no one. There are the shy and clinging who crave protection. And there are the maternal types, forgetful of self and eager to cherish and support.

If not heredity, what explanation does literature offer for these variants? Sometimes none. Lyrics poets in particular simply register their sentiments and leave readers to search elsewhere for explanations of the enigma. In a different fashion the same is true in unsympathetic narratives, and those where interest lies in plot alone. In these cases, too, variants are presented, as it were, Minerva-born, but are assumed to be a recognized type sure to generate dramatic tensions. Usually, however, as in more conventional fiction, authors supply some personal history for main characters and often directly or implicitly hold it responsible for their anomalies. This last is, of course, especially noticeable in recent years since the spread of Freudian psychology. Even where no notion of causality seems to exist in the author's mind, the same sort of background may recur in more than one narrative. Thus it is possible to identify a number of conditions, some fairly universal, some characteristic of their period, which appear repeatedly as antecedents or accompaniments of variance.

Of the universal class the most prevalent factor is some degree of negative reaction to men. In psychiatric casebooks this is often the result of sexual violation in childhood or adolescence, or of the witnessing of intercourse at an early age, which is almost equally traumatic. But such experiences and their sequelae of neurotic antipathy are rare in fiction. There a less compulsive aversion may result from rough or undesired caresses, or from their antithesis, pointed physical repudiation. Or it may grow from social neglect or slighting by men, or from deliberate indoctrination by a puritanic guardian. It may also stem indirectly from conjugal discord at home or elsewhere, through observation of a hated man's unfaithfulness or cruelty, a beloved woman's frigidity or suffering.

The next most frequent causal factor comprises a large and varied constellation of troubled family relations. Among our hundreds of variant women, those who enjoyed the sort of family life that social psychologists now exhort all parents to provide could be counted on one hand. Even those living with both parents on any terms would not multiply the number many times. Most often, the mother is found wanting in some way; indeed, the percentage of outright motherless girls is impressive. But, it may well be asked, what about the number in ordinary fiction? In novels of psychological cast dealing with the vicissitudes of young unmarried women the count is certainly high. The margin in favor of variant novels is further narrowed when one considers that few of these are literary masterpieces, and that minor fiction has, from its beginnings, capitalized heavily on the orphaned or motherless heroine. The reasons are obvious: a girl thus deprived can be a sympathetic character despite unconventional conduct; this conduct affords the reader escape-through-identification; and the author is guilty of no profanation of the revered mother image. Nevertheless, after all these allowances are duly made, a lack of maternal tenderness and understanding bulks large among influences leading to variant behavior.

The comparable lack of a father is seldom stressed. Paternal harshness appears rather oftener than the same trait in the mother, and the father is also sometimes a party to general parental indifference or neglect, but by and large the variant girl actively mistreated by either or both parents is fairly rare. A father fixation, on the other hand, though infrequent, is significant when it does occur, and Balzac's Seraphita bears witness that it is not confined to the Freudian twentieth century. The badgering of a lone girl by a parental surrogate—stepmother, relative or guardian—is featured now and then, as in The Scorpion, but this sympathy-begging device is less overworked in variant than in other minor fiction. The influence of siblings in producing either sexual fixation or aversion is negligible, unless their conspicuous absence is significant, for a considerable number of variant girls are presented as actually or virtually "only" children.

All this wide variety of subjective situations apparently contributes to the equally diverse range of variant experiences; yet none in the two lists is so consistently paired as to establish certainty of explicit cause and effect. In fact, more than one family factor and a measure of sex antagonism often occur simultaneously or successively in the same narrative.

In addition to subjective influences there remains the category of external circumstances which encourage variance. And while the psychological situations remain fairly constant from one period to another, environmental factors vary considerably with time. The more strictly convention limits a woman's activities, the more certain is her mere overstepping its bounds to produce significant results. From medieval times through the nineteenth century, to wear men's clothing was taboo. Therefore, when Clémentine or Fragoletta assumed man's dress, grave emotional consequences were inevitable. Today the donning of slacks or hunting costume produces little emotional impact. Similarly in nineteenth-century France or early twentieth-century England, when modesty forbade revealing the feminine body, a glimpse of uncovered breasts might stir a woman to passion, or Proust's Albertine and her friend might enjoy a half-hour's dalliance in a beach cabin because they had undressed together. Today, when beach, pool and gymnasium showers are communal affairs, their dressing-cubicles are unlikely to be the scene of tender passages. Furthermore, in days when woman's sphere was definitely the home, girls who claimed independence outside it exerted a strong imaginative appeal. Artists, actresses or mere bachelor girls attracted one another as strongly as they fascinated more sheltered women. But how many such "bohemians" have aroused general excitement since the 1920s? Few, certainly, in fiction.

One objective setting, however, has for decades remained basically constant as a hotbed of variance—those institutions which restrict young women to the company of their own sex. Until well into the nineteenth century, convents or convent schools were the segregating agency. After 1850, secular boarding schools took over the role, without the occasional compensating outlet of religious emotion. With the spread of higher education in our own times, women's colleges joined the list, and the latest additions have been reform schools, military barracks, sorority houses and metropolitan residence clubs. The results of a cloistered existence, then, might seem to argue for environment as a cause of variance just as strongly as recurrence of the "Maupin" type argued for heredity. But we have already seen that when many women wear men's clothes at one time or another, the effect of even the most boyish is less pronounced than it used to be. As for environment, excepting disciplinary and military quarters, twentieth-century cloisters allow their residents so much more freedom than their predecessors that variant or lesbian developments within them can no longer be laid wholly to pressure of circumstance.

Thus, it appears that literary testimony from a score of centuries confirms the current psychiatric verdict: variance is one possible solution of pressing emotional problems; but arrival at this particular solution depends upon so many variables that as yet no certain predictive formula has been derived.

An aspect of the current scene not yet duly recognized in literature is the relation of variant experience to gainful employment. In the heyday of feminism a good deal of concern was voiced by anti-feminists lest women's financial and social independence might breed lesbianism on a grand scale. But a comparison of French fiction from 1870 to 1900, when women were still dependent, with the English and American record since World War I suggests that the fear was unjustified. The issue at stake in our own time is not the influence of earning upon variance but the reverse effect of variance on a woman's capacity to hold a paid position. Before 1900 it was normal for the unmarried girl or the estranged wife to be supported by her parents or her long-suffering husband. For the last fifty years more and more women have been obliged to earn their own livings in ordinary unromantic jobs, and to this trend fiction has not done full justice. To be sure, creative license has always allowed the freedom of an independent income to more persons than are so favored in everyday life. It is true also that in recent variant novels a good many occupations have at least made an appearance. We have met actresses, modiste's assistants, novelists, interior decorators, social workers, a number of teachers, a trio of nurses, a department store executive and a minor clerk, and several girls employed in business offices. But in general these positions have served only as realistic backdrops for action which did not impinge upon them. In less than half a dozen cases has variance interfered with earning capacity. It gravely affected the actresses in *Queer Patterns;* the schoolmistresses in *The Children's Hour;* a college instructor in *Diana;* and it constituted a serious risk for nurses in *Promise of Love* and government employees in *Either is Love.* This meagre proportion, especially at the level of mere risk, does not reflect "things as they are" according to factual evidence in psychiatric literature, and the failure of variant fiction to come to grips with this aspect of reality is a count against it. It is also a waste of one fertile potential source of dramatic tension.

There remains a final ticklish question which leads straight into controversial territory, but to which a wide range of possible answers must be considered: why are variant belles-lettres so generally ignored? When so much has been written on the theme, why has it been slighted in library collections, histories of literature, and bibliographic records? One immediate answer will be that it is generally inferior, which is to a certain extent true; but it is not inferior to a deal of ordinary literature which has not been so slighted, notably that by the same authors who have produced variant titles. According to their generation or to their more considered convictions, different persons will explain this comparative neglect by claiming that variance is immoral, or abnormal, or the concern of an eccentric few and of no importance or interest to humanity at large. None of these claims can be summarily dismissed as neglibible.

Without going deeply into what the term "abnormal" connotes in different intellectual fields, it may be stated categorically that many psychiatrists no longer regard ordinary homosexual experience as pathological. Nor is the phenomenon too remote even from a statistical norm. In addition to literary evidence, anthropology and uncensored history and biography indicate that homosexuality has existed if not flourished in all times and places; and Dr. Kinsey's quantitative studies show that twenty-eight percent of women now living have experienced "sexual arousal" by their own kind at some time in their lives. Only rarely in either literature or life are women who have known this experience distinguishable from their fellows, and many who are perceptibly masculine in physique and temperament have never known it. Variants, then, are fairly numerous, not "abnormal" in an alienist's sense of the term, and not perceptibly eccentric.

The moral charge is less simply disposed of because it is so generally and often so unthinkingly advanced. It should be stated at once that in this discussion the morality of a course of action is referred to its effect upon the actor and his social group, as social anthropologists believe it was referred originally in the shaping of moral codes now regarded in some quarters as absolute. It should also be said, and underlined, that marriage and motherhood, despite the frequent failure of the one and the heavy burdens imposed on women by the other, appear more ultimately satisfying to the majority of women than other emotional experiences, and are certainly more beneficial to society. They are therefore the goals toward which personal and social effort should be directed, and obstacles to their success should be minimized. To what extent is variance such an obstacle and how pernicious is it in other respects?

Since human survival depends upon childbearing, if any large number of women should substitute homosexual relations for marriage and motherhood, the long range results would be socially deleterious. But heterosexual and maternal drives seem an effective guarantee against any such eventuality, and as long as numerous groups are advocating birth control as a check to overpopulation, this sociological argument against variance operates only in the realm of pure abstraction. As to conventional strictures upon all sex activity save legitimate intercourse, their apparent function is to curtail the social dangers of heterosexual license. Since even the most active lesbianism cannot be the cause of illegitimate offspring or of abortion, there is no valid case against variance on this score. A more practical argument stems from the now generally admitted psychological bearing of early upon later sexual experience. A number of marriage counselors, for instance, maintain that extensive pre-marital petting and homosexual activity are handicaps to later marital adjustment, and are therefore harmful to the young. So far as is known this claim has not been unquestionably validated by quantitative evidence, and certain authorities pronounce it a rationalization of unadmitted prejudice, but it must be recognized as the consensus of a good many popular advisors. For married women also, of course, lesbian relations or merely a consuming variant passion can prove as detrimental to marital happiness as similar heterosexual infidelties. On the other hand, for women deterred from marrying by lack of opportunity, financial or family burdens, inadequate sex appeal, or invincible disinclination, variant attachments may provide the sole chance for the experience of passionate love, and some psychiatrists consider such fulfillment preferable to lifelong deprivation.

Clearly, then, variance is not, like sadism for example, a limited aberration consistently destructive per se. It seems more nearly a lesser category of emotional experience parallel to the heterosexual and capable of as much variety. If governed by the standards of moderation, integrity, and mutual consideration which should prevail in all passionate relationships, it should not be harmful oftener than heterosexual passion. But in actual experience utopian conditions seldom prevail. We have heard from "Diana" some reasons why variant passion, unregulated by any legal or social codes of its own, is apt to be irresponsible and impermanent. Working against it also is the negative influence of sweeping social condemnation. Most neuroses among variant women have resulted from the conflict between their impulses and feelings of anxiety, guilt, or even sin. Thus the forces which would control variance are often responsible for making it a destructive experience.

Here actually is an important reason for such inferiority as variant literature exhibits. The age-long prejudice against variance, deriving as it does from religious taboo, retains something of the hysteria which motivated witch-burning and inquisition. For this reason the whole subject is surrounded by a surcharged atmosphere to which no sensitive mind is impervious. Even the best authors are scarcely able to free their work of all controversial overtones, and partisanship in creative writing has never made for artistry. As we have seen, lesser writers on both sides of the issue may descend to outright zealotry. Fervent antagonists choose variants who would be hateful without emotional irregularity, and who, with it, become monsters, usually the more dangerous for being picturesque to the eye or otherwise seductive. Negative writing of better quality presents less-sinister characters, but manipulates circumstances to the end that variant experience shall always prove disastrous. In *Mme Adonis* and *Die Schwester* the relatively sympathetic title figures meet violent death; in *Méphistophéla*, *The Island*, *The Captive*, and *Pity for Women*, they end in madness or severe neurosis. In minor French tales of the last century, variant couples destroy one another by excessive physical indulgence, and in virtually all censorious novels they bring much harm or suffering to those with whom they are associated. Frank champions of variance are guilty of parallel artistic offenses. Some make society the villain and variants its romanticized victims, and become shrill in denunciation of the one and defense of the other. Even *Diana* and *Either is Love,* temperate as they are in tone, would be artistically disqualified by their inclusion of outright argument even were they more excellent than they are. The subtler defenders are also no better than their opponents. Fearing public opinion too much to betray unqualified sympathy, they, too, strain circumstance to prevent their appealing characters from enjoying happiness. Granted that in life popular prejudice makes the chance of happiness precarious, case studies and other factual records show no such proportion of suicide and tragedy as do tolerant variant novels of the minor sort. Even writers of power sometimes fall into similar tragic exaggeration, as for example Miss Sackville-West in *Dark Island* or Masefield in *Multitude and Solitude.*

There are, however, a fair number of works guilty of no gross shortcomings, and a few of outstanding excellence. When their authors' total output merits serious literary study, critics as far as possible ignore those titles in which variance figures. Where no inclusive critical appraisals of an author are made, reviewers of individual variant works are apt to exercise less restraint, praising them grudgingly for their manner but deprecating their matter with disapproval, regret, or—what is worse—ironic or patronizing superiority. It has already been remarked that sympathetic literary treatments of variance are seldom written by men. Now the parallel circumstance must be noted—most literary criticism and the majority of book reviews are masculine work. It is only natural that men should react negatively to writing so oblivious of their own kind as is much variant literature. And this reaction must not be viewed as mere prejudice; its roots go deeper. Statistical studies of the reading done by some 20,000 persons have established the fact that the prime factor affecting reading interests, more basic than education, occupation or age, is sex.[1] The personality inventories constructed by psychologists and derived from probably even more numerous observations show that sex also determines many other interests and attitudes.[2] Thus men and women live to a certain extent in different subjective worlds—a fact recently dramatized by Philip Wylie in *Disappearance.*

With regard to variant literature, this means that men, who pass some nine-tenths of the judgments upon it, are attempting to evaluate a realm of experience in which first-hand knowledge is impossible to them. Naturally, they do best in rating variant material written by men, and next best with unsympathetic works by women. Some few project themselves with comparative success into tolerant studies by women whose mental idiom and emotional outlook is somewhat masculine. Djuna Barnes, Henry Handel Richardson, Mary Renault, and even Gail Wilhelm in her first novel, fared rather well at the hands of reviewers. In contrast, pertinent titles by Rosamond Lehmann, Elizabeth Bowen, Dorothy Richardson, Helen Anderson, Anais Nin and Kay Boyle, were either slighted or treated with unjustified harshness considering the admitted quality of their authors' other work. "Thin," "nebulous," "unconvincing," "insignificant," "futile," "overwrought," and "hysterical" were among the evaluative terms applied to these titles by male reviewers.[3] Women on the other hand had much to say in their favor, the most significant and frequent comment being that they were peculiarly sensitive and accurate in emotional interpretation.

Neither group of critics should be labeled "right" and the other "wrong." To most women and to such men as are endowed with unusual imaginative sensibility, perceptive and well-written variant works will always seem good literature. And they *are* good by the established canons of truth to experience, sound character analysis, artistic structure, convincing background, vivid objective detail, and beauty of expression. To most men and—for a different reason—some women, such works will seem bad in varying degrees from nonessential to intolerable. They *are* bad, then, in that they lack universality of appeal. For the same reason much non-variant fiction written by men—work predominantly objective in plot and violent in action, full of casual and unimaginative sex activity—is uninteresting or distasteful to the majority of women, though it too may fulfill the other requirements of good literature.

Variant fiction is of course not alone among feminine efforts in being disparaged by the opposite sex. The battle over the quality of feminine writing is old; to do it full justice would require a small volume in itself. But a brief comment is required to conclude this long discussion. Male critics (who comprise better than nine-tenths of the whole) can be roughly divided into three schools of opinion. The least charitable maintain that women lack creative power in all artistic fields because nature has designated them for biological creation alone. (Otto Weininger[4] is the extreme example of this school, but he is not alone in his opinions.) The largest group make the point that women's artistic efforts are almost exclusively imitative rather than original, and, without investigating reasons, they argue that this fact demonstrates patent creative inferiority. A few—Nathaniel Hawthore was among the first—feel that

> Generally women write like emasculated men and are only to be distinguished from men by greater feebleness and folly; but when they throw off [imitative] restraints . . . and come before the public stark naked as it were—then their books are sure to possess character and value.[5]

Hawthorne did not, however, live up to his convictions; he gave up writing fiction in the 1850s and fled the country because it was full of "damned scribbling females." The average quality of the scribbling perhaps justified his flight, but his apostasy was symbolic of his sex.

The women who began in the mid-nineteenth century to write like women were writing also largely *for* women, and on a level to be printed in newspapers and in the newly born "home" magazines. They wrote from the limited conventional experience that was known to them and their numerous audience; sentimental religious exaltation and dreams of romantic love supplied the only emotional color in their lives. The common lot of marriage brought mainly domestic drudgery and constant childbearing, with the loss of so many children that even the universal experience of the death of a child lost its keen edge. Had such lives been presented with the austere truth to experience demanded of good literature, the results would have been read no more widely than are starkly realistic novels at any time. And most of those women authors needed to earn money. Thus, feminine fiction concentrated upon blameless romantic passion, took wild liberties with reality, and was altogether unrelated to art. But it sold in the hundreds of thousands, and it set a style in popular feminine narrative which has altered in detail from decade to decade but has not yet gone out. Until well after 1900 few women authors rose above this level save those who more or less successfully imitated men, and chiefly such men as Dickens and Trollope. This sentimental tide has always been completely alien to men, both as individuals and as critics, and it has done much to solidify the majority male opinion that women are not creative artists. Even those men who achieve some intellectual appreciation of the best feminine writing find that, in general, they, like Hawthorne, cannot accept it completely. One might say that, beginning with Dorothy Richardson and Katherine Mansfield, women have attempted to raise essentially feminine writing to a level of absolute quality. No pretense will be made here to trace this growing trend, or to separate the more from the less "feminine" authors. The trend has run to more and more subjective content, as is evident in such current authors as Shirley Jackson and Jean Stafford.

Variance is, of course, more than any other subject, exclusively feminine. Had it not suffered the handicap of taboo, probably more literature of high quality would have grown up around it. Indeed, had such inhibited spirits as Emily Brontë, Emily Dickinson and Rose O'Neill, to mention only the most obvious, been less paralyzed emotionally, they might have had richer experience from which to write as well as more courage to write about it. This is not a plea for the cultivation of either homosexual experience or variant literature. It is simply a suggestion that if those women who are irremediably so constituted, and who happen also to be artists, were less shackled, the world's literature might be by that slight degree the richer. Before that comes to pass, of course, two changes must occur: public opinion in general must come closer to the most lenient psychiatric evaluation of variance. And men must become aware of the unconscious prejudice in their literary evaluation of all, and particularly of variant, feminine writing. If they cannot surmount this prejudice, they should leave the variant field to feminine critics. Also, more women should enter the field of literary criticism.

To conclude: we have seen that feminine variance has persisted in human experience since the beginning of literary records. It has repeatedly aroused sufficient interest to be the subject of literature, some of it good enough to have survived through many centuries against all odds. The odds have been of two very different sorts—religious taboo and masculine distaste. The first operated stringently from the beginning of the Christian era to the Renaissance, and is not yet dead. The second was apparent in classical times and has been especially evident whenever the neo-classical spirit prevailed, for that spirit exalts objective and intellectual experience, stresses the physical aspects of sex, and is contemptuous of subjective emotional preoccupation. In Romantic periods when emotion was glorified—that is, when essentially feminine values prevailed—variant literature has at least comparatively flourished. In our own day the ancient religious taboo has weakened and psychiatric values have to some extent been substituted. Now immaturity rather than sin is the socioethical argument against variance. To each age its own new wisdom seems a social panacea more cogent than all that have gone before, but none has ushered in Utopia. Momentarily, however, we have attained—or at least it seems to us that we have attained—to somewhat more tolerance than the elder moralists. If variance is to be always with us, calm acceptance of that fact may become as prevalent as the recognition of human evolution has come to be. And since variant literary expression appears equally persistent, it may conceivably become a narrow but similarly recognized field, permitted to come to fruition according to its own laws, and to contribute the best of which it is capable to the total sum of world literature.

AFTERWORD

While working in the catalog department of the Kansas City, Kansas, Public Library in the winter of 1956, I came across a reference in the Cumulative Book Index to a new book, *Sex Variant Women In Literature*, by a Jeannette H. Foster. I was then twenty-three and I had been collecting Lesbian literature for seven years. Having gathered nearly one hundred books I felt that I had achieved some sort of record and I had long since planned to write a book about this special genre. So my joy at finding this book was mixed, momentarily, with sadness. Calling a local bookstore to order a copy, I had the good fortune to be told that they had "heard" that the author was right in the Kansas City area, connected with the University of Kansas City (now University of Missouri at Kansas City). I called the university library and found that, indeed, Dr. Jeannette H. Foster was on their staff, away for the day, but right in my area. With the brashness that only a twenty-three-year-old might have, I found her telephone number and called her up. Thus began my life-long friendship with the author, and my love affair with the book. Beside me as I write this is my first copy of it, and its inscription reads "For Barbara Grier, This Volume's First Fan. Jeannette H. Foster". The world of Lesbian literature has changed a great deal in these past twenty years, but, as those of you who are reading this afterword in its proper place know, there is no replacement for this book, and no substitute for its in-depth analysis of the genre.

The publishing history of *Sex Variant Women In Literature* is an example of the amount of prejudice against Lesbians and Lesbianism in our culture. Completed in 1955, the book was first scheduled for publication in its logical place, a university press. This fell through, however, when the editor of the press died and his successor was afraid to honor the commitment. There was no way of knowing then that this book was destined to become a best-seller in a cult sense. No effort was made at that time to place it with a commercial trade publisher and, instead, Dr. Foster contracted for its publication and distribution through Vantage Press.

In 1974, the Gay Task Force of the Social Responsibilities Round Table of the American Library Association gave this book the Third Annual Gay Book Award, and a serious effort was made to arrange its republication. It is indeed wonderful that Diana Press recognized that this book properly belongs in the canon of feminist publishing and undertook to reissue it.

My job here is to talk about what has happened since the time this book was first published, or, more accurately, what has happened since 1954, the cut-off time for included titles in SVWIL. Twenty-one years later, there are records on well over 2,500 "quality" titles and over 2,500 others that need not be recorded here or anywhere. In the same year that saw this book published, 1956, there also began a Lesbian magazine called *The Ladder*, which soon instituted a careful recording of Lesbian literature. Utilizing review-checking techniques pioneered by Dr. Foster, and taught to me by her, I began keeping detailed records of new titles as well as searching out the "missed" titles from prior years. In those days reviewers seldom said specifically that titles contained Lesbians or Lesbian material, and it was a matter of learning to sense the tone of the reviews. During the 1960's an enormous quantity of Lesbian material became available through the burgeoning field of the "paperback original novel". Much of this proliferation was in the field of trash, but a small percentage of titles from this market became "pop" classics with writers such as Valerie Taylor, Ann Bannon, Paula Christian and Artemis Smith achieving a kind of coterie popularity that makes their now yellowed-page books nearly priceless. In all, about ten per cent of the paperback titles published during the decade roughly between 1960 and 1970 have some merit.

At the same time, the increasing freedom in subject matter in literature was growing yearly, and from 1960 on each year saw about one hundred books added to the lists, most of them quality hardback publications. Reviews of these books appeared in the pages of *The Ladder*, and in 1960, 1961 and 1962, *Checklists* were published privately by Marion Zimmer Bradley and myself (under my pseudonym, Gene Damon) covering the titles we had located after Jeannette's book. These are no longer available. In 1967, with a copyright cut-off date of 1966, *The Ladder* published a bibliography, *The Lesbian In Literature*, co-authored by myself and Lee Stuart. This contained about 2,000 titles, half of them in the "trash" category. So the actual growth in numbers of titles from *Sex Variant Women In Literature's* primary listing of 324 titles was only about 675 titles with real value. This year, 1975, *The Ladder* has published a second edition of *The Lesbian In Literature* with over 2,000 titles of merit.

At the end of this chapter I have added a list of bibliographies and related titles that need to be read after this book to provide the overview of the field of Lesbian literature today. I have also appended a short list of titles I feel are major contributions to the field. Admittedly they are personal choices and must be so viewed. There is no doubt in my mind that in ten or twenty years the field will be beyond classifying in any sense, because with the growth of freedom and individual choice, in part created by the growth of the women's liberation movement, the incidence of admitted and overt Lesbianism on and off the printed page will make "lists" obsolete. But, for lovers of literature, the books will go on and on and on.

Other changes since the first publishing of this book make areas of it seem cautious. Today authors can and do flatly state the Lesbian proclivities of this or that writer, without fear of either legal or scholarly scorn. Collections of poetry, such as Louise Bernikow's *The World Split Open: Four Centuries Of Women Poets In England And America, 1552—1950*, openly discuss the Lesbianism of many of the collected poets in the introduction to the volume, going so far as to analyze the male tendency to search endlessly in the lives of so many of these women for some *man* on whom they can pin the romantic expressions of the poets.

When *Sex Variant Women In Literature* was first published, there was not *one* title in the general field of non-fiction that dealt authoritatively with the Lesbian accurately. There are several such titles now, and because they also deal to some extent with the literature of this field, some of these are included in the brief bibliography at the end of this chapter.

While Dr. Foster was able only to "speculate" about the variance of her biographical subjects in 1954, today book after book comes out from every major publisher outlining the lives of the famous Lesbians of the past.

The field of Lesbian literature has grown beyond the possibility of another book quite like *Sex Variant Women In Literature*, for no one book can hope to adequately discuss more than 2,500 titles, let alone cover the supplemental works available. More accurately, it may just be that there has not yet been another scholar of Jeannette Foster's stature to attempt it.

Barbara Grier

TITLES OF SPECIAL INTEREST

Because I cannot list all of the titles that have been published since *Sex Variant Women In Literature* was published, nor those that have come to light from the past, I have chosen only those I feel Jeannette Foster would have been most pleased to discuss, and I have continued to use her method of listing, chronological order.

Dr. Foster expressed very early a fear that many titles might be found with copyrights earlier than 1954 after her book was published. As it turned out, several hundred titles have been uncovered, but the important point remains true, that very few books of great value and substance in the field were missed by her. The one really major exception is *Surplus* by Sylvia Stevenson (N.Y., Appleton, 1924).

1955
Bertin, Celia. *The Last Innocence.* N.Y., McGraw-Hill, 1955.
Franklin, Rose. *Intimate Story.* Garden City, N.Y., Doubleday, 1955.
Hackett, Paul. *Children Of The Stone Lions.* N.Y., Putnam, 1955.

1956
Kramer, N. Martin (Beatrice Ann Wright). *The Hearth And The Strangeness.* N.Y., Macmillan, 1956.
Rehder, Jessie. *Remembrance Way.* N.Y., Putnam, 1956.
Smith, Shelley. *The Lord Have Mercy.* N.Y., Harper, 1956.

1957
Brophy, Brigid. *The King Of A Rainy Country.* N.Y., Knopf, 1957.
Creal, Margaret. *A Lesson In Love.* N.Y., Simon and Schuster, 1957.
Faviel, Frances. *Thalia.* N.Y., Farrar, Straus, 1957.
Hill, Pati. *The Nine Mile Circle.* Boston, Houghton-Mifflin, 1957.

1958
O'Brien, Kate. *As Music And Splendour.* N.Y., Harper, 1958.

Phelps, Robert. *Heroes and Orators.* N.Y., McDowell, Obolensky, 1958.
Rinser, Luise. *Rings Of Glass.* Chicago, Henry Regnery, 1958.
Sandburg, Helga. *The Wheel Of Earth.* N.Y., McDowell, Obolensky, 1958.

1959
Berkman, Sylvia. *Blackberry Wilderness.* Garden City, N.Y., Doubleday, 1959.
Garrett, Zena. *The House In The Mulberry Tree.* N.Y., Random House, 1959.
Jackson, Shirley. *The Haunting Of Hill House.* N.Y., Viking, 1959.
Lee, Marjorie. *The Lion House.* N.Y., Rinehart, 1959.

1960
Mahyere, Evaline. *I Will Not Serve.* N.Y., Dutton, 1960.
Verel, Shirley. *The Dark Side Of Venus.* London, Quadriga, 1960.
    (N.Y., Bantam, 1962, paperback only).

1961
De Jong, Dola. *The Tree And The Vine.* London, John Calder, 1961.
Sarton, May. *The Small Room.* N.Y., Norton, 1961.
Sherman, Susan. *Give Me Myself.* N.Y., World, 1961.

1962
Baker, Dorothy. *Cassandra At The Wedding.* Boston, Houghton-Mifflin, 1962.
Grumbach, Doris. *The Spoil Of The Flowers.* Garden City, N.Y., Doubleday, 1962.
Prokosch, Frederic. *Seven Sisters.* N.Y., Farrar, Straus, 1962.
Suyin, Han. *Winter Love In Two Loves.* N.Y., Putnam, 1962.

1963
King, Louise. *The Day We Were Mostly Butterflies.* London, Michael Joseph, 1963. Garden City, N.Y. Doubleday, 1964.
McCarthy, Mary. *The Group.* N.Y., Harcourt, Brace and World, 1963.
Morrison, Jessamy. *The No-Road.* London, Chapman and Hall, 1963.

1964
Randall, Vera. *The Inner Room.* N.Y., Knopf, 1964.
Rule, Jane. *The Desert Of The Heart.* London, Secker and Warburg, 1964. N.Y., World, 1965.

1965

Mezvinsky, Shirley. *The Edge.* Garden City, N.Y., Doubleday, 1965.
King, Louise W. *The Velocipede Handicap.* London, Michael Joseph, 1965.
    Garden City, N.Y., Doubleday, 1966.
Sarton, May. *Mrs. Stevens Hears The Mermaids Singing.* N.Y., Norton,
    1965. (Note: As a result of the women's liberation movement, Norton
    reissued this Lesbian classic in 1974.)
1966
Duffy, Maureen. *The Microcosm.* N.Y., Simon and Schuster, 1966.

1967
Frankau, Pamela. *Over The Mountains.* N.Y., Random, 1967.
Gardiner, Judy. *Waltzing Matilda.* S.N. in *The Power Of Sergeant Mettle-
    ship.* London, Michael Joseph, 1967.
Kilpatrick, Sarah. *Ladies Close.* London, Gollancz, 1967.

1968
Barker, A.L. *The Middling.* London, Hogarth Press, 1967.
Villa-Gilbert, Mariana. *A Jingle Jangle Song.* London, Chatto and Windus, 1968.
Walton, Su. *Horace Sippog And The Siren's Song.* N.Y., Morrow, 1968.

1969
Elliott, Janice. *Angels Falling.* N.Y., Knopf, 1969.
Harris, Bertha. *Catching Saradove.* N.Y., Harcourt, Brace and World, 1969.
Lees, Hannah. *The Sweet Death Of Candor.* N.Y., Harcourt, Brace and World,
    1969.
Miller, Isabel. *A Place For Us.* N.Y., Bleecker Street Press, 1969. (Reissued
    in 1972 as *Patience And Sarah* by McGraw-Hill.)

1970
Rule, Jane. *This Is Not For You.* N.Y., McCalls, 1970.

1971
Haggerty, Joan. *Daughters Of The Moon.* Indianapolis, Bobbs-Merrill, 1971.
Powell, Lily. *The Bird Of Paradise.* N.Y., Knopf, 1971.
Rule, Jane. *Against The Season.* N.Y., McCalls, 1971.

1972
Harris, Bertha. *Confessions Of Cherubino.* N.Y., Harcourt, Brace and Jovano-
    vich, 1972.

Howard, Elizabeth Jane. *Odd Girl Out.* N.Y., Viking, 1972.

1973
Brown, Rita Mae. *Rubyfruit Jungle.* Plainfield, Vt., Daughters, 1973.
Carpenter, The. *The Cook And The Carpenter.* Plainfield, Vt., Daughters. 1973.

1974
Aldridge, Sarah. *The Latecomer.* The Naiad Press, 1974.
Shockley, Ann Allen. *Loving Her.* Indianapolis, Bobbs-Merrill, 1974.

BIBLIOGRAPHIES AND RELATED TITLES

Damon, Gene and Lee Stuart. *The Lesbian In Literature: A Bibliography.* San Francisco, The Ladder, 1967.

Damon, Gene and Jan Watson and Robin Jordan. *The Lesbian In Literature,* 2nd Edition. Reno, The Ladder, 1975.

Klaich, Dolores. *Woman Plus Woman: Attitudes Towards Lesbianism.* New York, Simon and Schuster, 1974.

Kuda, Marie J. *Women Loving Women: A Select And Annotated Bibliography Of Women Loving Women In Literature.* Chicago, Lavender Press, 1974.

Rule, Jane. *Lesbian Images.* Garden City, N.Y., Doubleday, 1975.

Watson, Jan, et al *Index To "The Ladder".* Reno, The Ladder, 1974.

Women And Literature: An Annotated Bibliography Of Women Writers. Sense and Sensibility Collective. 2nd Edition, Revised and Expanded. Cambridge, MA, 1973.

Wysor, Bette. *The Lesbian Myth.* New York, Random House, 1974.

ADDENDA TO TITLES OF SPECIAL INTEREST

JEANNETTE HOWARD FOSTER (died July 26, 1981) was not able to follow the surge of Lesbian literature that began in the middle 1970s and has continued to this day. This is a real tragedy for I know of no woman who would have more enjoyed these years . . . it would have been the fulfillment of her lifetime dream. On the other hand, she would have been very pleased to know that her book is still being used and is still needed and has been restored to print indefinitely. As I did in the 1975 edition of SEX VARIANT WOMEN IN LITERATURE, I am here listing a few major titles from each year from that time until now.

Barbara Grier
March, 1985

1975
Arnold, June. *Sister Gin*. Plainfield, Vt., Daughters, 1975.
Boucher, Sandy. *Assaults and Rituals*. San Francisco, Mama's Press, 1975.
Bulkin, Elly & Joan Larkin. *Amazon Poetry*. Brooklyn, Out & Out Books, 1975.
Harris, Bertha. *Lovers*. Plainfield, Vt., Daughters, 1975.
Russ, Joanna. *The Female Man*. Bantam, 1975.

1976
Brown, Rita Mae. *In Her Day*. Plainfield, Vt., Daughters, 1976.
Grier, Barbara. *The Lesbians Home Journal*. Oakland, Ca., Diana Press, 1976.
Guy, Rosa. *Ruby*. N.Y., Viking, 1976.

1977
Beal, M. F. *Angel Dance*. Plainfield, Vt., Daughters, 1977.
Broumas, Olga. *Beginning with O*. New Haven, Ct., Yale University Press, 1977.

1978

Gearhart, Sally. *The Wanderground.* Watertown, Ma., Persephone Press, 1978.
Grahn, Judy. *The Work of a Common Woman.* Oakland, Ca., Diana Press, 1978.
Rich, Adrienne. *The Dream of a Common Language: Poems 1974–1977.* N.Y., Norton, 1978.
Scoppettone, Sandra. *Happy Endings Are All Alike.* N.Y., Harper & Row, 1978.
Stockwell, Nancy. *Out Somewhere and Back Again: The Kansas Stories.* Washington, D.C., (No publisher listed), 1978.

1979

Aldridge, Sarah. *All True Lovers.* Weatherby Lake, Mo., Naiad Press, 1979.
Brady, Maureen. *Give Me Your Good Ear.* Argyle, N.Y., Spinster's Ink, 1979.
Grumbach, Doris. *Chamber Music.* N.Y., Dutton, 1979.

1980

Rule, Jane. *Contract with the World.* N.Y., Harcourt Brace Jovanovich, 1980.
Toder, Nancy. *Choices.* Watertown, Ma., Persephone Press, 1980.
Wilson, Anna. *Cactus.* London, Onlywomen Press, 1980.

1981

Koertge, Noretta. *Who Was That Masked Woman?* N.Y., St. Martin's Press, 1981.
Rule, Jane. *Outlander.* Tallahassee, Fl., Naiad Press, 1981.
Taylor, Valerie. *Prism.* Tallahassee, Fl., Naiad Press, 1981.

1982

Shockley, Ann Allen. *Say Jesus and Come to Me.* Avon, 1982.
Taylor, Sheila Ortiz. *Faultline.* Tallahassee, Fl., Naiad Press, 1982.
Walker, Alice. *The Color Purple.* N.Y., Harcourt Brace Jovanovich, 1982.

1983

Azpadu, Dodici. *Saturday Night in the Prime of Life.* Iowa City, Ia., Aunt Lute Books, 1983.
Birtha, Becky. *For Nights Like This One.* Palo Alto, Ca., Frog In The Well, 1983.
Forrest, Katherine V. *Curious Wine.* Tallahassee, Fl., Naiad Press, 1983.

1984
Forrest, Katherine V. *Daughters of a Coral Dawn.* Tallahassee, Fl., Naiad
    Press, 1984.
Grahn, Judy. *Another Mother Tongue.* Boston, Beacon, 1984.
Grumbach, Doris. *The Ladies.* N.Y., Dutton, 1984.
Schulman, Sarah. *The Sophie Horowitz Story.* Tallahassee, Fl., Naiad Press,
    1984.

NOTES

Notes refer to items in the bibliography by letter and number only.

Foreword
I. *An earlier edition of C 72*
Introduction
1. C111
2. C 153, 154
I. *Ancient Record*
1. A 250
2. A 251
3. B 199
4. A 213
5. A 251:15
6. A 250 & B 199, notes
7. A 251:67
8. *ibid.*:39
9. *ibid.*:97, 3
10. *ibid.*:90
11. A 250
12. B 174:134; B 199:319
13. A 250:155
14. *ibid.*:166
15. *ibid.*:155 & note
16. B 173:209
17. A 251:30
18. A 28:209, note 2;
    A 28a:235, note 1
19. A 28:210; A 28a:236
20. B 39 v.2:665
21. B 18
22. B 162 v.1:101
23. C 72 v.1 pt.4:197

24. A 7 v.2 (VII) :718;
    v.4 (XII) :365
25. A 8 v.2:151; C 72 v.2 pt.2:41
26. B 69 v.2 Chap. 6
27. B 199:108, 109
28. A 8 v.1:203 & B 65
29. Bloomington, Ind., news-
    paper
30. C 192
31. A 8 v.1:395
32. *ibid.* v.2:191-93
33. *ibid.* v.2:41
34. *ibid.* v.2:89
35. A 214 v.1:35-41
36. *ibid.* v.2:107-13
37. *ibid.* v.1:91-92
38. *ibid.* v.2:51-60
39. *ibid.* v.2:60, note
40. *ibid.* v.1:199-205
41. A 140
42. A 183: I.
43. *ibid.*:VII
44. A 7 v.2:11, 345, 450
45. A 171 v.1 (V) :100-05
46. *ibid.* (XII) :130-42
47. A 2:192

II. *Dark ages to Age of Reason*
1. B 148
2. *ibid.*

3. B 97
4. B 119
5. B 18
6. B 71
7. A 211x
8. B 76
9. A 9 v.2:9
10. A 261:174-75
11. B 27
12. A 280:35
13. A 191a
14. A 191; C 72 v.1 pt.4:245
15. A 96:47
16. *ibid.*:29
17. A 37:128
18. A 117 v.2:89
19. A 277:145
20. A 187

III. *Romantic to modern*
1. C 220
2. C 72 v.1 pt.4:66-67
3. C 213; C 72 v.1 pt.4 1896 ed.;
   C 119
4. B 74:21
5. *ibid.*:16
6. A 74 pref.
7. C 72 v.1 pt.4:199
8. B 134
9. B 82:18
10. A 310:44
11. *ibid.;* 51
12. B 192:120
13. A 310:97
14. *ibid.*:76
15. *ibid.*:187
16. B 160:82, 88
17. *ibid.*:232
18. *ibid.*:313
19. A 20:23
20. A 14:110
21. *ibid.*:164

22. *ibid.*:425
23. B 185:11
24. A 107
25. B 47 v.1:52-61
26. A 150 v.2
27. C 72 v.1 pt.4:200
   p. 415, notes 28-51
28. A 150 v.2:223
29. *ibid.*:166
30. B 127 Chap. 6
31. C 158:396
32. A 98:46-47
33. *ibid.*:47
34. *ibid.*:204
35. *ibid.*:205
36. *ibid.*:209
37. *ibid.*:244
38. *ibid.*:273
39. C 158:396
40. B 90:147
41. B 16:24-51
42. A 50:85-86
43. B 185:249-303
44. A 22
45. B 185 loc. cit.
46. B 8:42
47. A 281:121-22
48. B 120 v.1:307
49. B 210:238
50. A 269:115
51. *ibid.*:164

IV. *Later 19 Century*
1. B 78
2. A 25:242
3. A 319:356
4. *ibid.*:376
5. C 269:285
6. See B 155
7. A 32a:37 (nothing further in
   French language edition)
8. B 56

9. A 230a:91
10. A 230:xvi
11. A 230a:9
12. B 141 v.5, 1892 mai
13. B 153:221ff.
14. *ibid.:* footnotes on pp. 42, 84, 145-46, 170, 217
14a. A 118:58
15. B 160:128
16. A 256:351-52; see also 256x: 202 for a young married woman's reverie of being a man.
17. A 137:vi, ix
18. *ibid.*:144
19. *ibid.*:283
20. *ibid.*:325
21. *ibid.*:ix
22. A 267:301
23. *ibid.*: pref.
24. B 155
25. B 165: v-ix
26. A 189:348
27. *ibid.*:488
28. *ibid.*:12
29. *ibid.*:6-9
30. Paris, E. Dentu, 1890
31. B 34:150; B 108 v.1:301
32. B 141 v.23:523, 1897

V. *Conjectural interlude*
Labé
1. B 64 v.41:72; B 152 v.28:347-49
2. B 152 loc. cit.
3. A 37:205
4. A 146a: dedication
5. See note 1. above
6. A 146a:78
7. *ibid.*:87
8. *ibid.*: introd.
9. B 152 v.7:82-83 *(Bourges)*

10. A 146 v.2
Charke
1. C 72 v.1 pt.4:245
2. A 45:77
3. *ibid.*:52
4. *ibid.*:90
5. *ibid.*:80-89, 139
Llangollen
1. B 95
2. A 24
3. B 145:22-27
4. A 51:155, 161
5. *ibid.*:177
Günderode
1. A 10:1-67
2. A 11
3. A 113
4. B 64 v.97:167-231
5. See note 1. above
6. A 11; A 113, biog. introd.
7. A 298 v.1.; 298a.
Sand
1. A 249 v.13:187-373
2. *ibid.*:267-68
3. B 196
4. B 181:244
5. B 138:163
Brontë
1. B 20x:42 (both quotations)
2. B 144 Chap. 20
3. *ibid.*:84
4. *ibid.*:86
5. *ibid.*:89
6. B 168: pref.
7. *ibid.*:255-56
Eliot
1. B 94
Fuller
1. B 3
2. B 197:xv
3. *ibid.*:196

Menken
1. B 212 Chap. 4
2. B 115
3. B 212:57
4. *ibid.*:58
5. B 107 v.1:278
6. A 190:75-76
7. *ibid.*:28
8. *ibid.*:13
9. B 203
10. B 212:65

Field
1. A 92:xvi
2. *ibid.*:27
3. A 91:50
4. A 92:ix
5. *ibid.*:16
6. *ibid.*:57
7. *ibid.*:63

VI. *20 Century. Int. & Poetry*
1. C 123
2. B 74:16
3. C 164-175
4. C 146:119
5. See especially C 276, the best available brief résumé of the current psychoanalytic opinion on homosexuality
6. A 20:22-26
7. *ibid.*:176ff.
8. B 86 no. 4
9. *ibid.* no. 8
10. B 85 Dec. 12
11. A 19:10ff: In these quotations and some later ones from poetry, line indentations and stanza divisions have been disregarded for economy.
12. *ibid.*:108
13. *ibid.*:19

14. *ibid.*:111
15. B 79
16. A 283 v.2:78-80
17. *ibid.*:112
18. B 48
19. A 283 v.2:52-55
20. *ibid.*:50
21. *ibid.* v.1:38-39
22. *ibid.*:36
23. *ibid.*:87-88
24. *ibid.*:31
25. *ibid.*:32
26. *ibid.*:195
27. B 141 v.49, mars.
28. *ibid.* v.50, avril.
29. *ibid.* v.89:181-82
30. A 283 v.2:219
31. *ibid.*:189
32. *ibid.*:230
33. B 141 v.89:181-82
34. A 19:235
35. A 20; B 49
36. B 151x v.9:488 (Je.20, 1914)
37. A 240
38. B 49:249
39. B 25 Chap. 13
40. A 176
41. A 122 v.1:7-27
42. *ibid.* v.2:176-80
43. A 263, from B 101 v.5
44. A 257:53
45. B 74:46; from W. L. George, Literary chapters, 1918, p. 127
46. A 167:97-105
47. B 144:189-90
48. B 212:288
49. A 212:114
50. The Loves of Edwy
51. B 217:60
52. Harold Cook (B 217 introd.)

and Elizabeth Atkins (B 10:34 footnote & 242)
53. A 197:20-21
54. A 196:17
55. A 194:55
56. B 10:37-38
57. A 193:38, 39; A 194:70, 71
58. A 194:70, 71
59. A 196:20
60. *ibid.*:42
61. Djuna Barnes & Natalie C. Barney. See A 196:index
62. B 10:200
63. A 185:52-53
64. *ibid.*:54
65. A 3:21
66. A 248:24
67. *ibid.*:9
68. *ibid.*:29
69. *ibid.*:5
70. A 179:142-43
71. *ibid.*:17-18

VII. *Fiction in France*
1. A 52a:289
2. A 54:220
3. A 55 Chap. 18, end.
4. A 51:185-218
5. B 35
6. A 55a:244-50
7. A 56:117
8. B 141 v.38:229-34; B 101 v.3:439
9. B 141 v.40:781-82
10. B 101 v.5:1120
11. B 141 v.45-50, var. pag.
12. B 141 v.55:254; B 101 v.9:584
13. A 227
14. A 228
15. A 222
16. A 227

17. A 225
18. A 20:74; A 51:186
19. A 242:155
20. *ibid.*:102
21. *ibid.*:153
22. *ibid.*:164-65
23. A 182:22-23
24. *ibid.*:191-97 passim
25. *ibid.*:128-144 passim
26. A 148:201
27. A 31:x
28. *ibid.*:149-50
29. Seen only via advertising résumés in C.-E.'s other novels, back pages.
30. B 136 v.35:176-213

VIII. *Fiction in Germany*
1. A 292 v.5:285-87
2. B 101 v.2:41ff
3. *ibid.* v.3:431
4. *ibid.* v.3:462
5. *ibid.* v.3:449
6. *ibid.* v.5:1115
7. *ibid.* v.3:453?
8. *ibid.* v.3:489
9. B 25 Chap. 13
10. B 101 v.5:1080
11. *ibid.* v.5:1106
12. *ibid.* v.5:1070
13. C 121:171-79
14. B 101 v.7:885
15. *ibid.* v.9:606
16. *ibid.* v.9:613
17. B 144x:317
18. A 178:222
19. *ibid.*:229
20. A 295:188
21. B 98
22. B 101 v.17:129
23. A 274:10
24. *ibid.*:11

25. *ibid.*:11-12

IX. *Fiction in English* (1)
 1. A 116:pref.
 2. C 153, 154
 3. A 102:12
 4. *ibid.*:13
 5. *ibid.*:14
 6. *ibid.*:56-57
 7. A 175:6
 8. *ibid.*:288
 9. *ibid.*:269-70
10. *ibid.*:135
11. *ibid.*:182
12. A 215:833
13. B 204
14. A 256:4
15. *ibid.*:7
16. *ibid.*:13
17. *ibid.*:8
18. *ibid.*:9
19. *ibid.*:57
20. *ibid.*:88
21. A 184:79
22. *ibid.*:108
23. A 239:271
24. A 260:262
25. *ibid.*:390
26. Publ. in book form by
    Century
27. A 155:324
28. B 143
29. A 294:334
30. A 61:37-38
31. *ibid.*:37
32. *ibid.*:402-03
33. *ibid.*:407
34. A 173:267-68
35. *ibid.*:37
36. *ibid.*:276-81
37. A 97:22, footnote
38. *ibid.*:348

38. A 6:304
40. *ibid.*:305
41. A 131:69-70
42. *ibid.*:268
43. *ibid.*:290-91
44. A 129:320-21, 149
45. A 93:125-256
46. *ibid.*:148
47. *ibid.*:222
48. A 210:198
49. A 311:46-47
50. *ibid.*:48, 50-52
51. *ibid.*:53
52. A 245:139-40
53. *ibid.*:287
54. B 63:64 and New York
    Times, Sun. Nov. 7,
    1926, VIII:10, col. 1
55. New York Times Feb. 1,
    1927, p. 3, col. 6
56. A 313:29
57. *ibid.*:300
58. A 116:pref.
59. B 54
60. A 312:117-18
61. *ibid.*:138
62. *ibid.*:221-22
63. *ibid.*:298
64. *ibid.*:258

X. *Fiction in English* (2)
 1. A 207:63
 2. *ibid.*:64
 3. A 199:343-44
 4. A 218:266
 5. A 152:333
 6. A 160:221-36
 7. A 244:24
 8. *ibid.*:158
 9. *ibid.*:167
10. A 237:243
11. *ibid.*:245

12. *ibid.*:231-32
13. *ibid.*:257
14. *ibid.*:230-31
15. A 23:49
16. *ibid.*:58
17. British edition: Stamboul
    Train, late 1932
18. A 42:382
19. *ibid.*:380-81
20. Nov. 1932 p. 2 col. 4.
21. A 206:2
22. A 238:132-33
23. *ibid.*:137
24. *ibid.*:138
25. A 276:162
26. *ibid.*:230
27. A 76:32; A 157:125
28. A 76:234
29. A 78:74
30. *ibid.*:82-83
31. A 78a:72; cf. also p. 79-80
32. A 316:107
33. A 158:112-14; cf. also p. 38
34. A 64:208, 219
35. A 59:147

36. Time Mag. Oct. 25,
    1937:26-28
37. A 36:203, 205
38. A 35:203
39. *ibid.*:204
40. A 104
41. e.g. *ibid.*:196-97
42. A 144:156
43. A 43:92
44. A 264:320,396
45. A 209:[7]
46. *ibid.*:107
47. *ibid.*:136
48. A 271:24
49. A 272:23
50. A 203:246
Conclusion
1. e.g. B 71
2. See C 105, 139, 207, 254, 255,
   257, *273*, 287, 300
3. Cf. excerpts in Book Review
   Digest for any title in *A*
   list.
4. C 284
5. B 158:111

BIBLIOGRAPHIES

* An asterisk indicates titles of which only a review, an abstract, or a précis was seen.
List A: Primary belletristic titles, in some cases including biographical or critical material. The editions listed are those used in the study. Original dates of publication or composition appear in the text.
List B: Bibliographic, biographical, critical and historical references, including psychiatric studies of specific authors or titles.
List C: Medical, psychological, psychiatric and psychoanalytic background reading, with special reference to etiology (e.g., in studies of exclusively male subjects.)

A. PRIMARY MATERIAL

1. ADAMS, FAY. Appointment in Paris. N. Y., Fawcett, 1952.
2. ALCIPHRON. Letters from town and country. (tr. F. A. Wright) Lond., Routledge, n.d.
3. ALDINGTON, RICHARD. The loves of Myrrhine and Konallis. Chic., Pascal Covici, 1926.
4. ANDERSON, HELEN. Pity for women. N. Y., Doubleday, 1937.
5. ANDERSON, SHERWOOD. Dark laughter. N. Y., Boni & Liveright, 1925.
6. ——. Poor white. N. Y., B. W. Heubsch, 1920.
7. ANTHOLOGIA GRAECA. (tr. R. W. Paton) N. Y., Putnam, 1915-26. 5v.
8. APOLLODORUS. The library. (tr. J. G. Fraser) Cambridge, Mass. Harvard Univ. Press, 1946, 2v.
9. ARIOSTO, LUDOVICO. Orlando furioso. (tr. W. S. Rose) Lond., Bell, 1907. v. 2.
10. ARNIM, ELISABETH VON. Goethe's correspondence with a child. Bost., Ticknor & Fields, 1859.
11. ——. Die Günderode. (Sämmtliche Werke, bd. 2) Berlin, Propylaenverlag, 1920.
12. BAKER, DOROTHY. Trio. Bost., Houghton, 1943.
13. ——. Young man with a horn. N. Y., New American Library, 1953.
14. BALZAC, HONORÉ DE. Cousin Betty. (tr. James Waring) Bost., Dana Estes, 1901.

15. ———. Seraphita. Lond., Dent, 1897.
16. ———. The girl with the golden eyes. (tr. Ernest Dowson) [N. Y.], DeLuxe Éditions, 1931.
17. BARBEY D'AUREVILLY, JULES. Les diaboliques. Paris, Dentu, 1874.
18. BARNES, DJUNA. Nightwood. N. Y., Harcourt, 1937.
19. BARNEY, NATALIE CLIFFORD. Actes et entr'actes. Paris, Sensot, 1909.
20. ———. Aventures de l'esprit. Paris, Emile-Paul, 1929.
21. BAUDELAIRE, CHARLES. Prose and poetry. (tr. Arthur Symons). N. Y.. Boni, 1926.
22. ———. Les fleurs du mal. (tr. George Dillon and Edna St. Vincent Millay) N. Y., Harper, 1936.
23. BEER, THOMAS. Mrs. Egg and other barbarians. N. Y., Knopf, 1933.
24. BELL, MRS. G. H., ed. The Hamwood papers of the ladies of Llangollen and Caroline Hamilton. Lond., Macmillan, 1930.
25. BELOT, ADOLPHE. Mlle Giraud, ma femme. Paris, Dentu, 1870.
26. BENNETT, ARNOLD. Elsie and the child. N. Y., Doran, 1924.
27. ———. The pretty lady. N. Y., Doran, 1918.
28. BIBLE. Revised version. Oxford, University Press, 1891.
28a. ———. American standard version. N. Y., Nelson, 1901.
29. BOLTON, ISABEL. Ruth and Irma. New Yorker 23:21-24. Jan. 26, 1947.
30. *BORYS, DANIEL. Carlotta Noll. Paris, Albin Michel, 1905.
31. BOURDET, EDWARD. The captive. (tr. Arthur Hornblow, jr.) N. Y., Brentano, 1927.
32. BOURGET, PAUL C. J. Un crime d'amour. Paris, Lemerre, 1886.
32a. ———. A love crime. Paris, Société des Beaux Arts, 1905.
33. BOWEN, ELIZABETH. The hotel. N. Y., MacVeigh, 1928.
34. BOWLES, JANE. Two serious ladies. N. Y., Knopf, 1943.
35. BOYLE, KAY. The bridegroom's body. (In: The crazy hunter. N. Y., Harcourt, 1940)
36. ———. Monday night. N. Y., Harcourt, 1938.
37. BRANTÔME, P. DE B. DE. Lives of fair and gallant ladies. (tr. A. R. Allinson) N. Y., Liveright, 1933.
38. BROCK, LILYAN. Queer patterns. N. Y., Greenberg, 1935.
39. BRONTË, EMILY. Complete poems (edited from manuscripts by C. W. Hatfield) N. Y., Columbia University Press, 1941.
40. ———. Gondal poems. (ed. Helen Brown and Jean Mott) Oxford, Blackwell, 1938.
41. BROWNRIGG, GAWEN. Star against star. N. Y., Macaulay, 1936.
42. BURT, STRUTHERS. Entertaining the islanders. N. Y., Scribner, 1933.
43. CALDWELL, ERSKINE. Tragic ground. N. Y., Duell, 1944.
44. CASANOVA DE SEINGALT, G. G. Memoirs. (tr. Arthur Machen) N. Y., Regency House, 1938. 8v.

45. CHARKE, CHARLOTTE. Narrative of the life of . . . written by herself. Lond., W. Reeve, 1755.
46. CHARLES-ETIENNE. La bouche fardée. Paris, Editions Curio, 1926.
47. ——. Les désexuées. Paris. Editions Curio, 1924.
48. ——. & Nortal, Albert. Inassouvie. Paris, Editions Curio, 1927.
49. [CHOISEUL-MEUSE, FÉLICITÉ DE]. Julie, ou j'ai sauvé ma rose. Priv. print., 1882.
50. Coleridge, S. T. Christabel. (In: Page, C. H. British poets of the nineteenth century. N. Y., Sanborn, 1917)
51. COLETTE, SIDONIE GABRIELLE. Ces plaisirs. Paris, Ferenczi, 1932.
52. ——. Claudine à l'école. Paris, Ollendorff, 1903.
52a. ——. Claudine at school. N. Y., Boni, 1930.
53. ——. Claudine à Paris. Paris, Ollendorff, 1903.
53a. ——. Young lady of Paris. N. Y., Boni, 1931.
54. ——. Claudine en ménage. Paris, Mercure de France, 1902.
54a. ——. The indulgent husband. (In: Short novels of Colette. Glenway Wescott, ed. N. Y., Dial, 1951).
55. ——. Claudine s'en va. Paris, Ollendorff, 1903.
55a. ——. The innocent wife. N. Y., Farrar, 1934.
56. ——. La retraite sentimentale. Paris, Mercure de France, 1947.
57. COUPERUS, LOUIS. The comedians. N. Y., Doran, 1926.
58. COWLIN, DOROTHY. Winter solstice. N. Y., Macmillan, 1943.
59. CRAIGIN, ELIZABETH. Either is love. N. Y., Harcourt, 1937.
60. CUISIN, P. Clémentine, orpheline et androgyne. Bruxelles, J. J. Gay, 1883.
61. DANE, CLEMENCE. Regiment of women. N. Y., Macmillan, 1917.
62. DASCOM [BACON], JOSEPHINE. Smith College stories. N. Y., Scribner, 1916.
63. *DAUTHENDEY, ELISABETH. Vom neuen Weib und seiner Liebe. ed. 3. Berlin, Schuster & Löffler, 1903.
64. DAVENPORT, MARCIA. Of Lena Geyer. N. Y., Scribner, 1936.
65. DAVIES, RHYS. The trip to London. N. Y., Howell Soskin, 1946.
66. *DEHMEL, RICHARD. Weib und Welt. (In: Gesammelte Werke, bd. 2. Berlin, Fischer, 1913).
67. DESVIGNONS, MAX. Plaisirs troublants. Paris, Librairie Artistique, n.d.
68. DEVAL, JACQUES. Club de femmes [film]. Review: Time v. 30 pt. 2, Oct. 25, 1937.
69. DICKINSON, EMILY. Bolts of melody; new poems. N. Y., Harper, 1945.
70. ——. Letters of . . . (Mabel Loomis Todd, ed.) Cleveland, World Publ. Co., 1951.
71. ——. Letters to Dr. and Mrs. Josiah Gilbert Holland. Cambridge, Mass., Harvard University Press, 1951.
72. ——. Life and letters of . . . by her niece, Martha Dickinson Bianci. Bost., Houghton, 1924.

73. ———. Poems. (Martha Dickinson Bianci and Alfred L. Hampson, ed.) Bost., Little Brown, 1937.
74. DIDEROT, DENIS. La religieuse. Paris, Editions de Cluny, 1938.
75. DINESEN, ISAK. Seven Gothic tales. N. Y., Smith and Haas, 1934.
76. DONISTHORPE, SHEILA. Loveliest of friends. [N. Y.], Claude Kendall, 1931.
77. DOSTOEVSKY, FEODOR. The friend of the family. Lond., Heinemann, 1920.
78. DRESSER, DAVIS. Mardigras madness. N. Y., Godwin, 1934.
78a. ———. Peter Shelley. One reckless night. N. Y., Godwin, 1938.
79. DRUON, MAURICE. The rise of Simon Lachaume. (tr. Edward Fitzgerald) N. Y., Dutton, 1952.
80. DUBUT DE LAFOREST, J. J. La femme d'affaires. Paris, Dentu, 1890.
81. *———. Mlle Tantale. Paris, Dupont, 1897.
82. *DUC, AIMÉE. Sind es Frauen? Berlin, Echstein, 1903.
83. DUMAURIER, ANGELA. The little less. N. Y., Doubleday, 1941.
84. *EICHHORN, MARIA. Fraülein Don Juan.
85. EICHRODT, JOHN. Nadia Devereux. (In: Sextet. Whit and Hallie Burnett, ed. N. Y., McKay, 1951.)
86. EISNER, SIMON. Naked storm. N. Y., Lion Books, 1952.
87. ELLIS, JOHN BRECKENRIDGE. The Holland wolves. Chic., McClurg, 1902.
88. EULENBERG, HERBERT. Der Maler Rayski. (In: Casanovas letztes Abenteuer. Dresden, Reissner, 1928.)
89. FEYDEAU, ERNEST. La comtesse de Chalis. Paris, Michel Levy 1871.
90. FIELD, MICHAEL. Long ago. Portland, Me., Mosher, 1897.
91. ———. Underneath the bough. ibid. 1898.
92. ———. Works and days. From the journal of Michael Field. (T. and D. C. Sturge Moore ed.) Lond., Murray, 1933.
93. FIRBANK, RONALD. Five novels. Norfolk, Conn., New Directions, 1949.
94. FIRMINGER, MARJORIE. Jam today. Paris, n. publ., 1931.
95. FISHER [PARRISH], MARY. F. K. Not now but NOW. N. Y., Viking, 1947.
96. FITZMAURICE-KELLY, JAMES. The nun ensign. Lond., Fisher Unwin, 1908.
97. FITZROY, [SCOTT] A. T. Despised and rejected. Lond., Daniel, 1918.
98. FLAUBERT, GUSTAVE. Salammbo. N. Y., Rarity Press, 1932.
99. FLORA, FLETCHER. Strange sisters. N. Y., Lion Books, 1954.
100. FORREST, FELIX. Carola. N. Y., Duell, 1948.
101. FOSTER, GERALD. Strange marriage. N. Y., Godwin, 1934.
102. FOWLER, ELLEN T. The Farringdons. N. Y., Appleton, 1900.
103. *FRAUMAN, LUZ. Weiberbeute. Budapest, Schneider, 1906.
104. FREDERICS, DIANA. Diana; a strange autobiography. N. Y., Dial, 1939.

105. FULLER [OSSOLI], MARGARET. Günderode. Boston, Peabody, 1942.
106. ——. Memoirs. Bost., Phillips, Sampson, 1852. 2v.
107. GAUTIER, THÉOPHILE. Mlle de Maupin. Chic., Franklin, n.d.
108. GEORGIE, LEYLA. The establishment of Madame Antonia. N. Y.,
     Liveright, 1932.
109. GIDE, ANDRÉ. The school for wives; Robert; Genevieve . . . (tr.
     Dorothy Bussy) N. Y., Knopf, 1950.
110. GOURMONT, REMY DE. Le songe d'une femme. Paris, Mercure de
     France, 1899.
111. *GRAMONT, LOUIS DE. Astarte; opéra en quatre actes . . . (Aca-
     démie Nationale de Musique, Feb. ?, 1901).
112. GREENE, GRAHAM. Orient express. N. Y., Doubleday, 1933.
113. GÜNDERODE, KAROLINE. Gesammelte Werke. Berlin, Goldschmidt-
     Gabrielli, 1920-22. 2v.
114. GUNTER, A. C. A Florida enchantment. N. Y., Home Publ. Co.,
     1892.
115. HALL, RADCLYFFE. The unlit lamp. N. Y., Jonathan Cape, 1924.
116. ——. The well of loneliness. N. Y., Covici, Friede, 1929
117. HAMILTON, ANTHONY. Count de Grammont. Lond., Grolier So-
     ciety, n.d.
118. HARDY, THOMAS. Desperate remedies. N. Y., Harper, 1896.
119. HARRIS, SARA. The wayward ones. N. Y., Crown, 1952.
120. HELLMAN, LILLIAN. The children's hour. (In: Plays. N. Y., Ran-
     dom, 1942.)
121. HEMINGWAY, ERNEST. The fifth column and the first forty-nine
     stories. N. Y., Collier, 1938.
122. HILLE, PETER. Gesammelte Werke. Berlin, Schuster & Löffler,
     1904. 2v.
123. HENRY, JOAN. Women in prison. N. Y., Permabooks, 1953.
124. *HÖCHSTETTER, SOPHIE. Selbstanziege. Die letzte Flamme. Jena,
     Landhausverlag, 1917.
125. HOLMES, O. W. Elsie Venner. N. Y., Burt, n.d.
126. ——. The guardian angel. Bost., Houghton, 1890.
127. ——. A mortal antipathy. Bost., Houghton, 1892.
128. HULL, HELEN R. The fire. Century Magazine 95:105-114, Nov.
     1917.
129. ——. Labyrinth. N. Y., Macmillan, 1923.
130. ——. Quest. N. Y., Macmillan, 1922.
131. HUNEKER, J. G. Painted veils. N. Y., Modern Library, n.d.
132. HUON OF BORDEAUX. (tr. Lord Berners) Lond., Trubner & Co.,
     1884.
133. *HURLBUT, THOMAS. Hymn to Venus. Review: New York Times,
     Nov. 7, 1926; VIII:10.
134. HURST, FANNIE. Lonely parade. N. Y., Harper, 1942.
135. IRA, IRIS. Lesbos: Gedichte. Priv. print., 1930.

136. JACKSON, SHIRLEY. Hangsaman. N. Y., Farrar, 1951.
137. JAMES, HENRY. The Bostonians. N. Y., Dial, 1945.
138. ——. The turn of the screw. (In: Novels and tales. N. Y., Scribner, 1922. v. 12.)
139. *JANITSCHEK, MARIA. Neue Erziehung und alte Moral. (In: Die Neue Eva. Leipzig, Seeman, 1903.)
140. JUVENAL. Satires . . . (tr. Lewis Evans) Lond., Bell, 1895.
141. KALTNEKER, HANS. Die Schwester: ein Mysterium. Berlin, Zsolnay, 1924.
142. KEOGH, THEODORA. Meg. N. Y., New American Library, 1952.
143. [KING, WILLIAM]. The toast . . . Written in Latin by Frederick Scheffer. Done into English by Peregrine O'Donald, Esq. Dublin, 1732.
144. KOESTLER, ARTHUR. Arrival and departure. N. Y., Macmillan, 1943.
145. LABÉ, LOUISE. The debate between Folly and Cupid. (tr. E. M. Cox) Lond., Williams & Norgate, 1925.
146. ——. Oeuvres, publiées par Charles Boy. Paris, Lemerre, 1887. 2v. (v. 2: Recherches sur la vie et les oeuvres de Louise Labé.)
146a. ——. Oeuvres complètes . . . (P. C. Boutens, ed.) Maestricht, Stols, 1928.
147. ——. Love sonnets. (tr. Frederic Prokosch) N. Y., New Directions, 1947.
148. LACRETELLE, JAQUES DE. Marie Bonifas. Lond., Putnam, 1927.
149. LAFARGE, CHRISTOPHER. The sudden guest. N. Y., Coward-McCann, 1946.
150. LAMARTINE, A. M. L. Regina. (In: Nouvelles confidences. Paris, Levy, 1855.)
151. LANDON, MARGARET. Never dies the dream. N. Y., Doubleday, 1949.
152. LAPSLEY [GUEST], MARY. Parable of the virgins. N. Y., R. R. Smith, 1931.
153. LATOUCHE, HENRI DE. Fragoletta. Paris, Lavasseur, 1829. 2v.
154. *LAVAUDÈRE, JANE. Les demi-sexes. (In: Le Figaro) 1896.
155. LAWRENCE, D. H. The rainbow. N. Y., Modern Library, n.d.
156. LEE, JENNETTE. The cat and the king. Ladies Home Journal 36:10, Oct. 1919.
157. LEHMANN, ROSAMOND. Dusty Answer. N. Y., Holt, 1927.
158. ——. The weather in the streets. N. Y., Literary Guild, 1936.
159. LEWIS, SINCLAIR. Ann Vickers. N. Y., Doubleday, 1933.
160. LEWIS, WYNDHAM. The apes of God. Lond., Arthur Press, 1930.
161. *LIEBETREU, O. Urningsliebe. Leipzig, Fischer, 1905.
162. LODGE, LOIS. Love like a shadow. N. Y., Phoenix, 1935.
163. LOFTS, NORA. Jassy. N. Y., Knopf, 1945.
164. LOUYS, PIERRE. Aphrodite. Priv. print., 1925.

165. Louys, Pierre. Les aventures du roi Pausole. Paris, Fayard, n.d.
166. ———. The songs of Bilitis. N. Y., Godwin, 1933.
167. Lowell, Amy. A dome of many-colored glass. Bost., Houghton, 1912.
168. ———. Pictures of the floating world. N. Y., Macmillan, 1919.
169. ———. Sword blades and poppy seeds. Bost., Houghton, 1914.
170. ———. What's o'clock. Bost., Houghton, 1925.
171. Lucian. (tr. C. Jacobitz) v. 1, The ass, Dialogues of the courtesans, and The amores. Athens, Athenian Society, 1895.
172. Mackenzie, Compton. Extraordinary women. Lond., Secker, 1932.
173. MacLane, Mary. I, Mary MacLane. N. Y., Stokes, 1917.
174. ———. My friend Annabel Lee. Chic., Stone, 1903.
175. ———. The story of Mary MacLane; by herself. Chic., Stone, 1902.
176. Madeleine, Marie. Auf Kypros. Berlin, Vita, n.d.
177. Mallet, Françoise. The illusionist. (tr. Herma Briffault) N. Y., Farrar, 1952.
178. Mann, Heinrich. Die Göttinen: Venus. Berlin, Zsolnay, 1925.
179. Mansfield, Katherine. The scrapbook . . . N. Y., Knopf, 1940.
180. ———. Journal. N. Y., Knopf, 1928.
181. Marchal, Lucie. The mesh. (tr. Virgilia Peterson) N. Y., Appleton, 1949.
182. Margueritte, Victor. La garçonne. Paris, Flammarion, 1922.
182a. ———. The bachelor girl. Lond., A. M. Philpot, 1924.
183. Martial. Epigrams. (tr. W. C. Aker) Lond., Heinemann, 1930, 2v.
184. Masefield, John. Multitude and solitude. N. Y., Macmillan, 1925.
185. Masters, Edgar Lee. Domesday book. N. Y., Macmillan, 1929.
186. Maupassant, Guy de. La femme de Paul. (In: La maison Tellier. Paris, Ollendorff, 1899.)
186a. ———. Paul's mistress. (In: Works of . . . Aldus de luxe ed. N. Y., National Library, 1909. v. 4.)
187. [Mayeur de St. Paul?] Confessions d'une jeune fille; Suite; Suite et fin. (In: [Mairobert, M. F. P. de? et al.] L'espion anglais. Lond., n. publ., 1784. t. 10.)
188. *Meebold, Alfred. Dr. Erna Redens Thorheit und Erkenntnis. (In: Allerhand Volk. Berlin, Vita, 1900.)
189. Mendes, Catulle. Méphistophéla. Paris, Dentu, 1890.
190. Menken, Ada Isaacs. Infelicia. Phila., Lippincott, 1875.
191. Middleton, Thomas and Dekker, Thomas. The roaring girl. Lond., Vizetelly, 1890.
191a. ———. Ibid. (In: Works. A. H. Bullen, ed. Lond., Nimmo, 1885-86. v. 4.)
192. Millay, Edna St. Vincent. Fatal interview. N. Y., Harper, 1931.

193. ———. A few figs from thistles. N. Y., Harper, 1922.
194. ———. The harp-weaver and other poems. N. Y., Harper, 1923.
195. ———. The lamp and the bell. N. Y., Harper, 1921.
196. ———. Letters. (Alan Ross Macdougall, ed.) N. Y., Harper, 1952.
197. ———. Renascence. N. Y., Kennerly, 1924.
198. ———. Second April. N. Y., Kennerly, 1924.
199. MILLAY, KATHLEEN. Against the wall. N. Y., Macaulay, 1929.
200. MITCHISON, NAOMI. The delicate fire. N. Y., Harcourt, 1932.
201. *MOLLER, O. W. Wer kann dafür? (tr. from Danish, Richard
     Meienreis) Leipzig, Spohr, 1901.
202. MONTFORT, CHARLES. Le journal d'une saphiste. Paris, Offen-
     stadt, 1902.
203. MORGAN, CLAIRE. The price of salt. N. Y., Coward-McCann,
     1952.
204. MOSS, GEOFFREY. That other love. N. Y., Doubleday, 1930.
205. *MUHSAM, ERICH. Die Psychologie der Erbtante. Zurich, Schmidt,
     1905.
206. NATHAN, GEORGE JEAN. Design for loving. American Spectator
     1:2-3, April 1933.
207. NEFF, WANDA FRAIKEN. We sing Diana. Bost., Houghton, 1928.
208. *NIEMANN, AUGUST. Zwei Frauen. Dresden, Pierson, 1901.
209. NIN, ANAIS. Ladders to fire. N. Y., Dutton, 1924.
210. O'HIGGINS, HARVEY. Julie Cane. N. Y., Harper, 1924.
211. OLIVIA. [Dorothy Bussy] Olivia. N. Y., William Sloane, 1949.
211x. Oriental stories. (La fleur lascive orientale) . . . trans. from
     Arabian . . . (etc.) Athens, priv. print., 1893.
212. O'NEILL, ROSE. The master-mistress. N. Y., Knopf, 1922.
213. OVID. Heroides and Amores. (tr. Grant Showerman) Lond.,
     Heinemann, 1931.
214. ———. Metamorphoses. (tr. Frank Justus Miller) Lond., Heine-
     mann, 1946. 2v.
215. Oxford Book of Victorian Verse. (A. T. Quiller-Couch, ed.)
     Oxford, University Press, 1912.
216. PACKER, VIN. Spring fire. N. Y., Fawcett, 1952.
217. PARKER, DOROTHY. After such pleasures. N. Y., Viking, 1934.
218. PATTON [WALDRON], MARION. Dance on the tortoise. N. Y., Dial,
     1930.
219. PELADAN, JOSEPHIN. La gynandre. Paris, Dentu, 1891.
220. ———. La vertu suprême. Paris, Flammarion, 1900.
221. *POUGY, LIANE DE. Idylle saphique. Paris, Librairie de la Plume,
     1901.
222. PROUST, MARCEL. The captive. (tr. C. K. Scott-Moncrieff) N. Y.,
     Modern Library, 1929.
223. ———. Cities of the plain (tr. ibid.) N. Y., Modern Library, 1930.
224. ———. The Guermantes way. (tr. ibid.) N. Y., Modern Library,
     1925.

225. PROUST, MARCEL. The past recaptured. (tr. F. A. Blossom) N. Y., Boni, 1932.
226. ———. Swann's way. (tr. C. K. Scott-Moncrieff) N. Y., Modern Library, 1928.
227. ———. The sweet cheat gone. (tr. ibid.) N. Y., Boni, 1930.
228. ———. Within a budding grove. (tr. ibid.) N. Y., Modern Library, 1924.
229. RACHILDE. [Marguérite Aymery Vallette]. Madame Adonis. Paris, Ferenczi, 1929.
230. ———. Monsieur Vénus. (Maurice Barrès, ed.) Paris, Felix Brossier, 1889.
230a. ———. Monsieur Vénus. (tr. Madeleine Boyd, Maurice Barrès, pref.) N. Y., Covici, Friede, 1929.
231. REMARQUE, ERICH. Arch of triumph. N. Y., Appleton, 1945.
232. RENAULT, MARY. The middle mist. N. Y., Morrow, 1945.
233. ———. Promise of love. N. Y., Morrow, 1939.
234. *REUSS, PAULE. Le génie de l'amour. Paris, Oeuvres Représentatives, 1935.
235. *REUTER, GABRIELE. Aus guter Familie. Berlin, 1897.
236. RICE, CRAIG. Having wonderful crime. N. Y., Simon & Schuster, 1943.
237. RICHARDSON, DOROTHY. Dawn's left hand. N. Y., Knopf, n.d. (In: Pilgrimage, v. 4).
238. RICHARDSON, HENRY HANDEL. The end of a childhood . . . Lond., Heinemann, 1934.
239. ———. The getting of wisdom. N. Y., Duffield, 1910.
240. *RIGAL, HENRY. Sur le mode saphique. Paris, Mercure de France, 1902.
141. ROLAND-MANUEL, SUZANNE. Le trille du diable. Paris, Deux Rives, 1946.
242. ROLLAND, ROMAIN. Annette and Sylvie. (tr. B. R. Redman) N. Y., Holt, 1935.
243. RONALD, JAMES. The angry woman. N. Y., Bantam, 1950.
243x. ROSSETTI, CHRISTINA. Goblin Market. (In: Stephens, James, et al., ed. Victorian and later English poets. N. Y., American Book Co., 1937.)
244. ROYDE-SMITH, NAOMI. The island. N. Y., Harper, 1930.
245. ———. The tortoiseshell cat. N. Y., Boni, 1925.
246. *RULING, THEODOR. Ratzelhaft. (In: Welcher unter Euch ohne Sünde ist. Leipzig, Spohr, 1906.)
247. SACKVILLE-WEST, VICTORIA. The dark island. N. Y., Doubleday, 1934.
248. ———. King's daughter. N. Y., Doubleday, 1930.
249. SAND, GEORGE. Gabriel-Gabrielle. (In: Oeuvres complètes. Paris, Perrotin, 1843. v. 13).

250. SAPPHO. (tr. and ed. J. M. Edmonds) (In: Lyra Graeca. Cambridge, Mass., Harvard Univ. Press, 1934, v. 1).
251. ——. The songs of Sappho, in English translation by many poets. Mt. Vernon, N. Y., Peter Pauper Press, n.d.
252. ——. Songs; including the recent Egyptian discoveries. (tr. Marion Mills Miller, into rimed verse; [ed. &] tr. into prose by D. M. Robinson) N. Y., Macon, 1925.
253. SARTON, MARY. A shower of summer days. N. Y., Rinehart, 1952.
254. SARTRE, JEAN PAUL. No exit. The flies. (tr. Stuart Gilbert) N. Y., Knopf, 1947.
255. SAYERS, DOROTHY. The Dawson pedigree. N. Y., Harcourt, [c1928].
256. SCHREINER, OLIVE. Story of an African farm. Bost., Little, Brown, 1920.
256x. ——. From man to man. N. Y., Harper, 1927.
257. SCHWABE, TONI. Komm kühle Nacht. München, Miller, 1908.
258. *SEYDLITZ, R. VON. Pierre's Ehe: psychologisches Problem. München, Schupp, n.d.
259. SHAKESPEARE, WILLIAM. The complete works of . . . (ed. W. G. Clark and W. A. Wright) N. Y., Cumberland Publ. Co., n.d.
260. SIDGWICK, ETHEL. A lady of leisure. Bost., Small, Maynard, 1914.
261. SIDNEY, PHILIP. The Countess of Pembroke's Arcadia. Cambridge (England), University Press, 1912.
262. *SINOWJEWA, ANNIBAL. Dreiunddreissig Scheusale. St. Petersburg, 1907.
263. *STADLER, ERNST. Freundinnen. Ein lyrisches Spiel. Magazin für Literatur, 2 Feb., 1904.
264. STAFFORD, JEAN. Boston adventure. N. Y., Harcourt, 1944.
265. STEIN, GERTRUDE. Things as they are. Pawlet, Vt., Banyan Press, 1950.
266. STERLING, GEORGE. Strange waters. Priv. print., n.d.
267. STRINDBERG, AUGUST. The confession of a fool. (tr. Ellie Schleussner) N. Y., Viking, 1925.
268. ——. Lady Julie. (In: Lucky Peter's travels and other tales. Lond., Cape, 1930.)
269. SWINBURNE, A. C. Lesbia Brandon. (Randolph Hughes, ed.) Lond., Falcon Press, 1952.
270. ——. Poems and ballads. Series I. London, Chatto, 1893.
271. TEY, JOSEPHINE. Miss Pym disposes. N. Y., Macmillan, 1948.
272. ——. To love and be wise. N. Y., Macmillan, 1951.
273. THAYER, TIFFANY. Thirteen women. N. Y., Claude Kendall, 1932.
274. THEISS, FRANK. Interlude. (tr. Caroline Fredrick) N. Y., Knopf, 1929.
275. THOMAS, ELISABETH W. Ella. N. Y., Viking, 1930.

276. THORNE, ANTHONY. Delay in the sun. N. Y., Literary Guild 1934.
277. TILLY, ALEXANDRE DE. Memoirs. (tr. Françoise Delisle) N. Y., Farrar, 1952.
278. TOLSTOI, L. N. Anna Karenina. N. Y., World, 1931.
279. TORRES, TORESKA. Women's barracks. N. Y., Fawcett, 1950.
280. (D'URFÉ). MAGENDIE, MAURICE. L'Astrée d'Honoré d'Urfé. Paris, Société Française d'Editions Littéraires..., 1929.
281. VERLAINE, PAUL. Parallèlement. Paris, Leon Vanier, 1894.
282. VIRGIL. Aeneid. Minor poems. (tr. H. R. Fairclough) Lond., Heinemann, 1925. 2v.
283. VIVIEN, RENÉE. Poésies complètes. Paris, Lemerre, 1948. 2v.
284. ——. Brumes de fjords. Paris, Lemerre, 1902.
285. ——. Du vert au violet. Paris, Lemerre, 1903.
286. ——. Le Christ, Aphrodite, et M Pépin. Paris, Sansot.
287. *——. Une femme m'apparut. Paris.
288. *[—— and NYEVELT, HÉLÉNE DE] "Paule Riversdale." Echos et reflets. Paris, Lemerre, 1903.
289. *——. L'être double. Paris, Lemerre, 1904.
290. *——. Netsuké. Paris, Lemerre, 1904.
291. *——. Vers l'amour. Paris, Maison des Poètes, 1903.
292. WAGNER, ERNST. Isidora. (In: Sammtliche Schriften. Leipzig, Fleischer, 1828. v. 5.)
293. *WASSERMANN, JACOB. Geschichte der junge Renate Fuchs. Berlin, Fischer, 1930.
294. WEBSTER, H. K. The real adventure. Indianapolis, Bobbs Merrill, 1916.
295. WEDEKIND, FRANK. Erdgeist. (In: Gesammelte Werke. München, Miller, 1919. v. 3.)
296. ——. Mine-haha. München, Langen, 1905.
297. ——. Franziska. München, Miller, 1913.
298. WEIRAUCH, ANNA ELISABET. Der Skorpion. Berlin, Askanischer Verlag, 1930, 3v.
298a. ——. The scorpion. (tr. Whittaker Chambers) N. Y., Greenberg, 1932.
298b. ——. The outcast. (tr. S. Guyendore) N. Y., Greenberg, 1933.
299. WELLS, CATHERINE. The beautiful house. Harper's Magazine 124:503-11, 1912.
300. WHEELER, HUGH C. The crippled muse. N. Y., Rinehart, 1952.
301. WILDER, ROBERT. Wait for tomorrow. N. Y., Bantam, 1953.
302. WILHELM, GALE. Torchlight to Valhalla. N. Y., Random, 1938.
303. ——. We too are drifting. N. Y., Random, 1935.
304. WILLIAMS, IDABEL. Hellcat. N. Y., Dell, 1952.
305. WILLIS, GEORGE. Little boy blues. N. Y., Dutton, 1947.
306. WILSON, EDMUND. Memoirs of Hecate County. N. Y., Doubleday, 1946.

307. WILSON, ETHEL D. Hetty Dorval. N. Y., Macmillan, 1948.
308. WINSLOE, CHRISTA. The child Manuela. (tr. Agnes N. Scott)
     N. Y., Farrar, 1933.
309. ———. Girl alone. (tr. Agnes N. Scott) N. Y., Farrar, 1936.
310. WOLLSTONECRAFT, MARY. Mary, a fiction. Lond., Johnson, 1788.
311. WOOLF, VIRGINIA. Mrs. Dalloway. N. Y., Modern Library, 1928.
312. ———. Orlando. N. Y., Harcourt, 1928.
313. ———. To the lighthouse. N. Y., Modern Library, 1937.
314. WYLIE, PHILIP. Disappearance. N. Y., Rinehart, 1951.
315. ———. Opus 21. N. Y., Rinehart, 1949.
316. YOUNG, F. B. White ladies. N. Y., Harper, 1935.
317. ZOLA, EMILE. La curée. Paris, Charpentier, 1887.
318. ———. Nana. N. Y., Pocket Books, 1942.
319. ———. Pot-bouille. Paris, Charpentier, 1883.

Addenda
320. FLORA, FLETCHER. Strange sisters. N. Y., Lion Books, 1954.
321. HALES, CAROL. Wind woman. N. Y., Woodford Press, 1953.
322. SHAW, WILENE. The fear and the guilt. N. Y., Ace Books, 1954.
323. WOOD, CLEMENT. Strange fires. N. Y., Woodford Press, 1951.
324. WOODFORD, JACK. Male and female. N. Y., Woodford Press, 1935.

B. BIBLIOGRAPHIC, BIOGRAPHICAL, HISTORICAL AND CRITICAL MATERIAL

 1. ALDINGTON, RICHARD. D. H. Lawrence; portrait of a genius but
    . . . N. Y., Duell, 1950.
 2. ALPERS, ANTONY. Katherine Mansfield: a biography. N. Y.,
    Knopf, 1953.
 3. ANTHONY, KATHERINE. Margaret Fuller: a psychological biogra-
    phy. N. Y., Harcourt, 1920.
 4. ARTIMAN, ARTINE. Maupassant criticism in France, 1880-1940.
    N. Y., Kings Crown Press, 1941.
 5. ASCHAFFENBURG, GUSTAVE. [Harmful effects of homosexual peri-
    odicals: editorial in German, untitled] Aerztl. Sachverst. Zei-
    tung 34:351-54, Dec. 1928.
 6. [ASHBEE, H. S.] Pisanus Fraxi. Catena librorum tacendorum.
    Lond., priv. print., 1885.
 7. ———. Centuria librorum prohibitorum. Lond., priv. print., 1879.
 8. ———. Index librorum prohibitorum. Lond., priv. print., 1877.
 9. ASHLEY MONTAGU, M. F. The natural superiority of women.
    Sat. Rev. Lit. 35 (9) :8-9, 1952.
10. ATKINS, ELIZABETH. Edna St. Vincent Millay and her times.
    Chic., University of Chicago Press, 1936.
11. AYNARD, JOSEPH. Les poètes lyonnais, précurseurs de la pléiade.
    Paris, Bossard, 1924.

12. BALDENSPERGER, FERNAND. L'avant-guerre dans la littérature française: 1900-1914. Paris, Payot, 1919.
13. ———. La littérature française entre les deux guerres, 1919-1939. Los Angeles, Lyman House, 1941.
14. BARRY, P. B. Twenty human monsters. Lond., Jarrolds, 1929.
15. BARZUN, JACQUES. Romanticism and the modern ego. Bost., Little, Brown, 1944.
16. BASLER, ROY. Sex, symbolism and psychology in literature. New Brunswick, N. J., Rutgers University Press, 1948.
17. BEARD, MARY R. On understanding women. Lond., Longmans, 1931.
18. ———. Woman as a force in history. N. Y., Macmillan, 1946.
19. BEAUVOIR, SIMONE DE. The second sex. N. Y., Knopf, 1953.
20. BELL, MARGARET. Margaret Fuller. N. Y., Boni, 1930.
21. BENTLEY, PHYLLIS E. The Brontës. Denver, Alan Swallow, 1948.
22. BERGLER, EDMUND. Psychoanalysis of writers and of literary production. (In: Psychoanalysis and the social sciences: an annual. Geza Roheim, ed. v. 1, 1947.)
23. BINGHAM, MILLICENT T. Ancestors' brocades: the literary debut of Emily Dickinson. N. Y., Harper, 1945.
24. ———. Emily Dickinson: a revelation. N. Y., Harper, 1954.
25. BITHELL, JETHRO. Modern German literature: 1880-1938. Lond., Methuen, 1939.
26. BLACKSTONE, BERNARD. Virginia' Woolf: a commentary. N. Y., Harcourt, 1949.
27. BLOCH, IWAN. Sex life in England . . . N. Y., Panurge Press, 1934.
28. BOUTEN, JACOB. Mary Wollstonecraft and the beginnings of female emancipation in France and England. Amsterdam, A. H. Kruyt, 1922.
29. BRACHFELD, OLIVER. Das androgynen Problem in der Gegenwart. Ztschr, f. sex. Wissensch. 17:425-31, 1931.
30. BRAGMAN, L. J. The case of Algernon Charles Swinburne: a study in sadism. Psychoanal. Rev. 21:51-74, 1934.
31. BRAITHWAITE, W. S. The bewitched parsonage. N. Y., Coward-McCann, 1950.
32. BRAUNSCHWIG, MARCEL. La littérature française contemporaine (1850-1925). Paris, Armand Colin, 1925.
33. BRITTAIN, VERA. Lady into woman. N. Y., Macmillan, 1953.
34. BROOKS, VANWYCK. The pilgrimage of Henry James. N. Y., Dutton, 1925.
35. BROWNE, F. W. Stella. Der weibliche Typus Inversus in der neueren Literatur. Neue Generation 18:90-96, 1922.
36. BRUN, CHARLES. Pauline Tarn. Notes & Quer. ser. 11. 10:151, 1914.
37. CALVERTON, V. F. & SCHMALHAUSEN, S. D. Sex in civilization, N. Y., Macaulay, 1929.

38. CARPENTER, EDWARD. Iolaus: an anthology of friendship. N. Y., Kennerly, 1917.
39. CHADWICK, H. M. and N. K. The growth of literature. v. 1. The ancient literatures of Europe. Cambridge (Eng.), University Press, 1932.
40. CHARCOT, J. M. & RICHTER, PAUL. Les démoniaques dans l'art. Paris, Delahaye, 1887.
41. CHASE, R. V. Emily Dickinson. N. Y., Sloane, 1951.
42. CHAUVIÈRE, CLAUDE. Colette. Paris, Firmin Didot, 1931.
43. CHESTER, ELIZA. [Harriet E. Paine]. Girls and women. Bost., Houghton, 1890.
44. ———. The unmarried woman. N. Y., Dodd, 1892.
45. CIBBER, COLLEY. An apology for the life of Mr. Colley Cibber, written by himself. Lond., Nimmo, 1889. 2v.
46. CLARKE, ISABEL C. Haworth parsonage. Lond., Hutchinson, 1927.
47. CLAYTON, ELLEN C. Queens of song. Lond., Smith, Elder, 1863 2v.
48. Columbia dictionary of modern European literature. (Horatio Smith, ed) N. Y., Columbia University Press, 1947.
49. COOPER, CLARISSA B. Women poets of the twentieth century in France: a critical bibliography. N. Y., Kings Crown Press, 1943.
50. COREY, D. W. The homosexual in America. N. Y., Greenberg, 1951.
51. CRAIG, ALEC. Above all liberties. Lond., Allen, Unwin, 1942.
52. CROSLAND, MARGARET. Colette: a provincial in Paris. N. Y., British Book Centre, 1954.
53. CURTIS, E. R. European literature and the Latin middle ages. N. Y., Bollingen Foundation, 1953.
54. DAICHES, DAVID. Virginia Woolf. Norfolk, Conn., New Directions, 1942.
55. *DAUTHENDEY, ELISABET. Die urnische Frage und die Frau. Leipzig, Spohr, 1906. (Review: Jahrb. sex Zwisch. 7:285-300, 1906.)
56. DAVID, ANDRÉ. Rachilde, homme de lettres. Paris, Nouvelle Revue Critique, 1924.
57. DEEGAN, DOROTHY Y. The stereotype of the single woman in American novels . . . N. Y., Kings Crown Press, 1951.
58 DENOMY, ALEXANDER. Courtly love and courtliness. Speculum 28:44-63, 1953.
59. DONALDSON, JAMES. Woman: her position and influence in ancient Greece and Rome and among the early Christians. N. Y., Longmans, 1907.
60. DRY, FLORENCE S. Brontë sources. I. The sources of Wuthering Heights. Cambridge (Eng.), W. Heffer, 1937.
61. EBERHARD, E. F. W. Die Frauenemanzipation und ihre erotische Grundlagen. Wein u. Leipzig, Braumüller, 1924.
62. EDMONDS, J. M. Sappho in the added light of the new fragments. Lond., Bell, 1912.

63. ERNST, MORRIS & LINDEY, ALEXANDER. The censor marches on. N. Y., Doubleday, 1940.
64. ERSCH, J. S. & GRUBER, J. G. Allgemeine Encyclopädie der Wissenschaften und Künste. Leipzig, Brockhaus, 1878. v. 97.
65. FIRESTONE, C. B. The coasts of illusion. N. Y., Harper, 1924.
66. FLAT, PAUL. Figures et questions de ce temps. Paris, Sansot, n.d.
67. ——. Nos femmes de lettres. Paris, Perrin, n.d.
68. FLEISCHMANN, HECTOR. Mme Polignac et la cour galante de Marie Antoinette. Paris, Bibliothèque des Curieux, 1910.
69. FORBERG, F. K. Manual of classical erotology. Manchester, Julian Smithson, 1844.
70. FORSTER, E. M. Virginia Woolf. N. Y., Harcourt, 1942.
71. FOSTER, JEANNETTE H. An approach to fiction through the characteristics of its readers. Library Q. 6:129-74, 1936.
72. FOX, RALPH. The novel and the people. N. Y., International Publishers, 1945.
73. FRASER, J. G. The golden bough. Lond., Macmillan, 1905-16. 12v.
74. FREIERSON, W. C. The English novel in transition, 1885-1940. Norman, Okla., University of Oklahoma Press, 1942.
75. FULLER [OSSOLI], MARGARET. Woman in the nineteenth century. Bost., Roberts, 1874.
76. GARDNER, E. G. King of court jesters [Ariosto]. N. Y., Dutton, 1906.
77. GAUNT, WILLIAM. The aesthetic adventure. Lond., Cape, 1945.
78. [GAY, JULES]. Bibliographie des ouvrages relatifs à l'amour . . . Paris, Lemonnyer, 1894-1900. 4v.
79. GERMAIN, ANDRÉ. Renée Vivien. Paris, Crès, 1917.
80. GILBERT, O. P. Women in men's guise. Lond., John Lane, 1932.
81. GIRAUD, VICTOR. Les maîtres de l'heure. Paris, Hachette, 1914.
82. GODWIN, WILLIAM. Memoirs of Mary Wollstonecraft. N. Y., Richard Smith, 1930.
83. GOLDSMITH, MARGARET. Christina of Sweden: a psychological biography. N. Y., Caxton House, 1939.
84. GOURMONT, JEAN DE. Muses d'aujourd'hui . . . Paris, Mercure de France, 1910.
85. GOURMONT, REMY DE. Lettres intimes à l'Amazone. Paris, Mercure de France, 1927.
86. ——. Letters to the Amazon. (tr. R. Aldington) Lond., Chatto, 1931.
87. GREGORY, HORACE & ZATURINSKA, MARYA. A history of American poetry, 1900-1940. N. Y., Harcourt, 1946.
88. GRIBBLE, FRANCIS. The court of Christina of Sweden and the later adventures of the queen in exile. N. Y., Kennerly, 1914.
89. ——. George Sand and her lovers. N. Y., Dutton, 1928.
90. GUÉRARD, ALBERT. French civilization in the nineteenth century. N. Y., Century, 1918.
91. HALLAM, HENRY. Introduction to the literature of Europe in the

fifteenth, sixteenth and seventeenth centuries. N. Y., Armstrong, 1882. 4v. in 2.

92. [HAMILTON, COSMO]. Wants citizen censor. N. Y. Times, Feb. 4, 1927. p. 17, col. 2.

93. HANSON, LAWRENCE. The four Brontës. Lond., Oxford University Press, 1949.

94. —— & HANSON, ELISABETH. Marian Evans and George Eliot. Lond., Oxford U. Press, 1953.

95. HARDY, BLANCHE C. The Princesse de Lamballe. N. Y., Appleton, 1909.

96. HARRISON, G. ELSIE. The clue to the Brontës. Lond., Methuen, 1948.

97. HEROLT, JOHANNES. Miracles of the blessed Virgin Mary. Lond., Routledge, 1928.

98. HILLER, KURT. Wo bleibt der homoerotik Roman? Jahrb. sex. Zwisch. 14:338-42, 1914.

99. HINKLEY, LAURA L. The Brontës, Charlotte and Emily. N. Y., Hastings House, 1946.

100. HIRSCH, C. H. De Mlle de Maupin à Claudine. Mercure de France 42:577-88, 1902.

101. [HIRSCHFELD, MAGNUS]. Numa Praetorius. Bibliographie der homosexuellen Belletristik . . . Jahrb. sex. Zwisch. bd. 1-20, passim.

102. [——] THEODOR RAMIEN. Sappho und Socrates; wie erklärt sich die Liebe der Männer und Frauen zu Personen des eigenen Geschlechte? Leipzig, Spohr, 1922.

103. HOCHSTETTER, SOPHIE. Die Königin Kristina. Jahrb. sex. Zwisch. 9:168-98, 1908.

104. HOFFMAN, F. J. Freudianism and the literary mind. Baton Rouge, La., State University Press, 1945.

105. ——. The little magazine. Princeton, N. J., University Press, 1947.

106. HUIZINGA, J. The waning of the middle ages. Lond., Arnold, 1924.

107. HUNEKER, J. G. Steeplejack. N. Y., Scribner, 1928.

108. JAMES, HENRY. The letters of . . . (Percy Lubbock, ed.) N. Y., Scribner, 1920. 2v.

109. JAMES, H. R. Mary Wollstonecraft: a sketch. Lond., Milford, 1932.

110. KARSCH, F. Mlle de Maupin. Jahrb. sex. Zwisch. 5:694-706, 1903.

111. KIEFER, OTTO. Sexual life in ancient Rome. Lond., Routledge, 1935.

112. KINSLEY, EDITH E. A story of Bramwell Brontë and his sisters. N. Y., Dutton, 1939.

113. KLEIN, VIOLA. The feminine character: history of an ideology. Lond., Kegan Paul, 1946.

114. KOCK, HENRY DE. Histoire des courtisanes célèbres. Paris, Bunel, Vernay, 1869.
115. KUNITZ, S. J. & HAYCRAFT, HOWARD, ed. American authors, 1600-1900. N. Y., H. W. Wilson.
116. ———. British authors before 1800. N. Y., H. W. Wilson.
117. ———. British authors of the nineteenth century. N. Y., H. W. Wilson.
118. ———. Twentieth century authors. N. Y., H. W. Wilson, 1942.
119. LACLAVIÈRE, R. DE M. Les femmes de la renaissance. Paris, Perrin, 1898.
120. LAFOURCADE, GEORGES. La jeunesse de Swinburne. Oxford, Humphrey Milford, 1928. 2v.
121. LAMBALLE, MARIE T. L. DE S. C. Secret memoirs of . . . ed. and annotated by Catherine . . . Hyde, marquise de . . . Scolari. N. Y., M. W. Dunne, 1901.
122. LANGDON-DAVIES, JOHN. A short history of women. N. Y., Literary Guild, 1927.
123. LANGE, VICTOR. Modern German literature: 1870-1940. Ithaca, Cornell University Press, 1945.
124. LANSON, GUSTAVE. Histoire de la littérature française. Paris, Hachette, 1916.
125. LAW, ALICE. Emily Jane Brontë and the authorship of Wuthering Heights. Altham, Old Parsonage Press, n.d.
126. LeBRETON, ANDRE. Le roman au dix-septième siècle. Paris, Hachette, 1890.
127. LEWANDOWSKI, HERBERT. Das Sexualproblem in der modernen Literatur und Kunst . . . seit 1800. Dresden, Aretz, 1927.
128. LEWIS, C. S. The allegory of love: a study in medieval tradition. Lond., Oxford University Press, 1951.
129. LEWIS, EILUNED & PETER. The land of Wales. N. Y., Scribner, 1937.
130. LICHT, HANS. [Paul Brandt] Sexual life in ancient Greece. Lond., Routledge, 1932.
131. LINFORD, MADELINE. Mary Wollstonecraft. Bost., Small, Maynard, 1924.
132. [Literature and sexual inversion. Untitled editorial] Urol. & Cutan. Rev. 37:920-21, 1933.
133. LUCAS, F. L. The decline and fall of the romantic ideal. N. Y., Macmillan, 1936.
134. LUNDBERG, FERDINAND & FARNHAM, MARYNIA. Modern woman: the lost sex. N. Y., Harper, 1947.
135. MARCHAND, H. L. Sex life in France, including a history of its erotic literature. N. Y., Panurge Press, 1933.
136. MARGES (PARIS). Enquêtes sur l'homosexualité en littérature. Marges, mars-avril, 1926.
137. MARTENAU, HEINZ. Sappho und Lesbos. Leipzig, Eva-Verlag, 1931.

138. MAUROIS, ANDRÉ. Lélia: the life of George Sand. N. Y., Harper, 1953.
139. ———. The seven faces of love. N. Y., Didier, 1944.
140. MAURRAS, CHARLES M. P. Romantisme et révolution . . . Paris, Nouvelle Librairie Nationale, 1922.
141. Mercure de France, v. 1-106, 1890-1913; v. 131-144, 1919-20: all reviews of Poèmes, Romans, Théâtres. v. 107-130, 1914-1918; v. 145-   : sampling of reviews.
142. MONTAIGNE, MICHEL DE. Journal of Montaigne's travels in Italy . . . in 1580 and 1581. Lond., John Murray, 1903. v. 1.
143. MOORE, HARRY T. The life and works of D. H. Lawrence. N. Y., Twayne, 1951.
144. MOORE, VIRGINIA. The life and eager death of Emily Brontë. Lond., Rich & Cowan, 1936.
144x. MORE, PAUL ELMER. Selected Shelburne essays. N. Y., Oxford Univ. Press, 1935. (Christina Rossetti, pp. 47-62.)
144y. MORECK, CURT. . . . Sittengeschichte der neuesten Zeit. Dresden, Aretz, 1929.
145. MORTON, H. C. V. In search of Wales. N. Y., Dodd, 1932.
146. MULJI, KARSANDAS. History of the sect of Maharajas . . . in western India. Lond., Trubner, 1865.
147. MURAT, MARIE. La vie amoureuse de Christine de Suède. Paris, Flammarion, 1930.
148. MURRAY, MARGARET A. The witch cult in western Europe: a study in anthropology. Oxford, Clarendon Press, 1921.
149. Mythology of all races. (L. H. Gray, ed.) Bost., Marshall Jones, 1916-32. 13v.
150. NEUMANN, ALFRED. Christina of Sweden. Lond., Hutchinson, 1935.
151. NITZE, W. K. & DARGAN, E. P. A history of French literature . . . N. Y., Holt, 1922.
152. Nouvelle Biographie Générale. (Dr. Hoefer, ed.) Paris, Firmin Didot, 1853-66. 46v.
153. OBERNDORFF, CLARENCE P. Psychiatric novels of Oliver Wendell Holmes. N. Y., Columbia University Press, 1943.
154. ———. Psychoanalysis in literature. (In: Psychoanalysis and the social sciences: an annual. Geza Roheim, ed. v. 1, 1947.)
155. OFFENBACHER, E. Contributions to the origin of Strindberg's Miss Julia. Psychoanal. Rev. 31:81-87, 1944.
156. O'CONNOR, DOROTHY. Louise Labé: sa vie et son oeuvre. Paris, Les Presses Françaises, 1926.
157. O'MALLEY, ISABEL B. Woman in subjection: a study of the lives of Englishwomen before 1832. Lond., Duckworth, 1933.
158. PATTEE, F. L. The feminine fifties. N. Y., Appleton, 1940.
159. PAULY, A. F. VON. Encyclopaedie der classischen Altertumwissenschaft. Stuttgart, Metzler, v.d. v. 9, 1916.

160. PENNELL, ELIZABETH R. Mary Wollstonecraft. Bost., Roberts, 1888.
161. PERCEAU, LOUIS. Bibliographie du roman érotique au XIX siécle. Paris, Fourdrinier, 1930. 2v.
162. PLUTARCH. Lives (tr. A. H. Clough) N. Y., Colonial Co., 1905. 5v.
163. PORCHÉ, FRANÇOIS. L'amour qui n'ôse pas dire son nom. Paris, Grasset, 1927.
164. [PORCHÉ, SIMONE BENDA]. Emily Brontë: pièce en 3 actes . . . Paris, Nagel, 1945.
165. POTTIER, EDMOND. Mme Dieulafoy [biographical note] (In: Dieulafoy, Jane. La reine de Castille. Paris, Hachette, 1920.)
166. PRAZ, MARIO. The romantic agony. Lond., Oxford University Press, 1951.
167. PUNER, HELEN. Freud: his life and mind. Lond., Grey Walls Press, 1949.
168. RATCHFORD, FANNIE E. The Brontës' web of childhood. N. Y., Columbia University Press, 1941.
169. REINACH, SALOMON. [Renée Vivien]. Notes & Quer, ser. 11. 9:488, 1914.
170. REYNIER, GUSTAVE. La femme au XVII siècle. Paris, Tallandier, 1927.
171. REUILLY, JEAN DE. La Raucourt et ses amies. Paris, Daragon, 1909.
172. "Revue de la quinzaine." Mercure de France 89:181-82, 1911.
173. RILKE, R. M. The notebook of Malte Laurids Brigge. Lond., Hogarth Press, 1930.
174. ROBINSON, D. M. Sappho and her influence. Bost., Marshall Jones, 1924.
175. ROSS, T. A. A note on the Merchant of Venice. Brit. Med. Psychol. 14:303-11, 1934.
176. ROUGEMONT, DENIS DE. Love in the western world. N. Y., Harcourt, 1940.
177. RÜLING, ANNA. Welches Interesse hat die Frauenbewegung an der Lösung des homosexuellen Probleme? Jahrb. sex. Zwisch. 7:131-51, 1905.
178. SAURAT, DENIS. Modern French literature: 1870-1940. N. Y., Putnam, 1946.
179. SCHERMERHORN, ELIZABETH. Seven strings of the lyre: the romantic life of George Sand. Bost., Houghton, 1927.
180. SENIOR, DOROTHY. The life and times of Colley Cibber. N. Y., Henkle, 1928.
181. SEYD, FELIZIA. Romantic rebel: the life of George Sand. N. Y., Viking, 1940.
182. SHORTER, CLEMENT K. The Brontës and their circle. N. Y., Dutton, 1914.

183. SIMPSON, CHARLES W. Emily Brontë. N. Y., Scribner, 1929.
184. SINCLAIR, MAY. Three Brontës. Bost., Houghton, 1912.
185. SPOELBERGH DE LOVENJOUL, ALFRED C. J. DE. Les lundis d'un chercheur. Paris, Calmann Lévy, 1894.
186. STEAD, CHRISTINA, comp. Modern women in love. N. Y., Dryden Press, 1945.
187. STERN, MADELEINE B. The life of Margaret Fuller. N. Y., Dutton, 1942.
188. SUSMAN, MARGARETE. Frauen der Romantik. Jena, Diederichs, 1929.
189. SYMONS, ARTHUR. Studies in strange souls. Lond., C. J., Sawyer, 1929.
190. TAGGARD, GENEVIEVE. The life and mind of Emily Dickinson. N. Y., Knopf, 1930.
191. TAYLOR, ALBERT B. An introduction to medieval romance. Lond., Heath Cranton, 1930.
192. TAYLOR, G. R. S. Mary Wollstonecraft: a study in economics and romance. Lond., Secker, 1911.
193. TREVERRET, ARMAND DE. L'Italie au XVI siècle. Ser. I. Paris, Hachette, 1877.
194. VARIN, RENÉ. Anthologie de l'érotisme: de Pierre Louÿs á J. P. Sartre. Paris, Nord-Sud, 1948.
195. ———. L'érotisme dans la littérature étrangère de D. H. Lawrence à H. Miller. Paris, Nord-Sud, 1951.
196. *VINCENT, M. L. George Sand et l'amour. Paris, Champion, 1919. (Review: Mercure de France 194:690).
197. WADE, MASON. Margaret Fuller: whetstone of genius. N. Y., Viking, 1940.
198. WARDLE, RALPH W. Mary Wollstonecraft: a critical biography. Lawrence, Kans., University of Kansas Press, 1951.
199. WEIGALL, ARTHUR. Sappho of Lesbos: her life and times. N. Y., Stokes, 1933.
200. WEINDEL, HENRI DE & FISCHER, F. P. L'homosexualité en Allemagne. Paris, 1906.
201. WELLS, H. W. Introduction to Emily Brontë. Chic., Hendricks House, 1947.
202. WILLAMOWITZ-MOELLENDORFF, ULRICH. Sappho und Simonides. Berlin, Wiedmann, 1913.
203. WILLARD, FRANCES & LIVERMORE, MARY. Woman of the century: 1470 biographical sketches. . . . N. Y., C. W. Moulton, 1893.
204. WILSON, EDMUND. Gertrude Stein as a young woman. New Yorker 27:108-15, Sept. 15, 1951.
205. ———. Postscript on Edna St. Vincent Millay. (In: The shores of light. N. Y., Farrar, 1952.)
206. ———. The ambiguity of Henry James. (In: The triple thinkers. N. Y., Oxford University Press, 1948.)

207. WILSON, MONA. Sir Philip Sidney. London, Duckworth, 1931.
208. WILSON [O'BRIEN], ROMER. All alone: the life and private history of Emily Jane Brontë. Lond., Chatto, 1928.
209. WINWAR, FRANCES. The life of the heart: George Sand and her times. N. Y., Harper, 1945.
210. ——. Poor splendid wings: the Rossettis and their circle. Bost., Little, 1933.
211. WOOD, CLEMENT. Amy Lowell. N. Y., Vinal, 1926.
212. ——. Poets of America. N. Y., Dutton, 1925.
213. *WOODS, MISS MARIANNE and MISS JANE PIRIE, vs. DAME HELEN CUMMINGS GORDON. Trial. Edinburgh, 1811-19. [Citation; U. S. Surgeon General's Catalog of the Army Medical Library, ser. I, v. 14, 1893].
214. WOOLF, VIRGINIA. The common reader. N. Y., Harcourt, 1925.
215. WRIGHT, F. A. Feminism in Greek literature from Homer to Aristotle. Lond., Routledge, 1923.
216. WRIGHT, RICHARDSON. Forgotten ladies. Phila., Lippincott, 1928.
217. YOST, KARL. A bibliography of the works of Edna St. Vincent Millay. With an essay in appreciation by Harold Lewis Cook. N. Y., Harper, 1937.
218. ZOLA, EMILE. Ein Brief an Dr. Laupts über die Frage der Homosexualität Jahrb. sex. Zwisch. 7:371-84, 1905.

C. SCIENTIFIC AND PSYCHIATRIC MATERIAL

(Exclusively male studies included for references to etiology)
*—seen only in abstract.

1. ADLER, ALFRED. Das Problem der Homosexualität. Leipzig, Hirzel, 1930.
2. ——. Zum Thema: sexuelle Perversionen. Int. Ztschr. individ. Psychol. 10:401-409, 1932.
3. ALLEN, CLIFFORD. The sexual perversions and abnormalities. Lond., Oxford, 1940.
4. ALLEN, F. H. Homosexuality in relation to the problem of human differences. Amer. J. Orthopsychiat. 10:129-36, 1940.
5. ALLPORT, GORDON. Personality: a psychological interpretation. N. Y., Holt, 1937.
6. "Anomaly." The invert and his social adjustment. Balto., Williams & Wilkins, 1929.
7. BACK, GEORG. Sexuelle Verirrungen des Menschen und der Natur. Berlin, Standard, 1910. 2v.
8. BARAHAL, H. S. Constitutional factors in male homosexuals. Psychiat. Q. 13:391-400, 1939.
9. *——. Testosterone in psychotic male homosexuals. Psychiat. Q. 14:319-29, 1940.

10. BAUR, JULIUS. Homosexuality as an endocrinological, psychological and genetic problem. J. Crim. Psychopathol, 2:188-97, 1940.

11. BENDER, LAURETTA & PASTER, SAMUEL. Homosexual trends in children. Amer, J. Orthopsychiat. 10:730-44, 1941.

12. BENEDEK, THERESE. Psychosexual functions in women. N. Y., Ronald, 1952.

13. —— & RUBENSTEIN, BORIS. The sexual cycle in women . . . National Research Council, 1942.

14. BERGLER, EDMUND. The basic neurosis . . . N. Y., Grune & Stratton, 1949.

15. ——. Eight prerequisites for psychoanalytic treatment of homosexuality. Psychoan. Rev. 31:353-86, 1944.

16. ——. Lesbianism, facts and fiction. Marr. . . . Hyg. 1:197-202, 1948.

17. ——. Neurotic counterfeit sex . . . N. Y., Grune & Stratton, 1951.

18. ——. The present situation in genetic investigation of homosexuality. Marr. Hyg. 4:16-29, 1937.

19. ——. The respective importance of reality and fantasy in the genesis of female homosexuality. J. Crim. Psychopathol. 5:27-48, 1943.

20. ——. The writer and psychoanalysis. N. Y., Doubleday, 1950.

21. *——. Kinsey's myth of female sexuality. N. Y., Grune & Stratton, 1954.

22. BESTERMAN, THEODORE. Men versus women: a study of sexual relations. Lond., Methuen, 1934.

23. BLANCHARD, PHYLLIS & MANASSES, CAROLYN. New girls for old. N. Y., Macaulay, 1930.

24. BLOCH, IWAN. Anthropological studies in the strange sexual practices of all races in all ages . . . N. Y., Anthropological Press, 1933.

25. BLOCH, IWAN. Der Ursprung der Syphilis. Jena, G. Fischer, 1911.

26. BONAPARTE, MARIE. Female sexuality. N. Y., International Universities Press, 1953.

27. BOURGET, PAUL. Physiologie de l'amour moderne. Paris, Crès, 1918.

28. BRACHFELD, OLIVER. Sexuelle Lebensschwerigkeiten. Int. Ztschr. individ. Psychol. 8:142-151, 1930.

29. BRIERLEY, MARJORIE. Specific determinants in feminine development. Int. J. Psychoanal. 17:163-80, 1936.

30. BRILL, A. A. Homoerotism and paranoia. Amer. J. Psychiat. 13:957-74, 1934.

31. ——. Sexual manifestations in neurotic and psychotic symptoms. Psychiat. Q. 14:9-16, 1940.

32. BRODY, M. W. Analysis of the psychosexual development of the female, with special reference to homosexuality. Psychoan. Rev. 30:47-58, 1943.
33. BROMLEY, DOROTHY D. & BRITTEN, FLORENCE E. Youth and sex: a study of 1300 college students. N. Y., Harper, 1938.
34. BROSTER, L. H. et al. The adrenal cortex and intersexuality. Lond., Chapman, 1938.
35. BROWNE, F. W. STELLA. Studies in feminine inversion. J. Sexol. & Psychoan. 1:51-58, 1923.
36. BRUNON, ROGER. L'inversion est-elle un snobisme? Med. Variétés 68:245; annexe:iv-v, 1928.
37. BURGESS, E. W. & COTTRELL, L. S. Predicting success or failure in marriage. N. Y., Prentice-Hall, 1939.
38. *BRYAN, D. Bisexuality. Int. J. Psychoan. 11:150-166, 1930.
39. BUTTERFIELD, O. L. Love problems of adolescence. N. Y., Emerson, 1939.
40. CAPRIO, FRANK. Female homosexuality. N. Y., Citadel Press, 1954.
41. CARPENTER, EDWARD. The intermediate sex. N. Y., Kennerly, 1912.
42. ———. Intermediate types among primitive folk. N. Y., Kennerly, 1914.
43. ———. Love's coming of age. N. Y., Kennerly, 1911.
44. *CASAN, V. S. El amor lesbio. ed. 8. Barcelona, 1896.
45. CASE, IRENE & SHERMAN, MANDEL. The factor of personal attachment in homosexuality. Psychoan, Rev. 13:32-37, 1925.
46. CAWADIAS, A. P. Hermaphroditos: the human intersex. Lond., Heinemann, 1943.
47. CHESSER, EUSTACE. Sexual behavior, normal and abnormal. N. Y., Roy, 1949.
48. CHIDECKEL, MAURICE. Female sex perversions . . . N. Y., Eugenics Publishing Co., 1935.
49. CLENDENING, LOGAN. Love and happiness: intimate problems of the modern woman. N. Y., Knopf, 1938.
50. COLLINS, JOSEPH. The doctor looks at love and life. N. Y., Garden City, 1929.
51. CORFAT, I. H. Homosexuality, its psychogenesis and treatment. N. Y. Med. J. 97:589-94, 1913.
52. CORRÉ, ARMAND. L'ethnographie criminelle . . . Paris, Reinwald, [1894].
53. COSTLER, A. et al. Encyclopedia of sexual knowledge. N. Y., Coward-McCann, 1934.
54. CURRAN, DESMOND. Homosexuality. Practitioner 141:280-87, 1938.
55. DAUTHENDEY, ELISABETH. Die urnische Frage und die Frau. Jahrb. sex. Zwisch. 8:285-99, 1906.

56. DAVIS, KATHERINE B. Factors in the sex life of 2,200 women. N. Y., Harper, 1929.
47. ———. The periodicity of sex desire. Amer. J. Obstet & Gyn. 14:345-60, 1927.
58. DEUTSCH, HELENE. Homosexuality in women. Psychoan. Q. 1:484-510, 1932.
59. ———. Psychology of women. v. 1. N. Y., Grune & Stratton, 1944.
60. DEVEREUX, GEORGE. Institutionalized homosexuality of the Mojave Indians. Human Biol. 9:498-527, 1937.
61. ——— & MOOS, M. C. Social structure of prisons and the organic tensions. J. Crim. Psychopathol. 4:306-24, 1942.
62. DICKINSON, R. L. & BEAM, LURA. One thousand marriages: a study of sex adjustments. Balto., Williams & Wilkins, 1931.
63. ———. The single woman: a medical study in sex education. Balto, Williams, 1934.
64. DICKS, G. H. & CHILDERS, A. T. Social transformation of a boy who lived his first fourteen years as a girl. J. Psychol. 18:125-30, 1944.
65. DUNBAR, FLANDERS. Emotions and bodily changes. N. Y., Columbia Univ. Press, 1938.
66. ———. Mind and body: psychosomatic medicine. N. Y., Random, 1947.
67. EAST, W. N. Sexual offenders (In: Mental abnormality and crime. Lond., Macmillan, 1944. Ch. 9.)
68. ELIASBERG, W. The closeup of psychosexual gratification. J. Nerv. & Ment. Disease. 99:179-196, 1944.
69. ELLIS, ALBERT. Sexual psychology of the human hermaphrodite. Psychosom. Med. 7:108-25, 1945.
70. ———. The folklore of sex. N. Y., Boni, 1951.
71. ELLIS, HAVELOCK. Sexual inversion in women. Alienist & Neurologist 16:141-58, 1895.
72. ———. Studies in the psychology of sex. N. Y., Random, 7v. in 2, 1940.
73. FENICHEL, OTTO. Outline of clinical psychology. N. Y., Norton, 1934.
74. ———. The psychology of transvestism. Int. J. Psychoan. 11:211-27, 1930.
75. FÉRÉ, C. S. Social and esoteric studies of sexual degeneration in mankind and in animals. N. Y., Anthropological Press, 1932.
76. -FIELDING, WILLIAM J. Sex and the love life. N. Y., Dodd, 1927.
77. FINESINGER, J. E. et al. Clinical, psychiatric and psychoanalytic study of a case of male pseudohermaphroditism. Amer. J. Obstet & Gynec. 44:310-17, 1942.
78. FLUGEL, J. C. A hundred years of psychology. N. Y., Macmillan, 1933.

79. FORD, C. A. Homosexual practices of institutionalized females. J. Abnorm. Psych. 23:442-48, 1929.
80. FORD, C. S. & BEACH, FRANK A. Patterns of sexual behavior. N. Y., Harper, 1951.
81. FOREL, A. H. The sexual question. N. Y., Medical Art Agency, 1922.
82. FREUD, SIGMUND. The basic writings of . . . N. Y., Modern Library, 1938.
83. ———. Certain neurotic mechanisms in jealousy, paranoia, and homosexuality. Int. J. Phychoan. 4:1-10, 1923.
84. ———. Psychogenesis of a case of female homosexuality. Int. J. Psychoan. 1:125, 1920.
85. FRIEDMANN, A. Beitrag zur pädagogischen Menschenkenntnis. Int. Ztschr. individ. Psychol. 7:129-43, 1929.
86. *FROMM, ERIKA & ELONEN, ANNA. Projective techniques in the study of a case of female homosexuality. J. Project. Tech. 15:185-230, 1951.
87. GALLICHAN, WALTER. The great unmarried. N. Y., Stokes, 1916.
88. ———. The poison of prudery; an historical survey. Bost., Stratford, 1929.
89. GATES, R. R. Human genetics. N. Y., Macmillan, 1946.
90. *GEISE, HANS. Zur Psychopathologie der homosexuellen Partnerwahl. Jahrb. Psychol. Psychother. 1:223-25, 1953.
91. GILBERT, J. A. Homosexuality and its treatment. J. Nerv. & Ment. Dis. 52:297-322, 1920.
92. GOLDSCHMIDT, R. Intersexualität und menschliches Zwittertum. Deutsch. med. Woch. 30:1288-92, 1931.
93. GRANT, V. W. A major problem of human sexuality. J. Soc. Psychol. 28:79-101, 1948.
94. ———. Preface to a psychology of sexual attachment. J. Soc. Psychol. 33:187-208, 1951.
95. GREENSPAN, HERBERT & CAMPBELL, J. D. The homosexual as a personality. Amer. J. Psychiat. 101:682-89, 1945.
96. GROVES, ERNEST. Marriage. N. Y., Holt, 1933.
97. ———, & GROVES, GLADYS. Sex in childhood. N. Y., Macaulay, 1933.
98. GUYON, RENÉ. The ethics of sexual acts. N. Y., Knopf, 1948.
99. ———. Sexual freedom. Lond., Lane, 1939.
100. HALL, W. S. & WINTER, JEANNETTE. Girlhood and its problems . . . Phila., Winston, 1919.
101. HAMILTON, D. M. Some aspects of homosexuality in relation to total personality development. Psychiat. Q. 13:229-44, 1939.
102. HAMILTON, G. V. A research in marriage. N. Y., Boni, 1929.
103. HAMMER, WILHELM. Die Tribadie Berlins. Berlin, Seemann Nachfolger, 1906.

104. ——. Uber gleichgeschlechtliche Frauenliebe mit besondere Berücksichtigung der Frauenbewegung. Monatschr. f. Harnskr. u. sex. Hyg. 4:395-405, 439-447, 1907.

105. Harvard University Psychological Clinic. Explorations in personality . . . N. Y., Oxford, University Press, 1938.

106. HENNESSEY, M. A. R. Homosexual charges against children. J. Crim. Psychopathol. 2:524-32, 1941.

107. HENRY, G. W. and GALBREATH, H. M. Constitutional factors in homosexuality. Amer. J. Psychiat. n.s. 13:1249-70, 1934.

108. HENRY, G. W. The homosexual delinquent. Ment. Hyg. 25:420-42, 1941.

109. ——. Psychogenic and constitutional factors in homosexuality. Psychiat. Q. 8:243-64, 1934.

110. ——. Psychogenic factors in overt homosexuality. Amer. J. Psychiat. 93:889-908, 1937.

111. ——. Sex variants: a study of homosexual patterns. N. Y., Hoeber, 1941. 2v.

112. —— & GROSS, A. A. Social factors in case histories of 100 underprivileged homosexuals. Ment. Hyg. 22:591-611, 1938.

113. HESNARD, A. L. M. Psychologie homosexuelle. Paris, Stock, 1929.

114. ——. Strange lust: the psychology of homosexuality. N. Y., Amethnol Press, 1933.

115. HILL, W. W. Status of hermaphrodite and transvestite in Navaho culture. Amer. Anthrop. 37:273-79, 1935.

116. HINKLE, BEATRICE. On the arbitrary use of the terms masculine and feminine. Psychoan. Rev. 7:15-30, 1919.

117. HINSIE, LELAND. Concepts and problems of psychotherapy. N. Y., Columbia University Press, 1937.

118. [HIRSCHFELD, MAGNUS]. Numa Praetorius. Die Homosexualität in dem romanischen Ländern. Sex. Probleme, 5:183-203, 1909.

119. HIRSCHFELD, MAGNUS. Die objektive Diagnose der Homosexualität. Jahrb. sex. Zwisch. 4:35, 1899.

120. ——. Sexual pathology: being a study of the abnormalities of the sexual function. Newark, Julian Press, 1932.

121. ——. Die Transvestiten; eine Untersuchung über den erotischen Verkleidungstreib . . . Berlin, Pulvermacher, 1910.

122. ——. Le troisième sexe; les homosexuels de Berlin. Paris, Rousset, 1908.

123. HODANN, MAX. History of modern morals. Lond., Heinemann, 1937.

124. HOFFMANN, M. H. Intersexual manifestations of non-endocrine origin. Journal-Lancet 62:446-49, 1942.

125. HORNEY, KAREN. Flight from womanhood; masculinity complex in women, as viewed by men and by women. Int. J. Psychoan. 7:324-39, 1926.

126. ———. The neurotic personality of our time. N. Y., Norton, 1937.
127. ———. On the genesis of the castration complex in women. Int.
       J. Psychoan. 5:50-65, 1924.
128. HORTON, C. B. & CLARKE, E. K. Transvestism or eonism. Amer.
       J. Psychiat. 10:1025-1030, 1931.
129. HOWARD, W. L. Effeminate men and masculine women. N. Y.,
       Med. J. 71:686, 1900.
130. HURLOCK, E. B. and KLEIN, E. R. Adolescent crushes. Child
       Devel. 5:63, 1934.
131. HUSTED, H. H. Personality and sex conflicts. N. Y., McBride,
       1952.
132. HUXLEY, ALDOUS. Do what you will, and other essays. N. Y.,
       Doubleday, 1930.
133. HUTTON, LAURA. The single woman and her emotional problems.
       Balt., Wood, 1935.
134. IOVETZ-TERESCHENKO, N. M. Friendship-love in adolescence.
       Lond., Allen & Unwin, 1936.
135. "JACOBUS, X." Crossways of sex: a study in erotic pathology.
       N. Y., American Anthropological Society, 1935.
136. ———. Untrodden fields of anthropology . . . Paris, Carrington,
       1898.
137. JASTROW, JOSEPH. Character and temperament. N. Y., Appleton,
       1915.
138. JOHNSON, WENDELL. People in quandaries: the semantics of per-
       sonal adjustment. N. Y., Harper, 1946.
139. JOHNSON, WINIFRED, et al. Highlights in the literature of sex
       differences published since 1920. Psych. Bull. 36:569, 1939.
       [Precis of paper read at American Psychological Assoc. 47th
       annual meeting].
140. JONAS, C. H. An objective approach to personality and environ-
       ment in homosexuality. Psychiat. Q. 18:626-41, 1944.
141. JONES, ERNEST. Early development of female sexuality. Int. J.
       Psychoan. 8:459-72, 1927.
142. JONES, WILLIAM. Fox texts. Amer. Ethnol. Soc. Publications
       1:51-52, 1907.
143. JOUX, OTTO DE. Die hellenische Liebe in der Gegenwart. Leipzig,
       Spohr, 1897.
144. JUNG, C. G. Psychology of the unconscious. N. Y., Dodd, Mead,
       1925.
145. KAHN, SAMUEL. Mentality and homosexuality. Bost., Meador,
       1937.
146. KALLMANN, FRANZ J. Heredity and health in mental disorder . . .
       N. Y., Norton, 1953.
147. ———. Modern concepts of genetics in relation to mental health
       and abnormal personality development. Psychiat. Q. 21:535-
       53, 1947.

148. KARDINER, ABRAM. Sex and morality. N. Y., Bobbs Merrill, 1954.
149. KARSCH, F. Uranismus oder Päderastie und Tribadie bei den Naturvölkern. Jahrb. sex. Zwisch. 3:72-201, 1901.
150. *KEISER, SYLVAN and SCHAFFER, DORA. Environmental factors in homosexuality in adolescent girls. Psychoan. Rev. 36:383-95, 1949.
151. KIERNAN, J. G. Sexology [current notes] Urol. & Cutan. Rev. 18:550, 1914.
152. KINSEY, A. C. Homosexuality: criteria for hormonal explanation of the homosexual. J. Clin. Endocrinol. 1:424-28, 1941.
153. ———. Sexual behavior in the human female. Phila., Saunders, 1953.
154. ———. Sexual behavior in the human male. Phila., Saunders, 1948.
155. KNIGHT, R. P. Relationship of latent homosexuality to the mechanism of paranoid delusions. Bull. Menninger Clin. 4:149-59, 1940.
156. KNOPF, OLGA. The art of being a woman. Bost., Little, 1932.
157. *KOUVER, B. J. Die sociale waardering van die sexuele inversie. Nederl. Tjdschr. Psychol. 7:364-78, 1952.
158. KRAFFT-EBING, RICHARD VON. Psychopathia sexualis. Brooklyn, N. Y., Physicians & Surgeons Publishing Co., 1935.
159. KRETSCHMER, ERNST. Physique and character. New York, Harcourt, 1925.
160. KRICH, A. M., ed. Women; the variety and meaning of their sexual experience. N. Y., Dell, 1953.
161. LAIDLAW, R. N. A clinical approach to homosexuality. Marr. & Fam. Living 14:39-45, 1952.
162. LANDES, RUTH. Cult matriarchate and male homosexuality. J. Abnorm. & Soc. Psych. 35:386-397, 1940.
163. LANDIS, CARNEY, et al. Sex in development: a study . . . of 153 normal women and 142 female psychiatric patients. N. Y., Hoeber, 1940.
164. *LANG, THEODOR. [Genetic factors in homosexuality] Ztschr. Ges. Neurol. & Psychiat. 155:702-13, 1936.
165. *———. [. . . further studies] ibid. 157:557-74, 1937.
166. *———. [Short methodological remarks on my work on genetic theory] ibid. 160:804-09, 1938.
167. *———. [Genetic factors in homosexuality] Dritter Beitrag. ibid. 162:627-45, 1938.
168. *———. Ergebnisse neuer Untersuchungen zum Problem der Homosexualität. Monatschr. Krim. Biol 30:401-13, 1939.
169. *———. [Hereditary conditioning of homosexuality and basic significance of research on intersexuality for human genetics] Allgem. Ztschr. Psychiat. 112:237-54, 1939.
170. *———. Vierter Beitrag zur Frage nach der genetische Bedingheit

der Homosexualität. Zeitschr. Ges. Neurol. & Psychiat. 166:255-70, 1939.

171. *———. Weitere methodologische Bemerkung zu meiner Arbeiten über die genetische Bedingheit der Homosexualität. ibid. 169:567-75, 1940.

172. *———. Fünfter Beitrag zur Frage nach der genetische Bedingheit der Homosexualität. ibid. 170:663-71, 1940.

173. ———. Studies in the genetic determination of homosexuality. J. Nerv. & Ment. Disease 92:55-64, 1940.

174. *———. Erbbiologische Untersuchungen über die Entstehung der Homosexualität. Med. Wochenschr. 88:961-65, 1941.

175. *———. Untersuchungen an männlichen Homosexuellen und deren Sippschaften mit besondere Berücksichtung dere Frage des Zusammenhangs zwischen Homosexualität und Psychose. ibid. 171:651-79, 1941.

176. *LAYCOCK, S. R. Homosexuality: a mental hygiene problem. Canad. Med. Assoc. J. 63:245-50, 1950.

177. LELAND, C. G. The alternate sex, or female intellect in man and the masculine in woman. N. Y., Funk & Wagnalls, 1904.

178. LEUBA, J. Hermès ou Aphrodite? Le côté biologique du problème. Rev. Franç. Psychoan. 8:194-207, 1935.

179. LEVETSOW, KARL VON. Louise Michel. Jahrb. sex. Zwisch. 7:307-70, 1905.

180. LICHTENSTEIN, P. M. The "fairy" and the "lady lover." Med. Rev. of Revs. 27: 369-74, 1921.

181. ——— and SMALL, S. M. Handbook of psychiatry. N. Y., Norton, 1943.

182. *LIEBIG, C. Die Frau als Ehemann. Krim. Monatsheft 9:131-33, 1935.

183. LOMBROSO, CESAR, & FERRERO, WILLIAM. The female offender. London, Unwin, 1895.

184. LONDON, L. S. Psychosexual pathology of transvestism. Urol. & Cutan. Rev. 37: 600-04, 1933.

185. LORAND, SANDOR. Perverse tendencies and fantasies: their influence on personality. Psychoan. Rev. 26:178-90, 1939.

186. LOWIE, G. H. The Assiniboine. Amer. Mus. Nat. Hist. Anthropol. Papers 4:223, 1909.

187. LUCKA, EMIL. The evolution of love. Lond., Allen & Unwin, 1922.

188. LYDSTON, F. The biochemical basis of sex aberrations. Urol. & Cutan. Rev. 23:384, 1919.

189. McDOUGALL, WILLIAM. Introduction to social psychology. Bost., Luce, 1912.

190. McHENRY, F. A. A note on homosexuality, crime, and the newspapers. J. Crim. Psychopathol. 2:533-48, 1941.

191. McKINNON, JANE. The homosexual woman. Amer. J. Psychiat. 103:661-65, 1947.

192. McMurtrie, Douglas. Legend of lesbian love among North American Indians. Urol. & Cutan. Rev. 18:192-93, 1914.
193. ——. Manifestations of sexual inversion in the female . . . ibid. 18:424-26, 1914.
194. ——. Principles of homosexuality and sexual inversion in the female. Amer. J. Urol. 9:144-53, 1913.
195. ——. Record of a French case of feminine sexual inversion. Maryland Med. J. 57:179-81, 1914.
196. ——. Sexual inversion among women in Spain. Urol. & Cutan. Rev. 18:308, 1914.
197. ——. Sexually inverted infatuation in a middle-aged woman. ibid. 18:601, 1914.
198. ——. Some observations on the psychology of sexual inversion in women. Amer. J. Urol. 9:38-45, 1913.
199. Malinowski, Bronislaw. Sex and repression in savage society. N. Y., Harcourt, 1927.
200. Mantegazza, Paolo. The sexual relations of mankind. N. Y., Eugenics Publ. Co., 1936.
201. Markey, B. & Noble, H. An evaluation of the masculinity factor in boarding-home situations. Amer. J. Orthopsychiat. 6:2, 1936.
202. Martineau, Louis. Leçons sur les déformations vulvaires et anales par la masturbation, le saphisme, la défloration et la sodomie. Paris, Delahaye, 1884.
203. Mauclair, Camille. De l'amour physique. Paris, Ollendorff, 1912.
204. Mead, Margaret. Male and female. N. Y., Morrow, 1950.
205. ——. Sex and temperament in three primitive societies. N. Y., Morrow, 1939.
206. Meagher, J. F. W. Homosexuality: its psychobiological and pathological significance. Urol. & Cutan. Rev. 33:505-18, 1929.
207. Menninger, K. A. Somatic correlations with the unconscious repudiation of femininity in women. J. Nerv. & Ment. Disease 89:514-27, 1939.
208. Merzbach, H. Homosexualität und Beruf. Jahrb. sex. Zwisch. 4:187-98, 1902.
209. Meyer, J. J. Sexual life in ancient India. N. Y., Dutton, 1930. 2v.
210. Modern attitudes in psychiatry. N. Y., Columbia University Press, 1946.
211. Moll, Albert. Handbuch der Sexualwissenschaft. Leipzig. Vogel, 1912.
212. ——. Libido sexualis . . . N. Y., American Ethnological Press, 1933.
213. ——. Les perversions de l'instinct génital . . . Paris, Carre, 1893.
214. ——. Perversions of the sexual instinct. Newark, N. J., Julian Press, 1931.
215. ——. The sexual life of the child. N. Y., Macmillan, 1912.

216. MONAHAN, FLORENCE. Women in crime. N. Y., Ives Washburn,
     1941.
217. *MÜLLER, F. C. Ein weiterer Fall von conträrer sexual Empfin-
     dung. Friedrichs Blät. f. Gerichtl. Med. 4; 1891.
218. MÜLLER-FREIENFELS, RICHARD. The evolution of modern psy-
     chology. New Haven, Conn., Yale Univ. Press, 1935.
219. *NEDONIA, KAREL. Homosexuality in sexological practice. Int.
     J. Sexol. 4:219-24, 1951.
220. NEUGEBAUER, FRANZ VON. Zusamenstellung der Literatur über
     Hermaphroditismus beim Menschen . . . Jahrb. sex. Zwisch.
     7 (1) :471-670, 1905.
221. NEUSTADT, R. & MYERSON, A. Quantitative sex hormone studies
     in homosexuality, childhood, and various disturbances. Amer.
     J. Psychiat. 47:524-51, 1940.
222. NIEMOLLER, A. F. American encyclopedia of sex. N. Y., Panurge
     Press, 1935.
223. NUNBERG, H. Homosexuality, magic and aggression. Int. J. Psy-
     choanal. 19:15, 1938.
224. OBERNDORF, C. P. Diverse forms of homosexuality. Urol. & Cutan.
     Rev. 33:518-22, 1929.
225. OPHUIJSEN, J. H. W. VAN. Contributions to masculinity complex
     in women. Int. J. Psychoanal. 5:39-49, 1924.
226. OWENSBY, N. M. Homosexuality and lesbianism treated with
     metrazol. J. Nerv. & Ment. Disease 29:65-66, 1940.
227. PAGE, J. & WERKENTIN, J. Masculinity and paranoia. J. abnorm.
     & soc. Psychol. 33:527-31, 1938.
228. PARENT-DUCHÂTELET, A. J. De la prostitution dans la ville de
     Paris. Paris, J. B. Baillière, 1857. 2v.
229. PARKE, J. R. Human sexuality. Phila., Professional Publ. Co.,
     1906.
230. PERLOFF, W. H. The role of the hormones in human sexuality.
     Psychosom. Med. 11:133-39, 1949.
231. PLANT, J. S. Personality and the cultural pattern. N. Y., Com-
     monwealth Fund, 1937.
232. PLOSS, D. H. & BARTELS, MAX. Das Weib in der Natur- und
     Völkerkunde. Leipzig, Grieben, 1905. 2v.
233. *POE, J. S. Successful treatment of a . . . homosexual based on
     the adaptational view of sexual behavior. Psychoanal. Rev.
     39:23-33, 1952.
234. POTTER, LAFOREST. Strange loves; a study in sexual abnormali-
     ties. N. Y., Dodsley, 1937.
235. Problems of sexual behavior. N. Y., American Social Hygiene
     Assoc., 1948.
236. REIK, THEODOR. A psychologist looks at love. N. Y., Rinehart,
     1944.
237. ——. The psychology of sexual relations. N. Y., Rinehart, 1945.

238. REISS, MAX. The role of sex hormones in psychiatry. J. Ment. Science 86:787-90, 1940.
239. RHEINE, THEODOR VON. Die lesbische Liebe. . . . Berlin, Aris & Ahrens, 1933.
240. RIGGALL, R. M. Homosexuality and alcoholism. Psychoanal. Rev. 10:157-69, 1923.
241. *ROBIE, T. R. Oedipus and homosexual complexes in schizophrenia. Psychiat. Q. 1:468-84, 1927.
242. ROBINSON, VICTOR, ed. Encyclopedia sexualis. N. Y., Dingwall-Rock, 1936.
243. ROBINSON, W. R. America's sex and marriage problems. N. Y., Eugenics Publ. Co., 1928.
244. ROHLEDER, H. Die Homosexualität: eine biologische Variation oder eine Krankheit? Jahrb. sex. Zwisch. 22:3-4, 16-21, 1922.
245. ROSANOFF, A. J. Human sexuality, normal and abnormal, from a psychiatric standpoint. Urol. & Cutan. Rev. 33:523-30, 1929.
246. ROSENZWEIG, S. An hypothesis regarding cycles of behavior in a schizophrenic patient. Psychiat. Q. 16:463-68, 1942.
247. RUDOLPH, G. DE M. Experimental effect of sex hormone therapy upon anxiety in homosexual types. Brit. J. Med. Psychol. 18:317-22, 1941.
248. RÜLING, ANNA. Welches Interesse hat die Frauenbewegung an der Lösung des Homosexuellen Probleme? Jahrb. sex. Zwisch. 7:131-51, 1905.
249. SCHMALHAUSEN, S. D. & CALVERTON, V. F., ed. Woman's coming of age; a symposium. N. Y., Liveright, 1931.
250. SCHWARTZ, OSWALD. Uber Homosexualität. Leipzig, Thieme, 1931.
251. *———. Zur Psychologie des Welterlebens und der Fremdheit: 2. Uber die weibliche Homosexualität. Ztschr. Ges. Neurol. & Psychiat. 143:478-505, 1933.
252. SELLING, L. S. The pseudo family. Amer. J. Sociol. 37:247-53, 1931.
253. SELTZER, C. C. Relationship between masculine components and personality. Amer. J. Phys. Anthropol. 32:33-47, 1945.
254. SHELDON, W. H. Varieties of human physique. N. Y., Harper, 1940.
255. ———. Varieties of human temperament. N. Y., Harper, 1942.
256. SILVERMAN, DANIEL, & ROSANOFF, W. R. Electro-encephalographic and neurological studies of homosexuals. J. Nerv. & Ment. Disease 101:311-21, 1945.
257. SMITH, S. Age and sex differences in children's opinion concerning sex differences. J. Genet. Psychol. 54:17-25, 1939.
258. SPRAGUE, G. S. Varieties of homosexual manifestations. Amer. J. Psychiat. 92:143-54, 1935.

259. STEINACH, EUGEN. Sex and life; forty years of biological and medical experiments. N. Y., Viking, 1940.
260. STEKEL, WILHELM. Bi-sexual love. Milwaukee, Caspar, 1933.
261. ——. Die Geschlechtskälte der Frau. Berlin, Urban, 1927.
262. ——. Is homosexuality curable? Psychoanal. Rev. 17:443-51, 1930.
263. ——. The homosexual neurosis. N. Y., Physicians & Surgeons Book Co., 1935.
264. STRAIN, FRANCES. The normal sex interests of children from infancy to adolescence. N. Y., Appleton-Century, 1948.
265. STRAKOSCH, FRANCES M. Factors in the sex life of seven hundred psychopathic women. Utica, N. Y., Hospitals Press, 1934.
266. STRECKER, E. A. Fundamentals of psychiatry. Phila., Lippincott, 1943.
267. SYMONDS, J. A. A problem in Greek ethics. Lond., priv. print., 1908.
268. ——. A problem in modern ethics. Lond., [priv. print.], 1896.
269. TALMEY, BERNARD. Love: a treatise on the science of sex attraction. N. Y., Practitioners Publ. Co., 1919.
270. TARNOVSKI, V. M. L'instinct sexuel et ses manifestations morbides. Paris, Carrington, 1904.
271. ——. Anthropological, legal and medical studies of pederasty in Europe. N. Y., Falstaff Press, 1933.
272. TENNENBAUM, JOSEPH. The riddle of woman: a study in the social psychology of sex. N. Y., Lee Furman, 1936.
273. TERMAN, L. M. & MILES, CATHERINE C. Sex and personality: studies in masculinity and feminity. N. Y., McGraw Hill, 1936.
274. THOM, D. A. Normal youth and its everyday problems. N. Y., Appleton, 1932.
275. THOMPSON, C. J. S. Mysteries of sex: women who posed as men and men who impersonated women. Lond., Hutchinson, 1938.
276. THOMPSON, CLARA. Changing aspects of homosexuality in psychoanalysis. Psychiatry 10:183-89, 1947.
277. THORPE, L. P. Psychological foundations of personality. N. Y., McGraw Hill, 1938.
278. [ULRICHS, KARL]. Numa Numantius. Vindex; Inclusa, 1864; Vindicta; Formatrix; Ara spei, 1865; Gladius furens, 1867; Memnon I, II, 1868; Incubus; Argonauticus, 1869; Prometheus; Araxis, 1870. [All privately printed.]
279. VELIKOWSKY, I. Tolstoy's Kreutzer Sonata and unconscious homosexuality. Psychoanal. Rev. 24:18-25, 1937.
280. VORONOFF, SERGE. Rejuvenation by grafting. Lond., Allen, Unwin, 1925.
281. ——. The study of old age and my method of rejuvenation. Lond., Gill, 1928.
282. WATSON, JOHN. Psychological care of infant and child. N. Y., Norton, 1928.

283. WEINDEL, HENRI DE. L'homosexualité en Allemagne. Paris, C. Juven, 1908.
284. WEININGER, OTTO. Sex and character. N. Y., Putnam, 1906.
285. WESTERMARCK, E. Homosexualität. Sex-Probleme 4:248-80, 1908.
286. WESTPHAL, C. VON. Die conträre Sexualempfindung. Archiv. f. Psychiat. & Nervenkrankh. 2 (1) :73-108, 1869.
287. WHITE, LYNN. Educating our daughters. N. Y., Harper, 1950.
288. WHITE, W. A. Twentieth century psychiatry: its contribution to man's knowledge of himself. N. Y., Norton, 1936.
289. WILE, I. S. Sex life of the unmarried adult. . . . N. Y., Vanguard, 1934.
290. *WINNER, ALBERTINE L. Homosexuality in women. Med. Praxis. 217:219-220, 1947.
291. WITSCHI, E. & MENGERT, W. F. Endocrine studies on human hermaphrodites and their bearing on the interpretation of homosexuality. J. Clin. Endocrin. 2:279-86, 1942.
292. WITTELS, FRITZ. Mona Lisa and feminine beauty. Int. J. Psychoanal. 15:25-40, 1934.
293. ———. Motherhood and bisexuality. Psychoanal. Rev. 21:180-93, 1934.
294. ———. The position of the psychopath in the psychoanalytic system. Int. J. Psychoanal. 19:471-88, 1938.
295. WORTIS, JOSEPH. Intersexuality and effeminacy in the male homosexual. Amer. J. Orthopsychiat. 10:567, 1940.
296. WRIGHT, C. A. Endocrine aspects of homosexuality; further studies. Med. Record 147:449-52, 1938.
297. WULFFEN, ERICH. Woman as a sexual criminal. N. Y., American Ethnological Press, 1934.
298. YARROS, RACHELLE S. Modern woman and sex: a feminist physician speaks. N. Y., Vanguard, 1933.
299. YAWGER, N. S. Transvestism and other cross-sex manifestations. J. Nerv. & Ment. Disease 42:41-48, 1940.
300. YOUNG, KIMBALL. Personality and problems of adjustment. N. Y., Crofts, 1940.
301. ZILBOORG, GREGORY. A history of psychiatric medicine. N. Y., Norton, 1941.
302. ———. Masculine and feminine: biological and cultural aspects. Psychiatry 7:257-296, 1944.
303. ———. Mind, medicine and man. N. Y., Harcourt, 1943.
304. *ZIMMERLEIN, K. Verschämte "lesbische" Liebe als Brandstiftmotiv. Krim. Monatsch. 7:112-113, 1933.

INDEX

420

Sex Variant Women in Literature

Against the Season by Jane Rule. A novel. 224 pp.
ISBN 0-930044-48-7 $7.95

Lovers in the Present Afternoon by Kathleen Fleming. A novel.
288 pp. ISBN 0-930044-46-0 $8.50

Toothpick House by Lee Lynch. A novel. 264 pp.
ISBN 0-930044-45-2 $7.95

Madame Aurora by Sarah Aldridge. A novel. 256 pp.
ISBN 0-930044-44-4 $7.95

Curious Wine by Katherine V. Forrest. A novel. 176 pp.
ISBN 0-930044-43-6 $7.50

Black Lesbian in White America by Anita Cornwell. Short stories,
essays, autobiography. 144 pp. ISBN 0-930044-41-X $7.50

Contract with the World by Jane Rule. A novel. 340 pp.
ISBN 0-930044-28-2 $7.95

Yantras of Womanlove by Tee A. Corinne. Photographs.
64 pp. ISBN 0-930044-30-4 $6.95

Mrs. Porter's Letter by Vicki P. McConnell. A mystery novel.
224 pp. ISBN 0-930044-29-0 $6.95

To the Cleveland Station by Carol Anne Douglas. A novel.
192 pp. ISBN 0-930044-27-4 $6.95

The Nesting Place by Sarah Aldridge. A novel. 224 pp.
ISBN 0-930044-26-6 $6.95

This Is Not for You by Jane Rule. A novel. 284 pp.
ISBN 0-930044-25-8 $7.95

Faultline by Sheila Ortiz Taylor. A novel. 140 pp.
ISBN 0-930044-24-X $6.95

The Lesbian in Literature by Barbara Grier. 3d ed. Foreword by
Maida Tilchen. A comprehensive bibliography. 240 pp.
ISBN 0-930044-23-1 $7.95

Anna's Country by Elizabeth Lang. A novel. 208 pp.
ISBN 0-930044-19-3 $6.95

Prism by Valerie Taylor. A novel. 158 pp.
ISBN 0-930044-18-5 $6.95

Black Lesbians: An Annotated Bibliography compiled by
J. R. Roberts. Foreword by Barbara Smith. 112 pp.
ISBN 0-930044-21-5 $5.95

The Marquise and the Novice by Victoria Ramstetter. A novel.
108 pp. ISBN 0-930044-16-9 $4.95

Labiaflowers by Tee A. Corinne. 40 pp.
ISBN 0-930044-20-7 $3.95

Outlander by Jane Rule. Short stories, essays. 207 pp.
ISBN 0-930044-17-7 $6.95

Sapphistry: The Book of Lesbian Sexuality by Pat Califia. 2nd
edition, revised. 195 pp. ISBN 0-930044-47-9 $7.95

All True Lovers by Sarah Aldridge. A novel. 292 pp.
ISBN 0-930044-10-X $6.95

A Woman Appeared to Me by Renee Vivien. Translated by
Jeannette H. Foster. A novel. xxxi, 65 pp.
ISBN 0-930044-06-1 $5.00

Cytherea's Breath by Sarah Aldridge. A novel. 240 pp.
ISBN 0-930044-02-9 $6.95

Tottie by Sarah Aldridge. A novel. 181 pp.
ISBN 0-930044-01-0 $6.95

The Latecomer by Sarah Aldridge. A novel. 107 pp.
ISBN 0-930044-00-2 $5.00

VOLUTE BOOKS

Journey to Fulfillment	by Valerie Taylor	$3.95
A World without Men	by Valerie Taylor	$3.95
Return to Lesbos	by Valerie Taylor	$3.95
Desert of the Heart	by Jane Rule	$3.95
Odd Girl Out	by Ann Bannon	$3.95
I Am a Woman	by Ann Bannon	$3.95
Women in the Shadows	by Ann Bannon	$3.95
Journey to a Woman	by Ann Bannon	$3.95
Beebo Brinker	by Ann Bannon	$3.95

These are just a few of the many Naiad Press titles. Please request a
complete catalog! We encourage and welcome direct mail orders from
individuals who have limited access to bookstores carrying our publications.